DATE DUE

Rio del

Rio del Norte

People of the Upper Rio Grande
From Earliest Times to the Pueblo Revolt

Carroll L. Riley

University of Utah Press
Salt Lake City

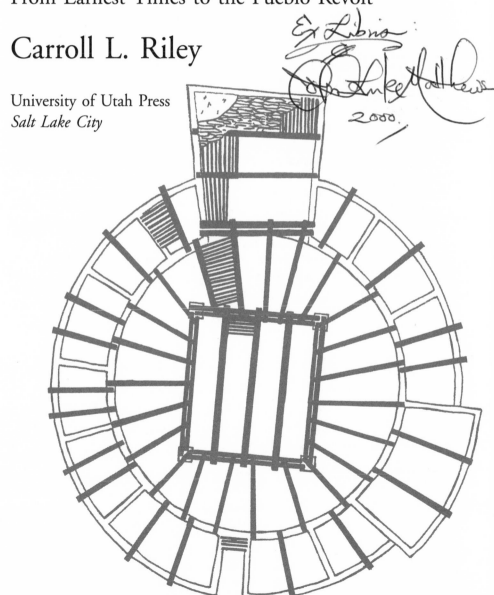

1999   1998   1997   1996   1995

∞ Printed on acid-free paper

LIBRARY OF CONGRESS CATALOGING-IN-PUBLICATION DATA

Riley, Carroll L.
    Rio del Norte : people of the Upper Rio Grande from earliest times
to the Pueblo revolt / Carroll L. Riley.
            p.   cm.
    Includes bibliographical references and index.
    (alk. paper)
    ISBN 0-87480-466-3 cloth
    ISBN 0-87480-496-5 paper
    1. Pueblo Indians—History.   2. Pueblo Indians—Government
relations.   3. Pueblo Indians—Social conditions.   4. Spain—
Colonies—America—Administration.   5. Rio Grande—History.   6. Rio
Grande—Social life and customs.   I. Title.
E99.P9R535   1995
976.4′4—dc20   94-40475

To my grandchildren

Rowyn Louise Evans
Jessica Olyn Evans
Nicholas James Evans

Contents

CONTENTS

Illustrations

Maps

Plates

ILLUSTRATIONS

Figures

Acknowledgments

A number of people helped with this book, and I wish to thank them all. Early chapters benefited from comments by members of the Las Vegas Fiction Workshop, especially Elizabeth Clarke, Ann Garcia, Edith Gold, Lillian Jones, Bernadine Meadows, and Brent Riley. Various points of the book have been strengthened by discussion with my old friend, the anthropologist and novelist J. A. (Courtway) Jones. Caroline H. Henry read the archaeology sections of the book from the viewpoint of the nonspecialist, and J. Reviere assisted in solving the mechanical problems of computer editing.

Robert Mishler of New Mexico Highlands University made available archaeological collections from the Gallinas and Tecolote valleys. Charles H. Lange gave me the benefit of his expert knowledge of Pueblo ethnology. Richard Flint read the entire manuscript in an early stage and made helpful suggestions on a number of important points. I was advised on ceramic matters by David H. Snow of Santa Fe and on the situation in pre-Hispanic central Mexico by Robert L. Rands of Southern Illinois University, Carbondale. My daughter, Victoria R. Evans, an archaeologist by training, discussed a number of the archaeological chapters with me.

I also wish to acknowledge the generous assistance of staff members of the Laboratory of Anthropology, Museum of New Mexico, especially librarian Laura J. Holt, to whom I owe a great debt. I also appreciate the fine help of assistant librarian Tracey Kimball, curator of ethnology Edmund J. Ladd, and Rosemary Talley, formerly of the Archaeological Records Management Section. I acknowledge the generous assistance of Tim Seaman, Keri Chalker, and Steve Townsend of the Archaeological Survey. I am especially grateful to Curtis F. Schaafsma, curator of anthropology and former New Mexico State Archaeologist, a longtime and sophisticated researcher in the diverse materials of the protohistoric period. Curt's comments and

ACKNOWLEDGMENTS

guidance at various stages of the manuscript have indeed enriched the final product.

I also wish to thank archivists Richard Rudisill and Arthur L. Olivas of the Museum of New Mexico for supplying photographs from the photo archives at the Governor's Palace. I thank Willow Powers, archivist, and Sibel Milik, assistant archivist, at the Laboratory of Anthropology for their good help in choosing photographic materials. Special thanks go to Shirley Cushing Flint, who not only read the manuscript and gave helpful criticism but also drew the maps, charts, and figures.

Finally, I wish to acknowledge the valuable advice of my wife, Brent Locke Riley, my in-house consultant on all things Southwestern.

Shortcomings in the book are my responsibility alone.

Preface

The upper Rio Grande basin is an area of great and continuing fascination, not least because humans have lived there for so many thousands of years. Today, ruins of Native American pueblos dot the landscape, many of them built long before any Europeans arrived in the Southwest. These aboriginal towns form the centerpieces for a number of national and state parks, monuments, and recreation areas, and they are enormous attractions to visitors from all over the world.

This book is about the Pueblo people of the northern Rio Grande, their adaptations, and their struggles with the natural environment as well as with hostile human forces. It is also about the sixteenth- and seventeenth-century Spaniards, especially in their tangled relationships with the Pueblos. After a century and a half of contact, ranging from assimilation to passive resistance and outright war, Pueblo Native Americans reached an uneasy accord with the Spaniards, which set the stage for the growth and development of Pueblo society today.

Although I am not a Native American, I am an anthropologist who has lived around and sometimes with Pueblo groups for nearly fifty years. A long-held concern of mine is that standard histories of the Southwest are often biased or indifferent in their treatment of Pueblos and other native peoples of the region. I am not alone in this concern. The Tewa Indian anthropologist and scholar Edward P. Dozier, a close friend from our student days together at the University of New Mexico and the University of California at Los Angeles, once said to me that he found it painful reading Southwestern history. His point was that historians traditionally have concentrated on the Spaniards to the virtual exclusion of indigenous peoples.

This was especially true of the widely read popular histories that appeared around 1940, the four-hundredth anniversary of Coronado's expedition to the

Southwest. Even today, in accounts of the early historic Southwest, one sometimes finds that the Native Americans are so much scenery, occasionally entering the picture as allies or antagonists, but only as they interact with Europeans. Natives who helped the Spaniards are praised; those who attempted to protect their people against the Spaniards are vilified, no matter how great their sacrifices or their courage. Not only historians but also many of the first generation of anthropologists who worked in the Southwest took this extreme Eurocentric attitude. Since the early decades of the twentieth century, however, anthropologists have tended to see things from the point of view of the Native American.

Of course, this kind of ethnic chauvinism was not true of every historian in the past. In the pre–World War II period, scholars like France V. Scholes were certainly exceptions. Today, there are many fine historians working specifically in the Pueblo area—Eleanor Adams, John Kessell, and Mark Simmons, along with the late Myra Ellen Jenkins, to mention only a few—who carried and carry on Scholes's tradition of intercultural sensitivity.

In this book I hope to show the Rio Grande Pueblo people and their various nomadic neighbors as the primary protagonists in the drama of Southwestern life. The main actors during prehistoric times were the men and women who produced the inventions and innovations that gradually enriched Native American life. Once the Spaniards arrive, I try to see the resulting events through Native American eyes, even though I must use Spanish documents to tell the story. Coronado and Oñate will be part of the tale, but so will such Indian heroes as "Turk" and Popé. My emphasis is not on Spanish institutions but on the shaping, over long millennia, of native institutions that were maintained even after the Southwest was overtaken by the cultural world of the Europeans.

Most of my writings in the past have been primarily for professional audiences, and indeed, I hope this book will be useful to my professional colleagues. It offers a number of new ways of looking at the archaeological and documentary data, and I welcome criticism and challenge. But I would also like to reach out to the general reader who is interested in the long history of the Southwest.

Because I hope to have a diverse audience, I have tried to minimize the book's scholarly apparatus. Although I attempt to document my statements comprehensively and to cite specialists who may disagree with my interpretations, I place this documentation in a special reference section at the end of the book, arranged by chapters for easy comparison with the text. It will allow professional anthropologists, cultural geographers, historians, and their students convenient access to my sources. Those who wish to read the volume for pleasure, without worrying about academic argumentation, may simply skip the reference section.

Rio del Norte

Introduction

The Rio Grande, the "big river," originates in the mountains of southern Colorado and flows southward through the heart of New Mexico. Curving to the east, the river then forms a long border between Mexico and the American state of Texas. About two hundred miles from where it leaves New Mexico, the river is joined by its most important tributary, the Rio Conchos, flowing in from the south and quadrupling the amount of water moving on to the Gulf of Mexico. The northern portion of this river—the segment that flows through New Mexico—has been the scene of human settlement for at least eleven thousand years. It became heavily populated only about seven hundred years ago.

This book sketches the human story of the upper Rio Grande beginning with its first settlers, whose origins lay in Asia. The story becomes more detailed with the "golden age" of the Pueblos, which started around A.D. 1300, and it continues through the Spanish invasion and its powerful aftermath.

By A.D. 1300, there was a quickening up and down the Rio Grande basin. This quickening reached its climax at the beginning of what is called the *protohistoric period* in the Southwest—a period that is the subject of the major part of this book. The term *protohistoric* is generally used by archaeologists and ethnohistorians for those periods in prehistory and history when nonliterate peoples first invent writing or come into contact with cultures that can supply written records. In the Southwest, such records began to be made by Spaniards in 1533 and continued, sporadically at first, until the end of Spanish occupation of the region.

Spanish accounts not only tell us about events of the sixteenth and seventeenth centuries but also, when used in conjunction with archaeological excavation, cast some light on the period just before the Spaniards arrived. Because of this "backlighting," we normally think of the Southwestern peoples as having entered the protohistoric period sometime around A.D. 1450. This book follows the history of the Pueblo peoples and the European newcomers on through the seventeenth century, by which time Spanish institutions and culture had greatly eroded native culture.

In Part I, "The Native Americans," we will be concerned with the natural setting and the long human history of the upper Rio Grande, and especially with the way the Pueblo Indians developed their rich riverine culture. The years from A.D. 1300 to 1450 saw the Pueblo world respond to this rich environment and open a far-flung trading system that reached away to the east, west, and south. In the century after A.D. 1450, this culture was stabilizing and maturing. Had the Europeans not come, it seems very likely that the Pueblos would have taken another leap forward, eventually to produce their own native American civilization. Such a civilization would have been similar to those of the Tarascans, Aztecs, and Mayas to the south and east but also distinctive, flavored in a particular, Southwestern Pueblo way. But that was not to happen: the Spaniards *did* come, and they changed the Rio Grande region in dramatic and often tragic ways.

To properly understand the Pueblos in their early *historical* setting, it is necessary to know the story of the early Spaniards in North America. Spanish armies destroyed the Aztec kingdom, and by the early 1520s the newcomers had a firm hold on central Mexico. During the next decade the Spaniards pushed up the Mexican west coast to the very edge of the Southwest. In 1540, Coronado led a large invasion force into Pueblo territory. Others followed, and at the end of the sixteenth century Spain achieved political control over the Rio Grande region. In the centuries that followed, Spanish culture made its own large and unique contribution to the Southwest.

Part II of this book, "The Invaders," is about the Spanish intrusion and what happened when the two very different lifeways met and clashed in the Rio Grande basin. It is a story of how the Pueblo Indians and their nomadic neighbors and sometime enemies, the Querechos and Teya-Jumanos, met the European invaders, reacted to them, and attempted to maintain their cultural integrity in an increasingly alien world.

At the end of the first period of Spanish conquest came one concerted effort by both Pueblos and Apachean nomads to throw off the European overlords. The effort ultimately failed, but it did give a certain new life to the Rio Grande Pueblos, for after the revolt they were able to maintain some portion of their religion and social life, which they retain to the present day.

In one sense this book is about the flexibility of the Pueblo lifeway. During the fifteen hundred years of Basketmaker-Pueblo history, settlers of the

INTRODUCTION

Rio Grande and (to the west) the San Juan River basin faced many challenges. There were military threats presented by hungry nomads and European empire builders, and there were internal pressures caused by the increasing complexity of Pueblo society. Added to these were recurring problems brought about by the vagaries of weather. The Pueblos met these challenges with a cultural system that was rigid at its core but flexible in its details.

The dramatic rise in Native American population that took place in the San Juan basin over a thousand years ago led to major town building in the upper Southwest and to social alliances, still not completely understood, that served the needs of the new semiurban polities. After the collapse of the San Juan as a homeland, the whole Pueblo world seems to have been threatened by disruption from both outside enemies and rivalry within and among the various Pueblo communities. Then, in the fourteenth century, a broad new religious system, the *kachina cult,* began to crosscut the older social groups and to act as a bonding mechanism within and between the massive towns of the "golden age." The sociopolitical groupings seen and named by the Spaniards in the mid-sixteenth century—Cíbola, Tiguex, and so forth—demonstrated the success of this bonding.

The kachina cult seems to have been installed without any real disruption of the Pueblo social system. Nor were other religious practices fundamentally changed by the coming of the kachinas. Of course, not too much can be read into the archaeological record, but ceremonies continued to be kiva-based, and the mute evidence of art and architecture suggests a continuity to religious life.

The Spaniards presented a more considerable threat. Not only did they replace Pueblo political organizations with alien institutions, Spanish in form and function, but the Franciscan missionaries made a powerful attempt to destroy the very bases of Pueblo religion. They failed in this, but many elements of Christianity became incorporated into Pueblo ceremonial life nonetheless.

The last chapter of the book tells of the desperate revolt of the Pueblo Indians against their Spanish overlords in 1680 and its aftermath over the next twenty years. Beginning in the eighteenth century, a gradual equilibrium was struck between the Pueblos and their Spanish (and later Mexican) co-dwellers along the Rio Grande. When the Americans arrived in the mid-nineteenth century, this equilibrium continued to hold, although Anglo-American culture has gradually impinged on the Pueblos, offering alternative patterns of behavior and glittering (if sometimes ephemeral) rewards.

Even though the Pueblo Indians in the twentieth century maintain something of their religious, linguistic, and political life, these neo-Pueblos differ greatly from their ancestors of prehistoric times. But more remarkable than the differences are certain broad similarities—the essence of "Puebloness"—that link the prehistoric, the protohistoric, and the historic Indians of the Rio Grande region. It is this long history of stability within massive change that is the major theme of this book.

PART ONE
The Native Americans

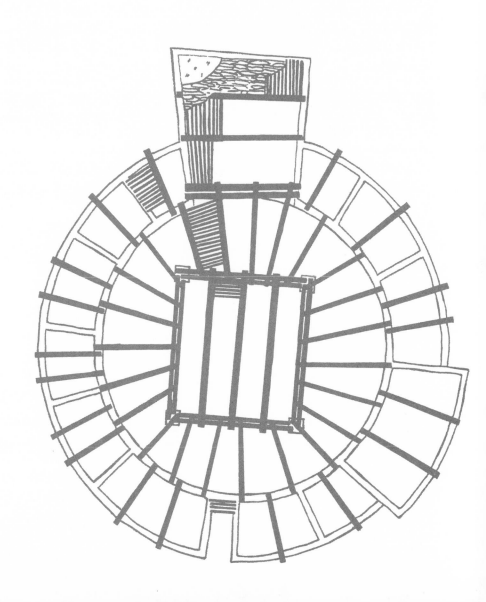

CHAPTER ONE

What's in a Name?

The words *Rio Grande* are Spanish, of course, but by no means did the Spaniards always give Hispanic names to Southwestern rivers. They often used native terms—though not necessarily *river* names—for streams and washes. Rivers such as the Pecos, Chama, Sonora, Yaqui, and Mayo all derive their names from Indian words. The English and their Anglo-American descendants in North America also tended to borrow words from Indian languages when they named rivers: Alabama, Allegheny, Kansas, Mississippi, Missouri, Ocmulgee, Ohio, Potomac, Tennessee, and many, many others. In the case of the Rio Grande, however, the Spaniards—after experimenting with several terms—settled on Spanish names: Rio del Norte (river of the north, or northern river) for the upper stream and Rio Bravo (fierce or rapid river) or Rio Grande del Norte for the lower. Americans, coming into the region in the nineteenth century, simplified things still further, using the one name, Rio Grande, for the whole river basin.

Human beings have lived in or visited the valley of the Rio Grande for many thousands of years. Over time they doubtlessly gave the river various names, but most of these have been irretrievably lost. Our first recorded Indian names for the Rio Grande come from Pueblo Indians who lived along the river in Coronado's day and who live there still (map 1). These names probably go back at least two or three centuries before Coronado's time, and in translation they mean much the same thing. The Keresan-speaking Indians of Cochiti Pueblo refer to the river as *mets'ichi chena,* which simply means "big river." The Tewa speakers call the river *posoge,* which also means "big river," and the northern Tiwa use the name *paslápaane,* with roughly

Plate 1. The Rio Grande south of San Ildefonso Pueblo, early twentieth century. Photograph courtesy Archives of the Laboratory of Anthropology/MIAC, Santa Fe, N.M., no. 70.4/368.

the same meaning. The Towa speakers of Jemez Pueblo say *hañapakwa,* which means "place of the great waters."

The seminomadic Navajo Indians, who lived near but not on the Rio Grande, have two names for that stream. One, in translation, simply means "Mexican river" and is obviously fairly late in time. The other and more common name, *tó ba-ade,* may have considerable antiquity. It means "female river," a name that is related primarily to direction. In Navajo cosmology, femaleness is identified with the south, and the section of the Rio Grande known best to the Navajos flows almost directly to the south.

The designation "big" or "great," used throughout the eastern Pueblo world, makes it clear that the Rio Grande impressed native peoples as a special river. The Chama River, the major tributary of the upper Rio Grande, is also a relatively large stream, but none of the Indians referred to it as "big," using instead such names as the Tewa *popinga* (red river) or the Cochiti *tñetepo-chena* (northwest river).

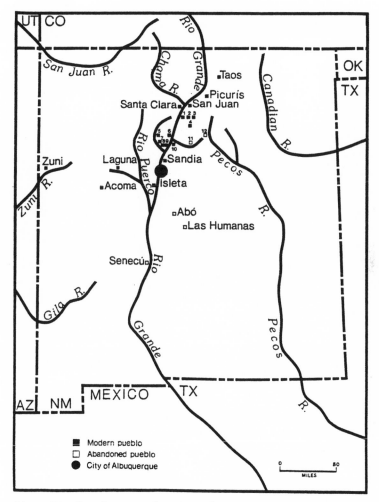

Map 1. Rio Grande area with native tribes. Key: 1, San Ildefonso; 2, Pojoaque; 3, Nambé; 4, Tesuque; 5, Jemez; 6, Cochiti; 7, Zia; 8, Santa Ana; 9, San Felipe; 10, Santo Domingo; 11, Galisteo; 12, Pecos.

You will notice that all these Pueblo Indian names are basically descriptive. As the Tewa Indians living on its banks could plainly see, the Chama often ran reddish brown from its sediment load. The river runs northwest of the pueblo of Cochiti. And "big river" referred to the largest running body of water around.

A few Pueblo Indians may actually have seen a comparable or larger river.

Though we have no records of this, it seems likely that people from the Rio Grande sporadically visited the San Juan River, which runs through a region of northwest New Mexico and southwest Colorado that was the center of heavy population as late as the thirteenth century. Pueblo Indians had deserted the San Juan basin by around A.D. 1300, and hunting and gathering peoples filtered into the region. In early historic times the Apacheans, especially, were pressing the Rio Grande Pueblos in the Rio Chama valley and along the line of the Jemez Mountains. Contacts were often hostile, but there was trade as well, and the occasional Pueblo trader surely got to the valley of the San Juan. A little farther afield, it is a reasonable assumption that a few eastern Pueblo people visited the lower Colorado River, just north of the Gulf of California. The western Pueblos visited those parts regularly, and traditional accounts tell of trading expeditions from the Rio Grande to the lower Colorado as well.

Pueblo pottery and turquoise found in the middle Red River valley on the Texas-Arkansas border make it also likely that a handful of Pueblo traders reached eastward to that stream. And in Coronado's time, there were travelers' tales of even larger rivers. Indians from the Great Plains—Pawnee, Caddo, and Wichita—visiting Pueblo land on trading missions brought hearsay accounts of a mighty river to the east, probably the Mississippi. But it is doubtful that any Pueblo Indian ever journeyed so far afield. In any case, to most native New Mexicans the Rio Grande was *the* great river, a river without equal.

Although parties of Spaniards had sighted the mouth of the Rio Grande before 1520, they had no idea of the extent of the river and no information whatsoever on the upriver area. In 1535 a shipwrecked Spaniard named Alvar Nuñez Cabeza de Vaca and his three companions probably reached the Rio Grande at La Junta in what is now southwestern Texas and northern Chihuahua, where the heavy flow of the Rio Conchos enters the mother river. Cabeza de Vaca may even have traveled upriver along the Rio Grande as far as modern Las Cruces, New Mexico. Unfortunately, he and his companions were not given to naming natural features—or at least they left us very little record of such names.

Francisco Vázquez de Coronado, with a large party of both Spaniards and Mexican Indians, arrived at the Zuni towns of western New Mexico in July 1540. A month or so later, a captain of Coronado's, Hernando de Alvarado, and a priest, Fray Juan de Padilla, were sent with a few men eastward from Zuni to spy out the land of the eastern Pueblos. Around the seventh of September, 1540, they reached the Rio Grande at Tiguex, the towns of the southern Tiwa

Indians, in the present-day Albuquerque-Bernalillo region. Alvarado, or perhaps his companion, Father Padilla, gave the stream a Spanish name, Nuestra Señora ("Our Lady," that is, the Virgin Mary). A little later that same year another of Coronado's captains, Juan de Jaramillo, referred to the Rio Grande as the Rio Tiguex, after the important Indian district of Tiguex. So far as I know, this is the only time an early Spaniard gave the Rio Grande an Indian name. The designation "Tiguex River" did not survive the Coronado expedition.

Coronado retreated from the Rio Grande area in 1542 and the Spaniards did not return until the small Chamuscado-Rodríguez party journeyed by the Conchos to the Rio Grande at La Junta in 1581. This party first named the Rio Grande just above La Junta the Nuestra Señora de la Concepción, perhaps from a memory of Alvarado's name forty years earlier. The party went on upriver and, reaching the Pueblo region, called the Rio Grande there the Guadalquivir, after the large river that runs near Seville in southern Spain. The Pueblo area itself they christened San Felipe de Nuevo México, but the saint's name, San Felipe, was quickly dropped and the area has been known from that day to this simply as New Mexico.

A second expedition beginning in 1582 and led by Antonio de Espejo explored the Rio Grande northward from La Junta and, on its return, traveled south via the Pecos River. On the journey to New Mexico this group took the standard route down the Conchos river and used the term *Rio del Norte* for the Rio Grande at the Conchos junction—the first use of the term for which we have any record. However, Diego Pérez de Luxán, chronicler for the Espejo expedition, remarked that he obtained the name from members of the Chamuscado expedition. So it may be that some member or members of the earlier party used Rio del Norte as an alternative to either Nuestra Señora or Guadalquivir. Different members of these parties of exploration often had their own ideas about what each natural feature should be called. Luxán, for example, suggested that the Río del Norte at La Junta should be called the Río Turbio because of its muddy and turbulent nature.

The various alternate names for the river quickly disappeared, and Rio del Norte became the term of choice for the upper Rio Grande. Gaspar Castaño de Sosa, who led an illegal expedition to New Mexico in 1590–91 and who first crossed the Rio Grande far downstream in the Del Rio, Texas, region, referred to that part of the river as the Rio Bravo. The upstream portion, however, he called Rio del Norte, as did Juan de Morlete, who led a party north in early 1591 to arrest Castaño and break up the expedition.

By the time of Juan de Oñate and the colonization of New Mexico in

1598, the term Río del Norte had become fixed; it was standard usage in the Oñate documents over the next two decades. Likely the Spaniards used the name because this was the main river of the "far north" province of New Mexico, although one of Oñate's priests in 1605 made an alternative suggestion that "Rio del Norte" was used because the river itself flowed from the north.

European map makers in the sixteenth century were rather slow to absorb the new and rapidly increasing information from Spanish exploration parties. Their maps gave a wildly inaccurate picture of the far northwest of New Spain, and the rivers they showed usually did not conform to any real geography. The Cornelius Wytfliet map of 1597, for example, has both a Rio Grande and a Rio Bravo in the region labeled "Quivira." The detailed Hakylut map of 1599 has two Rio Grandes and a Rio Bermejo (red river). Earlier sixteenth-century maps—for example, the great Ortelius world map of 1570 and the Mercator world map of 1587—list a number of Southwestern names: Quivira, Tiguex, Tontonteac, Granata [Granada], Marata, Cicuic, and others. Rivers are drawn in, some of them draining in the wrong direction, but no river names are given.

On the other hand, the Enrico Martínez map of 1602, which was drawn in Mexico specifically for the Southwest, is reasonably accurate. On it, the relationships of the Rio Grande, the Pecos River, and the Rio Conchos are clearly shown. The upper Rio Grande is called Rio del Norte; the Rio Grande below the Conchos has the designation Rio Bravo.

The upper river was called Rio del Norte throughout the Spanish period. It is the name given in the Oñate reports, on maps, and in the documents of church and state in the seventeenth and eighteenth centuries. The name continued to be used during the Mexican period, which ended around the middle of the nineteenth century. The lower portion of the Rio Grande was occasionally called the Rio Bravo during the seventeenth century, but by the eighteenth century it was more often referred to in Spanish documents as Rio Grande del Norte—although the term "R. del Norte ou R. Bravo" appears on the 1780 Bonne map published in France.

The names Rio del Norte and Rio Bravo were both current in the early United States. For example, in an 1803 letter to Meriwether Lewis (of Lewis and Clark fame), President Thomas Jefferson wrote concerning "the North River or Rio Bravo, which runs into the Gulph of Mexico." At the time of American contact with New Mexico via the Santa Fe trail, Rio del Norte was still the common usage for the New Mexico section of the river. In 1846, the explorer and trader F. A. Wislizenus came over the Santa Fe Trail, reaching

Santa Fe on the last day of June, a few weeks before S. W. Kearney arrived with an invading American army. Wislizenus used the name Rio del Norte, and his map, drawn the next year, shows the upper Rio Grande and the middle river between the Conchos and the Big Bend country as Rio del Norte, while the lower river is labeled "Rio del Norte or Rio Grande."

The modern term Rio Grande, used without the *Norte,* was picked up by early American settlers in Texas and appears in English-language documents of the early nineteenth century. For a period of twenty or thirty years, Rio Grande and Rio del Norte competed for favor as names for the upper river. By the later part of the nineteenth century, the term Rio Grande (sometimes mispronounced "ree-o-grand" or even "rye-o-grand") for the total river system, from Colorado to the Gulf of Mexico, had been firmly established, and that is the name by which the stream is known today.

CHAPTER TWO

Sun, Rain,
and Growing Things

 The upper Rio Grande basin has been home for human beings for perhaps 11,500 years, quite possibly continuously—although at times the population was very small. But in terms of heavy and intensive human settlement, the last seven hundred years have been the most important. The towns of the Rio Grande Pueblo Indians seen by the Spanish conquistador Francisco Vázquez de Coronado were already two or three hundred years old when he came in 1540, and many of them are still vigorous today.

The center of the eastern Pueblo Indian world in Coronado's time was a collection of towns stretching from the Chama River to below present-day Belen, New Mexico, and including portions of the Santa Fe, Jemez, and Galisteo rivers. The motorist can see a large portion of it simply by driving down Interstate Highway 25 from Santa Fe to Albuquerque. But mile after mile of that drive will be without human habitation, past or present. The barren brown uplands south of Santa Fe mostly contain desert grasses interspersed with scattered trees. Twenty miles south of Santa Fe, the highway winds down the eight-hundred-foot escarpment known since early Spanish times as La Bajada (the descent), into the Rio Grande valley. Although the viewer can trace a line of green off to the west, the immediate landscape is one of barren, eroded terraces and low sandy hills covered by bushes and the occasional straggling juniper. It is an empty land.

Empty, but relative to what? Modern visitors to New Mexico get the impression of vast expanses of unpopulated desert and remote, wooded mountains. But the Indians who met Coronado (and likely Coronado himself) would consider our modern New Mexico to be crowded beyond belief. In the mid-sixteenth century, the Rio Grande pueblos probably housed no

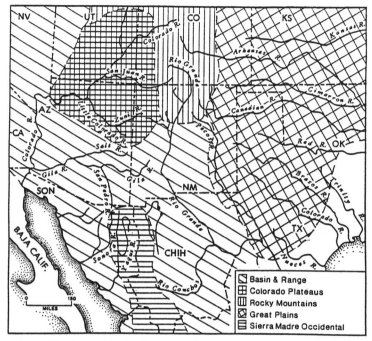

Map 2. Physiographic provinces of the Southwest and Great Plains.

more than fifty thousand people. Today, fifteen times that number live in the old Pueblo area.

This region of the Rio Grande Pueblo people, or eastern Pueblos, as they are sometimes called, is one of mixed mountains, river basins, rolling plateaus, and high plains contained in three great physiographic provinces (map 2). The first of these, the Rocky Mountain province, extends into northeastern New Mexico as the Sangre de Cristo Mountains—the highest range in New Mexico, with individual peaks reaching more than thirteen thousand feet. The Sangre de Cristo range is separated from the slightly lower Jemez and Tusas mountains by the Rio Grande rift, a major break in the earth's surface that extends from Colorado down through New Mexico and on into Mexico. Generally speaking, the region to the west of the Rio Grande rift is one of considerable instability. Today, the valley has earthquakes, though generally not very serious ones. A Pacific rim citizen of San Francisco or Tokyo would envy the relative safety of the Rio Grande depression. But in the fairly recent geological past, devastating volcanoes have erupted west of the river.

East of this rift and its adjacent uplifted mountains, and extending for hundreds of miles, are the Great Plains, our second physiographic province. These plains were formed millions of years ago by deposit after deposit of sediment, now thousands of feet deep. The present surface slopes gently to the east, and its western edge is a mile or more above sea level. These high, generally flat or rolling plains have in the past been home to vast herds of grazing animals. The most famous is the bison, or American buffalo, animals that could be counted in the millions less than two centuries ago.

The Great Plains abut the Sangre de Cristos in the northern part of New Mexico and, farther south, merge westward into the third important province. This Basin and Range region covers the southern half of New Mexico and much of southern Arizona; it reaches north into Utah and Nevada and south to Sonora and Chihuahua. It is a region where broad, flat upland basins surround isolated mountain ranges. These mountains are lower than those of the southern Rockies. One peak, Sierra Blanca, near Alamagordo, New Mexico, reaches twelve thousand feet, but most of the peaks are under ten thousand feet. Salt flats, the dry remnants of earlier lakes, sometimes form in the center of the basins, some of them tiny but others covering many square miles. The lakes themselves have virtually disappeared in New Mexico, but the Great Salt Lake, the remnant of a vast Ice Age inland body of water, still exists in Utah, and shallow lakes are still found in Chihuahua, Mexico.

Two other geographical provinces were of some importance to the eastern Pueblos. Some of the people living on the Colorado Plateaus moved into Rio Grande pueblos during the later prehistoric period. The Colorado Plateaus are a vast region of high, timbered mesas through which the Colorado River and its various tributaries cut great canyons. The San Juan area, discussed in chapter 6, falls partly in the Colorado Plateaus. The Sierra Madre Occidental, extending into the Basin and Range country of northwest Mexico, was secondarily important to the Rio Grande Pueblos. These rugged mountains served as a hinterland for the commercial towns of northeast Sonora, which transshipped trade goods from Mesoamerica to the Southwest, especially in protohistoric times.

Historically, most of the eastern Pueblo Indians lived in the valley of the Rio Grande or on its tributaries, building their cluttered villages and farming along the main stream or along the Pecos, Taos, Santa Fe, Galisteo, Chama, Jemez, and Puerco rivers. Only the Tompiros managed to maintain a toehold in the high Salinas region of the Estancia valley, east of the Manzano Mountains.

RIO DEL NORTE

Since A.D. 1300, the northern Rio Grande basin has seen wet years and periods of drought, and some fluctuations in animal and plant life. The Indian populations, in their long tenure, did relatively little to landscape the upper river region. The operative word here is *relative:* I do not mean that the Rio Grande area was left pristine until the depredation of the region by modern industrial society. The Pueblo Indians changed their environment mainly by stripping off vegetation to provide house timbers and fuel. Their continuous removal of wood goes a long way toward explaining why even the largest Pueblo Indian settlements were deserted after fifty to one hundred years of habitation. In pre-Spanish times, carriage had to be on human shoulders, and it took a century or less for firewood and building materials to become exhausted for many miles around any one pueblo. Of course, the destructive effect on the environment was somewhat lessened because populations were relatively low during Pueblo times. There was, however, considerable erosion in the uplands, and cutting down the small stands of timber in the *bosque,* the heavy river-bottom growth, often led to local flooding.

The Spaniards, too, were heavy users of wood, and they introduced large herds of domestic sheep. These animals, by their close cropping of vegetation in the semiarid Southwest, contributed to rapid runoff and soil erosion, especially along some of the tributary streams. But it was not until the American period, and especially the twentieth century, that major water control systems, a huge increase in human and stock-animal populations, and an insatiable urban demand for water began to fundamentally modify the Rio Grande region.

Indeed, there has been so much human tinkering with the environment in the last three-quarters of a century that today it is very difficult to reconstruct the older conditions, especially in the river valleys. Fortunately, a considerable amount of hydrological fieldwork was carried out in the Rio Grande basin before the great dam projects and heavy industrialization began in earnest. Descriptions of the river and the general area of north-central New Mexico as of the end of the nineteenth century give us information from which (allowing for modest Hispanic changes in the landscape) we can extrapolate conditions back to prehistoric times.

The upper portion of the Rio Grande—the Rio del Norte of this book—extends from its source on the northern slopes of the San Juan mountains of Colorado to the region around San Marcial, New Mexico, at the northern end of present-day Elephant Butte Lake. Actual Pueblo Indian settlement in this Rio Grande province did not extend significantly north of the Taos valley. However, people likely undertook sporadic hunting and collecting throughout the northern Sangre de Cristos and the San Juan Mountains, and we may justifiably consider the northern drainage to have been part of a borderland area used by some Pueblo Indians.

In pre-Spanish times, along the river south of San Marcial and in the adjacent mountains, lived both nomadic hunters and gatherers and farming villagers who had moved eastward from the Mogollon region of western New Mexico and eastern Arizona. These *Jornada Mogollon* Indians of southeast New Mexico and the El Paso area considerably influenced the Rio Grande Pueblo Indians. As the Jornada culture faded, sometime around A.D. 1400, much of the Rio Grande valley south of San Marcial, as well as the mountains east of the Rio Grande and the adjacent Pecos valley, continued to be occupied by people who, at least in part, were the descendants of the Jornada people—low-level agriculturalists and hunter-gatherers, the Manso, Suma, and Teya.

From its birthplace in the mountains of southern Colorado, the Rio Grande courses into New Mexico through a deep, narrow gorge. A few streams coming in from the east were, and still are, important in terms of human habitation, especially the Taos River. But the two most important rivers, both as suppliers of water and as living areas for Pueblo Indian farmers, flow from the west and northwest and join the Rio Grande below this gorge. These two rivers are the Chama, which heads in Colorado and flows around the northeast side of the Jemez Mountains, and the Jemez, which drains the central and southern sections of the Jemez range. The lower Chama and adjacent Rio Grande were the Puebloan population centers for what is often called the *Rio Arriba,* or "upper river" country.

Between the Chama and Jemez rivers lies the high wall of the Pajarito Plateau, a large, rugged region partly covered by tuff, a compacted volcanic ash. At some point in the past a tremendous volcano in the northern Jemez Mountains exploded, creating the vast caldera (volcanic crater) of Valle Grande and spreading deep layers of lava and ash over the region. This massive explosion must have been an impressive sight—and a deadly one for animals and plants in the vicinity. No human eye watched the volcano explode, however; at the time, the Old World ancestors of modern human beings were still in the early stages of their experiments with tool making and language. Many millennia of cultural and physical evolution were yet to come before the first human groups reached North America. When they finally came, they would find the Valle Grande as it is today—a broad valley, lush with vegetation.

The east-draining streams reaching the Rio Grande from the Pajarito

Plate 2. The ancient volcanic caldera of Valle Grande. Photograph courtesy Archives of the Laboratory of Anthropology/MIAC, Santa Fe, N.M., no. 70.1/ 1141.

Plateau are small, and some of them run only during the rainy season. The valleys of these streams, however, offered limited stretches of fertile soil, and the soft volcanic rock of south-facing canyon walls was pocked with shallow caves. During the two or three hundred years before the Spaniards came, these caves, often artificially improved, provided warm, secure homes for generations of Pueblo Indians. Streams draining from the east into this segment of the Rio Grande did not, for the most part, flow year-round. Still, the most important drainages—the Santa Fe and the Galisteo—contained rich soils and supported considerable Indian habitation aboriginally.

South of the Jemez Mountains, the Rio Grande flows through a relatively wide, flat floodplain, easy of access. Part of this broad valley today contains the urban sprawl of Albuquerque and its satellite towns to the north and south. No rivers worthy of the name flow in from the east. Below the Jemez, other rivers that join the Rio Grande from the north and west are irregular in their flow, sometimes dry and at other times discharging huge amounts of muddy water into the main river. The largest of these streams is the Rio Puerco, which heads on the west side of the Jemez range and flows southeastward for some 130 miles before converging with the Rio Grande between modern-day Belen and Socorro. Its major tributary, the San José, rises in the

high country west of present-day Grants, New Mexico, and drains the La-
guna-Acoma region, joining the parent Rio Puerco about thirty-five miles
from its mouth. In spite of its irregular water supply, the Rio Puerco supported at least one large pueblo in late prehistoric times—a great trading center now called Pottery Mound, which was occupied perhaps into the latter
part of the fifteenth century. In the sixteenth century this part of the Rio
Grande was the center of the important region of the Tiguex Indians. It is
sometimes called the *Rio Medio,* the "middle river."

The section of the Rio Grande from the mouth of the Rio Puerco to the
San Marcial–Milligan Gulch area, the southern limit of Pueblo occupation,
formed the *Rio Abajo,* or "lower river" country. The Rio Grande at San Marcial drains an area of about twenty-seven thousand square miles, and before
dams and water basins controlled the river's flow, it was extremely variable.
Average annual discharge for the fifteen years from 1897 to 1911 was 1,170,000
acre feet (an acre foot is the amount of water that will cover one acre to a
depth of one foot: 43,560 cubic feet, or 326,000 gallons). In 1902, however—an extremely dry year—the river's flow measured only 201,000 acre
feet, whereas the wettest year, 1905, accounted for almost 2.5 million acre
feet. Life in the valley bottoms in the pre-dam period was always uncertain
and sometimes exciting as raging floods roared down the river valleys.

The people of the upper Pecos valley, because of their cultural similarity to
and close interaction with other Pueblo peoples, can be included with the
Rio Grande groups. The Pecos River is also a tributary of the Rio Grande,
but it reaches the mother river some hundreds of miles from the Pueblo
world. It flows almost directly south out of the Sangre de Cristo Mountains,
then turns east at about the modern town of Pecos and edges the southern
flank of the Sangre de Cristos. It then picks its way south along the eastern
escarpment of Rowe Mesa and, after a series of twists and turns in the rugged
country around Villanueva, New Mexico, breaks out onto flat land north of
Santa Rosa.

In Coronado's time there was only one pueblo, that of Pecos, a few miles
south of the modern town. The Pecos Indians utilized the valley of the Pecos
River, possibly as far south and east as Villanueva, and hunted along the Tecolote and Gallinas rivers. They also hunted and collected raw materials in
the mountains to the north and atop Rowe and Glorieta mesas to the south
and west. A major link between Pecos and the Rio Grande pueblos was Glorieta Pass, which connects the Pecos and Rio Grande valleys and breaks into
the Rio Grande drainage a few miles south and east of modern Santa Fe. A
second route from Pecos to the Rio Grande followed the tops of Rowe and

Glorieta mesas southwestward to the Galisteo country. The Pecos people also had a back entrance to the Rio Grande valley: an aboriginal trail worked its way along the east side of the Sangre de Cristo range to the Mora valley and then over Holman Pass to Picuris and Taos pueblos.

On the extreme upper Pecos River, we are dealing with a watershed of only some two thousand square miles. Annual runoff of the Pecos, like that of the Rio Grande, is extremely variable, but the river is a permanent stream, as are its main upper tributaries, the Tecolote and the Gallinas.

The amount of rain and snow falling in the Rio Grande basin varies considerably from year to year and decade to decade, but overall it has not changed significantly since Coronado's time. In the upper Rio Grande and upper Pecos drainages, altitude is a factor in climate. The higher one goes, the colder the weather becomes, with more rain in summer and much more snow in winter.

The very southern part of the Pueblo Indian area was occupied at the beginning of historic times by the Piro Indians. The southernmost part of Piro country lies a little below 4,700 feet, the lowest altitude for any of the Pueblo Indians, east or west (the highest Pueblo towns are Pecos and Taos, at around 6,900 feet). Rainfall in the Piro region, the Rio Abajo, varies from about eight to ten inches annually, but most of the rain falls during the summer growing season. Very little precipitation appears as snow, which averages only about six inches per year. The Piro groups faded away during the late seventeenth and early eighteenth centuries, their place being taken by Hispanic towns along the Rio Grande. As a result, modern visitors to New Mexico who visit still-functioning pueblos such as Taos, Santo Domingo, and Acoma have often never heard of the Piros. Many of the old Piro towns are now buried under modern settlements, and even ones whose ruins are still visible lie off the main modern roads and are seldom visited.

The same is not true, however, of the Piros' linguistic kinfolk, the group of Pueblo Indians called Tompiro. Impressive ruins of Tompiro pueblos and their great Spanish mission churches remain and have been developed into a tourist attraction at the National Park Service's Salinas Pueblo Missions National Monument. These Indians lived to the east of the Piros, across the Manzano range in the interior-draining basins of the Salinas country near the modern New Mexican town of Mountainair. Tompiro country is fifteen hundred to two thousand feet higher than Piro territory and so has considerably more snow and a far shorter frost-free growing season. This is a marginal area for agriculture because precipitation is relatively scanty and winters

are often bitterly cold. In spite of these difficult conditions, by skillfully using small-scale irrigation and carefully husbanding water, the Tompiros
flourished for several centuries. The area opens eastward to the Pecos River
and the High Plains, and this gave the Tompiros easy access to plains bison
and antelope. It also allowed them to tap the intertribal trade network that
extended up and down the Pecos valley.

Even though the Tompiros managed quite well during pre-Hispanic
times, their hold on this harsh environment was fragile, and Spanish missionization following Oñate's colonization in 1598 upset the balance. A Tompiro rebellion shortly after 1600 led to brutal Spanish reprisals and the beginning of Tompiro decline. The uprising, of course, was a rebellion only in
the eyes of the Spaniards; the Tompiros doubtlessly—and with reason—
thought of themselves as freedom fighters.

Spanish missions were firmly established in the Tompiro area by about
1630. The Indians, already weakened by Spanish military action, now had to
face the cultural assault and economic demands of Spanish overlords and the
loss of political independence. For many decades the Tompiros had maintained long-term trading relationships with nomadic tribes to the east. After
1600, new economic and political realities made the nomads, especially the
Apaches, increasingly hostile and belligerent. As a result, the Tompiro pueblos dwindled, and the area was deserted before the end of the seventeenth
century.

The pueblo of Pecos—that other Pueblo Indian outlier on the plains—
suffered the same fate as the Tompiro towns. Pecos, tucked into the upper
Pecos valley, was an important trade center, funneling goods from the Great
Plains to the Pueblo world. It continued to flourish for decades after the
Spaniards took control of New Mexico; its subsequent breakdown was
gradual, and a few Indians clung to their homes into the early nineteenth
century.

North of the Piro pueblos lay the province of Tiguex in the Rio Medio
around Albuquerque and Bernalillo. Here the altitude is 5,000 to 5,100 feet
along the river, a bit higher than in Piro country, but rainfall is about the
same eight to ten inches per year and there is only slightly more snowfall. Just
to the east, however, along the higher slopes of the Sandia and Manzano
mountains, precipitation measures twenty inches or more. This was not an
area normally used for settlement, but the Indians occasionally took refuge in
the highlands during times of trouble. One of those times was the Spanish
occupation of Tiguex in the years 1540–42, when the Spaniards tried to

pacify the area by armed conflict and forced the Tiguex Indians to flee to the mountains. For the most part, however, the high country was used for hunting, collecting, and religious ceremonies.

To the west of the Rio Grande, in the Puerco–San José drainage, the ten-inch precipitation average holds except along the flanks of Mt. Taylor. As one goes on upriver into Keresan, Tewa-Tano, and northern Tiwa country, both altitude and rainfall increase. Modern Santa Fe, at 7,000 feet, receives some fourteen inches of precipitation per year, and Taos, at 6,900 feet, about the same amount, whereas Pecos, at roughly the same altitude, gets nearly nineteen inches. Unlike the Piros, descendants of these various Rio Medio and Rio Arriba groups still live in the area today, and many of their ruined pueblos from earlier times remain as impressive landmarks.

Snowfall varies a great deal, with Taos and Pecos receiving forty inches of snowfall per year and the region around Santa Fe and the Jemez drainage, about thirty-five inches. Even the more northerly parts of the Rio Grande valley proper get relatively little snow—about eighteen inches at Española in the Rio Arriba, the center of the old Tewa region.

Along both the upper Rio Grande and the Pecos rivers, precipitation falls mostly in the summer and early fall. In the Piro area, for example, over 50 percent of the total precipitation budget comes in the months of July through September. The reason for this is that the "Bermuda High," an annual, subtropical high-pressure cell, moves into the Gulf of Mexico during the summer months and brings a clockwise circulation of moist air into New Mexico. In the winter, most precipitation is caused by Pacific storms. These storms normally lose most of their moisture mass by the time they reach New Mexico. In northern New Mexico, however, the southern edge of the north-Pacific storm track often deposits considerable snow in the mountains, which has led in modern times to a profitable ski industry.

The length of the growing season varies considerably up and down the Rio Grande valley. In the Piro region, the last killing frost can be expected in mid to late April, and the first fall frost around the end of October—in other words, there are 180 or more frost-free days. The Tiguex Indians also lived near the 180-day frost-free zone. North of the Tiguex area the growing season diminishes, and the number of frost-free days falls dramatically as one climbs out of the Rio Grande valley and onto the high plateaus or mountain slopes. Pecos and Taos often have their last frost around the end of May and the first frost of the fall season in late August.

As any modern New Mexican who has struggled to grow tomatoes knows all too well, frost is not the only factor in planting and harvesting. In areas above 6,000 to 6,500 feet, night temperatures are almost always cool or cold. At Pecos and Taos, during the early and late part of the growing season, it is hardly uncommon to measure predawn temperatures in the low forties or even high thirties. Another local peculiarity along the Rio Grande is that night temperatures in the river bottom may be several degrees colder than in the heights above the river. Fortunately, native agriculture was based on sturdy crops—corn, beans, squash, and a special, short-season cotton.

Even today, in spite of reckless and shortsighted commercial timber cutting, the Rocky Mountains and the upper slopes of isolated mountains in the Basin and Range province support great stands of conifers: pine, spruce, and fir in the higher mountains and piñon and juniper, along with gambel oak and sagebrush, in the lower elevations. On the High Plains there are mostly grasses: blue and sideoats grama, four-wing saltbush, and buffalo grass. In the mesa country below the higher slopes of the mountains grow sage, saltbush, and grama. Along the Rio Grande and its tributaries there is juniper, cottonwood, American plum, serviceberry, willow, and maple. In more southern regions are found stands of walnut, mulberry, mesquite, and screwbean (the last two limited to the Piro region), plus a variety of shrubs, grasses, and cacti.

Both riverine and mountain regions produce wildflowers and many medicinal plants used both aboriginally and in historic times. Important plants used in curing include datura (jimsonweed), which was taken internally or was applied to wounds as a poultice for anesthetic effect, and Mormon tea (ephedra), taken as a tisane for respiratory problems. The Pueblo Indians knew other medicinal plants as well: *yerba mansa,* horsemint, sage, and many more. Other plants were collected for eating. The Pueblo Indians utilized a number of *quelites,* or potherbs. They collected wild cereal grains, the chenopods and amaranths, wild sunflower seeds, and perhaps wild potatoes. Nicotiana was collected wild and also cultivated as smoking tobacco, used especially in ceremonies. I will have more to say about the Indians' uses of plants in chapter 8.

A variety of animals were hunted in prehistoric and early historic times. One large grazing animal, the bison, was important in native life. People ate its meat and utilized its hide for many purposes; bison hides were traded from the eastern Pueblo area as far west as the Colorado River and as far south as Mexico. There is documentation for this trade at the very beginning of historic times. In 1539, Fray Marcos de Niza, somewhere in the Magdalena-Altar region of northwest Sonora, saw shipments of prepared hides going south.

Plains antelope were also hunted for food and skins. In the mountains were a number of large game animals—deer, elk, black bear, and mountain sheep—as well as predators such as mountain lions and wolves. At lower elevations lived mule deer, antelope, various squirrels, badgers, skunks, and coyotes, as well as cottontails and jackrabbits. These last two animals, especially abundant in the riverine areas and in the basin country, were very important in the Pueblo Indians' livelihood.

There were large numbers of birds, including wild turkeys, grouse, various ducks, and teals. Owls, hawks, and eagles were important in native religion, hawk and eagle feathers being especially in demand for ceremonies, as were the imported feathers of macaws and parrots. Dangerous animals, but also important ones in the ceremonial life of the Pueblo Indians, were the western and diamondback rattlesnakes. In the Rio Grande and Pecos rivers and their main tributaries swam a number of edible species of fish: trout, catfish, and chub. Even so, fish do not seem to have been a particularly sought-after food source. The usual component of insects and arachnids were found in prehistoric times, as they are today.

When the Spaniards came into New Mexico, one of their keenest interests was in mineral wealth, especially gold and silver. As late as the early seventeenth century, missionary and government reports claimed that there were significant silver mines in the Rio Grande area. This wealth in precious metals proved to be largely a pipe dream. Mineral wealth abounded, however, in terms of what the native Indians needed and used. In the Sangre de Cristo mountains they found the beautiful, translucent schist called fibrolite that was in great demand aboriginally for axes and other tools. Lead ores used in glazing pottery were and still are found in the Cerrillos Hills south of Santa Fe and in many other parts of New Mexico. Various lead ores such as galena and copper ores, especially azurite and malachite with their beautiful blue and green hues, were used as paint pigments. Such minerals were mined in considerable quantity in the Cerrillos Hills, around present-day Glorieta, and in other districts.

Turquoise, the great jewel-stone of the Pueblo Indians, occurred in considerable quantity in the Cerrillos Hills, although the turquoise mines have largely been worked out today. Evidence of prehistoric trade in Cerrillos turquoise is found far south into Mexico and eastward into the Mississippi drainage. Obsidian, or volcanic glass, occurs in the Jemez Mountains. The semiprecious stones garnet, jasper, opal, and olivine (peridots) and workaday minerals like chert and flint are found in various places in New Mexico, especially in the Cerrillos region and in the Sangre de Cristo and Jemez mountains. Jet, a form of lignite coal, was used by Pueblo Indians for beads, inlays, and small objects. The modern visitor, shopping in Pueblo Indian markets and shops, often finds lapis lazuli and may assume that it had a long history in the Southwest. Not true: lapis is a twentieth-century import from Asia and South America.

Northern and central New Mexico were comfortable places to live, suited for a variety of human habitations, rich in mineral resources and plant and animal life. The first New Mexicans, coming into the region near the end of the Ice Age, found a climate much more lush than today's, with shallow lakes where now are dry basins and salt flats. The earliest Indians lived along the shores of these lakes, concentrating much of their hunting energies on very large mammals such as the Pleistocene elephants. Still, they did not spurn the teeming smaller animals. What may have been especially important to them were the wild ducks, geese, and other birds that migrated annually from the glaciated north to the warm lands of Mexico and Central America.

As time went by and glaciers shrank back from the face of North America, New Mexico became drier and a bit warmer. The basin lakes disappeared, rivers dwindled, and heavy tree cover retreated to the mountains. For thousands of years, small groups of hunting and gathering peoples made their way throughout this region, moving from river to uplands in a never-ending seasonal quest for food. Slowly they improved their tool kit, slowly they gained control over their environment, but their numbers were never large and life was always hard.

Then, some three thousand years ago, ideas about the domestication of plant foods crept up from the south, and the Indians of northern New Mexico began to sow as well as to reap. Even with these new discoveries, population growth was gradual and uncertain. It was only a thousand years ago that significant populations of sedentary Indians, with their little fields of corn, beans, and squash, became firmly entrenched in villages along the Rio Grande and its tributaries. In the thirteenth and fourteenth centuries sizable villages or towns, called by the Spaniards *pueblos,* began to form, and they remain today.

CHAPTER THREE

The First New Mexicans

There is still considerable controversy about when and how the earliest people, the original *Paleoindians,* reached the interior of North America and began the slowly developing saga of American Indian life. The term Paleoindian comes from the more general term *Paleolithic* (Old Stone Age), which refers to human societies of the *Pleistocene,* or Ice Age, a climatic period that came to an end sometime after ten thousand years ago. We do know that human beings first entered the American continents during the last stages of the Ice Age, a time when great glaciers covered the northern part of North America and portions of Europe and northern Asia. For tens of thousands of years the glaciers fluctuated, sometimes growing, sometimes shrinking. During colder weather conditions they spread out over the land, reaching thicknesses of many thousands of feet. Then warmer conditions would set in and the glacial ice shrank back. When the glaciers were thickest and most widespread, sea levels around the world dropped as much as two or three hundred feet. During periods of ice-melt the oceans filled again and spread onto the coastal plains.

The last great glaciation of the Pleistocene, called in North America the *Wisconsin,* began perhaps seventy-five thousand years ago. During the Wisconsin glaciation there were several advances and retreats of the glacial ice. When glaciers grew on the continents and sea levels dropped, the shallow Bering Sea between northeast Siberia and northwest Alaska became a broad belt of low-lying land (map 3). This region, called Beringia by geologists and paleontologists, was the corridor through which North and South America were colonized by the ancestors of the American Indians. In the last seventy or eighty millennia, there have been several periods when marshy lowlands

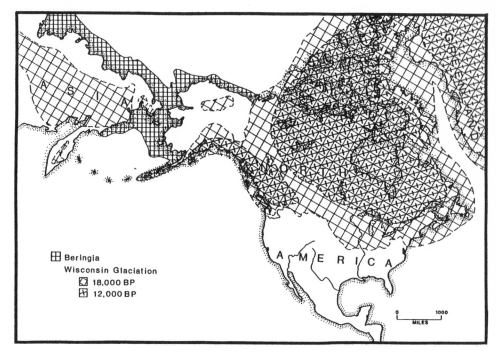

Map 3. Glaciation in North America, 18,000 and 12,000 B.P.

bridged Asia and America and there was a lively movement of animals from one continent to the other. Human beings, however, crossed the flat, cold plains of Beringia only toward the end of the Pleistocene.

Can we date the arrival of these first humans in the Americas? We have reasonable estimates of the dates for certain of these early peoples, owing primarily to radiocarbon, or carbon 14 (C14), dating. This technique measures the minute amounts of a radioactive and unstable type of carbon that has an atomic weight of 14 (distinguishing it from the much commoner carbon 12). All living things, through the process of metabolism, take in and discharge carbon 14 as a tiny fraction of the total carbon used by the body. On the death of any organism, plant or animal, no more carbon is absorbed, and the carbon 14 already in the organism undergoes radioactive decay at a steady rate, with a "half-life" of 5,730 years. This simply means that half the C14 disappears in about 5,730 years, half of the remainder in an additional 5,730 years, and so on.

This process sounds straightforward, but there are many pitfalls in carbon

14 dating. First, the amount of radioactive carbon in any carbon sample is extremely small, so that incorrect or uncertain readings are often obtained. Second, the material to be dated can be contaminated in a number of ways, both before and after collecting, thus giving incorrect high or low readings. Some organic materials—shell, for example—often give undependable dates. And third, the carbonaceous materials being dated are not always dependably associated with human artifacts. Even so, with modern, sophisticated techniques, including the use of computers, C14 samples can be dated as far back as thirty or forty thousand years into the past. After that length of time, only 1 to 2 percent of the original carbon 14 still remains in the plant or animal sample being tested.

Radiocarbon is not the only dating method for the late Pleistocene. Other techniques are used in specific cases. One whose use is increasingly common is called *archaeomagnetism.* This technique is based on the fact that magnetic north ("compass" north) varies from time to time and place to place. Iron particles in clay or other compounds can be fixed in their magnetic alignment by heating. In an ancient clay hearth, for example, these particles will be aligned to the magnetic north of the time the hearth was last in use. Archaeomagnetism, unfortunately, is not always reliable; it tends to be a "backup" method at the present time.

Other dating methods, such as the counting of "varves," or annual silt deposits in lakes or ponds, can be highly accurate, but they may date phenomena that are associated only accidentally with human bones or tools, or they may give a sequence of hundreds or thousands of years that cannot be tied into more recent times. For the Pueblo Indian period in the Southwest, the counting of annual tree-rings (to be discussed in chapter 5) can give exceptionally accurate dates, often to the very year of a tree's cutting.

Although there is still a great amount of work to be done, present evidence suggests that most modern Indians are descendants of a very small number of related people who crossed from Asia to America sometime in the late Ice Age. This idea is supported by recent work of the linguist Joseph Greenberg and his associates. I accept Greenberg's work in this book because it seems to best fit the early human scenario and the present distribution of American languages. I must caution readers, however, that many linguists (people who do scientific studies of languages around the world), question his methodology and results.

Greenberg believes that all North and South American languages are related and, except for two late language families, form a great superfamily called *Amerind.* The first of these latecomers are speakers of *Na-Dene* who entered the New World in post-Pleistocene times, probably sometime after eight thousand years ago—a time when the continental glacier had disappeared from much of western Canada. Today these Indians form the Athapaskan groups of Alaska and western Canada. Na-Dene speakers are also found in small pockets on the west coast of Alaska, Canada, and the United States. The southern Athapaskans, the Apaches and Navajos, reached the Southwest only a few centuries—possibly only a few decades—before the Spaniards. The second intrusive language group was that of the *Eskimo-Aleut,* which arrived in the northern fringes of North America perhaps no more than six thousand years ago.

All other American Indian languages, according to Greenberg, belong to the great Amerind stock, existing today in eleven major branches but descended from one original language in the same way that modern Spanish, French, and Italian are all descended from Latin. If all American Indian languages except for the latecoming Na-Dene and Eskimo-Aleut are related, it suggests a single major movement of human beings into the New World.

Another approach to early humans in the New World is the study of mitochondrial DNA (mtDNA). Deoxyribonucleic acid, or DNA, is the basic building matter of life. Contained in the chromosomes of the cell nucleus, it transmits the hereditary patterns of human beings and, indeed, all other life forms. However, DNA is also found in the mitochondrion, part of the cytoplasm, or outer (non-nucleus), portion of the individual cell. This mitochondrial material is not carried in that part of the male sperm that actually fertilizes a female egg, so a person's mtDNA can only be derived from the mother and passed from one generation to the next through women. Changes in mtDNA tend to be conservative, and similarities over large geographical areas suggest genetic relationships that may be thousands of years old.

In a test of Greenberg's linguistic hypothesis, mtDNA was collected from three American Indian groups (the Mayas of Central America, the Pimas of the southwestern United States, and the Ticunas from the Amazon rain forest) representing the northern, central, and southern branches of Amerind. According to the rather controversial method of dating by rate of mtDNA change, mitochondrial DNA from these far-flung branches of the American Indian linguistic stock suggests an original migration somewhere in the range of twenty-one thousand to forty-two thousand years ago. A possible second Amerind migration came more recently, but well before the Na-Dene migration. The mtDNA data suggest that the Na-Dene speakers formed a founding population in the time range of about five to ten thousand years ago.

What these mtDNA data may indicate is that *all* American Indians, with the exception of the Eskimo-Aleut and the Na-Dene, were originally descended from one, or at most two, small, homogeneous populations. There has even been put forward the (rather extreme) suggestion that American Indians are the descendants of one small band containing possibly as few as four women who crossed from Asia to America in late Pleistocene times.

The most securely dated early human sites in North America are those of the *Clovis* people (in the Southwest, sometimes called the *Llano period*). The Clovis Paleoindians moved southward sometime after twelve thousand years ago (10,000 B.C.). Within a few hundred years, Clovis culture was spreading throughout North America south of the great ice fields.

I will discuss the Clovis people in much more detail shortly, but first, what about people earlier than Clovis? In North America, various sites—Meadowcroft in western Pennsylvania, the Cooperton site in southwestern Oklahoma, and Sandia Cave in northern New Mexico, among others—have stratigraphic levels that, according to reports, date before twelve thousand years ago. In South America there are also sites that have been reported as older than twelve thousand years. These include, among others, Monte Verde in Chile, Los Toldos in Argentina, Toca de Boqueirao in Brazil, Taima Taima in Venezuela, Tabitó in Colombia, and Pikimachay and Guitarrero in Peru. It must be said, however, that every one of these sites, in both North and South America, has been challenged by experts on one ground or another.

One of the oldest claims for pre-Clovis people is that of Sandia Cave, a site excavated in the 1930s. Sitting high on the west flank of the Sandia Mountains north of modern Albuquerque, Sandia Cave contained distinctive projectile points called Sandia points. There are several types of these, but they usually are asymmetrical with a single shoulder (fig. 1). The Sandia culture was originally thought to be earlier than Clovis, with dates of 35,000 to 17,000 B.C. Such early dates have been largely discounted. Since the excavation of Sandia Cave, considerable numbers of Sandia points have been found in the upper Rio Grande region. None of them clearly pre-dates the Clovis culture, and some may even be from later periods. It may well be that Sandia points that actually date from Paleoindian times are simply specialized Clovis artifacts, perhaps knives.

Pendejo Cave, situated near the town of Orogrande in extreme south-central New Mexico, has yielded stratified animal remains from the late Pleistocene. Archaeologist Richard S. MacNeish believes that these bones were laid down in association with crude man-made scrapers, choppers, gravers, and other stone tools. A human finger- and palm-print were dated from a

POINTS

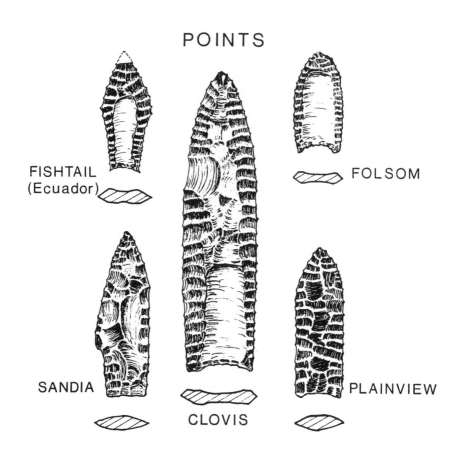

FISHTAIL
(Ecuador)

FOLSOM

SANDIA

CLOVIS

PLAINVIEW

KNIFE

CODY

Figure 1. Paleoindian projectile points and knife.

charcoal sample in an adjacent excavation square to around twenty-eight thousand years ago. A human hair has also been reported, its associated charcoal having (according to newspaper accounts) a C14 determination of around 19,000 B.P. (years before the present). MacNeish identifies three separate complexes in the cave, the earliest dating before forty thousand years ago and the latest extending to around 12,900 B.P., a possible precursor to Clovis. At the time this book went to press, the Pendejo Cave site had not yet been fully documented in professional publications. So far, these early dates have met with some skepticism.

The Orogrande finds certainly increase the possibility that pre-Clovis men and women were actually on the scene in the New World. Still, these early people must have been few in number because the extremely rapid spread of Clovis culture suggests little or no competition. Possibly the ancestors of the Clovis people represented only one tiny group in a very sparse New World population. Let me suggest that sometime around twelve thousand years ago, some unknown inventor among these proto-Clovis people devised a dramatically superior tool or weapon, the spear-thrower. Equipped with this new "state of the art" technology, Clovis people, in a matter of a few generations, spread over very large areas.

Recent work in western Beringia compounds the problem by suggesting that the area was uninhabited until around twelve thousand years ago. Perhaps in response to changing environmental conditions, especially the slow spread of an aspen, willow, and juniper forest, small groups of big-game hunters filtered into the area. Their tool kit somewhat resembled that of the later Clovis people. This *Nenana* complex, like the Clovis, involved the use of bifacial projectile points, end scrapers, gravers, and complex side scrapers, suggesting that Nenana was a founding population for Clovis. Lanceolate fluted points—the characteristeric artifacts of the Clovis culture—have yet to be found in clear stratigraphic associations with Nenana tools, so perhaps the fluted point was invented after the Nenana or proto-Clovis groups left Alaska. Around ten thousand years ago, at the beginning of the final Pleistocene cold oscillation, the Nenana were replaced by a new population whose most diagnostic tool was a small flake or blade (called a microblade) only an inch or two long.

Of course, if the Nenana tradition in Beringia is actually ancestral to Clovis *and* represents the first human occupation of that region, then by definition, nothing can be older than Clovis—except in the unlikely case of migrations by some other route from the Old World. However, earlier movements of human beings through Beringia—migrations of people whose traces have yet to be found—are a distinct possibility.

In any event, the hallmark of Clovis culture, the Clovis fluted point, appears in Canada, throughout the United States, in Mexico, and in Central America. In South America it reaches Peru, and a related type of projectile point, the "fishtail" point, is found as far south as southern Chile. Dates for Clovis sites in North America generally fall in the range of 11,500 to 11,000 years ago (9500 to 9000 B.C.). Indeed, a recent reevaluation of Clovis dates in the Southwest and western Great Plains heartland suggests an even tighter clustering, from approximately 11,200 to 10,900 years ago. In South America, the Clovislike culture at Fell's Cave in southern Patagonia dates to about 9000 B.C. It looks very much as if the Clovis people had at least an *almost* empty New World in which to expand. Even so, their spread was very rapid—so rapid, in fact, that some experts believe it unrealistic.

One possibility for both Clovis and hypothetical pre-Clovis populations is that they spread down the west coast of North and South America by boat. Evidence for Paleoindian boat transport along the western Pacific rim is generally lacking, but changes in the coastline and rising sea levels at the end of the Pleistocene have likely drowned many of the sites. Boat transport is certainly an idea that cannot be summarily discarded.

So far as the northern Rio Grande drainage is concerned, the first human beings for whom we have unequivocal evidence were these Clovis hunters. Indeed, the very name Clovis comes from a site in eastern New Mexico. These early citizens of New Mexico arrived a little before eleven thousand years ago. They were organized into small family bands of hunters who followed the herds of Pleistocene elephants along the region of shallow lakes and grasslands that now forms the southwestern plains. The Clovis Indians used a variety of stone implements, but especially an elegantly chipped stone point, usually of flint or chert, that was attached to a lance or perhaps a spear-thrower dart. The most noticeable feature of the Clovis point is what is called *fluting*, made when a flake was taken off the long axis of the point on either side (see fig. 1).

In the American west, the major collection of Clovis sites lies along the eastern line of the Rockies in what is today called the High Plains. In late Pleistocene times a series of shallow lakes dotted the region. Around these lakes, with their riches of great and small animals, birds of many kinds, and a huge variety of plant life, the Clovis Indians hunted and collected. The upper Rio Grande basin during the Clovis period seems to have been something of a backwater, for relatively few sites are found and these do not give a very complete idea of Clovis culture. The richer Clovis sites, however, lie only a few tens of miles to the east along the edge of the plains, and our picture of Clovis people can be drawn from them.

To the first Clovis hunter the Southwest was virgin territory, and incredibly rich. As we saw in chapter 2, the climate was wetter then, with a series of shallow lakes spread throughout the region. The Rio Grande valley itself may have been fairly marshy. Summers were cooler than they are today, and winters were probably damp and mild. It is hard to find a good equivalent in a modern climate; perhaps the area around Puget Sound (leaving out the ocean) would be a reasonably close match.

For some thousands of years, up to about twelve thousand years ago, the climate of the western United States had been equitable, with cool summers, mild winters, and considerable rainfall. It may have been this widespread favorable climate that permitted the flourishing of large animals known collectively as the Pleistocene megafauna. Beginning around twelve thousand years ago, however, there came dramatic changes in the climate that led to the geological period called the *Holocene,* or *Recent*—the climatic and biological period of about the last ten thousand years.

Twelve thousand years ago the Southwest was occupied by great herds of grazing animals—the mammoth, horse, American camel, tapir, caribou, musk ox, and big-horned bison. Other exotic plant-eating animals included the giant armadillo and the giant ground sloth. The area also supported large carnivores, including the saber-toothed cat, with its long, downcurving canine teeth, and the powerful dire wolf, among others. During the millennium between twelve thousand and eleven thousand years ago, these animals began to disappear. Elephants had died out by perhaps eleven thousand years ago, and other animals soon followed, although the Pleistocene bison (*Bison antiquus*) lasted until possibly nine thousand years ago. The great meat eaters disappeared around the beginning of Holocene times.

One thing that upset the delicate ecological balance, especially of the larger Pleistocene animals, was climate, which became sharply warmer and drier. Human beings may have been another upsetting factor. Some years ago the paleontologist Paul S. Martin suggested that humans moved out of the frozen north and down an ice-free corridor in western Canada around twelve thousand years ago. They rapidly spread south of the ice sheets, and in a matter of a few centuries populated the Americas, destroying the megafauna in the process. Martin, however, probably overstated the case. Although Clovis hunters may have killed wastefully and helped along the disappearance of some large animals, especially the slow-breeding elephants, climatic change was likely a major factor. Whatever the reasons, after about eight thousand years ago the animals of the plains and adjacent Southwest were much like those of today. In the higher elevations lived deer, pronghorn antelope, mountain sheep, and elk. The bison that roamed the Great Plains were intermediate between the modern species and the massively horned Pleistocene animals.

The archaeology of Clovis sites tells us something about Clovis Indian society, and consideration of modern hunter-gatherers can help fill in the edges of our knowledge. Clovis people lived in very small hunting bands, probably only a few families each. These bands subsisted by hunting large animals, especially the mammoth, the meat of which they sometimes stockpiled for future use. The Pygmies of central Africa in recent historic times hunted elephants singlehandedly with short spears. This may have been true occasionally for the Clovis hunters, but finds of multiple spear or dart points at kill sites suggest that group hunting was more likely the norm.

Testing of Clovis points bound to short spears, using dead elephants "harvested" in African game reserves, has produced some interesting results. The points penetrated the rib cavities of the elephants without much difficulty. But repeated experiments demonstrated that any flaw in the point or the foreshaft (or in the alignment of point to foreshaft) would cause the spear to lose penetration power or even to break on contact. If such a thing happened in a real hunting situation, it would be extremely dangerous for the hunter. We can be virtually certain that Clovis mammoth hunters did not always survive the pursuit of their powerful quarry.

Although the mammoth seems to have been the most important single animal hunted, bison, horses, camels, bears, and other large animals also formed part of the Clovis diet. The Clovis people also hunted rabbits and pronghorn, and likely a whole range of small animals.

In early Paleoindian sites on the eastern seaboard, there is evidence that both fruit and fish were consumed, and this surely was true for Southwestern Clovis groups as well. A few grinding tools have been found in Clovis sites; occasionally vegetable foods (for example, wild grass seeds) may have been ground up for food. But dependence on the processing of vegetable foods is far more pronounced among the Archaic Indians who followed the Paleoindians in North America.

We know most about the tool kit of the Clovis people. The Paleoindians came originally from eastern Siberia, and the stone technology found on Clovis sites is roughly comparable to that of Paleolithic sites in Siberia. The hallmark of the technology, however, was the Clovis fluted point, which seems to have been an American invention, for fluting was not used in Siberia. The fluted point averages around two inches long and was formed by delicate flaking on both sides. Then a flake was taken off each side of the basal end (where the point is hafted onto a shaft). These flakes ran up the midsection of the point, thus creating fluting. The reason for fluting is not entirely clear, but it may have enabled blood from the wounded animal to drain out freely.

Clovis points may have been hafted onto spear shafts. There is some reason to believe, however, that a composite machine, the spear-thrower, had reached the New World with the Clovis hunters or was invented by them in this hemisphere. The spear-thrower (sometimes called by its Aztec name, *atlatl*) is a flattened, narrow billet of wood, bone, or ivory about two feet long. One end of the billet is carved into a hand grip, and the other end is notched. Into this notch is fitted the butt end of a short spear or dart. To use the spear-thrower, the hunter holds the hand end of the thrower, and with a round swing of the arm casts the spear. By mechanically lengthening the hunter's arm, the spear-thrower increases the thrust of the dart over that of a spear by about 60 percent. The spear-thrower is both accurate and effective at a range of 150 feet.

To go with their fluted points, Clovis Paleoindians made a series of other stone implements from flint, chert, and obsidian. There were scrapers of various kinds, blades, and what seem to be tools for woodworking. Large flint cores, roughly flaked on both sides (bifaces), also apparently served as blanks from which other tools, including projectile points, could be made. But stone composed only a segment of the Paleoindian tool inventory. Points made of bone, suggestive of Paleolithic bone points in eastern Siberia, have been found, as well as cylinders of bone and ivory. A number of perishable materials were surely used: bone, antler, wood, hide, hair, and bark, among others. Clovis people used fire, as might be expected, although their method for making fire is not clear.

We have no firm evidence for Clovis houses. Indeed, it seems very likely that the Clovis people were constantly on the move, following the animal herds, and that what excavators find are temporary camps with their scatter of stone implements. Like modern peoples who depend a great deal on hunting—Eskimos, for example—Clovis people probably used tents. Alternatively, they may have made simple brush or wattle-and-daub (brush plastered with mud) houses, as did many later Indians in this region. There is evidence that the Clovis hunters ranged over a large territory. In a site in northeastern Colorado, archaeologists found a cache of Clovis points made

Plate 3. Quarry at Alibates. The Alibates flint, used and traded since Paleoindian times, is found only in a ten-square-mile area in the northern Texas Panhandle. Photograph courtesy Archives of the Laboratory of Anthropology/MIAC, Santa Fe, N.M., no. 70.1/1043.

from the beautiful, banded Alibates flint—the only source of which lies three hundred miles away in the Texas Panhandle.

Historic and modern hunter-gatherers usually have a period during the yearly cycle in which a number of individual bands come together. At this time people can trade, exchange gossip, and find husbands and wives for the younger family members. This behavior promotes outbreeding and maintains social ties over large distances. It also allows for new technological inventions to spread from one group to another, and over time it tends to stabilize and standardize the group's language. Ideas of a religious and ceremonial nature are also spread at such meetings. We have no direct evidence that Clovis Indians held these cyclic get-togethers, but the similarity of the Clovis tool kit over huge distances makes it likely.

We know very little about Clovis religion and ritual. Something occasionally found in association with Clovis burials is red ocher (red iron oxide). This blood-colored material was widely used around the world beginning in Paleolithic times. Among historic tribes it is often associated with the life force, a kind of antidote to death. A Clovis site in Montana yielded a cache of Clovis points with a cremated child burial; the cache was covered with red ocher.

Parenthetically, relatively little has been found in the way of physical remains of the Clovis people. A human cranium with a few additional fragments of bone was discovered in 1953 in a sand blowout near Midland, Texas. The skull, that of a female around thirty years old and completely modern, came from a late Pleistocene lake shore in what the investigators thought might be a Clovis occupation level. Unfortunately, no artifacts were definitely associated with the human remains. Recent redating of the Midland skull gave a C14 reading of 11,600 ± 800 years B.P. This redating has been challenged, but if it stands, it tends to confirm the Clovis date of this early American woman.

Although direct evidence is lacking, it seems highly likely that the practice of shamanism appeared during Clovis times. Shamanism is a religious system in which a trained person (the shaman) employs the help of spirit forces to ensure the capture of game, cure sickness, and generally promote group and individual welfare. In historic times shamanism was widespread both in Siberia and in northern and western North America; its roots must be very deep.

We can only speculate on sex differentiation in economic, social, or religious activities among the Clovis people. Recent years have seen increasing—and long overdue—attention paid to feminist social theory in archaeology. It is fair to say that the old truism "man the hunter, woman the gatherer" now meets with considerable and justified criticism. We really do not know what the sex roles were in Paleolithic times. Even such "masculine" occupations as flint knapping or hunting may have been, at least in part, women's work. Nor do we know which of the sexes took the roles of group leaders or shamans.

In 1950–51, I spent some time with a technologically rather primitive South American group living in the rain forest south of the Orinoco River. I remember being impressed and puzzled by a situation that seemed to violate what I had been taught in graduate school about "primitive" people. Although the people of this group could articulate what they considered to be male and female roles, reality was often different. Men were said to be the hunters, yet women often hunted, both alone and in sexually mixed groups. Men were supposed to weave baskets and usually did, yet I also saw women working on baskets. Women were considered the collectors of wild plants, but men often helped in collecting. Certain other activities were more generally sex restricted: men habitually manufactured weapons, and women normally prepared the family "pepper pot." But even those activities might occasionally have been performed cross-gender, or at least my informants indicated that it *could* happen. All in all, I got the feeling that everyday sex roles were much more fluid than the anthropologists of that period would generally admit. I think it is quite probable that the same flexibility was true of Paleoindians.

Around eleven thousand years ago the Clovis tradition began to give way to another, even better known, Paleoindian culture called *Folsom* after a site in northeastern New Mexico. Some experts have seen a transition period called the *Goshen* complex that produced a kind of projectile point intermediate between Clovis and Folsom. The Goshen complex is still not very well known, but it seems to have rapidly developed into full-fledged Folsom.

The Folsom people can be dated to a little after 9000 B.C., and they flourished in the Southwest for some six to eight hundred years. Although very likely an outgrowth of Clovis, the Folsom hunters had a smaller range, being essentially restricted to the western United States from Montana to south Texas. By Folsom times the New World was being filled in with little hunting bands, and the vast, empty spaces that allowed the explosion of the Clovis people over thousands of miles no longer existed. Folsom sites are distributed generally along the eastern edge of the Rockies and onto the adjacent High Plains. Unlike Clovis, there are a number of Folsom sites in the Rio Grande valley.

Like their Clovis forebears, Folsom hunters lived in small family bands and concentrated on hunting large game animals. By now, however, the mammoth, horse, and camel had disappeared, or at least were very rare. The favorite Folsom prey was a variety of the large Pleistocene *Bison antiquus,* but other animal bones—for example, rabbit, antelope, fox, coyote, and wolf— have also been found at Folsom sites. Like Clovis people, the Folsom bands utilized a variety of stone, bone, and antler tools. These included scrapers, various flake implements, gravers, bifacial knives, and fluted points. The beautifully flaked Folsom points, which, like the earlier Clovis ones, were hafted to a lance or throwing-stick dart, are distinguished by a particular kind of fluting. In the Folsom point, a long flake is chipped off the midsection of each side of the point, leading to extreme thinning of the point. The finished implement has a kind of "torpedo boat" look, and the base of the point has backward-projecting barbs on both sides. The middle of the basal region is scalloped out and ground to facilitate hafting (see fig. 1).

A great deal of nonsense has been written about the "lost art" of Folsom flint chipping. In fact, Folsom points in every stage of production have been found. They were made by first removing a large flake (called a preform) from a flint core. This preform was then fluted by detaching a long flake from each side. The tip of the preform was snapped off at the end of the shortest fluted surface. Finishing then involved delicate pressure-flaking to make sharp cutting edges and form the new tip. The Folsom preforms seem to have been carried with the hunters, who fashioned them into knives, scrapers, or projectile points as needed.

One significant invention documented for Folsom times is the eyed needle. So far as I know, these needles have not yet been found in Clovis sites, but it seems likely that the very first people migrating from eastern Siberia brought this implement with them. Tailored clothing was surely necessary in that very cold region. In addition to bone needles, bone projectile points are found in Folsom sites. It has been suggested that the Folsom (and probably also the Clovis) short spear, used with the spear-thrower, had a foreshaft or sleeve of bone, antler, or wood, with a socket in which the point could be fitted. This heavy foreshaft would allow optimal use of a spear-thrower, for it concentrated weight onto the front end of the projectile, something that the rather light point itself could not do.

The Folsom people used a variety of stone in making their tools. Folsom technology from the Hansen site in north-central Wyoming has been analyzed in detail. There, points, scrapers, hammerstones, and knives were made of chert, quartzite, and porcelainite (metamorphosed shale). Limestone was used for heavy choppers, and sandstone for abrading tools. There were a few examples of obsidian at the Hanson site, most likely from the Yellowstone area some two hundred miles away. At the Lindenmeier site in northern Colorado, there appeared obsidian from both Yellowstone, 350 miles to the northwest, and the Jemez Mountains, about the same distance to the south. Lindenmeier was used as a major campsite over a long period, and it may have been visited by bands from both north and south. Of course, long-distance trade in obsidian is another possibility.

Many Folsom sites have been found, and they are reminiscent of Clovis sites—hunting stations with nothing definitive in the way of house structures. Folsom people who hunted in the Rio Grande valley preferred camps near the shallow Pleistocene lakes or, less commonly, near running streams. The Folsom sites tend to sit on hill slopes or crests, averaging a hundred yards away and a dozen or so feet above the water. They normally are on the northeast side of their hunting and water areas, suggesting that camps were deliberately placed so as to be downwind of the game animals. From the general layout, it would seem that animals coming to drink at the adjacent lake or stream were the main victims of people from a given encampment.

Usually the camps were also located near arroyos or lava tongues that could be utilized to trap animals. Although there is no particular evidence for it in the Rio Grande valley, entrapment of bison in steep-sided arroyos was a favorite kill method of the Folsom hunters. The Folsom "type" site (from which the culture gets its name), near the little northeast–New Mexican town of Folsom, contains evidence for an early winter kill of a number of bison that were forced into a narrow arroyo. At other sites, groups of bison were driven over cliffs by hunters working in cooperation.

If the actual living structures of the Folsom people are unknown, the finding of eyed needles strongly suggests a skin-working tradition and skin tents. Most encampments, like those of the Clovis complex, were of small family groups. The large kill sites, however, might in some cases have involved larger groupings—perhaps cooperative hunting by a number of family bands. Very little is known of the religious or ceremonial life of Folsom people. One find at the Theo Lake site on the eastern edge of the Llano Estacado in west Texas seems to be a shrine of some sort. It is formed of a circular arrangement of bison long bones and jawbones fitted together and placed in a small hole. The shrine was then covered by bison bones discarded during butchering. As with the Clovis culture, it is likely that shamanism was practiced.

The tradition of fluting chipped-stone projectile points died out around ten thousand years ago, but Paleoindians continued to live in the Southwest and adjacent plains regions. In New Mexico, a variation of what is sometimes called the *Plainview* tradition—marked by a handsome, leaf-shaped projectile point—spread throughout much of the upper Rio Grande valley. Interestingly, Plainview sites tend to cluster near the rivers rather than along the shores of lake beds. It is clear that times and climates were changing, and the Southwest was slowly becoming warmer and drier.

By about 9,500 years ago (7500 B.C.) there appeared the final Paleoindian tradition, one called *Cody*. Cody sites in the Rio Grande area cluster around the Rio Grande, Puerco, San José, and other streams. It seems that by Cody times the shallow lakes that supported herds of animals in earlier times had turned into the dry playas existing today. The Cody people were still hunters, but in the Rio Grande valley there was less abundant game. Cody stone technology suggests more diverse hunting of a variety of small game. The Cody knife, which resembles a miniature modern meat cleaver, was perhaps a butchering tool (see fig. 1).

At some point, a bit after eight thousand years ago, the Cody tradition was replaced by that of the *Archaic*. It is still not clear who were the earliest Archaic peoples of the Rio Grande basin. Cynthia Irwin-Williams, who did much of the basic archaeological work on the Rio Grande Archaic, believed that Archaic peoples spread slowly from southern California and Arizona. This tradition eventually reached the Rio Grande basin, perhaps by 5500 B.C., and in New Mexico is called the *Oshara*. The relationship of this early Archaic complex to the Paleoindian Cody tradition is not entirely clear. Irwin-Williams believed that the Rio Grande may actually have been deserted between the end of Cody times and the beginning of the Oshara, but other experts see a Cody component in early Archaic life on the Rio Grande.

By about 5500 B.C., the end of a long era had come. Paleoindians had maintained their way of life in the Rio Grande valley for several thousand years, exploiting the rich animal and plant life along the shores of ancient lakes and in the mountain uplands. They had adapted to many changes over that vast span of time, but drastic alteration in the climate and the decline of large grazing animals finally made the Paleoindian type of economy impossible. Their inheritors—to some degree their descendants—gradually developed strategies to cope with the harsher conditions of the post-Pleistocene world.

CHAPTER FOUR

Small Societies
in a Large Land

 In order to understand what was going on in the Rio Grande basin at the end of Paleoindian times it is necessary to look at the climatic record. The geologist Ernst Antevs outlined a post–Ice Age climatic sequence that goes something like this. Beginning 10,000 years ago, there was a slow warming trend in the Southwest. It intensified around 7,500 years ago in what is known as the *Altithermal* (period of greatest warmth). The "long drought," as Antevs called it, stretched on for some 3,500 years. These extreme conditions began to change around 4,000 years ago (2000 B.C.), with a gradual moderating of temperatures and a climatic period called the *Medithermal* (moderate warmth), which has lasted to the present day. The long drought, with its general rise of temperature, caused the snowpack in the western mountains to shrink, Pleistocene lakes to dry up, and desert vegetation to spread. It was a period of hot, dry summers and cool, dry winters.

Today, some scholars question the concept of the Altithermal, at least for the Southwest proper. But it does seem that some climatic shift accompanied the disappearance of Pleistocene animals and the rise of tiny, impoverished hunter-gatherer societies in the Rio Grande area. The Altithermal probably represented the lowest point in the occupation of the northern Rio Grande. Tiny groups, containing in the aggregate no more than a few hundred people—perhaps only a few dozen—for the whole upper Rio Grande valley, struggled to live in the heat and dust of a landscape warmer and more barren than today's. In such an environment, water was the overriding factor, and life had to be centered on or near streams and water holes. The daily and seasonal round had to be planned so that water was always available.

By nine thousand years ago, Paleoindians in some parts of the greater

Southwest—California, western Arizona, and the Great Basin (the interior-draining region of present-day Utah and Nevada)—under pressure from a hostile environment, began to change themselves into what we now recognize as *Archaic* groups. These were gatherers and hunters who concentrated on a variety of plant and animal foods. The little bands foraged from one spot to another as particular seeds, roots, or fruits came into season, or they shifted location to take advantage of peak populations of rabbits and other small animals. To Indians of the Archaic, hunger and privation were never very far away.

An early and long-lived Archaic tradition called the *Cochise culture* formed in southern Arizona perhaps as early as 7000 B.C. Over several thousand years it spread gradually eastward into western and central New Mexico. Out of the Cochise eventually came two complex and far-flung cultural traditions, the *Hohokam* of the Gila-Salt area of modern Arizona and the *Mogollon,* originating in the mountains to the north of the Gila River in what is now eastern Arizona and western New Mexico. The direct ancestors of the Rio Grande Pueblo Indians, however, belonged to a somewhat different Archaic, one that slowly seeped eastward into Arizona and New Mexico, reaching the Rio Grande area sometime around 7,500 years ago (5500 B.C.).

The last of the Pleistocene hunters clung on in New Mexico until at least eight thousand years ago. What happened then is not entirely clear. New Mexico Archaic expert Cynthia Irwin-Williams believed that the end of the late Paleoindian Cody complex was followed by a period of several centuries in which nobody at all lived in northeastern New Mexico. Around 5500 B.C., new groups of people with an Archaic way of life drifted into the area. These constituted the Jay phase (5500–4800 B.C.), beginning a long-term Archaic culture called the *Oshara tradition.* The subdivisions, or phases, of the Oshara tradition are shown in figure 2.

A problem with the Oshara tradition is that detailed site excavation reports are not yet available for most of the phases. Not all experts agree with Irwin-Williams about the break in human occupation, preferring to see the Oshara tradition's Jay phase as growing out of the late Paleoindian Cody and representing a last-ditch attempt by small groups of people to continue in the big-game hunting tradition. They believe that the full Archaic economic adaptation came after the Bajada phase (4800–3200 B.C.), at the beginning of the San José phase (3200–1800 B.C.). In this book I shall assume that a very minimal population inhabited New Mexico throughout the seventh millennium B.C., bridging the Paleoindian and the Archaic periods. I will also treat the Jay and Bajada phases as somewhat separate from later phases, perhaps

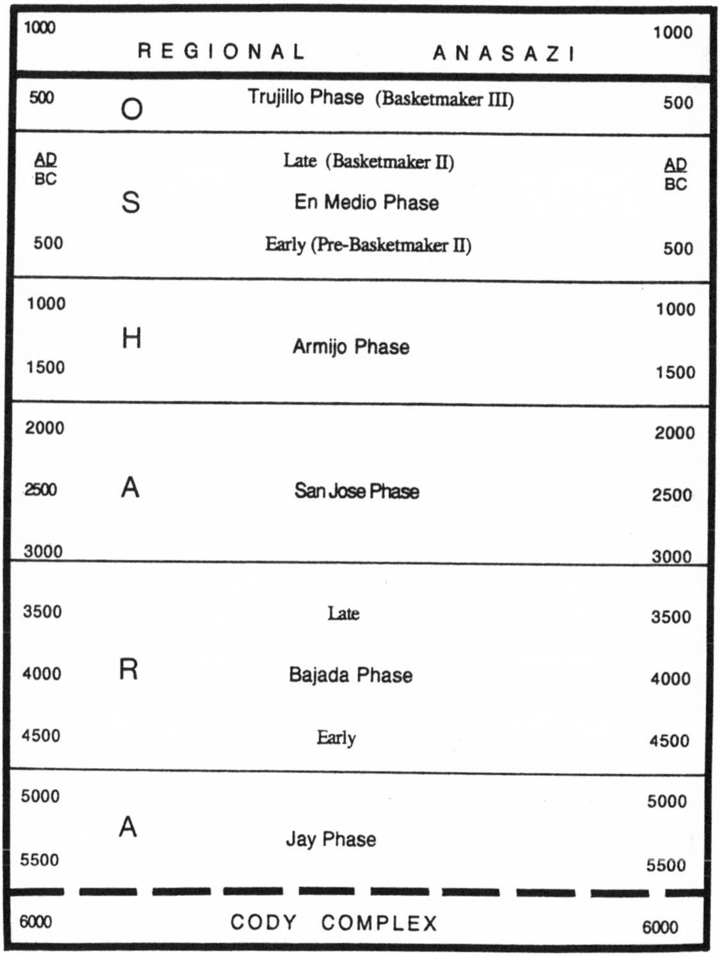

		REGIONAL ANASAZI	
1000		REGIONAL ANASAZI	1000
500	O	Trujillo Phase (Basketmaker III)	500
AD BC	S	Late (Basketmaker II)	AD BC
		En Medio Phase	
500		Early (Pre-Basketmaker II)	500
1000	H	Armijo Phase	1000
1500			1500
2000			2000
2500	A	San Jose Phase	2500
3000			3000
3500		Late	3500
4000	R	Bajada Phase	4000
4500		Early	4500
5000	A		5000
5500		Jay Phase	5500
6000		CODY COMPLEX	6000

Modified from Irwin-Williams, 1973

Figure 2. The Oshara tradition in northern New Mexico.

representing the tail end of Cody occupation, with some gene flow and cultural influence from small Archaic bands moving in from the west.

Irwin-Williams believed that the development of the upper Rio Grande area took the form of slow, incremental change over the centuries, with human populations continuing in an unbroken line for generation after generation. She has been criticized for this "gradualist" approach, but in my opinion it makes the best sense. This is not to say that outside influences were lacking or unimportant. Archaic peoples tended to cover large areas in their seasonal struggle to survive, and the archaeological record shows considerable evidence of intergroup contact. One very important example of contact, discussed later, is the introduction of agriculture to the northern Rio Grande from lands farther south.

Whatever the truth about its beginnings, the Oshara tradition was central to the human story along the Rio Grande. From Jay phase times onward, a continuum of human life can be traced, without any significant break, for seven and a half thousand years—to the Pueblo Indians of today's northern Rio Grande. The beginning of the Oshara coincided with the beginning of the long drought of the Altithermal. There is evidence from just about this time that the bison herds of the western and southern Great Plains had shrunk back, perhaps essentially disappeared, until about 4,500 years ago. It is doubtful that the Jay and Bajada people had any sort of big-game hunting strategy. The likelihood is that by the beginning of Jay times human beings were entering the diversified small-game hunting and gathering of Archaic culture.

Direct evidence for Archaic times in the upper Rio Grande basin is scanty but widespread. Most Oshara tradition fieldwork has been done in the mesas and valleys of the Arroyo Cuervo (map 4), a region of about two hundred square miles located between the Rio Puerco and Rio Jemez drainages on the east slope of Mesa Prieta (some twenty-five to thirty miles, as the crow flies, northwest of present-day Albuquerque). This is rugged canyon and mesa terrain, ranging from about five thousand to above seven thousand feet in altitude. Current precipitation is some ten inches per year, falling mainly as rain in the summer months. Stands of sage, piñon, and juniper dot the upper slopes of Mesa Prieta, the western rampart of Arroyo Cuervo. On the canyon floors and lower mesas are various wild grasses, including amaranth, yucca, cholla and other cacti, saltbush, squawberry, and bearberry. In Altithermal times there seems to have been more or less the same vegetation, though considerably sparser and with somewhat different proportions of the species involved. There was probably a bit less total rainfall than today, and it may have had a somewhat different seasonal distribution.

The vegetation is of a sort that produces food for human consumption mainly from March to November and is scattered in such a way that human groups making their living from plant gathering must move around a great deal. Sites of the early Oshara (Jay and Bajada phase) people are mostly found along cliff tops at the heads of canyons, along canyon floors, or at springs in the canyon sides. Occasionally, sites are found around seasonal

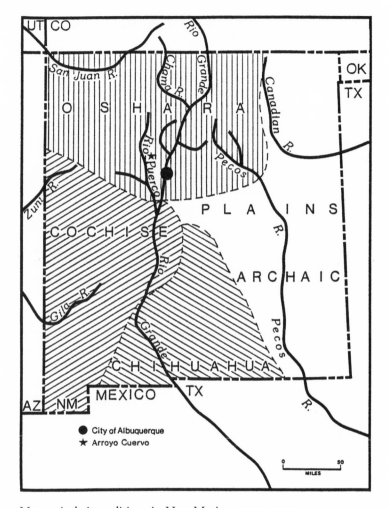

Map 4. Archaic traditions in New Mexico, 2000–1000 B.C.

water holes. A few hunting camps have been discovered in the Jemez Mountains to the east, and a few specialized quarry sites sit near good-quality outcroppings of the hard volcanic stone, basalt. Sites are very small, averaging less than five hundred square feet—about the floor space of a large modern living room. Often the exact core living area cannot be delineated. Instead, one finds simply a thin cover of tools and debris from stone flaking, especially along the heads of canyons. This pattern probably represents season after season of camping in the same spots.

53

Oshara stone implements are found in a number of areas of northwestern New Mexico and extending into the Four Corners region. They are widely spread north of Arroyo Cuervo in the upper Rio Grande basin and in southern and southwestern Colorado. There are Oshara materials in the Puerco drainage, as well as in the Pecos drainage as far north as the upper Gallinas valley and as far southeast as Santa Rosa in east-central New Mexico. Oshara points are also found in the upper Canadian drainage. The Oshara tool kit appears in the Estancia basin east and south of Albuquerque. Isolated early Oshara tools are reported from as far south as the Tularosa basin in south-central New Mexico. The stone implements in such sites may, perhaps, represent some of the Oshara bands on a seasonal round.

From around 3000 B.C., however, there seem to appear influences from the Cochise culture mentioned earlier. Cochise peoples, extending northward from what is now southwestern New Mexico, may have formed a shifting frontier with the Oshara people in an east-west line that cuts across the lower Puerco River valley, roughly on the line of modern Interstate Highway 40. There also seems to be a Cochise penetration into the Galisteo region south of modern Santa Fe. In the same general time period, a third Archaic culture, centered in the Chihuahuan Desert, was spreading northward into the Rio Grande valley. This *Chihuahua tradition* eventually extended into western and central New Mexico as far as the Socorro area and the San Agustin Plains. Given the tendency of Archaic foragers to move long distances in a seasonal round, it is not too surprising that people whose heartlands were hundreds of miles apart managed to contact each other and to trade tools and ideas. A fourth large tradition, the *Plains Archaic,* whose people extended to the drainages of the Pecos and Canadian rivers, also likely had contacts with the Oshara. The interaction of the Plains Archaic and Oshara traditions has not, as yet, been greatly explored by archaeologists.

Tools found in early Oshara sites include projectile points, bifacial (shaped on both sides) knives, side scrapers, chopping tools, and hammer stones. No living structures have been located. Since this is a region of quite cold winters, some sort of clothing and winter shelter would seem absolutely necessary, but we have very little evidence to go on. The people may have retreated to rock shelters in winter, and they probably wore some sort of skin clothing. So far as I know, no eyed needles have been found.

The early Oshara people seem to have eaten a wide range of plant foods, including yucca hearts, roots of various plants, seeds, and berries in season. By Bajada times there appear small, pebble-filled earth ovens. The projectile points of the Osharans, probably used with a spear-thrower, suggest considerable hunting. Judging from animal bones found in the Arroyo Cuervo region, it would seem that the Osharans mainly hunted small animals such as rabbits and hares but occasionally killed larger creatures such as the deer and antelope that lived on the grassy plains in the eastern part of Arroyo Cuervo.

In this region the seeds of various wild grasses, especially amaranth, make dependable food sources. But wild grass seeds need to be crushed or ground to break up the hard seed coats; otherwise, the seeds simply go through human intestines largely undigested. In native America, the commonest way to grind up seeds and other plants was to place them on a shallow slab of rock and scrub them back and forth with a hard, squared-off stone held in the hand. In modern times this smaller stone is usually referred to as a *mano,* the Spanish word for hand, and the larger flat slab as a *metate,* from the Aztec word *metatl.* The same implement, when found in early cultures in Eurafrica and Asia, is called a *quern,* but in the Americas *metate* is the term most often used.

The common alternative way to crush seeds was with a deep stone or wood bowl called a *mortar.* The seeds were placed in the mortar and ground with a drumsticklike implement, often fashioned of wood, called a *pestle.* The mortar and pestle were known but relatively little used in the ancient Southwest.

Although there is some evidence for ground stone tools as early as Jay phase times, it is not entirely clear whether or not early Osharans used a mano-metate set. If not, they probably had to forgo cereal grasses as part of the food supply. Picture tiny groups of people scattered over the mesas and along the canyons of the Arroyo Cuervo region. Their whole life revolves around water: springs and seeps near the canyon heads are crucial water sources. For part of the year people move in a very restricted area, perhaps only a few miles from the main encampment, hunting rabbits, ground squirrels, and other small mammals and collecting wild bulbs, roots, and the softer edible parts of various plants. Larger animals such as deer are great prizes, both for their supply of meat and for their skins—but a deer kill is not an everyday occurrence.

We have no direct evidence for how the early Osharans organized their society or what they had in the way of religion. On the analogy of historic bands at the same economic level, it seems likely that the groups contained, at most, three or four families. There were probably periods during the year—berrying season in the canyon bottoms, or times when piñon nuts were ripe in the uplands—when several bands came together, camping side by side, trading ideas, and arranging marriages for young people. Religion likely revolved around the skills of shamans who used their spirit powers to cure and to help fructify the land. We have no evidence for this, but as I mentioned in chapter 3, shamanism was and is widespread in America and Asia, and in all probability it goes back to Paleoindian times in North America.

The life of the early Osharans must have had high spots, periods when the weather was mild and this or that food source gave a few weeks of plenty. Ceremonies, shamanistic exhibitions of spirit power, and story-telling helped to pass the time and enrich life. But taken as a whole, this was a hard life, with food seldom in great supply and often lacking altogether. Death from disease, malnutrition, or accident was never far away. It was not a time for experimentation, and indeed, there is very little evidence that the tool kit increased in efficiency over the entire two-thousand-year span of the early Oshara. Innovation was a risk, and people had little time or stomach for risks.

But however slowly and uncertainly, change did come. Around or a little before 3000 B.C. the Oshara people began to develop a somewhat more elaborate way of life. The San José phase, which lasted from about 3000 to 1800 B.C., seems to show a response to the slow relaxation of the long drought, which finally came to an end about 2000 B.C., during the last centuries of the San José. This was a period of somewhat greater water availability as new springs and seeps formed and older ones increased in flow. Vegetation probably became slightly richer. Habitation sites grew larger (fifteen hundred or more square feet, the size of a small house), both hearths and earth ovens are found, and post-hole patterns suggest some sort of structure. There was an increase in the tool kit, with crude manos and metates and small, serrated projectile points, still probably used with the spear-thrower. Population increase is suggested by the larger site size and the larger number of sites. San José phase Oshara sites are found as far south as the Acoma area of central New Mexico and north to southern Colorado and Utah.

Around 1800 B.C., the San José phase gave way to the Armijo phase, in which for the first time there is evidence that people in the Arroyo Cuervo area were beginning to aggregate or cluster together during the fall and winter in rock shelters and other protected spots. The sites of the Armijo phase people are much larger, some of them as big as five thousand square feet, the size of an urban house lot. Winter populations in such spots as the Armijo rock shelter may have numbered as many as fifty individuals. The tool kit was considerably richer and included a variety of grinding implements, projectile points, scrapers, choppers, and stone drills. But the most important thing is that in late Armijo times a domesticated plant—maize, or corn—made its first appearance.

The question of agriculture in the Southwest is one over which there is still considerable disagreement. The outline, however, seems to be something like this. At some point before three thousand years ago, knowledge of a domesticated annual cereal plant called *Zea mays* began to trickle into the Southwest. *Zea mays* had been domesticated from its wild ancestor, teosinte *(Zea mexicana)*, as early as 5000 B.C., somewhere in the highlands of southeastern Mexico. The grain reached the Southwest as a rather primitive pod-popcorn variety called *chapalote.*

The early Mexicans had domesticated a number of other food plants, but of these, only four (counting maize) reached the Southwest in prehistoric times. In the same general time frame as maize came squash *(Cucurbita pepo* and *C. moschata)*. The bean *(Phaseolus vulgaris* and *P. acutifolius)* arrived much later; its more widespread species, *P. vulgaris* (the common brown bean or *frijol)*, reached the lower Southwest sometime around the beginning of the Christian, or common, era. The fourth plant was cotton (species of *Gossypium)*, which we do not normally think of as a food source but which was indeed utilized for its oil-rich seeds in early common-era times. A fifth domesticate appearing around the same time as squash was the bottlegourd *(Lagenaria siceraria)*, but gourds from this plant were probably used mainly or wholly as containers.

A firm commitment to maize and squash agriculture seems to have been made during the San Pedro phase of the Cochise culture, perhaps around 1000 B.C. Agriculture gradually spread northward, whether by migration of San Pedro–type people or by the diffusion of ideas is not clear. At least in the upper Rio Grande valley, the latter mechanism is more likely. The idea of agriculture and the plants themselves were passed along to Oshara groups who then engaged in their own experiments with the new techniques.

Cynthia Irwin-Williams believed that maize appeared early in the Armijo phase (1800–800 B.C.) at Arroyo Cuervo, but the evidence so far suggests later Armijo times. A few sites in the Chaco Canyon area, not far from Arroyo Cuervo, have produced maize pollen that seems to go back to the early second millennium B.C. There are uncertainties as to the validity of this date, however, because of the possibility of contamination. Maize pollen is small, and over a period of time, pollen from later agricultural activity can penetrate into lower levels of sites through small mammal or insect burrows. But at site LA 18091, a few miles west of Chaco Culture National Historical Park, maize kernels themselves have been dated at around 940 B.C. Whether this was an isolated adoption of agriculture that failed to catch on, leaving the formation of a continuous agricultural tradition several hundred years in the future, is not known.

We are not sure exactly how Mexican domesticated plants reached the Rio Grande. In all probability they spread northward out of Chihuahua and Sonora, carried through river valleys and along the adjacent lower flanks of the mountains. The San Pedro Cochise people may well have functioned as middlemen. The chapalote form of *Zea mays* may have been adapted to short growing seasons while still in Mexico.

With the plant must have come at least minimum ideas about how to store, protect, plant, and cultivate maize. Storage can be tricky. The seeds must be put in a cool, dry storage place to prevent premature germination and rot, and they must be protected from insects. The seeds must be planted late enough in the spring to avoid late frosts but early enough to take maximum advantage of damp soil conditions. Maize in the Southwest is not a crop that can be planted in the spring and left untended until the fall harvest. Guarding the plantings from birds and burrowing animals, weeding, thinning, irrigating the hills during dry weather, and protecting the mature corn from deer and other foragers all require a considerable investment in time and effort if the plants are to grow. Squash takes less care than maize, but the plants still need a certain minimum effort.

We are not sure what the sex division of labor may have been for early Archaic agriculture, although it has been argued for the Archaic of the eastern United States that women may have been the shapers and developers of maize agriculture.

Under what conditions would Archaic men and women in the Southwest turn to agriculture? Archaic life presented a constant series of challenges: where and when to find food, how to stay near dependable sources of water. The people of the upper Rio Grande valley and its tributaries were, by the nature of their economies, wanderers. Hunters and gatherers centered in the Arroyo Cuervo region must have roamed far afield during at least part of the year, and in fact, the arroyo may have been primarily a wintering area. It was during their wanderings that the people of the Armijo phase probably first got the idea of agriculture. They likely experimented with the new crops, trading for seed corn and squash and collecting information on planting and protecting the growing crops.

It was in late winter and early spring that Southwestern Archaic Indians were most at risk. This was a time when fats and carbohydrates were generally lacking in the diet. Even prey animals had lost their winter fat, and their flesh was mostly protein. This could cause problems because protein is hard for human beings to metabolize in diets lacking sufficient fats and carbohydrates. Maize supplies about three-fourths of its total calories in carbohydrates and also contains protein and a certain amount of vegetable fat. Squash (per weight) contains smaller but still significant amounts of carbohydrate and protein, plus a small amount of fat. Ripening as they do in late summer and early fall, and being easy to dry and store with little loss of food value, these two plants made an important contribution to the late winter diet.

In the northern New Mexico uplands, maize was near its ecological limits of growth. Modern hybrid corn requires fifteen to twenty or more inches of rainfall during the growing season, which must be about 120 days. Desert varieties of maize can reduce the amount of necessary moisture, although they often need a longer growing season. Certain parts of the Arroyo Cuervo region may reach 150 frost-free days per year, but rainfall there is deficient. It seems very likely that special areas around seeps and on south-facing slopes were planted, and perhaps some kind of hill irrigation was used.

It was partly because of these environmental problems that some centuries went by before agriculture became a truly important element in the diet of the Rio Grande peoples. Only slowly did the wandering family groups make the investment in sedentary behavior needed to maximize agricultural produce. Indeed, nowhere in the Southwest did gathering and hunting go out of economic style. Even the intensive irrigation agriculture of the Pueblo Indians in late pre-Hispanic times was done in parallel with the collection of wild plants and hunting of animals, both large and small. This is not to denigrate the importance of agricultural produce in the overall diet. By A.D. 500 (or perhaps by some centuries earlier) maize had become the Indians' single most important plant food. It retained this premier status throughout the prehistoric period.

During the late Oshara En Medio phase (800 B.C. to A.D. 400) and the Trujillo phase (A.D. 400–600), agriculture became a reasonably important part of life in the Arroyo Cuervo region. The later part of the En Medio phase represents what archaeologists have for many years called *Basketmaker II,* a complex found in a number of sites, especially in the area drained by the San Juan River to the west and north. The descriptions of Basketmaker culture that I will offer here are largely derived from the San Juan area. Sites in the Arroyo Cuervo and other parts of the upper Rio Grande valley were relatively impoverished during Basketmaker times.

The Basketmaker period was so called because of the excellent coiled and twilled baskets that appear in its sites, especially in dry cave sites. The "II" designation is simply a relic of an assumption made when the term was first coined—that an earlier, simpler *Basketmaker I* would eventually be found. It never has been, but perhaps the early part of the En Medio phase can be taken to represent Basketmaker I, at least in the upper Rio Grande valley.

Basketmaker people grew corn and squash, hunted with the spear-thrower, and dug small pithouses, often in rock shelters and caves, for living quarters and for storage. They domesticated the dog, probably for hunting. Their baskets came in several shapes, including bowls and trays, and were often decorated with black paint in geometric designs. Other woven items employed what were essentially basketry techniques, including sandals, carrying bags, and blankets. There were actually two traditions of basket making, in separate parts of the Basketmaker region. One seems to have originated in the San Pedro Cochise; the other probably had a northern Plateau origin. The southern, or San Pedro, tradition, with its two-rod foundation coiled basket, became important in the later Anasazi basket-weaving tradition. Cotton had not reached this far north, and weaving was done with human hair, apocynum (a brownish stemmed herb, also called black hemp or dogbane), yucca, and, for blankets, strips of rabbit or other skin.

Basketmaker II people placed their dead in shallow graves, often at the back of caves or rock shelters. The body was flexed—that is, the knees were drawn up toward the chin. There were grave offerings that might take the form of clothing, pipes, food, ornaments, or weapons. This habit of burying the dead with grave offerings and in a flexed position continued until the Spanish period, although in late prehistoric times two alternative fashions in burials—one with the body extended and the other by cremation—began to seep into the Anasazi region from farther south. Because of so many well-preserved burials, we know a fair amount about Basketmaker costume. In summer the Basketmaker people seem to have gone naked except for well-made sandals of yucca or juniper bark. In winter, they wore skins and skin-strip blankets. Small aprons of yucca or juniper fiber have been found and may have been primarily used by women during menstruation.

Babies were carried in cradles with shredded juniper bark forming a sort of diaper. Cradles that kept the infant strapped firmly in place were regularly used in the Pueblo world into historical times, and sandals likewise endured. Another long-lived item was the pipe, which in Basketmaker II times was a tube that looked a bit like a short, hollow cigar. The bowled pipe came in somewhat later in the Pueblo period. It is likely that wild tobacco *(Nicotiana rustica)* was smoked. Today, Pueblo Indians mix tobacco with other plants, a

practice probably followed in Basketmaker II times as well. Domesticated tobacco was being grown by Pueblo Indians in the Rio Grande area at least by
the fourteenth century.

The Trujillo culture in the Arroyo Cuervo region represents what is more
generally known as *Basketmaker III*. Arroyo Cuervo, however, and to some
degree the entire Rio Grande basin, were by Basketmaker times becoming
cultural backwaters. This period of ancient Southwestern history is much
better represented in the San Juan basin. The Basketmaker people of the San
Juan introduced several important new cultural elements into the Southwest,
and they eventually merged directly into the long lineage of the Pueblo
Indians.

CHAPTER FIVE

Setting the Scene

 Sometime around A.D. 400 to 500, peoples from the En Medio phase of the Oshara tradition and from the more prevalent Basketmaker II of the San Juan basin began to develop into the widespread tradition known as *Anasazi* or Basketmaker-Pueblo. This great cultural transformation, quickening the northern part of the Southwest, was not centered in the Rio Grande valley; indeed, the Rio Grande became for a number of centuries a sort of backwater, an area of relatively low population. The striking innovations that were to produce the Pueblo Indians of later prehistory and of historic and modern times took place mainly in the great basin of the San Juan River and on the Colorado Plateaus to the west and north.

The changes that made for dramatic new ways of living in the upper Southwest were already happening in southern Arizona and New Mexico, where people in an advanced phase of the Archaic Cochise culture had lived for millennia. Influences from more sophisticated peoples dwelling still farther south in Mexico had affected the Cochise for a long time. The pattern of south-to-north movement of ideas and goods was already two or three thousand years old, as the introduction of agriculture to Southwestern Indians witnesses. For centuries the Southwest represented a cultural "run-off" area for the higher cultures of central and western Mexico. This pattern dominated the way things were ordered in the Southwest not only during the last four thousand years of prehistoric times but on through the Spanish and Mexican occupation of the Southwest. Indeed, it was not until the building of the railroads in the second half of the nineteenth century that there came a major shift from south-to-north to east-to-west influences. Since that time,

Southwestern life has been dominated by the industrialized, Anglo-American east and west coasts.

Sometime after 500 B.C., ideas spreading from northern or western Mexico caused drastic changes in the lifeways of certain of the Cochise Indians, producing in a short time the beginning phases of the great Hohokam and Mogollon traditions. About the same time in the lower Colorado River area, coming from more westerly Archaic people, there appeared the *Patayan* tradition, which led eventually to the protohistoric Yuman speakers of the lower Colorado River. Except for sporadic trade, however, mostly in late times, the Patayan people had relatively little contact with the eastern Pueblo world, and they will not be considered further in this book. Map 5 shows the spatial relationships of the Anasazi, Hohokam, Mogollon, and Patayan.

By the early centuries of the common era, in the valleys of the Gila and Salt rivers, the Hohokam were already developing some of the traits that later affected much of the greater Southwest. The early Hohokam built irrigation canals, planted maize, squash, beans, and cotton, and lived in rectangular, semisubterranean houses. These were not true pithouses but what are sometimes called "houses in pits." In such structures the floors were often excavated slightly to reach a hard caliche layer, which often lies just below the surface in this desert area. The walls rise directly from the pit floors, and there are indications of substantial systems of posts to support grass or brush roofs.

Pottery appeared in the Hohokam area perhaps as early as 300 B.C.— brown and gray wares that were often decorated with red paint. Ceramic figurines made their appearance about the same time. Shell work began very early; shell carving and engraving and figurine production are hallmarks of Hohokam culture, lasting for around fifteen hundred years. Even though their irrigated fields could produce two crops a year, the Hohokam, like their Cochise forebears, also gathered and hunted. They collected saguaro, mesquite, and screwbeans and hunted cottontail, jackrabbit, and deer. Finds of small, serrated projectile points suggest that they used the bow and arrow.

The Mogollon people who lived in the mountains of west-central Arizona and east-central New Mexico began their development at roughly the same time as the Hohokam. By two thousand years ago in the Mogollon region there were already villages of true pithouses (that is, the excavated portions of the houses formed an integral part of the walls), brown and red pottery, maize, squash, and probably the common brown bean or *frijol.* The early brown-ware ceramics in both Hohokam and Mogollon sites seem to be from Mexico, although the exact point of origin is not known today. Like the Ho-

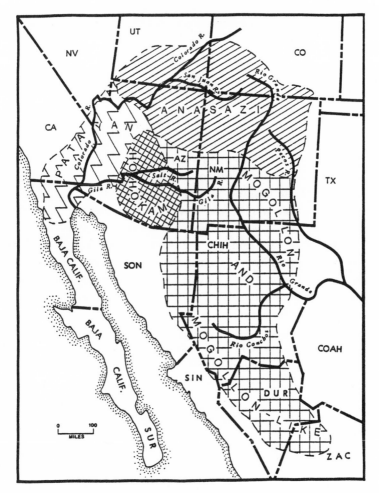

Map 5. Macro-traditions of the Southwest.

hokam, the Mogollon people collected various wild plants and hunted, using the bow and arrow.

This basic Mogollon way of life was quite widespread. By the early centuries of the common era, Mogollonlike cultures appear in a good portion of northwest Mexico. One group of Mogollonlike people in northwest Chihuahua was dramatically influenced by Mexican Indians off to the south and developed into the sophisticated *Casas Grandes* culture. Other groups in northeast Sonora were eventually to form the town-living groups, Opata and Piman speaking, that made up the *Serrana province* visited by Coronado and other early Spaniards. In Durango and Zacatecas, the long-lived *Loma San Gabriel* culture was basically Mogollon. It appeared in the early common-era centuries and was probably ancestral to the historic Tepehuan Indians.

A little later, the distinctive Mogollon brown and red wares and other Mogollon traits began to appear in the Rio Grande basin, extending north to around the region of present-day Elephant Butte Lake. These *Jornada Mogollon* Indians were to have considerable influence on the Rio del Norte province.

By about A.D. 400 or 500, certain ideas and influences and perhaps actual immigrants from the more southern groups, especially the Mogollon, were beginning to percolate into the San Juan and upper Rio Grande drainages. Basketmaker II people were spread widely, if thinly, throughout these two drainages and into the upper Pecos region, a frontier where the Basketmaker way of life seems to have hung on for some centuries after it disappeared elsewhere. In the upper Southwest the Basketmaker II groups, possibly intermixed with new people, became what archaeologists recognize as Basketmaker III, thus beginning the *Anasazi* period, a macrotradition on a par with those of Hohokam and Mogollon.

Basketmaker III, called the "Developmental" period by some archaeologists, especially in the Rio Grande region (fig. 3), was a time of considerable growth in population. The bulk of this growth took place in the San Juan area, although Basketmaker III occupation extended, with some eastern Mogollon influence, to the Salinas region east of the Rio Grande, and there are Basketmaker sites in the Nambe and Tesuque areas north of Santa Fe, around modern Albuquerque, and in the upper Pecos drainage.

Around the beginning of Basketmaker III times a minor climatic shift produced slightly cooler and perhaps wetter summers. This may have encouraged more wide-ranging agriculture; certainly during this period agriculture became increasingly important. Pottery, with its great potential for storing dry agricultural produce, meant an increase in the food supply during the winter months. The economic patterns of Anasazi life were clearly set during Basketmaker III times.

With the coming of Anasazi culture and its increased use of timber, archaeologists are able to use tree-ring dating, or *dendrochronology*. This dating system was developed in the Southwest during the 1920s by an astronomer, A. E. Douglass, who was investigating the effect of sunspots on Southwestern trees. It had been known that annual rings on trees vary in size from one ring to the next. This variation depends on the pressures of the environment on the tree. In the Southwest, moisture that reaches a given tree in a particular

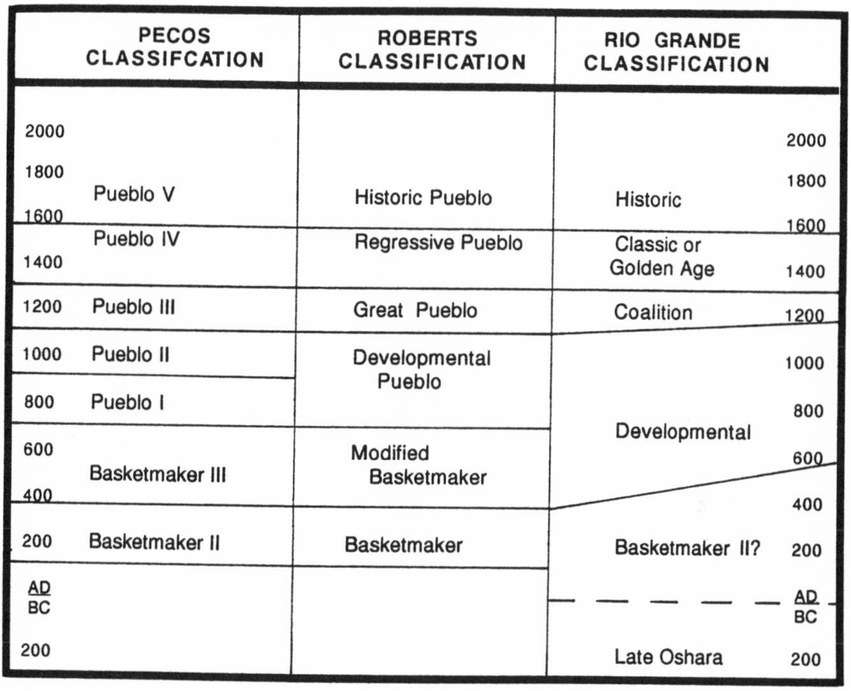

PECOS CLASSIFCATION		ROBERTS CLASSIFICATION	RIO GRANDE CLASSIFICATION	
2000				2000
1800	Pueblo V	Historic Pueblo	Historic	1800
1600				1600
	Pueblo IV	Regressive Pueblo	Classic or Golden Age	
1400				1400
1200	Pueblo III	Great Pueblo	Coalition	1200
1000	Pueblo II	Developmental Pueblo		1000
800	Pueblo I			800
			Developmental	
600		Modified Basketmaker		600
	Basketmaker III			
400				400
200	Basketmaker II	Basketmaker	Basketmaker II?	200
AD BC			— — — — —	AD BC
200			Late Oshara	200

Figure 3. Classificatory schemes for the Southwest from Basketmaker to historic times.

year is the key factor in the size of each year's rings. Wet years normally produce broad rings, and dry years, narrow rings (fig. 4).

Douglass and other investigators were able to demonstrate that this pattern of broad and narrow rings was repeated in tree after tree throughout a given area. They then built up a series of master charts showing patterns of tree-ring variation over many centuries. To do so, they matched the earliest inner tree-rings of living trees with the outer rings of timber used in Spanish mission construction during the seventeenth and eighteenth centuries, and then matched the inner rings of these mission timbers with the outer rings of logs used in pre-Hispanic Indian pueblos. Eventually, in some areas, tree-ring charts were constructed that reach back to the beginnings of Basketmaker III times.

Of course, tree-rings measure the cutting date of a tree, not necessarily the construction date of a building, because people often reused construction timbers pulled out of earlier buildings. Still, a study of tens or hundreds of

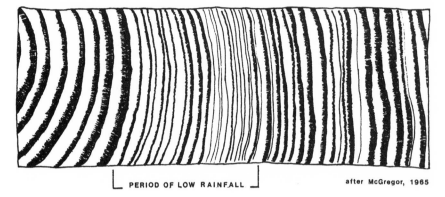

PERIOD OF LOW RAINFALL   after McGregor, 1965

Figure 4. Tree-ring section of Douglas fir. The bracketed area represents a cluster of low rainfall years in the late thirteenth century.

cuttings will generally give pretty accurate dates for buildings, often to within a year.

Dendrochronology, pioneered in the Southwest, has become important in other parts of the world as well, especially in the eastern Mediterranean region and Great Britain and Ireland. In Ireland, for example, there is a continuous record of tree-ring dates reaching back more than seven thousand years from the present.

One of most important innovations in Anasazi culture, certainly derived from Mexico, was that of pottery. Even in Basketmaker II times people had experimented by plastering mud mixed with bast (plant fiber) around the sides of baskets and then allowing the mud to dry, producing pseudo-pottery. This ware is worthless for anything except storage of dry materials, for if liquid is poured into the containers they will melt away. Whether this pseudo-pottery was purely a native invention or was stimulated by a vague knowledge of pottery to the south is unknown.

Somewhere around A.D. 400, or perhaps before, pottery appeared in the western part of the Basketmaker area. The raw material for this pottery was collected along streams and arroyos where the alluvial clays had a high iron content, giving the surface of the pottery a brown color. This brown ware was Mogollon in technique and surely derived from those more southerly Indians. Within a hundred years or so, Indians of the early Anasazi tradition began to produce their own gray or gray-white pottery using clays from other geologic formations. They rolled out thin ropes of clay by hand, then coiled the ropes around a flattened clay base, coil after coil, until the pot was the desired height. Next they scraped and smoothed the pot with a hand or with a river pebble. Because clay tends to crack upon firing, a material called temper—sand, crushed rock, ground-up potsherds, or sometimes plant material—was added to the clay paste to allow trapped moisture to escape during the firing process. As elsewhere in the New World, pottery was hand-made. The potter's wheel came to the Southwest with the Spaniards, but hand modeling of pots remains, even today, the normal practice of tradi-tional Pueblo potters.

Even before the end of the Basketmaker period, potters were experiment-ing with a black paint on the gray or white background—the beginning of a brilliant art form whose best historic and modern examples command huge prices in art markets. In some areas, such as the region around Quemado, New Mexico, south of Zuni, both Basketmaker and early Mogollon tradi-tions, as indicated by pottery, are represented in archaeological sites. There, over several hundred years, Native Americans using Mogollon pottery tech-niques and those following Basketmaker-Pueblo ceramic traditions worked and lived side by side.

Pottery is important to archaeologists because fired clay is next to imper-ishable in normal circumstances, and examples of pottery thousands of years old are not uncommon. Ceramic vessels do break easily, however, so over the years, vast numbers of pottery fragments (potsherds) build up around a habi-tation site. The walls of pots practically beg for decoration, and because decorative techniques change from generation to generation, they provide ar-chaeologists with a valuable tool for relative dating and for studies of the dynamics of art.

Aside from the value archaeologists place on ancient pottery today, the invention opened up many new possibilities for the potters and their groups. Clay pots can be placed directly on a fire, thus making certain kinds of cook-ing, especially boiling, much easier than before. This innovation was impor-tant in the Southwest, for protein-rich beans, when dried for transport or storage, require boiling to make them edible. It is probably no accident that beans appeared during the Basketmaker period, at about the same time as or a little after pottery. In addition, pottery makes a sturdier storage container for both water and dry foods than does basketry. Closed and sealed, the pot is essentially invulnerable to attacks by insects or rodents. And unlike bas-kets, pots will not become brittle with age.

By around A.D. 500 to 600, the Basketmaker period of the Anasazi was in full swing. Not only had pottery arrived but other important inventions had also appeared, again probably from the Mogollon region. The bow and arrow were introduced about this time, replacing that ubiquitous tool of Paleoindian and Archaic hunters, the spear-thrower. The common brown bean (*Phaseolus vulgaris*) was added to the food larder, and cotton, its seeds used for food, also began to appear (the weaving of cotton may not have taken hold until the early Pueblo period). People ate a variety of wild plant foods, including piñon nuts, prickly pear, purslane, goosefoot, and beeweed.

Another food source, the turkey (*Meleagris gallopavo*), hunted by the Basketmaker II people, was now probably domesticated. When the early Spaniards came, domesticated turkeys extended from the Southwest to Mesoamerica. In this case, there is a good chance that the origins of domestication lay in the Southwest—for once, Mesoamerican Indians were recipients rather than donors in their relations with the Southwest. A second domesticated animal, the dog (*Canis familiaris*), served primarily as a hunting companion. Domesticated dogs go back at least to early Basketmaker times in the Pueblo area.

About this time a new and superior type of house began to take hold: the pithouse, again likely derived from pithouses in the Mogollon area. A major advantage of the pithouse in the higher elevations of the upper Southwest was that it provided much better protection against the weather than did a rock shelter or the flimsy, mud-plastered brush house, or *jacal*, that was probably used in earlier times. Specialists have pointed out that pithouses are significantly warmer and easier to heat than are surface structures, with about 20 percent greater efficiency over surface buildings in terms of heat retention. In the Southwest we see a definite correlation between altitude and the depths of pithouses. For example, one study showed that among pithouses located at less than six thousand feet in elevation, only 21 percent were over six feet deep, whereas among pithouses located at between seven thousand and eight thousand feet, 78 percent measured at least six feet deep.

Generally, Basketmaker pithouses were some twelve to fifteen feet in diameter and were dug into the earth to a depth of three to six feet—or deeper in the higher elevations. Roof construction varied: some had cribbed timber roofs, others had a framework of slender poles held up with support logs, covered over with reeds or grass, and plastered with mud. The door might be connected to a short tunnel or crawl space, which also served as a ventilator shaft. A hole was left in the roof above the firepit to serve as an entryway as well as a smoke hole.

Despite these generalizations, pithouses in the northern Southwest showed considerable variation from earliest times. At Shabik'eshchee Village, about nine miles east of the great pueblo ruins in Chaco Canyon, a group of scattered pithouses—some round, others oval or even squared off, ranging from about ten to twenty feet in diameter—was associated with a much larger pithouse that the excavator called a *kiva*. This circular structure had an inside diameter of about thirty-six feet. It had probably four heavy support posts of a type that would hold a substantial roof. A low bench, or banquette, ran around the inner wall. This pithouse may possibly be the precursor of a type of ceremonial structure called the great kiva, which became important in Chaco Canyon and its environs some centuries later.

Even pithouses used primarily as living quarters seem also to have had a secondary ceremonial function. In the floors of many of them was a small hole, a feature known today as a *sipapu,* which in later times, at any rate, symbolized the ceremonial entry to the underworld, the origin place of all Pueblo Indians—indeed, of all human beings.

Beginning around A.D. 700, especially in the San Juan region, Anasazi Indians began to experiment with living in above-ground rooms. In many areas this was a gradual change beginning with flimsily built storage rooms associated with pithouses, which then slowly developed into more substantial square or rectangular stone and mud-mortar houseblocks. The pithouse dweller pattern of sinking pits for food storage outside the pithouse proper was now replaced by the use of special storage rooms in the houseblocks. The pithouse gradually lost its living functions but continued to serve as a ceremonial house or kiva, the Pueblo Indian equivalent of a church, temple, or mosque.

In the upper Rio Grande, pithouses continued in use until perhaps A.D. 950, and in some cases even later. One particular kind of pithouse had four posts supporting the roof and a ventilator shaft (often a crawl space or entryway) to the east or southeast. These pithouses, which have been found especially in the region around modern Albuquerque and northward to the lower Jemez region, seem to show Mogollon as well as Anasazi influence. They gave rise to a specifically northern Rio Grande type of kiva that characterized what is sometimes called the *Coalition period* and lingered, at least in the northern Tiwa area, into historic times.

I should say here that many names for Pueblo ceremonial items, including kiva and sipapu, are terms used by the modern Shoshonean-speaking Hopi Indians. This usage simply reflects the fact that Hopi ceremonial institutions were among the first to be studied by anthropologists. Other contemporary Pueblo Indians do not necessarily use the same names (although there has been some borrowing of ceremonial terms). The words used by the San Juan Basketmakers and early Pueblo peoples depended on the language or languages they spoke—about which we can only make educated guesses.

The crude pueblos that replaced the old dispersed pithouse towns were often built in houseblocks, that is, with contiguous rooms, and often with more than one story. The first centuries of their use belong to periods archaeologists call *Pueblo I* and *Pueblo II,* or sometimes in the Rio Grande basin, "Developmental" period. These "roomblock" pueblos may have evolved in part because of their greater thermal efficiency, since rooms sharing walls will experience less heat loss. They certainly represented a basic change in housing fashion. Their development was likely triggered by an increase in population, but also by a change in living preferences—perhaps a desire to get more sunlight into the individual rooms. They could also have had a military function, for a pueblo of roomblocks is much easier to defend than are scattered structures.

By around A.D. 1000, the transformation from pithouse to pueblo was largely complete, although there are examples from as late as the 1200s of pueblo dwellers reverting to pithouses, probably because of severe winters and economic hard times. In addition, along the eastern periphery of the Pueblo area, in the upper drainages of the Gallinas and Tecolote rivers, pithouse occupation had a long history. Its beginning date is not yet clear, but it lasted into the twelfth century and perhaps even to the early part of the thirteenth. I think it is likely, however, that when peoples from the Rio Grande valley moved into the region around A.D. 1250, it was largely or wholly deserted.

Generally, the Rio Grande valley remained somewhat backward up through Pueblo III times, but in the Four Corners area of the San Juan basin and in Chaco Canyon just to the south, there came remarkable cultural elaboration. Because these areas were important to the exuberant growth of Rio Grande towns in late prehistoric times, I will discuss the "Chaco phenomenon" and the heavily populated settlements in places like Mesa Verde in the following chapter.

CHAPTER SIX

The San Juan Co-Prosperity Sphere

 The best-known portions of the San Juan drainage, thanks to a century of intense archaeological work, are Chaco Canyon, Mesa Verde, and the Four Corners region. Chaco Canyon, lying at about 6,100 feet in elevation in its most heavily settled portions, is one of a series of broad, interconnected canyons that drain off the highlands west of the continental divide in modern-day Rio Arriba and Sandoval counties, New Mexico. The Chaco River (a dry wash most of the time) drains on westward and then almost straight northward, reaching the San Juan River near modern Shiprock. Vegetation in the canyon during Anasazi times was probably much like that of today—scattered juniper and piñon on the mesas, with a heavier growth of water-loving trees, shrubs, and grasses in the canyon bottoms. Ponderosa pine, used in construction of the Chaco towns, today grows at about 7,100 feet but may once have existed at slightly lower altitudes, especially in the period before A.D. 1100.

Farther north, in the San Juan River bottoms, elevation is considerably lower—about 5,300 feet in the Bloomfield-Farmington area. This is a fairly arid region but with somewhat warmer winters than those in Chaco Canyon. North of the San Juan, the uplands of Mesa Verde, the broad Montezuma valley, and the canyon country of Hovenweep to the west receive more rainfall. This is especially true for Mesa Verde, where the entire mesa was well timbered in early Anasazi times, as it is today.

In Chaco Canyon proper, Pueblo III times, or what is called the Classic period, are best exemplified by the massive pueblos of several hundred contiguous rooms standing several stories high. These great pueblos—Pueblo Bonito, Chetro Ketl, and others (fig. 5), almost all on the north side of

Plate 4. Pueblo Bonito before excavation. Photograph courtesy Archives of the Laboratory of Anthropology/MIAC, Santa Fe, N.M., no. 1116.17.

Chaco Canyon—were founded in the early tenth century A.D., but the main building period was the eleventh century. Some building activity continued in the Chaco after A.D. 1100, but the great Classic period in the region was coming to a close and people were drifting away.

Especially in the Chaco area there seems to have been considerable regional integration. At the height of the "Chaco phenomenon" in the mid-eleventh century, there were, by conservative estimates, as many as 4,500 to 5,000 people in Chaco Canyon alone, and some experts put the figure much higher. One problem with estimating population is that relatively few burials have been found at Chaco—the reasons for which are not clear. Perhaps burial grounds have been washed away, or deeply buried, by the erosion and deposition cycles of the Chaco wash. Possibly burial fields remain undiscovered in or around the large pueblos.

In spite of Chaco's heavy population, basic technology had not changed greatly since earlier Anasazi times, and the same trinity of food crops—corn, beans, and squash—underpinned the agricultural economy. Stone technol-

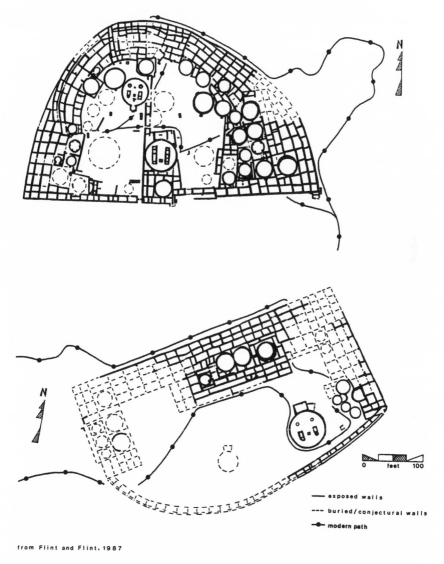

from Flint and Flint, 1987

Figure 5. Floor plans of Pueblo Bonito (top) and Chetro Ketl (bottom).

ogy advanced in minor ways; for example, the superior slab metate, often set in a grinding box, replaced the earlier "trough" metate, which featured a hollowed-out area, roughly oval or semicircular in cross section. Cotton, which had appeared as early as Basketmaker III times, was common by now, and it looks as if a simple loom was in use. It is still not entirely clear under what conditions cotton was grown in the San Juan region, but at Mesa Verde, studies of coprolites (prehistoric human feces) indicate that cotton seeds, rich in both protein and vegetable fat, were of considerable importance in the diet. Remains of turkeys are widespread in the Chaco towns, and because the canyon is outside the normal habitat of the wild turkey, we can presume that these were domesticated. Turkeys were probably raised both for food and for their feathers.

House-building skills increased but were not accompanied by any dramatic innovations in architectural technology. Builders used neither the true arch nor the corbeled arch; indeed, architecture remained technologically simple, and construction very much rule-of-thumb. One advance in technology, however, appeared in techniques for putting together building stone. Height was obtained by using a core-and-veneer technique, in which massive lower walls several feet thick support thinner-walled upper floors, and two carefully laid faces enclose a central core of rougher stones (fig. 6). Building techniques allowed the Chacoans to construct houseblocks of three or four floors, often to a preconceived plan.

Chacoan masonry had a certain elegance. Over time it evolved: early, simple walls were gradually replaced by varieties in which large and small stones alternated in bands. Room ceilings were made by crossbeams that in turn supported smaller poles, on which layers of reeds or grass covered with clay formed ceilings for the lower rooms and flooring for the ones above. Doors were squared up in the walls, with heavy wooden or stone lintels bearing the pressure of the stone wall above the doorway. The houseblocks surrounded courtyards that often contained large ceremonial structures, the "great kivas" of the San Juan region.

What I have been describing is called the *Bonito phase,* or perhaps better, the Bonito *style,* at Chaco, which is found in the great pueblos that line the north side of Chaco Canyon. A second tradition at Chaco, the *Hosta Butte style,* encompassed people who lived at the same time as the Bonito people in villages on both the canyon's north and south sides. Their houses were poorly constructed (compared to the great Bonito-style towns) and contained only small kivas. No great kiva is directly connected to a Hosta Butte village, although the very large Casa Rinconada—the one great kiva on the south side of the canyon—could have been associated with several nearby Hosta Butte sites. Not only was their house construction simpler, but the various luxury goods found in the great Bonito sites—turquoise, macaws, copper bells, inlay work—seldom if ever appeared in Hosta Butte sites (al-

Simple   **Compound**   **Core and Veneer**

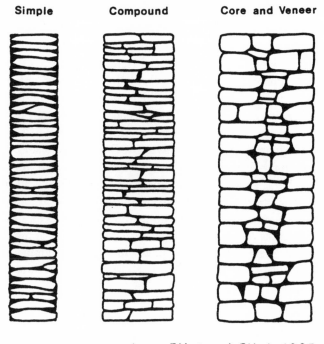

from Flint and Flint, 1987

Figure 6. Masonry wall types at Chaco Canyon.

though turquoise processing areas have been found in the canyon's south-side settlements).

Certainly the south side of the canyon lacked some of the advantages possessed by the north side. Less run-off water is available, and north-facing slopes are a distinct disadvantage in Southwestern winters. The Hosta Butte style does seem to be an "other side of the tracks" situation.

During the eleventh century, groups known as the *McElmo phase* people, whose cultural ties were with Mesa Verde north of the San Juan River, moved into the Chaco area and built pueblos, or added on to existing ones, along the north side of the canyon and on the heights above the canyon. There is some reason to believe that they mixed with remnant Bonito and perhaps Hosta Butte populations. These groups used a building technique that was common farther north: their houses were generally built with thicker blocks of sandstone, carefully pecked into a rectangular shape. These may have been Pueblo Indians with a different language and a somewhat different social system. This sort of infiltration of one Puebloan group by another happened in other times as well. In the historical period we can document the movement of Tano-Tewa and Tiwa-speaking Indians to Shoshonean-speaking Hopi during the late seventeenth and eighteenth centuries.

Bonito-style pueblos at Chaco were usually rectangular or semicircular, and they often incorporated kivas in their enclosed courtyards. The most spectacular building was the great kiva. Several of the big pueblos had these circular structures, and great kivas are found over a large area reaching well beyond the San Juan River into southwestern Colorado. Great kivas range in diameter from forty-seven to seventy-eight feet and in depth from about six to eight feet. These kivas, the most advanced architecture in all the Southwest, had roofs supported by four massive, upright logs or in some cases columns made of alternating layers of stone and wood. The logs or columns rested on great disks of sandstone, some of them three feet or more in diameter and several inches thick. These powerful support columns held heavy ceiling timbers, from which smaller logs reached from the center of the roof to rest on masonry walls that rose from the edges of the underground depression.

Great kivas vary in their number of entryways and placement of banquettes and wall niches, but they commonly have a central firepit flanked by troughlike, stone-lined, rectangular pits excavated into the floor of the kiva. How these pits were used is not certain; they may have functioned as resonators for foot drums, but evidence for plank coverings seems to be lacking. They may have been storage areas for ceremonial items or had some other, entirely different ceremonial function. Possibly they had multiple uses.

Niches in the kiva walls are square or rectangular openings usually only a few inches in depth. Probably they were used to store small ceremonial objects, perhaps prayer plumes. Some years ago, Pueblo architectural experts Richard and Shirley C. Flint measured the horizontal alignment of niches on the south and west walls of Casa Rinconada, the large kiva on the south side of Chaco Canyon. They measured seven niches and found that the horizontal variation of the niche bases over a sixty-foot stretch of the south and west walls was only two and one half inches. In other words, if a true horizontal line was projected around this arc of the kiva at the level of the central niche, no other niche would fall more than an inch above or an inch and a half below that line. Either the Chaco people had made an extremely level floor before they constructed the wall niches, and then measured upward, or they used some other, unknown method, perhaps a primitive leveling device, to ensure this high degree of accuracy.

Plate 5. Floor of the great kiva at Chetro Ketl, Chaco Canyon. Photograph courtesy Archives of the Laboratory of Anthropology/MIAC, Santa Fe, N.M., no. 1115.493.

There were smaller kivas, too, in the Chaco world. These greatly resembled kivas of the Mesa Verde area—to be described later—except that they tended to be somewhat larger and deeper. It has been suggested that the smaller kivas were used by clans or some other, relatively small social unit, while the great kivas served as community structures or were used by large entities such as moieties—divisions of a community into two large social groups. Moiety kivas and clan kivas are found among modern Pueblo Indians, but we really do not know the situation in Pueblo III times. The modern Pueblos use kivas not only for ceremonies but also as men's "clubs," places where men retreat to work and talk and where youngsters can learn the traditions of the pueblo. This may well have been the case during the Pueblo III period.

Today, most of the excavated Chacoan kivas stand open and empty. There is, however, one splendid example of a reconstructed great kiva at Aztec National Monument in Bloomfield, New Mexico. This monumental building,

79

restored by archaeologist Earl H. Morris in the 1930s, gives visitors a chance to step into the past and see a great ceremonial structure as it must have looked almost a thousand years ago (for details of the rebuilt roof, see fig. 7).

As the Chaco culture expanded, it produced political control of a kind likely never seen before in the upper Southwest. The nature of this political organization is not very clear, but it does seem as if a number of the great Chaco towns were interconnected and operating under some degree of central authority. Early fieldworkers noted roads in the Chaco area, and in more recent times, specialists using aerial remote-sensing techniques have mapped a connected web of these roads branching out from Chaco Canyon (map 6). Most Chaco scholars believe the roads were constructed in prehistoric times, beginning in the eleventh century and continuing into the twelfth.

If so, this network of roads inched out from the great Bonito centers to link pueblos along the San Juan River to the north and as far south and east as the Puerco–Rio Grande drainage. Westward, the roads extended nearly to present-day Gallup, and on the south, to about the line of modern Interstate 40. The major roads are each about thirty feet wide, and secondary ones, about half that width. They reach from the main Chaco centers in Chaco Canyon to various outliers such as Salmon Ruin on the north bank of the San Juan. Other roads run to Chacoan sites to the south and southwest. One problematic road reaches south and east to the Guadalupe site near the Puerco River.

The roads were probably laid out with primitive surveying instruments, because they march with determined straightness, going over hill and valley. Minor arroyos were sometimes filled in, making, in effect, tiny causeways. In steep areas, builders erected masonry ramps or occasionally cut steps into the sandstone of the canyon walls. Roadbeds were constructed with a gentle rise in the center to facilitate drainage, and the berm or curbing areas were sometimes outlined with stones.

Chaco roads and the great pueblos themselves suggest considerable centralization of power, or at least a powerful common purpose. A prodigious amount of timber, certainly representing some thousands of felled trees, was needed for the houses and kivas. Since Chaco Canyon, then as now, had very little timber growth, people had to transport the great ponderosa and other logs from the uplands at the headwaters of the Chaco wash thirty or forty miles to the east or from the high country along the continental divide west of Star Lake. The higher elevations of Chacra Mesa may have offered a somewhat nearer supply of timber. This great mesa, sloping from south to north,

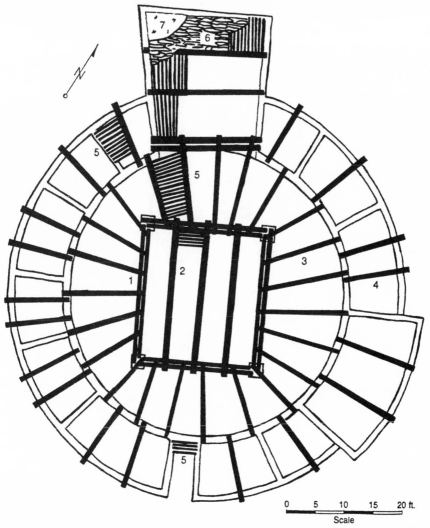

after Lister and Lister, 1987

Figure 7. Probable plan of great kiva roof, Aztec Ruins, New Mexico, as drawn by Earl A. Morris. Key: 1, large logs between tops of pillars; 2, large logs resting on pillar logs; 3, large logs radiating from pillar logs to peripheral room walls; 4, large logs across peripheral room walls; 5, small poles across large logs, between large logs and peripheral room walls, or across peripheral room walls; 6, cedar splints on top of small poles; 7, thick layer of dirt on top of splints.

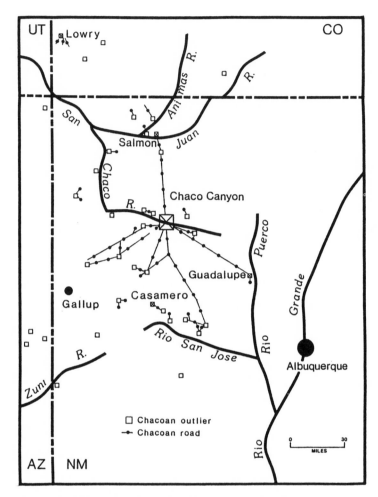

Map 6. The Chaco culture area with outliers and roads.

borders the Chaco River on the south and extends for about thirty-five miles in a northwest-to-southeast direction.

In the absence of pack animals, logs presumably were dragged or carried by human work squads. It has even been suggested that some timbers were floated down the washes, but in this semidesert environment such transport does not seem likely, at least as a regular and dependable thing. Work transporting trees obviously took considerable organization and the power to command fairly large labor gangs.

Another aspect of Chaco economic life that suggests considerable sophistication is that of water control. By at least Classic, or Pueblo III, times, the canyon's north side held a number of drainage-control features: dams, canals, ditches, and catch basins in the shallow hanging canyons along the north rim. There is also at least one such irrigation system along the south side of the canyon, and others have been found in outlying towns southwest of the main canyon settlements. To what extent the Chaco River, running through the center of Chaco Canyon, was used is not clear. The irrigation system does indicate reasonably intensive labor and probably cooperation between large populations involving several towns.

Perhaps the most suggestive feature of the Chaco Classic period is its large-scale trade in turquoise and other luxury goods. These goods have mainly been found in the large, north-side canyon towns such as Pueblo Bonito and Chetro Ketl. At least part of the turquoise came from the Cerrillos area of central New Mexico, although no specific mine or mines in the Cerrillos Hills have yet been identified as Chacoan sources. Other turquoise mines from as far away as Nevada may also have been involved in the Chaco turquoise trade.

The rich mines of Mt. Chalchihuitl and Mina del Tiro and certain other smaller mines in the Cerrillos range south of Santa Fe, have been producing turquoise for trade for a thousand years or more. The nature of the Cerrillos trade to Chaco and elsewhere is not entirely clear, because the Rio Grande valley had a relatively sparse population during earlier Anasazi times (Basketmaker and Pueblo I through III). But trade they did, for Cerrillos turquoise has been found as far east as the Spiro site in Oklahoma and as far south as the Alta Vista area of Zacatecas. Indeed, there is reason to believe that Cerrillos materials reached even farther south and east into central Mesoamerica.

Cerrillos turquoise for the great Chaco centers may have been dug out by miners who lived in certain small pueblos a short distance from the mines. These settlements, known today as the Bronze Trail Site Group, contain numbers of hammers and abrading stones used in working turquoise and considerable fragments of raw turquoise. In the sites are found potsherds from the Gallup, Mt. Taylor, and Chaco areas. Because these towns lie in an area poor for agriculture, it seems likely that the people who lived in them were primarily involved in processing turquoise. The main occupation period of the Bronze Trail sites seems to be the eleventh and early twelfth centuries, although there may have been some settlement there as early as A.D. 900.

Though the Bronze Trail sites were likely occupied to expedite the turquoise trade to the Chaco area, the routes over which the stones passed have

Plate 6. Basket covered with turquoise mosaic from Pueblo Bonito. Photograph courtesy Museum of New Mexico, neg. no. 21808.

not been fully worked out. It has been suggested that the Rio Grande site called simply LA-835, near Santa Fe—a Chaco outlier with a great kiva—

may have been somehow involved in the trade. And another outlier, the Guadalupe site on the Puerco River, likely was an entry point for Rio Grande trade. In any case, huge amounts of turquoise—estimates range from 200,000 to 500,000 pieces, including mosaics, pendants, and beads—have been found at Pueblo Bonito and other Bonito-style sites.

An extensive trade network connected Chaco Canyon with Mexico, out of which came, among other things, shells from the Gulf of Cortez, copper bells in considerable numbers, and techniques such as shell inlay and pseudo-cloisonné. The latter technique was widespread in western Mexico and consisted of painting pottery surfaces with a lacquerlike substance that dries by evaporation. In the Chaco area, the lacquer was applied to pieces of sandstone. Probably the most important import, however, was the scarlet macaw (*Ara macao*), which originated in tropical areas in Mesoamerica. It has sometimes been said that the Chaco people experimented with breeding macaws. Actually, there is no evidence for this practice, but it does look as if immature birds were actively traded, penned, and kept alive for their feathers.

The importance of macaws in Classic Chaco culture underlines a significant link between these Pueblo III peoples and historic and modern Pueblo Indians. One of the first things noticed by Spanish exploring parties in the early sixteenth century was the trade in parrots, macaws, and their feathers to the Southwest. The demand for brightly colored feathers, used in a variety of ceremonies, is as great in the Pueblo world today as it was in the sixteenth century—or the eleventh.

Not only do we have strong evidence of trade to and from Mexico, but certain structures in the great pueblos at Chaco Canyon also have what seem to be Mesoamerican features. Colonnades and free-standing columns, courtyard altars, room platforms, and perhaps even the core-and-veneer walls have tantalizing Mesoamerican analogies. Whether there were actual Mexican trading groups resembling the organized trading fraternity or *pochteca* of later Aztec times is still an unsettled question, but Mexican influences of some sort seem reasonably clear. All in all, it looks as if the Chaco people were engaged in a rather sophisticated trade, importing raw materials such as Gulf of California shells, including *Glycymeris* and *Olivella* species, Pacific coast shells such as abalone *(Haliotis* species), and Cerrillos turquoise and turning out finished goods—beads, pendants, and the like. I should stress, however, that some archaeologists see the Chaco trade as primarily a regional matter and downplay connections to the south, including the "Mesoamerican" structural features mentioned above.

A great deal has been written about the astronomical interests of the

Chaco people and their utilization of sun and moon positions for calendrical purposes. Certain rooms at Pueblo Bonito have windows that could have been used for winter solstice observances at sunrise. A window in the great kiva Casa Rinconada seems to be placed so that rays of light from the early morning sun mark the summer solstice. Perhaps the best-known manifestation is a vertical arrangement of flat stones near the top of isolated Fajada Butte a few miles east and south of Pueblo Bonito. Spirals pecked onto the cliff face are bisected or rimmed by a dagger of light that penetrates through cracks in the stones at certain times of the year. It has been vigorously argued (and equally vigorously disputed) that these stones and spirals not only represent solstice and equinox markers but also delineate aspects of the great nineteen-year lunar cycle.

Another observation of an astronomical event is possibly represented by a rock painting on the roof of a shallow cliff overhang near the great-house site of Peñasco Blanco, some two miles west of Pueblo Bonito. Here are pictured a circular, rayed figure, a crescent moon, and a human hand painted in red and yellow. It has been suggested that this rock painting represents the supernova of A.D. 1054, which produced the Crab Nebula.

The Bonito phase at Chaco Canyon, with its associated great pueblos and great kivas, went into decline after about A.D. 1100. There is some reason to believe that the McElmo phase, with its Mesa Verde–like structures, continued, though in a very reduced way, until possibly as late as A.D. 1200. The breakdown of complex society in Chaco may have had to do with depletion of the wood supply, and perhaps with the disruption of the Mexican trading system due to troubles in central Mexico at about this time. Climatic changes and social reaction to such changes also played a role. Archaeologist Lynne Sebastian has suggested a scenario in which patterns of overproduction in good crop years, to provide surplus for lean years, had characterized the San Juan basin people since Pueblo II times. Then, in Chaco Canyon during the early A.D. 900s, climatic downturns allowed those individuals controlling the most productive lands to increase their political control over the canyon region and to form elite groups. Variations on this socioeconomic situation continued for some two centuries, until catastrophic droughts beginning around A.D. 1130 finally overwhelmed the system.

Although the builders of the great houses of Chaco Canyon left truly spectacular ruins, people living in the Four Corners area—the great systems of canyons and plateaus that we know today as Mesa Verde, as well as the Montezuma valley and Hovenweep to the west—also underwent something of a fluorescence during the Pueblo III period. These San Juan basin people

Plate 7. Late Mesa Verde ruin (about A.D. 1250) in Square Tower Canyon, Hovenweep, north of Four Corners. Photograph by Jesse L. Nusbaum, courtesy Museum of New Mexico, neg. no. 60695.

lived in sizable towns and were at about the same technological level as the Chacoans. They differed from the Chaco people in using smaller kivas, normally less than twenty feet across. These kivas had the standard sipapu but lacked other features of great kivas. They were usually equipped with fresh-air intake shafts built into the kiva walls, and they often had cribbed log roofs.

The Mesa Verde groups produced an attractive black-on-white pottery painted with organic, or carbon-based, black pigments made from plant extracts. Mesa Verde pottery differed from the equally well-made Chaco black-on-white wares, for at Chaco the black pigment was made from inorganic minerals, especially the iron found in ochre. Mesa Verde Indians do not seem to have been very actively involved in the Mexican trade, nor does much turquoise appear in non-Chacoan sites of the Mesa Verde–San Juan area. In some ways the Mesa Verde people seem to have represented a kind of prosperous backwater, not plugged into the far-flung trade network as were their Chaco cousins.

We have seen that Pueblo III was a time of rapid population growth, especially in the San Juan basin. The upper Rio Grande valley, however, began the period with a smaller population. In the southern part of our area, around present-day Socorro, New Mexico, Indians whose culture shows mixed Mogollon and Anasazi influences entered what is called the *Tajo phase*. Some of them lived in pithouses, others in above-ground rooms called *jacal* by anthropologists. Jacal houses were made of poles interwoven with brush or reeds and covered with mud. Yet even in this early phase, there were some above-ground masonry structures.

The Tajo phase, roughly equivalent to Pueblo I in the Anasazi sequence, evolved into a regional culture that can be related to Pueblo II and is called the *Early Elmendorf phase*. The Pueblo III period, or *Late Elmendorf phase*, saw the development of fortified masonry sites, the largest encompassing about 150 rooms. Pottery from these sites includes both locally made black-on-white vessels and a continuation of the Mogollon-derived brown wares. One trade ware, known as Chupadero Black-on-white, developed by about A.D. 1150 on the Chupadero Plateau south of the Estancia region and east of Socorro. It became an important trade pottery during the "golden age" (after A.D. 1300) along the Rio Grande, and it may have been used to transport salt.

It should be stressed that a great many influences, especially in the southern portions of our Rio del Norte area, came not from the San Juan heartland of early Basketmaker-Pueblo culture but from the south and west. A dynamic balance of diverse major influences, partly from the Anasazi north and partly from the Mogollon–Casas Grandes region to the south and west, began to influence Rio Grande peoples at least by the early common-era centuries. This diversity of influences continued among Rio Grande populations into historic times.

THE SAN JUAN CO-PROSPERITY SPHERE

It is equally important not to ignore internal events in the upper Rio Grande. Whereas pottery distributions suggest considerable migration from the San Juan basin into the Rio Grande valley, kiva structures tell a story (often overlooked) of considerable continuity from earlier times. In chapter 5 I described a particular type of pithouse with four posts supporting the roof and a ventilator shaft oriented to the east—a type that lingered on, especially in the Rio Arriba area. These pithouses gradually developed into kivas in the later part of the Pueblo III, or Coalition, period. Among the northern Tiwa, this kiva style lasted for some seven centuries, into modern times.

East of the Rio Grande, on the eastern side of the Manzano and Los Pinos mountains, another Puebloan region, the Tompiro, was developing, again combining Mogollon and Anasazi influences. In this region pithouses remained common until about A.D. 1200, when they tended to be replaced by jacal structures. The Tompiro area was peripheral to main events in the Rio Grande region until about A.D. 1300, when large masonry pueblos appeared.

In the northern Rio Grande, an early development took place in the Gallina region north of the Jemez Mountains. This area is part of the Rio Grande drainage but is somewhat isolated from the Rio Grande valley proper. Gallina culture seems to have arisen out of what is called the *Rosa phase,* a largely pithouse Anasazi occupation that centered in the Gobernador Canyon area to the west and ended sometime around A.D. 950. Gallina culture itself began around A.D. 1100, so there may have been a hiatus of a century or more. Like the preceding Rosa phase people, the early Gallina Indians built pithouses, grouping them into villages and surrounding them with stockades. In the later part of the Gallina period (1200–1275?) there appeared masonry structures, towers (perhaps for defense), and kivas.

The decorated ceramics of the Gallina culture, a carbon-painted black-on-white ware, show some similarity to Mesa Verde ceramics of the same time period. This pottery was to have an influence on the much more widespread Santa Fe Black-on-white of the Rio Grande valley. One kind of Gallina utility vessel was the conical painted jar, similar to later Navajo plain wares. Navajos settled in the Chama River valley on the eastern flank of the Gallina area by at least the early Spanish Colonial period, but the Gallina culture had disappeared as a recognizable entity around A.D. 1300—perhaps owing to the same drought that affected Mesa Verde. As we will see in chapter 7, the Gallina Indians probably were ancestral to the Towa speakers who still inhabit the middle Jemez valley.

Pithouses lingered on in the upper Rio Grande, but by Pueblo II times a scatter of small, above-ground pueblos had sprung up. They sat, for the most part, in the uplands above the river bottoms of the Rio Grande and its major tributaries, and many of them now lie under later, Pueblo III ruins. During what is sometimes called the *Coalition period* (see fig. 3), a considerable number of people lived in the Rio Grande area, especially on the Pajarito Plateau—the tangle of mesas and narrow canyons that characterizes the country bounded by the Rio Grande on the east, the Jemez River on the south and west, and the Jemez Mountains on the north. Coalition period pueblos reached considerable sizes—over two hundred rooms in some cases—and were built in rectangular or L-shaped roomblocks constructed of stone and mud mortar, as were pueblos in the Chaco and San Juan regions.

In the later part of the thirteenth century, there was a movement of people eastward into the upper valleys of the Pecos and Tecolote rivers and the upper and middle drainage of the Gallinas River. At least some of the pueblos they built contain both Santa Fe and Galisteo Black-on-white pottery as well as Chupadero Black-on-white and a trade ware from eastern Arizona, St. Johns Black-on-red. Relatively little work has been done in this area, but a great deal of its human occupation (perhaps all of it) fits into a time frame of about A.D. 1250 to 1300. Why these rather rich river valleys were deserted just as a new surge of growth was taking place in the upper Rio Grande valley is something of a mystery. When Coronado arrived some two and a half centuries later, he found Querechos, nomadic ancestors of the Apaches and Navajos, operating not too far from the Pecos River line. Another group, the Teyas, also were in the region. I think the most likely explanation for the desertion of portions of the upper Pecos drainage is that Querechos were moving into the western Great Plains around 1300 and making life on this eastern fringe of the Pueblo world unacceptably dangerous.

One innovation that would become important later had already appeared by Pueblo II times in the Rio Arriba country: the use of puddled adobe for house construction. Around A.D. 1200 a widespread pottery type, Santa Fe Black-on-white, appeared; it was an outgrowth of an earlier type, Kwahe'e Black-on-white, but its makers copied the carbon paint tradition that was spreading from the San Juan area. Santa Fe Black-on-white remained a dominant pottery type until after A.D. 1300. About A.D. 1250, a new carbon-painted type began to appear in parts of the old Santa Fe Black-on-white area. This pottery, called Galisteo Black-on-white by anthropologists, bore striking resemblances to the late San Juan pottery now known as Mesa Verde Black-on-white. A coarsened version of McElmo–Mesa Verde Black-on-white had reached the Puerco valley by the early thirteenth century. It appears to have evolved into Galisteo Black-on-white, and the combined wares extended in a fairly continuous arc from the middle Puerco River and the Pajarito Plateau on the west to Pecos and its upper tributaries on the east.

THE SAN JUAN CO-PROSPERITY SPHERE

The Pajarito Plateau accommodated a major human occupation during these decades, and there was experimentation with new agricultural techniques. The Coalition period saw the beginnings of "grid gardens," small squares of mesa top enclosed with dark basalt cobbles. These chunks of stone trapped water on their cool undersides and also precipitated out water from the night air.

The mesa tops in regions such as the Pajarito Plateau became largely depopulated in the later part of the thirteenth century. People moved into the valley bottoms in places such as Frijoles Canyon and to the lower elevations along the Rio Grande and tributary streams such as the Santa Fe River and Galisteo Wash. On the Pajarito Plateau, especially, people tended to build using naturally occurring caves along the north sides of vertical-walled canyons, or actually to carve out cavelike structures in the soft volcanic tuff that forms the cliff walls—an echo of the kinds of cave or rock-shelter dwellings that were utilized at the same time on Mesa Verde. Some of the most spectacular of these cave dwellings can be seen today in Frijoles Canyon at Bandelier National Monument, northwest of Santa Fe. Indeed, impressive cliff houses were a general fashion during the thirteenth century. They were constructed in shallow caves or rock shelters, usually along the northern (south-facing) cliffs of the canyons, enabling the structures to catch maximum sunlight.

During the twelfth and thirteenth centuries, people with Mesa Verde–type culture continued to expand south and eastward, colonizing the region south of the Chaco heartland. For example, there seems to have been a late Mesa Verde movement onto Chacra Mesa, southeast of Chaco Canyon. In this high country near the continental divide, settlements of considerable size may date in some cases as late as A.D. 1300. From 1276 to 1299, however, a severe drought gripped the area, especially the San Juan drainage. By 1300, or a decade or two later, the entire San Juan region was deserted—a relocation of perhaps thirty thousand people.

Today, the reasons for this depopulation are not clear, but one thing that certainly contributed was the Pueblo Indians' voracious use of wood—for heating, especially in higher areas like Chaco and Mesa Verde, for cooking, for pottery making, and for various kinds of house construction. Stripping away forest and brush caused the often thin topsoil to erode, and in times of irregular rainfall this erosion became a serious problem. There are also hints of infighting: for example, watchtowers near waterholes suggest that choice watering spots were bitterly defended.

But surely regions like the valleys of the San Juan and Animas rivers must have supplied ample water, even in dry years, and sufficient wood for building and heating, especially for reduced numbers of people. It is possible that nomadic wonderers—early Utes or ancestors of the Navajos and Apaches—were beginning to drift into the area, posing an intolerable threat to Pueblo groups. Or, the decision to leave may have been a religious one. Perhaps because of practical or esoteric motives now unknown, the priestly leaders determined that the San Juan basin was no longer a proper homeland for the Pueblo people.

Whatever the reasons, family after family, clan after clan drifted off to the southwest or the southeast. The San Juan area became unappealing as a place in which to invest in a future, and the "psychological carrying capacity" dropped to zero. So the San Juan was deserted, and part of the San Juan population moved into the Rio Grande valley. It quickly produced a "golden age."

CHAPTER SEVEN

The Golden Age

 One of the most curious misclassifications in the history of Southwestern archaeology was made in 1935 by F. H. H. Roberts, Jr. In renaming the periods previously established under A. V. Kidder's Pecos Classification, Roberts called Pueblo IV the "Regressive Pueblo" period (see fig. 3). Presumably Roberts was so fascinated by the great Pueblo III towns in Chaco Canyon and Mesa Verde that he believed anything that came after them was bound to be inferior. The real oddity about Roberts's classification is that by 1935 a large amount of archaeological work had already been done on massive Pueblo IV sites. The extensive towns in the Galisteo basin had been explored and described, Kidder's own work at Pecos Pueblo was completed, and a great deal of other excavation and exploration had taken place both in and away from the Rio Grande valley.

In 1937, after criticism from Kidder, Roberts suggested a modification. "Regressive" would be used only for the first portion of the period, and "Renaissance" for the later part, especially in the Rio Grande valley. But this modified classification never really caught on. At the 1943 *mesa redonda* (round table) of the Mexican Society of Anthropology, J. O. Brew, of the Peabody Museum at Harvard University, suggested another term for the period from A.D. 1300 to Spanish conquest times. This last prehistoric period in the Southwest, according to Brew, should be called "the Golden Age of the Pueblos."

Indeed, Roberts's word "Renaissance" did not really reflect what went on in the Southwest. If one wished to borrow an apt term from early modern Europe, that word might best be "Reformation," that is, a *re-formation* of cultures and peoples. As we have seen, the Rio Grande area did seem to lag behind events in Chaco Canyon and elsewhere in the first part of Pueblo III times. It was not until around A.D. 1300 that new techniques of building, trading contacts, and innovations in pottery, house styles, and religion began to take hold. What happened after 1300 in the Southwest was a reformation of Pueblo culture, which now centered on the Rio Grande rather than the San Juan.

The rich San Juan valley was left to nomadic Indians, as was the upper Puerco drainage and much of central Arizona. The Mimbres culture of southwestern New Mexico, with its dazzling black-on-white pottery so beloved in the modern art world, had largely collapsed by A.D. 1150, although probable descendants of the Mimbres people held on along the upper Gila River until at least the mid-fifteenth century. The old heartland of the Mogollon was now becoming a *despoblado,* an empty land. It would be mainly Apache territory during the historic period.

On the middle Gila and lower Salt rivers, the Hohokam tradition, after a final surge in late Classic times, gradually transformed itself into the Pima-Papago culture that endures in southern Arizona today. Casas Grandes was functioning in A.D. 1300; indeed, its major period of expansion, the Paquimé phase of the Medio period, seems to have begun about this time. But when new trading routes sprang up west of the Sierra Madre Occidental a few decades after 1300, they increasingly bypassed this venerable trading center. There seems to have been curiously little direct trading influence from Casas Grandes into the Rio Grande of the golden age, and the great Chihuahuan center was in decay by the fifteenth century.

On the other hand, the region of northeast Sonora, an area I have called the Serrana Province or the "Sonoran statelets," witnessed a period of exuberant growth beginning just about the time of the Rio Grande Classic period. These warlike, urbanized, sophisticated statelets were still expanding when Spanish intervention and Old World diseases caused their collapse in the last part of the sixteenth century.

Settlement in the upper Rio Grande drainage had so far been mainly in the uplands, especially on the Pajarito Plateau. But around A.D. 1300 a shift into somewhat lower elevations, with an emphasis on riverine irrigation, took place. Within a century, very large towns grew up, and there appeared brilliant new art styles in ceramics and in murals on kiva walls. An enriched ceremonialism, based in part on the kachina cult, spread throughout the area. Not only this cult but other societies relating to war, hunting, and curing appeared, augmenting the older clan and lineage groups and helping to solidify and integrate relationships within the new, larger towns and perhaps between groups of linguistically related towns. It is not clear to what extent these new sodalities were necessitated by the rapid growth of the towns and to what extent they triggered that growth. Probably both factors were at work.

The regions to be held by particular groups of Pueblo Indians in historic times were now rapidly filled in. Many of the great sites in the Chama region, on the Pajarito Plateau in the Tiwa region, in the Galisteo basin, in the Piro and Tompiro areas, and in the upper Pecos valley were founded in either the late thirteenth or the fourteenth century. Other towns, from earlier modest beginnings, grew into very large settlements. A study by Paul F. Reed lists sites inhabited between A.D. 1325 and 1540 in the upper Rio Grande and Pecos valleys from the Chama area to Albuquerque. He finds more than seventy settlements of at least four hundred rooms *in this area alone*. Several sites had two thousand rooms or more, and there were even three-thousand-room pueblos. The large towns included Yungue, Sapawe, Ponsu, and Posi in the Chama valley; Tshirege, Puye, Tyuonyi, Tsankawi, and Otowi in the Pajarito region; Patokwa, Tovakwa, Wabakwa, and Guisewa in the Jemez country; Tunque and Kuaua in the Tiguex area north of Albuquerque; San Marcos, San Lázaro, San Cristóbal, Galisteo, and Shé in the Galisteo basin; Arroyo Hondo and Pindi near Santa Fe; and Pecos in the upper Pecos drainage.

South of the Tiguex, in the region around and south of modern Socorro, another group of Puebloan peoples was developing out of the Late Elmendorf phase, drawing from a mixed cultural background of Mogollon–Casas Grandes and Anasazi. Aggregation into very large towns lagged a little behind that of the northern Pueblo area, and during the fourteenth century sites averaged about one hundred ground-floor rooms. During the fifteenth century, however, the general northern Rio Grande trend toward concentration into fewer, larger villages took hold in the Rio Abajo. One site alone had fifteen hundred rooms and contained perhaps two thousand inhabitants. The fifteenth-century population in the Piro region has been estimated at seven thousand, a figure not reached again until the late nineteenth century.

One note of caution should be sounded here. It is not always possible to obtain Pueblo populations by a simple count of rooms at a given site. Some pueblos seem to have maintained a rather high rate of occupancy, but others, like the massive San Marcos Pueblo in the Galisteo basin, may have had some or most of their numerous roomblocks unoccupied at any given time.

Across the Manzano and Los Pinos ranges to the east, in the Salinas-Tompiro area, Pueblo IV began about A.D. 1300. Masonry structures replaced earlier jacal buildings, and, as in the Socorro area to the west, there was a movement toward consolidation into fewer and larger pueblos. This southeastern fringe of Pueblo IV culture—a mixture of southern and Anasazi traits—lagged behind the more active and innovative groups along the northern stretches of the Rio Grande. For example, stone masonry architecture built in courses or in continuous layers was introduced to the Tompiro area centuries after it appeared on the Rio Grande. Cooking pottery with its surfaces roughened by pinched areas, or corrugations, long manufactured in the San Juan region, now appeared among the Tompiro for the first time. Flat slab metates, sometimes placed side by side in a bin—also used in the San Juan area for hundreds of years—gradually replaced the older, scooped-out, trough metates. And the splendid glaze bichrome and polychrome pottery that burst on the northern Rio Grande scene around A.D. 1300 did not appear among the Tompiros for another 100 to 150 years.

By the beginning of historic times there were nine towns in this Salinas region, the northernmost being Chilili, Tajique, and Quarai on the eastern flanks of the Manzanos. Abó is situated at the east end of a pass that opens from the Rio Grande to the Estancia valley; Ténabo (LA 200) lies about five miles west of Abó; and Tabirá, Pueblo Pardo, Pueblo Colorado, and Humanas, or Gran Quivira, are clustered to the east and south of Abó.

In earliest Spanish times a language family called *Tanoan* extended from Taos on the north to around modern-day San Marcial on the south. The northernmost Tanoans, those of Taos and Picuris in historic times, spoke Northern Tiwa. In the lower Rio Chama valley and along the Rio Grande for some twenty or thirty miles south of the Chama junction, people spoke the Tewa language, while a closely related dialect, Tano, was spoken in the Santa Fe area and in the Galisteo basin. Towa, another Tanoan language, appeared among the Jemez pueblos of the middle Jemez River and at Pecos Pueblo on the upper Pecos. The great province of Tiguex, Southern Tiwa speaking, extended from about modern Bernalillo to a point north of present-day Socorro. Several pueblos east of the Sandia and Manzano mountains, including the three towns on the northwestern rim of the Salinas basin, also spoke Southern Tiwa. They may not have shared in the close social and political bond that seems to have characterized the Tiguex alliance.

Continuing downriver, from around Socorro south to the San Marcial region were the Piro speakers, and in the Salinas basin, their close linguistic kin, the Tompiros. Because Piro and Tompiro disappeared as living languages before proper linguistic studies could be made, their affiliation is uncertain—but the majority opinion among linguists is that Piro-Tompiro forms part of the Tanoan family, perhaps standing somewhat apart from the other Tanoan tongues.

It is reasonably clear that by around A.D. 1350 the northern and southern Tiwas, the Tewas, and the Tanos were living in areas where Coronado found them two centuries later. Sites dating to the fourteenth century along the middle Jemez River are normally thought to be ancestral to the historic Towas. There is little doubt that Pecos Pueblo, founded around 1300 and continuing to grow by amalgamation with other towns in the Pecos valley for the next century or so, was Towa speaking. Historic Tiwa towns seem to go back to the fourteenth century, and, as we have seen, the large Pueblo IV towns of the Piro and Tompiro areas are fourteenth or early fifteenth century in date. In other words, the Tanoan linguistic family extended in a long north-south line from the Taos area to the northern end of modern Elephant Butte Lake, with enclaves east of the Rio Grande to the southwest end of the Sangre de Cristo range, the west edge of Glorieta Mesa, the upper Pecos drainage, and the Estancia-Salinas region.

Tanoan is related to the plains Indian language Kiowa. Kiowa-Tanoan itself has ties to another speech family called Uto-Aztecan, which includes such languages as the Shoshonean Hopi and those of the Utes, Paiutes, and Comanches. It also includes, among others, Nahuatl, the language of the Aztec Indians of central Mexico; Tepiman, the language group of modern Pima-Papago and Tepehuan Indians; Taracahitan, a language group that includes Opata, Tarahumar, Yaqui, Mayo, and Cáhitan. The Suma and Manso languages are also considered Uto-Aztecan; their position within the greater family is not clear, but they may be related to Piro-Tompiro. Kiowa-Tanoan and Uto-Aztecan, along with another language family called Oto-Mangue that includes such languages as Otomi of central Mexico and Mixtec and Zapotec of southern Mexico, are included by Joseph Greenberg in the great branch he calls Central Amerind.

Crosscutting these areas of Tanoan speech were a series of towns whose residents spoke languages of the *Keres* or *Keresan* linguistic family. These pueblos included Acoma, on its high mesa south of modern Interstate 40, and towns on the lower Jemez River and along the Rio Grande from the Cochiti Dam area to the northern edge of present-day Bernalillo. In other words, the east-west distribution of Keresan-speaking Indians essentially intersected the north-south distribution of Tanoan.

The Keresan pueblos already had a history of several hundred years in the places where the Coronado expedition found them in 1540. The town of

Plate 8. Frijoles Canyon, site of large golden-age pueblos. Photograph by T. Harmon Parkhurst, courtesy Museum of New Mexico, neg. no. 31162.

Acoma probably dates from around A.D. 1200, and perhaps a century or so earlier. The Cochiti Indians believe that their ancestors came from Frijoles Canyon, which is dominated by the Pueblo IV site Tyuonyi, founded about 1300. For many years Keresan was considered an isolated language family with no known relatives. In Greenberg's classification, however, it is related to Iroquoian, the language of the Iroquois of eastern America; to Siouan and Yuchi, languages of the central and southern United States; and to Caddoan, a language group in the southern and central plains. Greenberg puts all these languages into a Keresiouan stock, a branch of what he calls Northern Amerind.

What all this means is that the neighboring Keresan and Tanoan speakers are separated *linguistically* by many thousands of years, a time scale perhaps comparable to that by which the Indo-European and Semitic language stocks of Eurasia-Africa are separated. Of course, people from, say, Cochiti Pueblo and San Ildefonso Pueblo—Keresan and Tanoan speakers respectively—have lived side by side for centuries, and there has been considerable borrowing from one language to the other. The same is true of Old World languages.

The Indo-European language English has words such as *algebra* and *almanac* that are clearly borrowed from the Semitic language Arabic—not to mention the flood of words, including many proper names, that have come from another Semitic language, Hebrew.

Parenthetically, the only other known Pueblo Indian language is Zuni, spoken by people to the west of the Rio Grande in extreme western New Mexico. Zuni is also part of Northern Amerind, but it is placed in a separate language group, Penutian, which also includes various California Indian languages and the Mayan languages of southeast Mexico and Central America.

What were the histories of the various language groups of the Rio Grande's golden age? There is no unity of opinion on the subject among either linguists or archaeologists. We would be better able to address the problem of ancient languages if we were sure of the sequence in which the various Tanoan languages split off from one another. One linguistic scenario puts this separation well before common-era times; another holds that Tewa, Towa, and Tiwa (and perhaps Piro) split off at a much later date, all the languages diverging about the same time. Obviously Northern and Southern Tiwa, even though the two dialects are not mutually intelligible today, represent the last separation of the Tanoan tongues. The purely linguistic evidence also seems to show that Tiwa and Tewa are more closely related to each other than either is to Towa.

A very tentative scheme for linguistic movements in the early Southwest might go something like this. An ancestral Tanoan or even Kiowa-Tanoan language may have been spoken at least by late Oshara times in the northern Rio Grande basin, and the same language perhaps extended into the San Juan region, including Mesa Verde and the Four Corners (map 7). In the Basketmaker and early Pueblo periods, this language began to separate into Towa, spoken in the upper San Juan region; Tewa, in the eastern part of the San Juan drainage and upper Puerco; Tiwa, in the upper Rio Grande basin; and Piro, in the Rio Abajo country (map 8).

My suspicion is that ancestral Piro was spoken in that region at least as early as the Tajo phase. Indeed, Piro or its ancestor may have been the language (or one of the languages) of the Jornada Mogollon. In such a scenario, languages related to Piro would extend into historic times with the descendants of the Jornada people, the Suma and Manso groups. In subsequent centuries, a trickle of Piro speakers reached the Salinas region to become Tompiros. By the thirteenth century, scattered Tompiro populations may have extended into the Pecos River valley in the vicinity of Santa Rosa. Some

Map 7. Linguistic distribution in the Rio Grande and adjacent areas,
500 B.C.

of them became bison-hunting nomads, the ancestors of the Teya-Jumanos
of early historic times—people who still retained some of their linguistic and
cultural ties with their Tompiro neighbors in the Salinas region.

It is not entirely clear where the Kiowa Indians fit into the scheme. They
may represent a movement into the Great Plains dating a thousand or fifteen
hundred (or more) years ago. In such a case the Kiowa language may have
split off from ancestral Kiowa-Tanoan many centuries in the past. On the

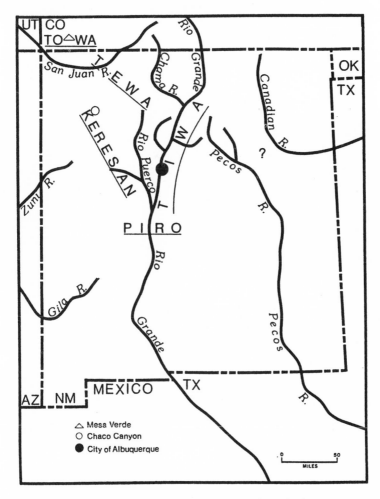

Map 8. Linguistic distribution in the Rio Grande and adjacent areas,
A.D. 1000.

other hand, an intriguing recent suggestion is that the modern Kiowas are, at
least in part, descendants of the Teya-Jumanos. This suggestion would make
Piro-Tompiro and Kiowa closely related tongues, closer than either is to the
other Tanoan languages.

Meanwhile, a more western and southern group of Archaic Indians spoke
an ancestral Keresan. These Indians were probably in residence at Chaco
Canyon by late Basketmaker times and were the main actors in the drama of

the Chaco Classic period. Sometime late in the first millennium A.D., groups of Keresan speakers spread east and south to Acoma, and a little later to the lower Jemez basin and the Pajarito Plateau (see map 8). It does seem that the western Keresans in the Acoma area were in place perhaps while Chaco Canyon was still occupied, and there may have been a movement of early Keresan speakers onto the Pajarito Plateau before—or right at the end of—the Chaco Classic period.

In late Pueblo III times in the San Juan basin, both Tewa and Towa Indians began to shift south and east. First were the Tewas, who moved across the north face of the Jemez Mountains to the lower Chama River and the Rio Grande, reaching the latter river sometime around the eleventh century. A century later, a second group of Tewas, speakers of the Tano dialect, trickled down the Puerco River valley and into the Galisteo basin. These two movements shattered the distribution of Tiwa peoples, eventually producing separate Northern and Southern Tiwa languages (map 9).

This complex series of language shifts was further complicated by a wedge of what became the eastern Keresan-speaking Indians, who moved into the lower Jemez valley and reached the Rio Grande before 1300. Their route likely was to the Jemez and then down that river. In any case, they quickly occupied the lower Jemez River basin and a portion of the Rio Grande valley between the Tiwa and Tewa, filling in what was perhaps a no-man's-land around the Jemez–Rio Grande confluence. Once reaching the Rio Grande, however, the Keresans moved north, penetrating the southern part of Tewa territory in the region north of historic Cochiti Pueblo, probably sometime in the late thirteenth or early fourteenth century. Traditional Pueblo Indian histories suggest that this invasion of Tewa territory by Keresan-speakers created a certain amount of hostility.

In the last centuries of habitation of the San Juan, Towa-speaking Indians were moving eastward, north of the Jemez range. Blocked by Tewa populations in the lower Chama valley, they spread—in the form of what we now call the Gallina culture—into the Gobernador–Largo Canyon region and then into the drainage of the Jemez, where they remain today. One group of these Towa speakers split off and, in some long-forgotten perambulation, reached the Pecos River, probably in the twelfth or thirteenth century. Early Towa speakers could also have been responsible for the brief colonization of the Pecos area east of Rowe Mesa and of the Tecolote and Gallinas valleys around A.D. 1250. I should stress once more that all these reconstructions are very speculative.

In chapter 6 I mentioned that the Gallina culture, as well as being ances-

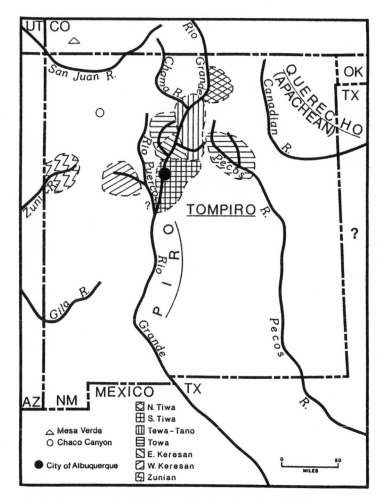

Map 9. Linguistic distribution in the Rio Grande and adjacent areas,
A.D. 1350.

tral Towa, also produced a very Navajo-looking kind of plain ware with a
pointed bottom. The Navajos were Southern Athapaskans or Apachean Indians, hunter-gatherers whose interaction with the Rio Grande peoples was
so important in protohistoric times. Navajos at some point settled along the
upper Chama River and in Gobernador and Largo canyons, near the old
Gallina culture homeland. It is interesting that the Jemez Indians, in part

descendants of the Gallina, maintained a close and special relationship with the Navajos in early historic times, and a number of Jemez people took refuge with Navajos in the aftermath of the Pueblo Revolt of 1680.

The early Navajos and Apaches were the southernmost extension of a language group called Na-Dene, the "Na" segment of which includes such Northwest Coast tribes as the Haida and Tlingit. Among the "Dene" wing are Northern Athapaskans of Alaska and northwest Canada (Tanaina, Kutchin, Kaska, Hare, Slave, Chipewyan, and other tribes), a few scattered Athapaskan groups on the lower Northwest Coast, and the Apacheans of the Southwest. If Joseph Greenberg's reconstruction of North American languages is correct, the Na-Dene groups were latecomers to the New World. It has been argued that Na-Dene may have an ancient connection to the Sino-Tibetan language stock, ancestor of modern Chinese, with a split at around nine thousand years ago. Another scheme relates Na-Dene to a basic Dene-Caucasian linguistic stratum from which Sino-Tibetan is also derived. A great deal more work needs to be done on these linguistic origins, but at any rate, Na-Dene seems to have arrived in the New World fairly late, no more than seven or eight thousand years ago.

The Apachean branch of the Athapaskans reached the Southwest in late prehistoric times; estimates range from about A.D. 575 to 1525, although both of these extremes seem unlikely. My own guess is that Apacheans (called Querechos by the Spaniards who first contacted them in 1540 or 1541) moved onto the Great Plains adjacent to the eastern Southwest about A.D. 1250–1300, thus explaining the Pueblo desertion of the area east of the upper Pecos River valley.

If one accepts these dates, then it is possible that the ancestral Querecho Apaches penetrated the San Juan basin either a century or so after the Anasazi left, or possibly even before the Anasazi exodus. If the latter, the Apaches likely became a factor in the desertion of the area by Puebloan peoples. David M. Brugge believes that such an early penetration explains why eastward-moving Shoshonean hunter-gatherers (Utes, for example) failed to expand into the San Juan basin and why the Pueblos did not reoccupy the region.

There is, however, archaeological and linguistic evidence to suggest that Shoshonean speakers had reached at least into southwestern Colorado by A.D. 1300 or earlier. Another Apachean specialist, Curtis F. Schaafsma, believes that it *was* Utes, not Apacheans, who became the first post-Pueblo intruders into the San Juan River basin. In such a case, at least some of the pre-Hispanic, non-Puebloan pottery found in the San Juan basin might have been introduced by early Shoshonean-speaking Indians, ancestors of the modern Utes. Schaafsma postulates that the Querecho Apaches filtered into the San Juan region during the second half of the sixteenth century. For an additional discussion of sixteenth-century "western Querechos," see chapter 16.

Along with movements of people and aggregation into large towns during the Pueblo IV period came innovations in Rio Grande material culture and in other aspects of society as well. I have mentioned the introduction of slab metates; another minor innovation was the spiral-grooved stone ax, which holds the axhead more firmly to the shaft. Arrow shaft straighteners appear at sites of this period, as do loom weights. I think it likely that the "true" loom, with batten and heddle, for weaving cotton was used by the Chaco and Mesa Verde people, but perhaps the golden age saw technical improvements and a general intensification in weaving.

Around A.D. 1300, new techniques for decorating pottery spread eastward from the White Mountains of Arizona, south and west of Zuni. A variety of pottery called White Mountain Red Ware, originating about A.D. 1000, became the basis for widespread ceramic types. One type, St. Johns Polychrome, painted in black and white on a red base (fig. 8), appeared in western Arizona sometime before A.D. 1200 and was traded and copied as far as Mesa Verde on the north, Casas Grandes on the south, the Chino valley of west-central Arizona on the west, and the Pecos River drainage on the east.

Certain of the White Mountain Red Wares became enhanced by the use of glazing, that is, by painting segments of the pot walls with a paste made from ground-up metallic compounds, primarily combinations of lead and copper. On firing, these metals become molten and glassy, making designs on the pottery surface. The idea of glazing seems to have come from western Mexico, where it appeared earlier than in the Southwest.

Rio Grande Glaze Wares derive in part from St. Johns Polychrome and in part from the early Zuni pottery type called Heshotauthla Polychrome, itself an offshoot of St. Johns. The glazed pottery was produced primarily by local potters copying the techniques of westerners, but there is a possibility that actual movements of Puebloan peoples from west to east brought potters' skills with them. Further experimentation took place in the Rio Grande basin. For example, in the central part of the valley, especially in the Galisteo basin, artisans used a basic yellow slip (a thin wash of clay) to paint the decorated surface of a pot, but elsewhere a red slip was preferred. This fashion in yellow background color may have originated in Mexico, and it spread west as well as east, reaching its apex in the superb, late prehistoric and early

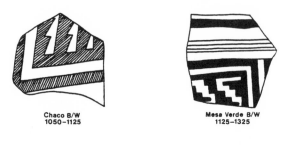

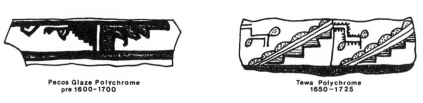

Figure 8. Selected pottery types of the Southwest.

historic Jeddito Yellow Ware made by the Hopis—one of the great ceramic traditions of the world and, in my opinion, the most magnificent aboriginal pottery ever made in North America

Although glaze painting flourished in the Rio Grande valley from A.D. 1300 until after 1700, the older black-on-white tradition hung on in the northern part of the region, with a considerable area of overlap among the Keresans and southern Tewa. The "biscuit wares," a puffy-pasted pottery, were widespread in the northern Rio Grande; their black designs were painted in carbon-based pigments that fired to a matte (dull) finish on a cream, gray, or off-white background. Eventually this local tradition led to the handsome Sankawi Black-on-cream and then to polychrome wares such as Tewa

Polychrome, which was being produced at the time of the initial Spanish settlement. Tewa Polychrome was made by slipping the lower half of a vessel's exterior in red, and the upper portion of the vessel in cream or white. The upper half was then painted with designs in a dull black (see fig. 8).

Another innovation that reached the upper Rio Grande—in this case probably from the Jornada area of southern New Mexico—was the use of adobe chunks or bricks in making house walls. This technique of building was common in the lower Southwest, appearing in Casas Grandes, in the Serrana region of Sonora, and among the Classic Hohokam. Its spread to some parts of the upper Southwest was restricted by higher rainfall, which makes adobe structures less desirable. But the area had a tradition of jacal structures that involved a great deal of mud overlay, and in some parts of the valleys adobe is easier to find than is usable stone. The Rio Grande valley often lacked good building sandstone; fortunately, its relative aridity made adobe practical. Whatever the reasons, the use of coursed adobe as a sporadic fashion took hold after A.D. 1150, and a number of pueblos were built of adobe rather than the more traditional stone and mud mortar. In the Tiwa area, the pueblo of Kuaua at present-day Coronado State Park, just across the Rio Grande from Bernalillo, New Mexico, is an example of an adobe pueblo.

During Pueblo IV times a variety of kiva forms appeared. We have seen how the northern New Mexico pithouse developed locally into a kiva type that persisted in the Taos-Picurís region into modern times. Other forms of kivas, round and square, below ground and above ground, small and large, eventually formed the golden-age inventory of ceremonial structures in the upper Rio Grande. Kivas of one variety, called by A. V. Kidder "corner kivas" because they are located near corners of roomblocks, are oval or D shaped. It looks as if some Rio Grande peoples were clinging to old architectural forms while others were experimenting with new kiva styles originating in the San Juan basin and in the Jornada region to the south.

At some point near the beginning of the Rio Grande Classic period, a new set of ceremonies, almost certainly originating in western Mexico, swept the Pueblo world. *Kachinas,* today most fully developed in the western pueblos of Zuni and Hopi, are ancestral gods who bring rain, harmony, and well-being to Puebloan peoples and to all humankind. They are represented by richly costumed, masked human dancers who are manifestations of the actual ancestor gods.

The kachina cult appears in all modern Rio Grande pueblos, though only traces remain in the Tiwa region. That the southern Tiwas, at least, may have had a full complement of kachinas in pre-Spanish times is suggested by the

Plate 9. Large kiva at Tyuonyi, Frijoles Canyon, excavated about 1911. Photograph by Jesse L. Nusbaum, courtesy Museum of New Mexico, neg. no. 130397.

fact that kachina representations are found in kiva mural paintings from late pre-Hispanic times at the Tiguex town of Kuaua and at Pottery Mound. There also are aboriginal representations of kachinas in rock art in what is called the *Rio Grande style* in the old Tiguex area and in the Piro and Tompiro regions. In addition, Spaniards reported masked dances at various Rio Grande pueblos in the sixteenth and seventeenth centuries. Today the kachina dances are organized somewhat differently in the different linguistic subregions of the Rio Grande, but everywhere kachinas are focused on the kivas. Those structures during the golden age were both round and square, probably representing Anasazi and Mogollon traditions. In chapter 8 I will discuss Pueblo socioreligious and political organization in more detail.

Although kachinas are associated with both round and square kivas, there does seem to be a correlation between square kivas and mural painting. The practice of painting on the walls of square kivas dates from around A.D. 1350, near the beginning of the golden age, and was in full force when the Spaniards came two centuries later. Kiva murals have been found at the sites of

Awatobi and Kawaika-a in the Hopi country, at Kuaua in Tiguex, at Pottery Mound, in the Cochiti and Picurís areas, and in the Tompiro region. They were reported (and wildly misinterpreted) by sixteenth-century Spanish explorers.

Kiva murals were painted in red, black, blue, green, gray, white, and yellow on a background of white plaster. At times, people renewed the paintings by covering them with fresh whitewash and then spreading another set of murals over the virgin white surface. At Kuaua, archaeologists distinguished eighty-five separate layers of plaster. This whitewashing and repainting of murals has strong parallels in Mesoamerica, where whole buildings were often covered over and rebuilt at important calendar intervals.

Many of the kiva walls display kachina figures and ceremonies. The Southwestern art historian J. J. Brody believes that the kachina cult, kiva mural paintings, and the Rio Grande style of rock art form "so interconnected a triad as to appear to be all parts of a single phenomenon." If there was indeed a southern or western introduction of the kachina cult, it would perhaps explain the favor shown to square or rectangular kivas—the Mogollon type of kiva—in mural art.

In the mural paintings are a variety of designs: masked figures representing either the kachina gods or the dancers that act for the gods during ceremonies; birds, including exotic parrots and macaws; and other animals and plants, mythological figures, and kilted human or god figures, often accompanied by ritual objects such as canes or staffs, quivers, and gourd water containers. In addition, there appear stylized elements that probably represent clouds, lightning, rain, and other weather symbols. The *avanyu*, the plumed or horned serpent, is seen sometimes with a star association.

The complex imagery of the kachina cult, with its elaborately masked dancers, was a rich addition to Pueblo religious life. Kachina costumes were probably adapted from southern models, and it seems likely that the mural paintings themselves derived from (now unknown) Mexican painting techniques.

It has often been suggested that the kachina cult derived from the Mesoamerican Quetzalcoatl cult. The name Quetzalcoatl means, on one level, "bird-snake," and on another level, "sacred-twin." Quetzalcoatl was one of the gods of the Aztec pantheon, but his worship goes back for centuries and was very widespread, certainly reaching the Yucatán Mayas several centuries before Columbus. In the north Mexican Chalchihuites culture of Zacatecas and Durango, dating well before A.D. 1000, ceramic vessels with balanced, paired bird and serpent figures are indicators of Quetzalcoatl. On other such vessels, quadrupeds being menaced by a monstrous toothed figure represent the god in his counterpoised relation to Xiuhcóatl, the earth monster, something that also appears in Aztec mythology.

There are clear Quetzalcoatl elements in the mural paintings, in kachina associations, and in the extensive ethnographical data on historic Pueblo peoples. The Southwestern plumed or horned serpent is one of these. Another is the star symbol, an important part of the Rio Grande art style, which may represent Quetzalcoatl as the morning star. Perhaps even more striking is the widespread ceremonial attitude toward twins in the Pueblo world.

But granting that Quetzalcoatl elements exist in the kachina ceremonies, it seems to me that the strongest candidate for kachina ancestor is Tlaloc, the Mesoamerican rain god (often thought of in the plural form, the *Tlaloco*). Tlaloc was important in Aztec times, but again was a much more widespread and ancient deity. Tlaloc was the god of rain and fertility and was worshiped in low, marshy, wet places. To him were sacrificed mainly children. The god could cure diseases such as rheumatism that were created by rain and wet. This deity has some very interesting parallels with the various Puebloan rain chiefs and their associations with colors and the cardinal directions. The ringed eyes of the Tlaloc god, in evidence at least by Teotihuacan times, are echoed by many kachinas. Indeed, some conventional representations of Tlaloc bear a generic resemblance to certain kachina masks (fig. 9).

Kachina ceremonies are, after all, rain dances, and the kachinas, like the Tlaloco, were associated with water and fertility, with curing in specific situations, and with the sacrifice of children. This human sacrifice motif must have been discarded by the Pueblos by 1540; at least, the suspicious Spaniards, who knew human sacrifice firsthand from Mexico, could find no trace of it in the Southwest. But elements of human sacrifice still exist in Pueblo folklore. One Pueblo motif is that of the kachinas coming for and carrying away children, and stories that suggest former child sacrifice were fairly common among the historic Pueblos. Pueblo tales of human sacrifice usually involve the horned serpent in a water manifestation, and pools of water.

Even though it is generally agreed that the kachina cult is Mesoamerican in origin, the exact route the kachinas took to reach the Southwest is not certain. Polly and Curtis F. Schaafsma believe the kachina complex diffused out of the Jornada Mogollon region of southern New Mexico, reaching the Rio Grande valley sometime after A.D. 1300 and from there spreading to the western pueblos. The Schaafsmas see artistic representations in rock art of the El Paso area as ancestral to kachina figures in the Southwest. Others question the identification of protokachinas in Jornada art. E. Charles

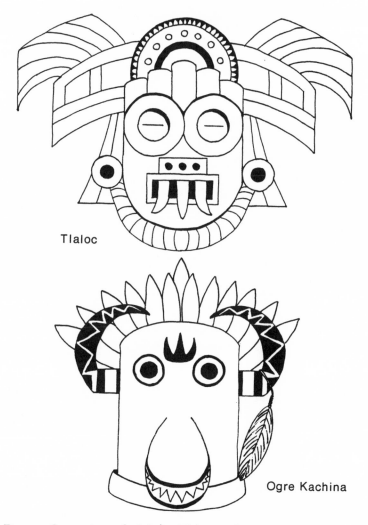

Tlaloc

Ogre Kachina

Figure 9. Comparison of a Mexica Tlaloc mask and a Hopi Ogre Kachina mask.

Adams has suggested that the cult developed in the Little Colorado area, perhaps around 1300, with original impulses from the south. Whatever its source, the kachina cult clearly had some relationship to various religious cults of central and western Mexico, and it appeared in the fourteenth century across the Pueblo world.

The strength of the cult and the rapidity of its spread suggest that it filled some deep need among the Pueblos. Kachinas appeared in their world at the end of a period of migrations, when new peoples were entering the Rio Grande valley and the western Pueblo area from the San Juan, and when the eastern Pueblo periphery in the Pecos, Tecolote, Gallinas, and Mora river valleys was collapsing. Most authorities believe the cult served as a bonding mechanism, cutting across kinship ties. This bonding, bringing more people into a strong ceremonial relationship, encouraged trade, promoted greater specialization, and allowed for more effective defense from the threat of outsiders—whether rival Pueblos or incoming nomads. It was likely the mechanism that held together the large Pueblo towns and in some cases helped link several towns in nascent sociopolitical associations.

After A.D. 1300, with increasing populations, greater demand for arable land, and the infiltration of hungry nomads into the Pueblo sphere, this bonding must have been extremely important. Rock art specialist Polly Schaafsma, discussing petroglyph evidence from the Tano area, suggests that warrior societies appeared about the same time as the kachina cult and also functioned as consolidating mechanisms. It is likely that the hunt and medicine societies also developed at this time and for the same reason. Like the kachina cult, the various war and medicine groups crosscut other Pueblo polities, linking pueblos and even groups of pueblos into a larger social whole.

One of the things that produced the golden age was the renewed influence of trade. We have seen how the extraordinary blossoming of the Chaco Canyon culture was made possible because the Chaco people managed to capture a significant part of the trade in turquoise, diverting the stone from its sources in the Cerrillos area and elsewhere, working it, and exporting it to Mesoamerica. I suggested in chapter 6 that one of the reasons for the collapse of the Chaco culture was that Mesoamerican civilization from the eleventh century to the thirteenth was in some disarray.

The Chaco trade routes have not been fully worked out. They probably involved Casas Grandes only peripherally (if at all), for the Chaco centers collapsed before the heyday of that great Chihuahuan site. At the beginning of the golden age in the Rio Grande area, Casas Grandes was still flourishing, but it was soon to have serious competition. Sometime around A.D. 1350 a new series of trade routes was established, this time running up the west coast of Mexico. The new routes probably competed for a time with Casas Grandes, but that great trade emporium was increasingly wracked with troubles. Casas Grandes may have continued to exert some influence, prob-

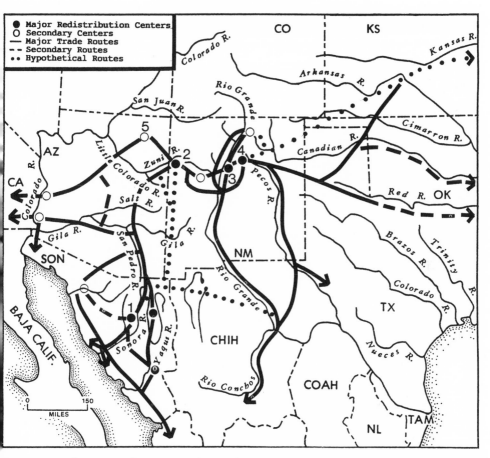

Map 10. Protohistoric trade routes in the Southwest. Key: 1, Corazones; 2, Zuni; 3, Tiguex; 4, Pecos; 5, Hopi.

ably up the Rio Grande route that in later centuries became the Spanish *camino real*, or royal road, but the main routes were now deflected westward. From the west coast of Mexico they reached the rapidly developing Sonoran statelets and then cut inland to the Gila and Salt river basins and Cíbola-Zuni. From that distribution center, routes were quickly developed northwest to Hopi and eastward to the Rio Grande and its tributaries (map 10).

As time went on, a series of secondary centers for trade began to develop. For example, the Hopi towns established their own routes to the lower Colorado River and the Pacific coast. On the east, pueblos that huddled on the edge of the plains, especially Pecos but also the Salinas pueblos and probably Taos and Picurís, began to extend long trading tendrils out into the western plains.

The impetus for this trade likely came originally from the demand for turquoise among Mesoamerican Indians. Once the routes were established, however, more than turquoise was exported south. Other semiprecious stones such as garnets and peridots were also sent along. Within a century or so, bison hides and products manufactured from those hides were beginning to get into the trade picture, as probably was salt and perhaps war captives exchanged as slaves. As they had done during Chaco days, the people of Mesoamerica offered seashells and brightly plumaged birds and their feathers, especially those of the scarlet macaw.

Gradually the nature and control of trade seems to have become more and more invested in certain "redistribution" centers that both bartered for and produced trade goods. One important center lay in the Serrana region of northern Sonora, where small, militarily active groups that I have called the "Sonoran statelets" gained control of much of the north-south trade. They stockpiled exotic goods from western Mesoamerica and the Gulf of California, especially bright-colored feathers and shells, shipping them north and probably adding locally produced cotton, both raw and woven. Several kinds of gulf shells were in wide demand, particularly the small, torpedo-shaped olive shells (*Olivella dama* and several other species) that were widely used as costume jewelry and for fringes on ceremonial robes. Other popular shell species were turret shells (*Turritella* species), cone shells (*Conus* species), and dog cockles (*Glycymeris* species), a bivalve especially used for bracelets (fig. 10).

The Zuni-Cíbola and Hopi towns also quickly developed into trade centers. These pueblos were in contact not only with people along the Gulf of California, with its treasures of shell, but also with those on the Pacific coast. The coast of what is now southern California produced olive shells and especially the creamy white shell of the abalone, source of the much-desired mother-of-pearl. Inhabitants of Santa Catalina Island, off the coast of southern California, exported the shiny talc known as steatite or soapstone. Early Spanish explorers heard of this steatite trade while exploring the lower Colorado River region, and, ever optimistic, they jumped to the conclusion that the item being traded was silver. Steatite reached as far east as the lower Colorado valley, and some was likely traded on east to the Pueblo world.

Hopi and Zuni-Cíbola parties may actually have reached the California coast, but much of the material originating there was collected by Yuman Indian trading parties and then transshipped eastward. Hopis conducted a

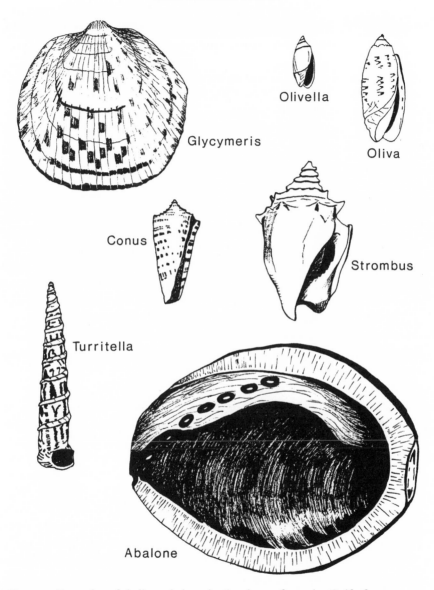

Figure 10. Examples of shells traded to the Southwest from the Gulf of California, the California coast, and the Gulf of Mexico.

flourishing trade with the lower Colorado people, importing shell from both the Gulf of California and the California coast. They were especially eager for red coral, which was much in demand all over the Southwest. Hopi traders transshipped some of the shell, especially abalone, sending it as far as Pecos. The Hopis were also cotton producers, trading for mineral pigments from the Verde River area of central Arizona to color the cotton cloth. Thanks to outcroppings of coal at the southern edge of Black Mesa, which made a superior fuel for firing pottery, the Hopi Indians also fashioned their exquisite bichrome and polychrome Jeddito wares. Both cotton cloth and Hopi pottery were avidly desired by the eastern Pueblos, and both were widely traded.

Semiprecious stones came from several locations, but areas rich in garnets and peridots were available to the Hopis and Zunis, and some of these, in the form of processed jewelry, must have been traded into the Rio Grande valley. They certainly reached as far south as Sonora; the shipwrecked Spaniard Alvar Nuñez Cabeza de Vaca obtained emerald-green stones while traversing the Sonora valley in 1536. These stones from the Pueblo area, shaped in the form of arrowheads, were bartered to the Sonora River people for parrot and macaw feathers. It has been suggested that these particular stones were peridots (olivine), but I think a more likely identification would be uvarovite garnets, which are found in the upper Southwest. Cabeza de Vaca, a sophisticated and educated man, took them to be true emeralds, and I doubt that he would have been fooled by peridots. Unfortunately, the "emeralds" were lost before Cabeza de Vaca reached central Mexico.

Another great center of redistribution and trade in the golden age was Tiguex on the Rio Grande. The Tiguex towns imported exotic goods from the west, and in return they seem to have controlled at least part of the distribution of turquoise from the Cerrillos Hills and obsidian from the Jemez Mountains. Tiguex sat at a great crossroads where a major trail running east to Pecos and west to Zuni-Cíbola met another stretching north and south along the Rio Grande valley. From the south came Gulf of Mexico shell, along with salt from the Salinas area of the Tompiro people. There was local production of turquoise, as well as copper, lead, and iron minerals, from mines in the Cerrillos Hills.

Obsidian came via the Towa towns in the Jemez valley or by way of Keresans and Tewas on the east side of the Pajarito Plateau. Obsidian, or volcanic glass, has been an important trade item in ancient societies in both the Old World and the New. Some of the earliest large towns in human history— settlements on the Anatolian plateau (modern Turkey)—rose in part because of local obsidian sources. The value of obsidian lies in the fact that it is extremely hard and can produce a cutting edge of incredible sharpness. It is also beautiful—translucent in thin section but shiny black, red, or even green in large cores.

Even more important trade goods came from the west, transshipped from Cíbola-Zuni: colorful macaw and parrot feathers and shells, especially *Olivella* and *Glycymeris* species, from the coast of the Gulf of California. Transshipped from Zuni and perhaps also obtained by direct contact were Hopi goods—the elegant Jeddito pots and cotton cloth.

The Tiguex people passed along cotton goods, Hopi pottery, southern and western shells, and feather goods to Pecos and on to the Great Plains. In return, bison products and a much-valued hard stone, fibrolite, in the form of highly polished axes, were shipped westward from Pecos. Much of the shell coming from the Gulf of Mexico, including conchs of the genus *Strombus* and olive shells of the genus *Oliva,* likely was shipped directly from Pecos Pueblo, although some was traded up the Rio Grande trail.

One town, known to archaeologists as Pottery Mound (its real name is now lost), on the lower Puerco River just a few miles west of Tiguex, was clearly another important redistribution center for western goods and ideas. Hopi pottery came into Pottery Mound, and traits such as cremation in Pottery Mound burials suggest strong influence from Zuni, where cremation was an important secondary burial trait. To what extent Pottery Mound functioned in the Tiguex hegemony is unknown, but because of its geographical location, Pottery Mound likely had some sort of association with Tiguex, and its inhabitants, or part of them, may have spoken Tiwa.

The Galisteo basin, too, was a great center from early in the golden age, with enormous towns covering many acres and containing up to three thousand rooms. After about A.D. 1450, the Galisteo towns became the major producers of yellow- or cream-slipped glaze pottery, probably because of nearby lead and copper ores in the Cerrillos region. They certainly had a share in Cerrillos turquoise mining, though not a monopoly.

Pecos Pueblo during the golden age was the major exporting center to the plains. From Pecos went the much-in-demand turquoise and shell, especially olive shells. Pecos people imported bison meat, hides, and horn from the High Plains and bois d'arc (Osage orange wood), which was used in making bows, from eastern Texas. A major source of fibrolite, a very hard, translucent schist, lies in the Sangre de Cristo Mountains around Pecos, where it was collected and worked by the Pecos Indians. However, there are other sources of fibrolite in the High Plains, and some axes may have come directly from plains groups. The beautiful Alibates flint, popular since Paleoindian days, was still traded, although evidence for it in the Rio Grande golden age is rather spotty.

The Pecos Indians stockpiled Gulf of Mexico shell, including alectrion (*Nassarius* species), strombus, and *Oliva sayana,* which were traded up the Pecos River. They also collected mussel shells (*Unio* species) from the local river and *Lapsilis purpurata* from east Texas. Both of these freshwater shells were used in making beads and pendants.

We are not too clear about the organization of trade. Judging from observations made by the earliest Spanish parties fifty years after Columbus and from later historic accounts, it seems that trading groups were organized by the religious leaders of the various pueblos and probably were directed by the heads of the warrior societies. There may even have been specialized leaders whose main function was to carry out trade. It *is* clear that trading groups often formed large parties; Coronado observed one in 1540. It was headed by two men from Pecos but contained Tiguex as well as Pecos members. Whatever else this points to, it seems realistic to believe that there were cooperative trade protocols between Pecos and the Tiguex towns. It is hardly an accident that a major trade route from Pecos went directly through Tiguex territory to Cíbola and beyond.

Toward the end of the fifteenth century and the beginning of the sixteenth, the golden age lessened somewhat in intensity. The important center of Pottery Mound was deserted before A.D. 1500, and others of the large towns were in decline. Part of this decline may have had to do with increasing hostility between Pueblos and nomadic peoples, which culminated in an attack on the Galisteo towns and on Pecos around 1525. Climatic conditions may have worsened slightly, and in some areas the large centers could have been consuming their wood resources too fast.

Yet overall, the Rio Grande Pueblo world on the eve of Spanish invasion was still vigorous, its trade networks in place and many of its large towns thriving. Garbled rumors of the Spaniards had been trickling into the Southwest probably since the 1520s, but they must have been both vague and conflicting. There is no sign that the Pueblo Indians really understood that their world was soon to be turned upside down.

CHAPTER EIGHT

1492 on
the Rio Grande

 In the fateful year 1492, an Italian navigator and ship's captain named Christopher Columbus managed to persuade the Spanish monarchs of Castile and Aragon to finance his visionary voyage across the Atlantic to eastern and southern Asia. A few years before Columbus's voyage, a Portuguese citizen named Ferno Dulmo, embarking from the Azores, attempted to reach what he thought to be the coast of east Asia and the rich islands that lay off that coast. Dulmo got no farther than the Sargasso Sea, hundreds of miles from the North American mainland, failing because of adverse winds and currents. Columbus, who certainly was aware of Dulmo's journey, had a more sophisticated knowledge of prevailing Atlantic winds and currents. He decided to sail far to the south before turning toward the sunset. Then, steering westward along what he thought to be the latitude of Japan, Columbus reached an unimagined new world, and he brought tragedy and profound change to the Native Americans.

For the Pueblo Indian tribes in the Rio Grande valley, 1492 was relatively uneventful except for one troublesome incident at the end of the year. In the Pueblo world, proper ceremonies were necessary to keep crops growing and the universe in harmony. In turn, fixing the planting calendar and setting the great annual ceremonies demanded painstaking measurements of the winter solstice. Measurements were made over a number of days by carefully observing the morning sun as it broke the plane of the eastern horizon. For six months, each sunrise had seen the sun inch slightly southward. Now, around December 20 or 21, there would be two or three days in which the sun seemed to rise in the same spot. The solstice was reached, and the sun's disk over the following days and weeks would slowly track northward along the horizon.

The solstice was fully dependable, but the weather-control priests also considered it important that the solstice coincide with a full moon. Every year they attempted to match these two events, and sometimes they succeeded. At other times, because of the nature of celestial mechanics—not fully understood by the Indians—the attempt would fail, and the solstice would come at or near a new moon. In 1492 the attempt failed miserably, for the solstice fell nearer the time of the new moon. Perhaps it was an omen!

Other aspects of the natural and cultural world, however, were reasonably satisfactory in 1492. Rainfall had been adequate for the past two or three years. A decade of extreme drought, reaching its peak in 1420, had taken a toll, but even folk memory of this grim time faded as the century wore on. Struggles over land, trade routes, and valuable resources were no greater this year than usual. Of late, Apachean nomads who lived to the east and north of the Pueblos had begun to press harder on the settled towns, but plains Indians would not become really threatening for another thirty years.

At the time of Columbus the names by which Pueblo peoples knew themselves and each other were probably about what they would be when Coronado entered the area in 1540. Spanish usage of Pueblo and other native names generally depended on their first source or sources of information. The Zuni towns were collectively called Cíbola by the earliest Spanish explorers. Cíbola is most likely a variation of *shiwana*, the Zuni name for the Zuni area (though it may possibly have been a misunderstanding of the Zuni word for bison, *si:wolo*). This term was picked up by Marcos de Niza from Indians in Sonora who were acquainted with the Zunis. The name Zuni itself was introduced in the 1580s by the two Spanish expeditions of that decade. These expeditions came into Zuni from the east rather than from the south and simply borrowed the tribal name used by the Keresan-speaking Acomas.

Spaniards of the Coronado expedition called the Hopi region Tusayán, which may possibly derive from a Navajo term, *tasaun,* meaning "country of isolated buttes." Such an identification might indicate that Apachean speakers were in the Hopi area by Coronado's time. However, Spaniards do not mention nomadic Indians at Hopi until the early 1580s. By that time Spaniards had started using an Acoma word for Hopi, rendering it *Mohose,* a term still current in the nineteenth century under its shortened form, *Moqui.* In recent times, however, outsiders have switched to *Hopi,* meaning "peaceful," "wise," or "good" people—the word used by the Hopi Indians to designate themselves.

For some reason the Spaniards tended to give Keresan towns their correct names—Acoma, Zia, and Cochiti—all appearing quite early in time. The term *Quirix* also turns up in the Coronado documents for the eastern Keresan towns. This word, borrowed by modern linguists for the Keres or Keresan language family, is of obscure origin. *Tiguex* (pronounced TEE-wesh), on the other hand, may well have been the southern Tiwas' name for themselves, with an atypical -*esh* ending.

In Coronado's day the pueblo of Pecos was called Cicúye or Cicúique, the designation *Pecos* not appearing in Spanish documents until around the end of the sixteenth century. Coronado's men presumably got the name Cicúye from the Pecos Indians. It may well be that Cicúye is a mispronunciation of *tziquite,* the Pecos Indians' name for themselves in their own Towa language. *Pecos* also seems to have been a Towa word.

The Rio Grande valley, with its great potential for irrigation agriculture and its rich bottomlands, was home in 1492 to a large number of towns, many of them quite sizable. People continued to aggregate in towns in certain portions of the northern Rio Grande basin, although population had shrunk some from its peak in the mid-fifteenth century. By 1492 the large Arroyo Hondo Pueblo south of Santa Fe had been deserted for thirty or forty years, and some marginal regions like Tijeras Canyon west of modern Albuquerque lost population during the fifteenth century.

Still, the Tiguex region, the Galisteo basin, the middle and lower Jemez valley, the east flank of the Pajarito Plateau, and the lower Chama valley continued to be heavily occupied, as did the Piro and Tompiro areas. Towns were built of sandstone blocks or river cobbles set in mud mortar or simply of coursed adobe. In some towns, houseblocks were three or more stories high. These "apartment houses" caught the imagination of Indians farther to the south, who, a few decades later, described them to the earliest Spanish explorers. Houseblocks might be separated by streets or lanes and generally were built around plazas in which the kivas were often located.

The political organization of the Pueblo Indians in the late fifteenth century is still a matter of some argument. There is a careless tendency on the part of certain specialists to call them "chiefdoms," meaning that political and economic (and perhaps religious) control was held by a group of high-status families who could divert surplus production to their own use and who were on their way to developing a stratified society. This may conceivably have been true of the Classic, or Pueblo III, period in Chaco Canyon, where the far-flung road system suggests some sort of overall control of a large area. To my mind, however, there is no real evidence for chiefdoms in golden-age New Mexico. It does look as if certain trade goods, especially turquoise and shell, were stockpiled as a hedge against bad times, when these easily storable items could be traded for more basic goods—food and clothing. But there is no indication that such warehousing or "banking" had anything to do with chiefdoms. More likely it was an economic function of the towns or of one or the other priesthoods representing the towns.

Certainly, the priests held ample power, as did quasi-religious political figures such as the war chiefs. Still, the Pueblos seem basically to have been egalitarian, with large social groups such as clans or moieties and the non-elitist societies handling matters of ceremonialism, war, social control, curing, and redistribution of surplus through trade. Nor does there seem to have been any domination of surrounding pueblos by a major primate town, as was the case with the Sonoran statelets.

This is not to say that cooperation among pueblos was completely lacking. At Zuni and Hopi in the west and at Tiguex in the Rio Grande valley there are signs of loose federations whose individual towns were tied by linguistic bonds and most likely ceremonial and familial bonds as well. The kachina cult and the war and other societies also helped cement ties between villages. In 1540 and 1541 the Tiguex pueblos cooperated in trying to defeat Coronado and his men—but even this cooperation seems to have been egalitarian in nature. Pueblo people could act together, but such action depended on decisions made by individual towns. They could and did unite for specific purposes, but it was an ad hoc sort of unity.

As I suggested in chapter 7, this sort of loose federation probably had developed during the golden age. In such an organization, individual town leaders, especially war experts, could rally neighboring towns. An example was Juan Alemán at Tiguex in 1541; another was the Hopi leader Francisco de Espeleta of Shungopovi in the late seventeenth century. The Hopi case is an especially striking one because of its long-term success. After forcing the Spaniards out of the Hopi mesas in 1680, the separate Hopi towns united to hold them out, destroying the one Hopi pueblo that dared to invite the Europeans to return. But the power of men like Alemán and Espeleta was limited to specific crisis situations, and their families never became hereditary aristocrats. The Hopis, for example, returned to village autonomy as soon as the threat from the Spaniards was over.

Rio Grande Indian economies in 1492 were based on production of basic foodstuffs: maize, beans, squash, and domesticated dogs and turkeys. By the golden age cotton was probably being grown in the southern and central part of the area, perhaps as far north as the Keresan, or even the Chama River Tewa, towns. Large amounts of cotton and cotton goods, however, continued to be imported from the Hopi towns. Tobacco seeds (*Nicotiana attenu-ata* and *N. trigonophylla*) have been found in the heart of our region at sites dating to early Pueblo IV times, and ceremonial use of the domesticated plant continued among the Pueblo Indians into modern times. The years after A.D. 1300 saw an elaboration in pipes. Tobacco was obviously important for ceremonies and probably also for medicinal purposes. Not only tobacco was smoked, but also various wild plants—sagebrush, snakeweed, manza-nita, thoroughwort, and sumac—were mixed with the tobacco or were smoked alone.

A variety of wild plants were collected for eating and for medical purposes. Common ones that have been found in golden-age archaeological contexts and are still used by Pueblo Indians today are mentioned below. The specific uses I describe for these plants are drawn partly from the historic Pueblos, but it is likely that they can be projected back into pre-Spanish times. Im-portant plants included goosefoot (*Chenopodium* species), the seeds of which were ground and treated much like maize flour. The garden green purslane was cooked with meat as a flavoring or was boiled and eaten as a separate dish. The Rocky Mountain bee plant (clammy weed) was collected both for seeds and for its leaves, which were cooked as greens. Wild potatoes were eaten, as were the seeds of the wild sunflower; there is even a possibility that the sunflower was domesticated in pre-Spanish times. Piñon nuts and the fruit of the yucca plant were also eaten. Mormon tea (*Ephedra* species) pro-duces tannin and a certain amount of an ephedrine-related alkaloid and was taken for respiratory problems and as a diuretic. (Ephedrine in a purified form is used today primarily as a bronchial dilator and decongestant.)

The datura or jimsonweed plant (*Datura meteloides*), whose active princi-pals are the tropane alkaloids hyoscyamine and scopolamine, was also used in medicine, its ground seeds or roots being rubbed on wounds for quicker healing and its seeds, leaves, and roots boiled to make a drink to control pain. Datura was in widespread use in central Mexico by the time of first Spanish contact there. In both Mesoamerica and the Southwest, small ce-ramic bowls and lidded jars decorated with spikes that mimic the spiny datura fruit have been found archaeologically. These are thought to have been used to carry or store datura, and in the Southwest they date as early as the ninth century A.D. It seems certain that the datura plant was both im-portant and widespread, used both medicinally and as a hallucinogen in re-ligious ceremonies in the Pueblo world of 1492.

Dogbane, or black hemp (*Apocynum* species), was also collected from early times. The plant contains apocynin and a variety of other active substances and has the medical properties of a stimulant and diuretic. Unlike the case for datura, however, there is no hard evidence that dogbane was used in medicine by pre-Hispanic Southwesterners, though its fibers were certainly employed by weavers.

Bones of a number of wild animals have been found in excavated sites of the late Pueblo IV period. Animal muscle consists of about 20 percent protein, and animal meat also provides valuable fat. The Pueblos ate rabbits, both cottontail and jackrabbit, as well as deer, antelope, and a number of smaller animals and birds, including the domestic turkey. Larger animals were hunted with bows and arrows, but rabbits were literally harvested by means of communal rabbit drives in which the animals were surrounded and killed with clubs or sticks—sometimes with the ubiquitous digging stick used in cultivation. Rabbit drives date back to Archaic times and represent a way of life thousands of years old.

Agriculture provided the staples of life, even though a considerable percentage of the food resources came from gathering and hunting. Like animal flesh, the *frijol,* or brown bean, is about 20 percent protein, but unlike meat, it does not supply a complete protein—that is, it lacks some crucial amino acids. Although maize yields only about 3.5 percent protein, it makes up the amino acid deficiency in beans. Maize was generally planted as soon as the frost season ended. For people on or near the main river, this was April or early May, with harvest time in September or early October. The Pecos area had a shorter growing season, as did Taos and the Tompiro country. Beans and squash tended to be planted in or around the cornfields. There were several ways of maximizing the amount of moisture the crops would receive. Tewas, for example, built grids such as those mentioned in chapter 6, spreading a gravel mulch on the garden plots. Sometimes these plots were associated with ditches and catchments. There was ditch irrigation along the main streams, although historic and modern activities have largely destroyed the ancient irrigation systems.

During the golden age the Rio Grande inhabitants often grew enough foodstuffs, especially maize, for trade. Plains nomads were particularly eager to trade bison meat, bison skins, and other items for dried or parched corn or cornmeal, and these commodities were important in the trade going eastward. It remained a very important exchange item into the nineteenth century.

The costume à la mode in 1492 was about the same as that of half a century later when the first Spanish explorers wrote down what they saw. Women wore a blanketlike garment usually woven of cotton but sometimes of yucca fiber or strands of apocynum, tied with a sash at the waist. Both breasts might be bare, or the garment might be fastened over one shoulder with the other shoulder and breast exposed. In cold weather a second blanket of cotton or skin would be draped over the first. Men wore loincloths, often decorated with tassels, or short, kiltlike skirts, and in cold weather covered their upper bodies with a draped blanket. Children went nude. According to one Spanish account of the years 1540–42, mature women also went nude until marriage—but if true at all, this probably held only for the summer months.

Costume jewelry included turquoise, garnets, peridots, and other semiprecious stones, along with shell, bone, and jet, all worn as pins, bracelets, finger rings, earrings, pendants, and brooches. Among the western Pueblos, one of the earliest chroniclers described the traditional squash-blossom hairdo in which the hair is put up in two large whorls, one on each side of the head. We are not certain whether this was the general custom in the Rio Grande.

The sociopolitical life of Rio Grande peoples in 1492 was closely intertwined with religion and ceremony. Even today, after four centuries of Spanish, Mexican, and American control, Pueblo religion still deeply influences every aspect of life. In attempting to understand social, political, and religious life among the late-fifteenth-century Pueblos, it might be well to summarize the situation today. Modern Pueblos have a series of secular offices derived from the Spanish town or *cabildo* officials in colonial New Spain. In the fifteenth and sixteenth centuries, it is likely that religious and political offices were so closely allied that no functional distinction was made.

Social organization among the modern Pueblos shows different levels of Spanish acculturation. Three kinds of sociopolitical organizations are usually described for Rio Grande Pueblos today. The first, which will be discussed more fully below, is, collectively, the various societies and kiva groups that share social and religious functions. Second is the moiety, the division of a society into two halves. A third type of organizational group is the clan. Now, the proper meaning of the word *clan* to anthropologists is "descent group"; classically, it meant *matrilineal* descent, that is, descent in which ancestors are traced primarily in the mother's line. Modern Anglo-Americans do not have clans, but they have a weak sort of *patrilineal*, or father's line, descent— though only to the extent that children usually take their father's surname. In our Euro-American system, relatives of both the father and the mother are called by the same kin names: "uncle," "aunt," "cousin," and so forth.

Among strongly clan-oriented societies, both father's and mother's families are important, but kinship titles and attitudes toward the father's relatives and the mother's relatives may differ considerably.

Leaving out the Piro-Tompiro Indians, who were acculturated out of existence before much could be learned about their social, political, and religious organization, the most culturally modified of the modern Pueblos are the southern Tiwas, the aboriginal Tiguex. Among them are found a summer and a winter moiety and also so-called clans, the corn groups associated with colors and directions. None of the social groupings has any particular kinship or marriage function. Among the northern Tiwas, what are sometimes referred to as clans are really kiva groups that have no kin functions. North-side kiva groups form one moiety, and south-side kiva groups the other. The Tewas also have a dual division of society into summer and winter moieties and so-called clans. Tewa clans, like the Tiwas', serve no kinship or marriage function.

The Keresan people have matrilineal clans and are organized into a turquoise and a squash or pumpkin moiety, turquoise being equated with the Tewa winter moiety and squash with the Tewa summer moiety. The Towas also have turquoise and pumpkin moieties. Their clans are matrilineal but very weakly developed and, like so much else of Towa socioreligious organization, are probably derived from the nearby Keresans. Indeed, the Tewa Indian anthropologist Edward P. Dozier believed that the "clan" structure of the Tanoans, Tewas, and Tiwas, as well as that of the Towas, represents no more than a fairly recent borrowing from Keresans.

The Tewas and Keresans picked up the term *cacique,* a word meaning "lord" or "chief," from Spaniards who had earlier borrowed it from the Taino Indians on the island of Hispaniola. In the Rio Grande area this word was used in historic times to refer to the ceremonial leader of the pueblo (Keresan) or the moiety (Tewa). The office itself probably had roots in the prehistoric Pueblo world. Another trait—an object once considered to have been Spanish-introduced—is the "cane of office." These canes, sometimes ornately decorated, were presented by Spanish officials to Pueblo political leaders. The cane of office, however, has strong Mesoamerican affinities, and it certainly came into the Southwest in prehistoric times. Such canes are found archaeologically as early as the Classic period in Chaco Canyon and are represented in rock paintings in various parts of the Pueblo world. Most likely, they were originally walking canes associated with traders of one sort or another.

Important in all the Rio Grande pueblos was the war chief, who took over from the peace-associated cacique in times of conflict. The functions of the war chief and associated war societies have become somewhat blurred by the fact that Spanish authorities in the seventeenth and eighteenth centuries encouraged the office of war captain (*capitán de la guerra*), winking at the Pueblo habit of collecting scalps from Apache or Navajo enemies. Scalp or war societies seem to have originally existed in all groups. As I pointed out in chapter 7, there is some reason to believe that they arose about the same time as the kachina cult, and like that cult served as an integrating mechanism for the pueblos.

The supernatural underpinnings for such societies were the Twin War Gods, or elder and younger twins, a mythological concept spread throughout much of Mesoamerica. At a guess, the situation of the warrior societies and officials in the Rio Grande pueblos in 1492 was somewhat like the historic Zuni situation, with an elder and younger bow priest representing the Twin War Gods. At any rate, scalp taking was an important part of socioreligious life in the pueblos until fairly recent times. If traditional Pueblo stories are to be believed, head taking was also practiced in the prehistoric past.

It should be stressed that individual offices such as war chief or bow priest, as well as social divisions such as moieties and clans, always had religious significance. In pre-Spanish times, talk of the "separation of church and state"—splitting apart the religious and secular functions of various sociopolitical groups—would have been quite meaningless.

Archaeologist Marc Thompson has traced the divine twin motif in Mesoamerica, where it appears as far south and east as the Maya country. The twins represent the sun and the moon, as do two totem animals, deer (sun) and rabbit (moon). In the course of their adventures the twins undergo death and are resurrected as fish or fish men. Not only are the divine twins part of the religious and political hierarchy, as at Zuni, but folktales and graphic depictions of these twins in various stages of their adventures are widespread in the Southwest. Such depictions form important parts of Mogollon-Mimbres scenes on pottery, and the fish motif appears in the Kuaua murals painted during the golden age.

Somewhere in the course of their travels the divine twins picked up a Quetzalcoatl association, but originally they seem to have been part of a separate religious complex. In prehistoric times it seems likely that a Quetzalcoatl identification with the war deities was part of the Pueblo ceremonial structure. In the historic pueblos the more obvious Quetzalcoatl affinities have dropped out, but the elder and younger war gods are still very important in Pueblo religion.

Two religious groups widespread among all the modern pueblos are clown societies and medicine societies. I suspect that clown societies may be quite old in the Southwest. Not only is ritual clowning prevalent there but it is also found in other parts of aboriginal North America. In the modern pueblos there are traces of two separate orders of clowns. They serve both to relieve religious tensions with their clowning activities and, more importantly, to perform police functions, maintain proper behavior, and guard community morals.

Medicine societies in all modern pueblos are lockstepped into the priestly religious organization. Members may join such societies by means of a vow or by being cured of an illness by a given society. I mentioned in chapter 3 that throughout North America (and beyond), curing is the function of the shaman, or curer, who heals by control of the spiritual and supernatural world. Shamans normally function as individual entrepreneurs in hunting-and-gathering societies. Among more complex agricultural groups, however, there tend to be associations of shamans and even specialization in curing skills, as, for example, among the Tepehuan and Pima-Papagos, neighbors of the Pueblos to the south. The Pueblos, with their extreme social compartmentalization of religion into priesthoods and societies, seem also to have absorbed these curing associations and fitted them into the priestly structures. Probably the sorts of shamans who worked their cures in Paleoindian and Archaic times became gradually incorporated into the Anasazi priesthood complex well before the golden age. But the specific development of medicine societies that crosscut clan and lineage structures may have taken place mainly after about A.D. 1300.

The cult of the kachinas—the ancestor gods who bring rain and harmony to Pueblo life—was everywhere focused on the kivas in 1492, as had surely been the case since its inception in the fourteenth century. The ceremonial house, or kiva, among modern Rio Grande Pueblo Indians varies from group to group. Tewas tend to have one very large ceremonial house shared by the two moieties, and this seems also to be true of at least the southern Tiwas. There are also rectangular moiety houses and society houses in the Tewa houseblocks, used for storing ceremonial equipment. The same situation holds among the Towas, whereas the Keresans normally have two large kivas for the two moiety groups, plus society houses. Modern Rio Grande kivas can be either round or rectangular, as was true in 1492 and, indeed, throughout the golden age.

To sum up, at the time of Columbus's first journey, both the sociopolitical and the religious structures of the Rio Grande pueblos possessed many of the same elements found today. But in many cases the organization of these elements was quite different. The kachina cult, so rich in the fifteenth century, barely survived the onslaughts of Christianity among the Tiwas and suffered much change among the Tewas and Keresans. Rio Grande Pueblo religion generally has been drastically affected by Christian dogma, ritual, and iconography. Social organization may not seem much altered in basic structure, but the introduction of Spanish secular officers has confused the old lines of command and diluted the once overpoweringly religious nature of social control.

By 1492 the far-reaching trading system had been in place for a century and a half, and the Rio Grande Pueblos received goods that originated as far away as central and eastern Kansas, Oklahoma, and Texas, the Pacific coast of California, and western Mexico. In addition, the Southwestern Pueblos were involved in an extremely important and rich internal trade.

If we were visiting one of the towns of the Tiguex region in 1492, we would see ample evidence of this trade. Tiguex parties were sent out both east and west, certainly as far as Zuni to the west and probably to Hopi. Such parties may occasionally have reached the Sonoran statelets, the Gulf of California, the lower Colorado River, or even the Pacific coast. We have descriptions of the makeup of Rio Grande Pueblo parties from the nineteenth century. At that time fifty or more men would be involved in a trading expedition, and they could be from more than one pueblo and even from more than one language group. In the nineteenth century the secular officials, including the war captains who were introduced in early colonial times, organized the trading parties, but it is likely that the heads of the war societies handled trade in pre-Spanish times. Travel to potentially hostile areas, especially out of the immediate Pueblo realm, meant that traders must also be equipped on a war footing.

As we saw in the last chapter, goods from those far-flung places were mostly transshipped, with Cíbola-Zuni acting as a major redistribution center. The same was true for trade going east. Though indications are that Tiguex and other Rio Grande Indians, especially the Galisteo groups, sent parties out to the High Plains, many of the goods from the central plains came through Pecos Pueblo, and those from the southern plains, through the Tompiro towns. Fifty years after Columbus, some of this trade was in the hands of Pecos Pueblo Indians, but part of it was carried out by Querecho-Apache and Teya Indians, and this likely was true in 1492. The southern trade in the later sixteenth century was in the hands of the Jumano Indians, who, I suggest, were linguistic kin of the Piro-Tompiros. It looks as if the Jumanos contacted by the Spaniards in the later part

Plate 10. Pottery Mound, south side of site. Photograph by the author.

of the sixteenth century were actually those Indians called Teyas by Coronado's party in 1541. The Teya-Jumanos and their ancestry will be discussed in more detail in chapter 13.

An observer at one of the Tiguex towns in the year of Columbus's first voyage would see a great deal of plains Indian goods, including bison hides, meat, bois d'arc, eastern river shell, and fibrolite, some of it already shaped and polished in the form of axes. From the west came shells, feathers, pottery, and other luxury goods.

Pueblos that were deserted before Coronado's time can sometimes be identified by name, and the linguistic affiliation of their inhabitants satisfactorily established. Unfortunately, this is not true for the great trading center of Pottery Mound, which was probably deserted by 1492 and whose name has not been preserved in modern Pueblo Indian traditions. Pottery Mound likely fell victim to its exposed position on the edge of the Puerco River, where generation after generation of townspeople had stripped away the riverine groves of cottonwood and willow and the scanty junipers and brush covering the surrounding hills. For several decades family had followed family in drifting away to join kinsmen in other towns. Whether these kinsmen were Tiwa, Piro, or Keresan is unknown.

Plate 11. Pottery Mound, looking north along the Puerco River. Photograph by the author.

During its heyday Pottery Mound had controlled a part—probably a very important part—of the Cíbola and Hopi trade. There may actually have been a settlement of Cíbola-Zuni traders at Pottery Mound, reminiscent of the barrios or town precincts set aside for families of traders in the Aztec kingdom. This is suggested by cremation burials, a cultural trait associated in the Southwest primarily with Zuni. Whether through Zuni or more directly from the Hopi towns, Pottery Mound handled a certain amount of Hopi Jeddito ceramics, as well as ceramics from Zuni. It is likely that Pottery Mound was also an entry point for the cotton cloth, shell, and coral that came through both Hopi and Zuni. In any case, these riches in traded materials now flowed directly into Tiguex to be retraded east to Pecos, southeast to the Salinas towns, and up and down the Rio Grande.

The Tiguex people were able to purchase these exotic goods with an outpouring of turquoise, the mines for which they shared with the river Keresans and the Tanos. Today, we are not clear about how rights of access to the mines were apportioned. From later ethnographic evidence, and from examination of Pueblo IV pottery from the Cerrillos sites, it would seem that certain towns claimed individual rights to the Cerrillos mines. An examination of broken pottery from Cerrillos sites indicated that Tiguex, the Galisteo Tano towns, and the Keresan centers were all involved. The Tiguex also had surpluses of maize, beans, and squash, some of which they shipped to the plains. This trade in foodstuffs was still going on a century later.

In 1492 the major center of Rio Grande pottery making was the Galisteo basin. There the large Tano towns produced red- and orange-slipped wares called by modern archaeologists San Lazaro Glaze Polychrome or Glaze D Polychrome, perhaps the apogee of the glaze tradition. In 1492 this pottery, with its lustrous glaze paintings in complex geometric designs, was just beginning to replace the earlier Glaze C pottery and would remain in style for about a quarter of a century. By the time Coronado arrived, another fashion in pottery, now called Glaze E, had replaced Glaze D. Over in the Pecos valley, a pottery today called Glaze IV, very similar to San Lazaro Glaze Polychrome, was widely used in the last decades of the fifteenth century. Glaze D pottery is found in the form of both jars and bowls; one form, the shouldered bowl, perhaps reflected some borrowing from the Caddoan area of east Texas. Farther north, potters produced the biscuit wares and black-on-cream pottery described in chapter 7.

All in all, life in the upper Rio Grande valley in 1492 was relatively uneventful and satisfying, with rich trade and beautiful and complex ceremonials to break up the drudgery of the agricultural round. Selected Pueblo traders were able to travel, sometimes great distances. Threats from neighboring nomads, the Querecho and Teya Indians, would trouble the Puebloan future, but in the year of Columbus's sailing there was no great indication that these nomads were a serious menace. Even the most indirect effects of the Spanish invasion of the New World would not seep into the Southwest for another two or three decades. Still, some of the babies born in the fateful year 1492 would live to see the invaders, and those babies' grandchildren would face a very different world indeed.

PART TWO
The Invaders

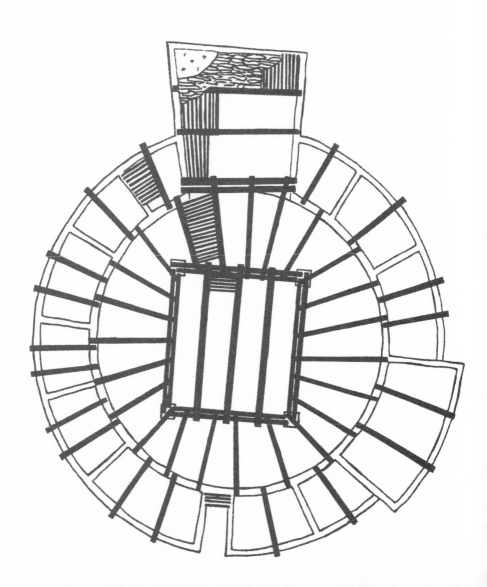

CHAPTER NINE

A Storm in
the South

In the wake of Columbus's 1492 voyage to the New World, Spain hastened to step up its transatlantic exploration, invasion, and domination. In the last years of the fifteenth century Spaniards quickly seized control of the island of Hispaniola and its Taino Indian population. From that base of operations they spread rapidly to nearby islands, overrunning Puerto Rico in 1508, Jamaica in 1509, and Cuba in 1511. The islands of the West Indies, which may have contained two million people or more, were soon depopulated by a combination of Spanish callousness and Euro-African diseases. African slaves began to be introduced shortly after 1500. Within half a century a new, genetically mixed population made up of Africans, Europeans, and remnant Indian groups had replaced the aboriginal Tainos.

Europeans had made tentative contact with the mainlands of the New World even before 1500, and in the first decade of the sixteenth century they began settling lower Central America and Colombia. Vasco Nuñez de Balboa reached the Pacific coast of what is now Panama in 1513. Meanwhile, in North America during that same year, Juan Ponce de León explored part of Florida. A movement into the Gulf of Mexico was inevitable, especially since rumors of gold-rich kingdoms to the west were beginning to trickle into the Indies.

The coast of Yucatán was touched by expeditions in 1517 and 1518, but they were mere preludes to the great enterprise of Hernán Cortés in the year 1519—a definitive invasion that was to destroy the mighty empire of the Aztecs of central Mexico and within a few years that of the west Mexican Tarascans. Since the Tarascans had at least indirect contacts with the Southwest, their fall sent ripples into that region. Even before the Tarascans were fully conquered, the Spaniards had leapfrogged to the west coast of Mexico.

Inevitably, sooner or later, the newcomers would move north to the greater Southwest. The thrust came rather sooner than later.

At the time of Spanish invasion, the central portion of Mexico was held by the powerful plunder empire of the Aztecs. Central Mexico had now been occupied by sophisticated, town-dwelling peoples for over two thousand years. A century or so before the beginning of the Christian or common era, a powerful and massive city now called Teotihuacan began to rise in the northeastern quadrant of the Valley of Mexico. The early centuries A.D. saw Teotihuacan reach its mature growth during a period called the *Classic,* to distinguish it from the earlier *Preclassic* or *Formative* societies of central Mexico and the later *Postclassic* in central Mexico, which was dominated by the Toltecs.

Teotihuacan's influences in the sixth century A.D. extended from Guatemala in the southeast to Zacatecas and Durango in the northwest. In the more remote regions these influences were likely a matter of trade rather than conquest. The center of this polity, Teotihuacan itself, covered several square miles and was resplendent with great pyramids, temples, palaces, and courtyards, many of them clustered along a broad avenue today called the Avenido del Muerto, which stretches for some two miles. Teotihuacan's leaders obviously held strong central control over their city and its surroundings, for they were able to command the labor of large numbers of people. That there was an elaborate priesthood is indicated by the splendid temples and by the cults of a number of gods and goddesses—especially the Feathered Serpent, Quetzalcoatl, and the rain god Tlaloc. Southwestern forms of these deities, found in such ceremonials as those of the kachina cult may well have originated in the expansion of Teotihuacan into the north and west of Mexico.

The great city and its unmeasured empire collapsed sometime during the seventh century A.D. After a period of troubles, a new people, the Toltecs, and a new center, Tula, north of the Valley of Mexico, rose during the late eighth century. For the next two hundred years they controlled much of central Mexico, and their influence stretched from Yucatán to the Mexican west coast. Much of Toltec culture was based on that of Teotihuacan, but the Toltecs did introduce copper metallurgy, probably obtaining copper from western Mexico, where metallurgy may have been invented or perhaps diffused from western South America. The Bonito phase Indians at Chaco Canyon were likely influenced by the Toltecs, though probably at second- or even thirdhand.

Tula collapsed in turn in the mid-twelfth century, and the Mexican area experienced another time of great instability. There is a good chance that trade networks leading into northern Mexico and the Southwest became disrupted with the end of Toltec rule. Assuming that the networks were

Plate 12. Fifteen-foot-high warrior figures in a temple in the Toltec capital of Tula, state of Hidalgo, Mexico. Photograph by the author.

already suffering strain in late Toltec times, this could help explain the disintegration of the Chacoan Classic period in New Mexico. At any rate, there was fragmentation in central Mexico as a number of small city-states struggled for control of the area.

At the beginning of the fourteenth century, one of the contending groups in the Valley of Mexico, a tribe called the Mexica (pronounced *meh-SHEE-ka*) began slowly to establish its supremacy over the central highlands of Mexico. The Mexica, or Aztecs, as they were later called, established themselves on a series of low, marshy islands in the southwest part of the Lake of Mexico. Their twin cities of Tenochtitlan and adjacent Tlatelolco just to the north (both now part of metropolitan Mexico City) have traditional founding dates in the first part of the fourteenth century. There may even have been an original joint settlement, with Tlatelolco splitting off a decade or so later. The Aztecs seem to have been a rather bloodthirsty people from the beginning. Their chief tribal god was the demonic Huitzilopochtli, whose priests demanded a steady diet of human sacrifice.

With several generations of skillful and forceful leaders, the Aztecs gradually gained control of the Valley of Mexico and then began to expand east and west. They did this through alliances as well as by warfare. The centerpiece of Aztec diplomacy was the triple alliance of Tenochtitlan-Tlatelolco with Texcoco on the east side of the Lake of Mexico and Tlacopan on the mainland to the west of Tenochtitlan. Texcoco, at least, was a more or less equal partner; during the fifteenth century, the single most prestigious figure in the Aztec world was the famous poet-king of Texcoco, Nezahualcoyotl (1402–72).

Still, the war machine was largely run by the rulers of Tenochtitlan. Such kings as Moteuczoma I (Moctezuma or Montezuma; 1440–68), Axayácatl (1469–81), Ahuítzotl (1486–1502), and the great kingmaker Tlacaelel (1398–1487) provided the military power and determination that extended Aztec power from the east Mexican coast of Veracruz south to the Tehuantepec area and southwestward to the Pacific (map 11). The Tarascan kingdom of the Lake Patzcuaro region was never overrun, nor were the Tlaxcalans of the Valley of Pueblo to the east. Failing to capture this latter enclave of hostile peoples proved fatal to the Aztecs when the Spaniards came.

The Aztec center of Tenochtitlan at the beginning of the sixteenth century may have housed a quarter of a million people, making it one of the great cities of the world. (London in 1500 had a population of less than a hundred thousand.) The twin cities of Tenochtitlan and Tlatelolco were located on a series of low islands, tied together and connected to the mainland by wide causeways. Centralization of the political system led to military efficiency and a regularized tribute system, which to all intents and purposes represented an annual tax on the various portions of the empire. This was partly a tax in kind, but it also employed a sort of primitive currency—cacao beans for small transactions, cotton blankets for mid-range ones, and quills filled with gold dust for large business operations. Metallurgy was now well established for copper, silver, and gold; there was even enough metal to allow copper to be used for agricultural and industrial tools as well as for armaments

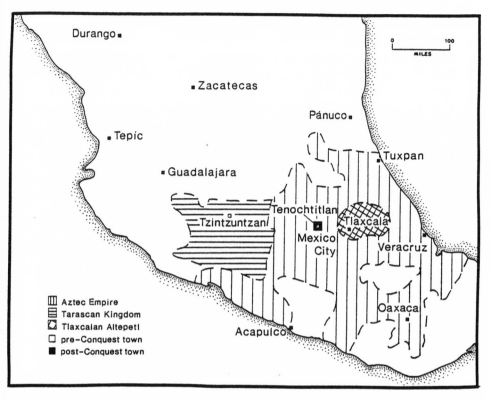

Map 11. Central Mexico around A.D. 1500.

and jewelry. A great market in the center of Tenochtitlan supplied a vast range of foodstuffs, cloth, slaves, and crafted goods of many kinds.

A class of merchants, called in Aztec times the *pochteca,* was centered in Tenochtitlan's twin, the commercial city of Tlatelolco. This group probably had fair antiquity among the Aztecs, and the pochteca idea may well have originated in the early high cultures of Mexico. In Aztec times the pochteca were a series of intermarrying families who controlled trade into central Mexico and who ventured beyond the limits of the empire, opening new markets and, incidentally, acting as spies for the central government. The pochteca were upwardly mobile, and though they took care to hide their wealth and not to challenge the nobility overtly, it is clear that by the time of the Spanish invasion, the pochteca, collectively, had developed considerable political clout.

The strength of Aztec class structure is indicated by descriptions left to us by Bernal Díaz de Castillo, one of Cortés's soldiers, of the luxury in which the king and his court lived. The ruler was considered semidivine and could be approached only with great ceremony and self-abasement, even by the highest nobles. His meals were extravagant affairs with beautiful servant women serving more than thirty courses, using handsomely decorated pottery dishes and cups of pure gold. The king was attended at meals by jesters. On his trips, the monarch rode in a litter and was surrounded by hundreds of richly attired attendants, many of them from the Aztec elite. His palaces boasted an aviary containing eagles, quetzal birds, and parrots, with their bright plumage, along with cranes and other exotic birds. There was a zoo that included not only highland and lowland animals but also deformed human beings.

The picture is one of a barbaric plunder empire, but there was also considerable sophistication of governmental function. Records were kept on bark paper using a mixture of picture elements, rebuses (graphic use of puns), and various ideograms in a kind of half-writing. The tribute system was efficiently organized and produced vast amounts of foodstuffs, cotton cloth, jewelry, metals, brightly colored feathers, and other luxury items. The pochteca played an important role, receiving goods from central governmental warehouses and trading them to areas beyond the Aztec domain.

In spite of its strong central organization, the Aztec world was already beginning to show strain even before the Spaniards arrived. The frenetic insistence on mass human sacrifice to propitiate the gods, especially the national deity, Huitzilopochtli, forced the Aztecs into the economically preposterous "flower wars," fought only to produce war captives. In their voracious appetite for sacrificial victims the Aztec leaders turned on their own lower classes. One deity who demanded an annual levy of children was the rain god, Tlaloc. Worship of this god involved the sacrifice of frightened, sobbing children whose tears were believed magically to produce rain. As I proposed in chapter 7, Tlaloc worship—perhaps including these darker elements—may have spread to the Southwest sometime after A.D. 1300. In Mesoamerica, Tlaloc can be documented to at least Teotihuacan times and probably has much greater antiquity.

Although human sacrifice is old and widespread in Mesoamerica, the Aztecs raised it to a central and all-important part of their religion. Away from its Aztec epicenter, however, human sacrifice was less important and seems to have died out in parts of west and north Mexico and in the upper Southwest by the sixteenth century.

It was not the mass slaughter of people in itself that contributed to the brittleness of the Aztec state. Other tribes and nations, past and present, have been grandly indifferent to human life—witness the continuing practice of genocide in the modern world. But the human sacrifice of the Aztecs had a terrible and immediate purpose. Aztecs believed that the gods, especially the monstrous Huitzilopochtli, must have a *constant supply* of freshly torn-out human hearts or life-warm blood. Failure to contribute these and other products of human sacrifice meant the destruction of the world. The gods would withdraw their presence and humankind would be overwhelmed in a violence of earthquake and fire. So the Aztecs lived under constant threat, with destruction only a day or a ceremony away. It was not a situation that could lead to rational planning.

The Aztec attitude toward mass sacrifice, reported in great detail by the early Spanish chroniclers, has fascinated scholars from the sixteenth century to the present day. The enormity of the sacrificial carnage has produced a number of revisionist attempts to deny or explain away these Aztec customs. Some students of Aztec society have doubted the extent of the human sacrifice, believing that the Spaniards, for propaganda purposes, deliberately overstated the situation. Others have offered ecological explanations for the practice; for example, one hypothesis holds that central Mexico was afflicted with chronic overpopulation and sacrifice functioned to reduce the possibility of famine. One rather outré explanation is that the people of the Valley of Mexico suffered from protein deficiency and consumption of sacrificial human flesh helped make up the lack.

On balance, however, there seems to be no real reason to doubt the word of soldiers, administrators, and priests who witnessed the human sacrifices or who heard the ceremonies described by Aztec informants. It is also hard to ascribe a function to the sacrifice that had any sort of positive value for Aztec society. It did have a certain tactical benefit as an instrument of terror. Rulers and important people from tribute cities were regularly brought to Tenochtitlan to see the bloody sacrifices—a kind of object lesson in the event they planned to rebel. But generally, human sacrifice among the Aztecs seems to be a case in which a set of religious ceremonies had become rampantly dysfunctional.

The instability of Aztec Mexico, with the enormities of its sacrificial cults and increasing tensions within the Aztec polity, was exacerbated by the appearance of Moteuczoma II, who became king in 1502. Previous kings of the Aztec empire had been military-minded pragmatists who permitted commoners considerable upward mobility into the nobility, especially in the army and the priesthood. Moteuczoma II, however, had an exalted and reactionary attitude toward royalty and the upper nobility, and he attempted to end this social mobility even for the most talented lower-class individuals. According to accounts of the time, commoners were forbidden even to look at Moteuczoma under pain of death. This rule must have created a constant series of difficult situations, so perhaps only on certain ceremonial occasions was Moteuczoma held sacrosanct from the eyes of his people. Be that as it may, he certainly brought a new and drastic emphasis on social rigidity. The pochteca, who by this time probably possessed much of the real power of the state, seem to have held their own, but the warrior societies were purged of commoners.

Moteuczoma's most serious shortcoming as a ruler, however, was his obsession with religion and his brooding, mystical approach to life. It was this mysticism that caused the king to treat the arrival of the Spaniards as a supernatural event, the return of the great god Quetzalcoatl. The god, according to legends dating from Toltec times, had left Tula some hundreds of year earlier, sailing eastward from the coast of Mexico on a raft of serpents. Quetzalcoatl had promised to return at some future time on the year of his birth date, *ce acatl* (one-reed) in the Aztec calendar, and reclaim his kingdom. In Moteuczoma's mind the Aztecs, successors to the Toltecs, were bound to accept the god when he came—and 1519 was, in fact, the year ce acatl.

The rest of the Aztec court had no such illusions about the godliness of the Spanish invaders, but Moteuczoma persisted in considering Cortés an epiphany of Quetzalcoatl, or at least as a representive of him. In spite of the increasingly frantic advice of his military leaders, the Aztec king vacillated until the enemy was literally within the gates.

Moteuczoma was especially unlucky in that his adversary, Hernán Cortés, was a skilled military commander with a good understanding of psychological warfare. He quickly evaluated the possibilities and difficulties of the Aztec military and political situation, and by his actions took advantage of every weakness. This Spaniard, the nemesis of the Aztecs, was a professional soldier of middle-class origins, the type of man who often rose to the top in the turbulent early decades of Spanish operations in the New World. Hernán Cortés came to Hispaniola in 1504, at the age of nineteen, and eventually settled in Cuba. He was sent on an exploring expedition to the mainland by Governor Diego Velázquez, to follow up on explorations made by Hernández de Córdoba in 1517 and Grijalva in 1518.

Cortés left Cuba in February 1519 in eleven ships with some six hundred men and sixteen horses. Stopping on the east coast of Yucatán, Cortés took on board a Spaniard, Jerómino de Aguilar, who had been shipwrecked some years before and had been living with the Yucatán Mayas and so spoke the

Mayan language. A few weeks later, in Tabasco, the Spanish party received a group of female slaves, one of whom could speak both Maya and Nahuatl, the language of the Aztecs. This woman's name, Malinal (from the day-sign *malinalli*), was transformed by the Spaniards into the baptismal name Marina (María), and in later years the honorific suffix *-tzin* was added. Because Nahuatl had no *r* sound, the Aztecs rendered the name Malintzin, which the Spaniards Hispanicized as Malinche. Under whatever name, Marina quickly became the expedition's prime interpreter. At first she worked with Aguilar, translating Nahuatl to Maya for him and then allowing him to rephrase it in Spanish. But Marina was good with languages and rapidly picked up Spanish. By the time Cortés reached the Valley of Mexico she could interpret directly.

Cortés landed on the Veracruz coast in April 1519, already knowing a great deal about the Aztecs. The Grijalva expedition of 1518 had contacted Aztec officials when one of Grijalva's ships sailed up the Papaloapán River, south of modern Vera Cruz, and its captain, Pedro de Alvarado, met officials of the Aztec court on this eastern outpost of the Aztec empire. Cortés interviewed Alvarado at length and also spoke with members of the earlier Córdova expedition. Alvarado was especially eager to cooperate, for he was to become Cortés's second-in-command during the 1519 expedition. Whether Cortés had heard the Quetzalcoatl story while still in Cuba is not certain. He may have received a preliminary account of it in Tabasco, perhaps from Marina herself.

On the coast in late April of 1519, with that curious regard for legalisms so characteristic of sixteenth-century Spaniards, Cortés set up a new town with its *cabildo,* or city officers, and called it Villa Rica de la Vera Cruz. Elected by the new officials of Vera Cruz to command the expedition, Cortés now completely threw off control by Governor Velázquez in Cuba and struck out on his own. It was a daring decision, for Cortés could well expect retribution from the Cuban authorities—as indeed he was dealt. To make sure his own men continued to follow him, Cortés took the drastic step of destroying his ships.

The Spaniards quickly consolidated the lowland area around Vera Cruz. The natives of that region, though subject to the Aztecs, were not especially friendly toward them. Everywhere the Spaniards destroyed temples and overthrew statues of gods, replacing them with Christian statues and images, especially those of the Virgin Mary. In mid-August, Cortés turned inland and began his march to Mexico City. By this time he knew a great deal about Aztec society and had collected detailed information on the personality of the Mexica king.

The savagely anti-Aztec Tlaxcalans, in the Puebla area, met Cortés with some suspicion, apparently thinking him a secret ally of Moteuczoma. After a series of battles in which Tlaxcalan forces were defeated, Cortés persuaded them to join the Spanish cause. This was a major diplomatic triumph for Cortés, and it set the pattern for the conquest of the Aztecs. Cortés's forces, now with an allied troop of Tlaxcalan warriors, inflicted a severe defeat on the Aztecs at Cholula, near the modern city of Puebla. Pushing on over the passes into the Valley of Mexico, the combined Spanish and Tlaxcalan army reached Tenochtitlan in November of 1519. Moteuczoma, with a chilling disregard for advice from his own governmental and military leaders, invited the Spaniards across the causeways into the island capital. Once ensconced in Moteuczoma's palace, Cortés imprisoned the emperor and ruled in his name. Sadly for the Aztecs, Moteuczoma cooperated for some months with his captor—whether out of fear or misplaced religious fervor is unknown.

Meanwhile, Cortés had to face a new danger. In the spring of 1520 a large Spanish party arrived at Vera Cruz. This group of several hundred men, under the command of Pánfilo de Narváez, had been sent by Governor Velázquez to arrest Cortés. The conquistador quickly divided his forces, leaving Pedro de Alvarado in charge in Tenochtitlan. Returning to the coast, Cortés outmaneuvered and outwitted Narváez, persuading the latter man's followers to desert. Cortés then led his greatly increased Spanish force back to the Valley of Mexico.

He found affairs in a shambles. Alvarado had massacred a large number of Aztec notables who were trying to hold the principal festival of the spring month of Toxcatl. The outraged Aztecs allowed Cortés, with his augmented army, to reenter the city but then closed around him, cutting off supplies.

Cortés and Moteuczoma now attempted to start negotiations with the rebellious Aztecs and took the gamble of releasing Moteuczoma's brother, Cuitlahuac, who had also been held captive. This proved an almost fatal step, for Cuitlahuac, whose enmity toward the Spaniards ran deep, immediately rallied the Aztec leadership to his cause. Moteuczoma was deposed and Cuitlahuac installed in his place. The emperor now disappears from history; whether he was killed by his own people or murdered by the Spaniards is uncertain.

The Spaniards' situation became more desperate each day. On the night of June 30–July 1, 1520 (the famous *noche triste,* or sad night, of Spanish-Mexican history), they broke out of the city. Spanish losses were staggering, and only fragments of the army managed to straggle off to the north and east, where they were aided by the Otomi, a mountain people generally hostile to the Aztecs. Cortés barely survived a battle on July 7 near the ruins of Teotihuacan, and with the remnants of his forces limped back across the mountains to the safety of Tlaxcalan-controlled territory. The Aztecs had managed a major victory, but by failing to completely destroy Cortés and his army they sowed the seeds of eventual defeat.

The Spaniards came back in force, with thousands of Tlaxcalan and other allies, early in 1521. By this time disease had become a new and powerful ally of the Spaniards. Smallpox, introduced by an infected member of the Narváez expedition, swept the Aztec capital and spread into other parts of east and central Mexico; the king Cuitlahuac was one of its victims. Indeed, it seems fair to say that Cortés might not have won Mexico had not the rapid spread of Old World diseases tipped the balance.

The death of Cuitlahuac in the fall of 1520 brought a new king to the throne, a nephew of Moteuczoma's named Cuauhtemoc. Under Cuauhtemoc, one of the heroic figures of Mexican history, the Aztecs fought on for a time. In the last stages of the fight the merchant groups of Tlatelolco became more powerful, and new blood entered the Aztec leadership. But Cortés now built brigantines which, with their superior firepower, controlled the Lake of Mexico. Still, Cuauhtemoc managed his dwindling forces with great skill and won a considerable victory on June 30, 1521.

The Spaniards, however, continued to collect allies from those central Mexican tribes and cities that had long been victimized by the Aztecs. The combined Spanish-Indian army launched a major attack and overran much of Tenochtitlan. Falling back on Tlatelolco, the Aztec forces fought on, street by street, plaza by plaza, temple by temple. Finally, on August 13, with most of the people dead and the rest starving, resistance collapsed and Cortés stood victorious in the ruins of the great twin capitals. The following day the gallant Cuauhtemoc surrendered, and the Aztec empire was no more.

CHAPTER TEN

Edging Northward

It is impossible to understand the actions of the Span-
iards when they finally reached the Rio Grande unless
we consider the reasons why Spain chose to treat all the
bands, tribes, and kingdoms of the New World in such
a high-handed way. Basically, their attitude stemmed
from the medieval Christian worldview in which all human beings were children of the primal couple, Adam
and Eve. To medieval people, the coming of Christianity was the defining
moment of the human species, the great watershed of all history. After
Christ, the Church Militant held the destiny of humankind, including the
benighted pagan segment of humanity. The church could assign powerful,
secular Christian rulers to bring this or that part of the world to Christianity.
This theory, however, broke down when the Christian states faced powerful
nations and empires like the Islamic countries of North Africa and western
Asia, or China and Japan in eastern Asia. In such cases purely secular ar-
rangements had to be made.

It was otherwise in the New World. Spain and Portugal had been the first
Christian nations to launch great sea explorations in the late fifteenth and
early sixteenth centuries. In 1493, Pope Alexander VI, in a "donation," divided the newly found lands between the two, the boundary being clarified
a year later in the Treaty of Tordesillas between Portugal and Castile. The
donation and the treaty awarded Spain the lands lately discovered by Columbus and gave Portugal the East Indies. In 1493, Portugal, after a decades-
long march down the coast of Africa, had already reached east Africa and
within five years would arrive in India. The line of demarcation was fixed at
370 leagues west of the Cape Verde Islands (between 48 and 49 degrees west
of Greenwich). This line inadvertently gave Portugal a segment of what later

became Brazil. Both Spain and Portugal were obligated to convert the aboriginal population.

The Spaniards legalized their claim by means of a pronouncement called the *requerimiento*. This statement, worked out by theologians at the request of King Ferdinand in 1513, was based on the papal donation of 1493. Read to the natives at the time of first contact, it informed them that the king of Spain was now their ruler. Any subsequent rebellion or hostilities would be construed as treason. The requerimiento was read by Cortés to the Aztecs, and Coronado later read it to the Pueblo Indians.

It is interesting to speculate that, given a little more time to adjust to European diseases (and slightly better luck in first contacts), some of the larger polities of the New World might, like Japan, have maintained their independence. Had the Aztecs managed to fight Spain to a standstill it certainly would have meant a very different history for the Southwest. But probably this was not in the cards. The Aztec state was unstable at best, and the rulers at Tenochtitlan had produced only a facade of national unity. Under this facade the individual aspirations, jealousies, and mutual rivalries of cities and peoples boiled busily away. The Aztecs, in spite of their less sophisticated military technology, could and should have destroyed Cortés during the *noche triste*. That they failed to do so indicates the vast difference between the Europeans' military set of mind and that of the Aztecs, and, indeed, between the Europeans and all other complex New World states.

Even sophisticated New World people like the Aztecs considered warfare a kind of game, hinged around with elaborate rules. Europeans in medieval times had somewhat the same concepts of war, exemplified by the courtly formality of El Cid's campaigns. This "play by the rules" attitude was still alive in fifteenth-century France, as witness the noble nincompoops who charged English longbows at Agincourt. But Europeans, and perhaps especially Spaniards, by the sixteenth century had taken a hard-headed attitude toward war. Winning was everything. Fighting the Spaniards, the Aztecs found themselves in the position of a football team whose opponents ignored the yard markers—and used guns.

Even had the Aztecs beaten and killed Cortés, another conqueror would surely have come along. The brittle confederation of the Aztecs, with its lunatic insistence on mass human sacrifice, probably could not have withstood the strain. In time, the Aztecs might have learned the uses of a more effective warfare, but time was the one thing they did not have.

With the defeat of the Aztecs, Cortés now moved rapidly to consolidate his control over central Mexico. He began to think of a westward thrust to destroy the other power in this part of Mesoamerica, the Tarascan kingdom centered at Tzintzuntzan in the Lake Pátzcuaro region (see map 11). Since the Tarascans had defeated the Aztecs only a few generations before, one might have expected them to battle the new Spanish forces sharply. Instead, opposition simply melted away. The reasons are not entirely clear, but certainly disease and depopulation were important factors. The last Tarascan *cazonci,* or king, was murdered by the brutal Nuño Beltrán de Guzmán in 1528.

In 1522, largely bypassing the passive Tarascan kingdom, Cortés reached what is now the state of Colima on the Pacific coast. In 1524, one of Cortés's captains, Francisco Cortés de Buenaventura, was sent north into present-day Tepic and southern Sinaloa. He found sizable towns, large populations, and sophisticated societies, though smaller and less well organized than the Aztecs and Tarascans, and much less warlike. The Tarascans were missionized by Franciscan friars in 1525 or early 1526. Two years later, Hernán Cortés having been recalled to Spain, the conquest of the west coast was undertaken by Nuño de Guzmán. He drafted a number of Tarascans into his army, perhaps mainly as *támenes,* or burden bearers. Then Guzmán launched a long raid up the west coast of Mexico, looting and burning as he went. He reached Sinaloa in late 1530 and the following year worked his way up the coast as far as Culiacán, where the Spaniards founded a settlement a few miles south of the present west coast metropolis.

Guzmán was, at heart, something of a medieval man with the medieval ability to believe far-fetched stories. He heard tales of an Amazon kingdom called Ciguatán somewhere to the north, and his raid up the west coast was aimed at seizing this mysterious province. Guzmán was disappointed in Ciguatán, finding it was very much like the surrounding statelets. Another story, which was to influence the Spaniards for a decade, was told to Guzmán by an Indian named Tejo who lived in the valley of Oxitipar in eastern Mexico. Tejo claimed that his father had been a trader to seven large cities, each the size of Tenochtitlan, located forty days' journey northwest of Oxitipar. The father had traded feathers for gold and silver.

Guzmán was probably motivated to believe this tall tale because of a durable European legend about the Seven Cities of Antillia. According to the story, Antillia was a large body of land west of Portugal—whether island or mainland was never made clear—that had been colonized in A.D. 714 by Portuguese refugees from the Moors. As the legend went, these Christian refugees were led by the archbishop of Oporto and six other bishops, each of whom founded a city. By the sixteenth century, the Seven Cities of Antillia had become one of those utopias that so fascinated the European mind in the early exploration period.

Guzmán's excesses were too much for the Spanish Crown, and the conquistador was ordered back to Spain to face trial and imprisonment. Meanwhile, Cortés, now operating from the lower west coast of Mexico and also influenced by the Ciguatán and perhaps by the "seven cities" story, began to send ships exploring up the Mexican coast. In 1532, one of these ships, under the command of Diego Hurtado de Mendoza, was lost somewhere around the mouth of the Sinaloa River. The crew wound up in the Fuerte River area, where they were killed by local Indians.

In 1533, one of Guzmán's lieutenants, a kinsman named Diego de Guzmán, launched a slaving raid from San Miguel de Culiacán. He reached as far north as the lower Yaqui River—the first Spanish party to get to the edge of the Southwest. Hurtado's sailors had already been murdered, but Diego de Guzmán found equipment from their ship, including iron objects that had entered the trade network and were being passed north and south from the Sinaloa River location where the Spaniards had come ashore.

The first Spaniards actually to traverse parts of the lower Southwest came on the scene in 1535 and 1536, when a party of four men led by Alvar Nuñez Cabeza de Vaca completed its trek from the Texas coast and reached the west coast of Mexico. Cabeza de Vaca and his companions had been part of the 1528 Pánfilo de Narváez expedition to Florida. Narváez, who had lost his army to Cortés at Vera Cruz, was determined to try again. Unfortunately, his leadership abilities had not improved, nor had his judgment. Having explored a portion of northern Florida, Narváez, in a miscalculation almost beyond belief, attempted to go by sea in hand-built boats from Florida to Pánuco, Mexico. He managed to get himself and most of his expedition killed in a storm somewhere off the western Louisiana or eastern Texas coast.

One by one, the remaining members of the expedition died at the hands of hostile natives or from starvation and exposure, finally leaving only Cabeza de Vaca's little party to reach New Spain. With Vaca were two other Spaniards, Andrés de Dorantes and Alonso de Castillo Maldonado. The fourth member, who later played a role in the first Spanish *entrada* into the upper Southwest, was a black slave of Dorantes's named Esteban de Dorantes. During the long journey from Texas to Sinaloa, Esteban, who picked up languages easily, functioned as interpreter and general contact person.

In the later part of the year 1535, Cabeza de Vaca and his group had worked their way westward to La Junta, the confluence of the Rio Grande and Conchos rivers. The route they took from that spot is uncertain. It is possible that they ascended the Rio Grande to around modern Las Cruces and then crossed the flat lands of southern New Mexico before turning southward into the Sonora River drainage. Alternatively, they may have gone west from La Junta, crossing the Sierra Madres and the upper Yaqui River drainage and eventually reaching the Sonora River.

Whatever their route, the little band arrived at the large towns of the Sonora valley in the spring of 1536. They stayed for a time at a place the Spaniards called Corazones (hearts) because they had been given six hundred dried deer hearts. Corazones, southernmost of the vigorous statelets in the Sonora River valley proper, was situated in the Ures basin about sixty miles northeast of modern Hermosillo. This part of the valley seems to have been populated by Piman-speaking Indians, unlike the Opata-speaking towns just to the north of the Ures Gorge. From Corazones, with a group of Indians who were mainly or wholly Piman speaking, the Vaca party reached Culiacán on the west coast of Mexico.

During their travels in Sonora, Cabeza de Vaca and his companions heard stories about people living to the north in great multistory houses, who traded turquoise and other goods for bright-colored parrot and macaw feathers. It was in that area that Vaca received the five "emeralds" mentioned in chapter 7, which were later lost on the trail.

Cabeza de Vaca's story caused a great deal of excitement in Mexico City, where the newly arrived viceroy, Antonio de Mendoza, began to think seriously about an expedition to the north. News of Pizarro's conquest of the Inca empire was flooding into Mexico, and it seemed that there was gold on every horizon. Mendoza, however, was cautious and made no immediate move into the Southwest.

One of Pizarro's captains in the conquest of the Peruvian Incas, Hernando de Soto, had no such qualms. Returning to Spain in 1536, the same year Cabeza de Vaca reached Mexico, de Soto petitioned King Carlos for territorial grants in Ecuador and Guatemala. These were refused, but in 1537 de Soto was granted permission to lead an expedition to Florida. In May of 1539, he left Havana with some six hundred soldiers and perhaps an additional hundred servants and slaves. The expedition was outfitted with two hundred horses, mules, pigs for food, and many other provisions. For the next four years, Spaniards under de Soto—and after his death in 1542, under Luís de Moscoso—explored parts of the eastern and southern United States. The expedition was a colossal failure, and the Spaniards lost more than half their men. But in the spring of 1539 it must have seemed to Mendoza that de Soto was going to steal a march on him and discover the "golden cities."

In any case, the viceroy decided to move. He made careful plans, aided by Francisco Vázquez de Coronado, a young protégé of Mendoza's who had been appointed governor of the newly founded province of Nueva Galicia, the fruits of Guzmán's campaigns a decade earlier. Coronado and Mendoza, both prudent men, decided to send a preliminary expedition under a Franciscan friar, Marcos de Niza, who had recently been reassigned to Mexico from Peru and who thus had had experience with gold-rich areas. Going north with Marcos was the black slave from the Vaca party, Esteban de Dorantes. Marcos also took a handful of Mexican and Tlaxcalan helpers and in Culiacán picked up some of the Piman Indians who had come south with Cabeza de Vaca three years before. In addition, if a statement made by Coronado is correct, Marcos had with him some eighty people from the region north of Culiacán, probably including both Tahue and Cáhitan speakers. A second Franciscan friar named Onorato was also assigned to the voyage, but he soon became ill and was left behind.

Marcos departed Culiacán on March 7, 1539, and continued northward, following the trail left by Spanish exploring and slaving parties. He kept fairly near the coast, crossing the various rivers that flow down from the Sierra Madre. There is a great deal of disagreement as to his route. My own opinion is that Marcos and party traversed the low desert country between mountain and ocean in northern Sinaloa and Sonora. Eventually cutting inland beyond the Sonora River, Marcos reached heavy settlements of Piman-speaking Indians somewhere in the Altar-Magdalena drainage. There he began to pick up stories of important provinces or "kingdoms" in the area, especially those of Totonteac, Marata, and Acus. I believe those names reflect memories of rich states, perhaps offshoots of Casas Grandes, that had collapsed a century or so before.

Marcos also heard of a rich land to the north dominated by the "Seven Cities of Cíbola." These were the Zuni pueblos of extreme western New Mexico. As I said in chapter 8, the word *Cíbola* was probably Marcos's attempt to pronounce the term used by the Zunis for their territory. At the same time, Marcos was told of "Ahacus," which he considered to be one of the seven cities but which likely was a garbled account of the pueblo of Acoma. With this rather vague mention, the Pueblo Indians of the Rio Grande drainage enter written history.

At a town called Vacapa, probably on the Magdalena River, Esteban was sent ahead with a number of the Indian servants. Marcos continued more slowly up the Magdalena and across to the San Pedro River. Clearly he was on one of the major trade routes angling down through Pima country toward the coast of the Gulf of California, for Marcos tells of rich shipments of turquoise, hides, and pottery. He followed the San Pedro River for a time, eventually cutting northeastward to the Gila. Because this part of the route was also followed by Coronado, I will discuss it in more detail when I consider Coronado's march to the Southwest.

Somewhere on the Gila River, Marcos de Niza received the news that Esteban had been killed at Cíbola. For once the slave's famous linguistic and negotiating skills, so valuable to the Cabeza de Vaca party, failed him. Now, four and a half centuries later, we have no real idea what happened. Esteban had a considerable reputation as a womanizer, and it may be that he insulted the Cíbolans by his attentions to their women; so, at any rate, reported Coronado the following year. More likely his death had to do with magic. Esteban carried with him a gourd rattle that he seems to have used to demonstrate shamanlike powers. For some reason, the people of Cíbola were offended by this rattle and by Esteban's activities. It sounds as if they suspected him of witchcraft and killed him for that reason. He may also have been considered a spy for the oncoming Spaniards, for the Cíbolans likely already had secondhand knowledge of Spanish slaving activities in Sinaloa and southern Sonora. Or, indeed, Esteban may have been branded both a witch *and* a spy.

Exactly what Marcos did after the alarming news of Esteban's murder is also uncertain. According to his own account, Marcos went on to Cíbola, where he viewed the first of the Cíbolan settlements, a city greater than Tenochtitlan–Mexico City. Writing twenty years later, Pedro de Castañeda, a chronicler for the Coronado party, told a story of how the friar, upon hearing the account of Esteban's death, immediately turned back to Mexico without ever having seen Cíbola. But Castañeda, like most of the secular Spaniards on Coronado's expedition, was bitter over Marcos's exaggerated account of Cíbola. His statement must be taken with some reservation.

I think there is a good chance that the friar actually did see one of the "cities of Cíbola," which is to say one of the Zuni towns in extreme western New Mexico. Whether this town was Hawikuh, where Coronado entered Zuni country the following year, or the more eastern pueblo of K'iakima, is not clear. Nor is it clear why Marcos exaggerated the size of whatever pueblo he saw. There is reason to believe, however, that Marcos did not really have a fluent command of Spanish (his native tongue was Provençal), and it may be

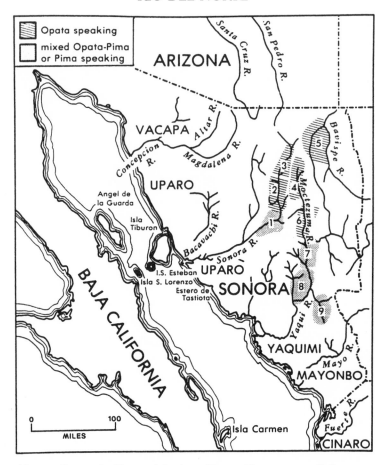

Map 12. Sonora in Coronado's time. Key: 1, Corazones; 2, Señora; 3, Guaraspi; 4, Cumupa; 5, Sahuaripa; 6, Batuco; 7, Pinebaroca; 8, Paibatuco; 9, Oera.

that his report was edited in Mexico City after his return in the late summer of 1539.

In any case, Marcos made no claims for riches in gold and silver at Cíbola. He did mention turning aside on the return trip and journeying up one of the river valleys to the edge of a large settled area, where he heard tales of "much gold." This side trip was very likely up the Sonora River, perhaps to the edge of the Ures basin where Cabeza de Vaca had found the settlements of Corazones (map 12). It is true that there was gold in this area of northeast Sonora—the only gold found by the Coronado expedition.

In one regard, Marcos gave incorrect information that had grave consequences. From the friar's account the Spaniards got the idea that Cíbola lay quite near the sea. By the time of Marcos's trip, Europeans had explored the Gulf of California to about the mouth of the Colorado River, and a supply route by sea for the Spanish exploratory expedition seemed logical. As a result, a portion of the equipment and, especially, the food and clothing needed by the Spaniards under Coronado was sent by sea.

The report of Marcos de Niza led to increased activity on the part of the Spaniards. In January 1540, Coronado, already governor of Nueva Galicia, was formally appointed commander or captain general of the expedition by Viceroy Mendoza. In February, a muster was held in the tiny town of Compostela, capital of Nueva Galicia, which had been founded only a few years before. Compostela in the early months of 1540 was located approximately where Tepic, modern capital of the state of Nayarit, lies today; the town was moved to its present site, some fifty miles south of Tepic, later that same year. Then the army moved on to Culiacán, where a second muster was held. Finally ready for the move northward, Coronado commanded about 350 European soldiers and some 1,300 Indian allies. Most of the Europeans were Spaniards, but there was a scatter of men from other parts of Europe— Portugal, France, Italy, Germany, and Scotland. A large number of them are known by name.

On the other hand, we have only a handful of names of the Indian allies and their groups. In the Tlatelolco *Anales* (annals) is an entry for 1540 stating that Mexican-Tlatelolcans went to conquer Yancuictlalpan (the "new lands"). Sometimes, when naming individual Indian allies, the chroniclers gave the town or area from which they came. Thus, we know that the Mexican Indian contingent was made up mostly of Tlaxcalans, Mexicas (Aztecs), and Tarascans, something that would seem logical in any case.

Most members of the expeditionary force were men, but three women married to Spanish soldiers are listed, and we know of at least two Spanish children. It is possible that there were also women and children in the Indian encampments. The expedition had fifteen hundred stock animals—horses, mules, sheep, and perhaps cattle. For its time and place, it was an ambitious undertaking.

The cautious viceroy, after hearing Marcos de Niza's account, decided to send still another exploring party northward to verify the friar's story. Mendoza chose for this trip the *alcalde mayor* (mayor) of Culiacán, Melchior Díaz. With fifteen horsemen, Díaz left Culiacán in November 1539 and wintered somewhere in the northern Sonora and southern Arizona region. His

Plate 13. Impressionistic mural depicting Coronado and party, by Gerald Cassidy. Photograph courtesy Museum of New Mexico, neg. no. 20206.

report, somewhat less enthusiastic than Marcos's but with essentially the same details, arrived in March 1540—too late to have much effect on the course of the expedition.

In April of 1540, Coronado left Culiacán with a force of Spaniards, mostly mounted, and some Indians allies—perhaps two hundred to three hundred men in all. The main army, under Tristán de Arellano, followed some twenty days behind. A sea arm of the expedition, under Captain Hernando de Alarçón, was directed to sail from Acapulco to resupply the trip. This naval expedition did indeed sail in May 1540 and reached the mouth of the Colorado River in late August. Although Alarçón ascended the Colorado as far as the mouth of the Gila River, he was confronted with the grim fact that Cíbola was still hundreds of miles across mountains and desert. Alarçón, with the army's supplies of food, equipment, and winter clothing, turned back to Mexico.

Coronado's own trip north was relatively uneventful. European diseases and Spanish slave raiding had drastically affected the native populations of Sinaloa and southern Sonora, and Indians who remained in those parts had no stomach for war with Coronado's large force. Even when Coronado's vanguard reached the warlike statelets of the Sonora River area, there seems to have been no great amount of hostility. This was probably because Coronado, under strict orders from Viceroy Mendoza, kept his men away from the native villages and conspicuously cultivated good behavior in his relations with the natives.

The main army, following behind the general, was less scrupulous. Coronado had ordered that a permanent settlement be built as a way station between Mexico and the Southwest, and this was placed at Corazones, the site visited a few years before by Cabeza de Vaca. Arellano and the army remained in Corazones through the rainy summer months, and then, with food short, he moved the settlement of San Gerónimo de los Corazones a few miles north, beyond the Ures Gorge and within the boundaries of the powerful statelet of Señora on the middle Sonora River. San Gerónimo de los Corazones eventually fell to the command of Diego de Alcaráz, a man both brutal and stupid. It was a dangerous combination of character traits for such a time and place, and, as we shall see in chapter 14, the ill-starred settlement of Corazones had a short and tragic history.

While at Corazones, Coronado sent an exploring party down the Sonora River to the sea, trying to make contact with Alarçón. The Spaniards encountered hunting-and-gathering Indians, presumably the Seri, but no sign of ships. In late May, Coronado left the statelet area, ascending the Sonora River and its tributaries to a point near modern Cananea. Then he struck out northward across the flat country north of Cananea to the headwaters of the San Pedro River. There Coronado intersected the route used by Marcos the previous year. Marcos was with Coronado's vanguard, and he may have had a hand in guiding the Spaniards over this last stretch of road. However, Coronado had depended on native guides going over well-worn trade routes, and he clearly continued doing so.

Going down the San Pedro, the party swung to the north and east, probably between the Winchester and Little Dragoon mountains. From there the Spanish forces reached Aravaipa Canyon and then turned northeastward between the Pinaleño and Santa Teresa Mountains, where they found the impressive ruins of Chichilticalli, the "red house." It was at Chichilticalli, as the route turned even farther northeast, that Coronado began to realize that he was moving steadily away from the Gulf of California.

But the immediate business of the expedition was to reach Cíbola.

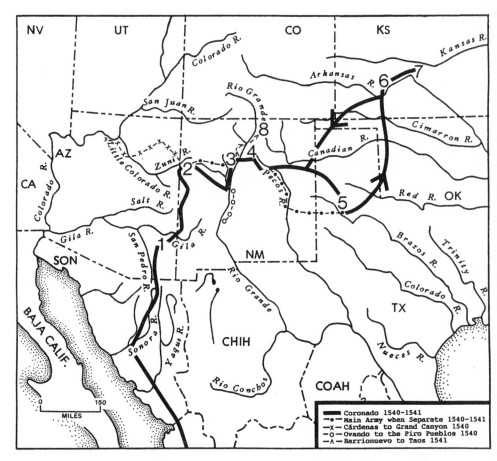

Map 13. Coronado's route from Sonora to Kansas. Key: 1, Chichilticalli; 2, Cíbola (Hawikuh); 3, Coofor (Santiago); 4, Cicúye (Pecos); 5, the deep barranca; 6, Quivira; 7, Harahey; 8, Braba (Taos).

Coronado entered the Gila valley, following the river to the vicinity of modern-day Virden, and then, crossing the Gila, he struck off up the San Francisco River, tracking it northward to near its headwaters. At that point the Spaniards turned westward again, following Carrizo Wash to near its junction with the Zuni River (map 13).

From Chichilticalli, the Spaniards' route, though wonderfully scenic, crossed a somewhat deserted area. The provisions they had brought from Culiacán now ran out, as did the large quantity of corn bread collected at

Corazones and Señora and made from the previous year's crop (the 1540 late winter or spring planting of maize had not yet ripened in the Sonora valley). Hunger began to stalk the Spanish camp. Attempts to live off the land were not particularly successful; in fact, several of the Indian allies, two black slaves, and a Spanish soldier died from eating poisonous herbs.

It was a desperately hungry army that finally followed Carrizo Wash westward toward the Zuni River. There, the Spaniards saw their first Cíbola natives. On reaching the Zuni River, Coronado crossed a trail that connected the various Cíbola-Zuni towns with the Zuni sacred site called Ko:thlu-wala:wa. This site, which lay at the junction of the Zuni and Little Colorado rivers some thirty miles southwest of the cluster of Zuni pueblos, seems to have been the focus of one of the important, multitown summer ceremonials. The Spanish intrusion at such a sacred time led to a flurry of hostilities. These did not slow up the Spaniards, and on July 7, 1540, the army reached the westernmost Cíbola town, the Zuni pueblo of Hawikuh.

CHAPTER ELEVEN

Spain Reaches the Rio Grande

 Because this book is basically about the native people of the Rio Grande—their adaptations and their struggles with the natural environment as well as hostile human forces—I shall try to interpret the mood of the Native Americans, their reactions to Spanish invasion, and their various strategies for contending with the invaders. For example, it is clear that the Indians made serious attempts to defeat the Spaniards militarily, as we will see later in a struggle at Tiguex. More dramatic was the plan, probably worked out at Pecos, for losing the Spaniards in the Great Plains. The Rio Grande people were undoubtedly willing to defend their land and their culture. Their great failure in 1540, like that during the Pueblo Revolt a century and a half later, was their inability to form and especially to sustain a unified front. In their first contacts with the Europeans, the Pueblo Indians had several chances to work together for a common goal. They failed in this, and Coronado, like Cortés before him, was able to divide and conquer.

The battle for Cíbola-Zuni was short and decisive. The requerimiento was read through an interpreter, without making any great impression on the Cíbolans. Likely they had no clue what it was all about. Coronado's vanguard then attacked Hawikuh with cavalry and artillery, and the Indians retreated to the sheltering walls of the town. They held the Spaniards off for a time, raining arrows and stones onto the attacking force. The town itself, typical of sixteenth-century pueblos, was built for defense. Its outer rooms had no external doorways and could be entered only from the flat roofs of the first terrace. A series of additional terraces made the center of the town several stories high, and the Cíbolans climbed from one terrace to the next by means of ladders. This kind of fortified town gave the Spaniards trouble throughout Coronado's journey.

The general deployed his cavalry to surround the pueblo. The Spaniards directed arquebus and crossbow fire at the walls, and Coronado himself, heavily armed, led an attack on foot. Cíbolan strategy was to shower the attackers with arrows and stones from the ramparts. It had some success, for several Spaniards were wounded. Coronado himself was knocked senseless by a blow from a heavy stone and was carried out of the action. Eventually, under the command of the *maese (maestro) de campo* ("campmaster," or chief aide), García López de Cárdenas, the attackers broke into Hawikuh. There was a truce; the natives withdrew and allowed the invaders possession of the town and the considerable amount of food it contained.

Cíbola was a stunning disappointment to the Spaniards, for there was no gold or silver—indeed, no great wealth of any sort. But for the moment, food was worth more to the starving invaders than gold. Coronado settled down in Hawikuh, the inhabitants withdrawing eastward to the protective heights of the great flat-topped mesa Dowa Yalanne, the Zuni sacred mountain near which lay the eastern Cíbola-Zuni towns.

Coronado immediately began to explore the area. He sent Melchior Díaz back along the trail to meet the main army at Corazones and to take charge of the way station being founded there. After accomplishing that task, Díaz was ordered to go west to the Gulf of California and meet Alarçón and his ships. Contact with Alarçón was certainly to be desired, but ironically, this decision to send Díaz to the gulf was one factor in the failure of Coronado's expedition. Díaz, efficient but brutal, reached the lower Colorado River just days after Alarçón had departed. After committing some pointless atrocities, Díaz was on his way back to San Gerónimo de los Corazones when a freak accident left him mortally wounded. He died in early January 1541, leaving Diego de Alcaráz in command of this important post. Within a few months Alcaráz had blundered his way into losing San Gerónimo, thus leaving Coronado without the vital connection to his home base in Mexico.

Coronado sent another expedition, under Captain Pedro de Tovar, to Tusayán, today's Hopi country of northeastern Arizona. He may have been making still another attempt to find a route to Alarçón and the lower Colorado River, for the Hopis had a long tradition of trade with that area. The Hopis received Tovar with considerable coldness. At the first pueblo he encountered—probably Kawaika-a, a town on Jeddito Mesa near the historic pueblo of Awatovi—the Indians came to meet him in battle formation and drew a line on the ground, telling the Spaniards not to cross it. This line was likely drawn with sacred corn pollen, and its function was to magically block the intruders.

According to Tovar's report, the Hopis, after a short fight, became conciliatory and offered presents of food and blankets. Forty years later, however, when the Espejo expedition reached Hopi, the chronicler Diego Pérez de Luxán heard that Coronado's party had totally destroyed a Hopi town which, from its location, appears to have been Kawaika-a. This story was repeated by Baltasar de Obregón, who got independent information firsthand from another member of the Espejo expedition. If Coronado's men treated the Hopis with the same ruthlessness they displayed in the Tiguex area a few months later, Kawaika-a may indeed have been destroyed. I should point out, however, that the post-expedition hearing into Coronado's treatment of native peoples failed to mention atrocities at Hopi.

In any case, Tovar did not get beyond Hopi, returning to Hawikuh in mid-August, 1540. A few days later the campmaster, Cárdenas, was sent via Hopi to travel west to the Colorado River and follow it downstream. Cárdenas collected Hopi guides, who took him on something of a wild goose chase across the Little Colorado River and then over the arid wasteland to the west. He and his men are usually credited with "discovering" the Grand Canyon, viewing it from the south rim. They probably reached the Grand Canyon, though conceivably they were viewing the western end of the Little Colorado gorge. In any case, they came nowhere near the lower portions of the Colorado River and were kept away from the real route, much traveled by the Hopis, which angled southwestward from the Hopi mesas to the Verde River region.

Shortly after Cárdenas left for the west, Coronado received exciting news of the region to the east. Sometime in August 1540, there arrived a trading party including people primarily from Pecos but probably also some from Tiguex. There was an interpreter with the party, and the leaders were two Pecos men. Their real names have been lost, but the Spaniards called the older man Cacique, perhaps understanding that he had an important leadership role. The younger man, who wore long mustaches, they called Bigotes (whiskers). Cacique and Bigotes may have been bow priests, or chiefs of the warrior society, at Pecos Pueblo. The party carried dressed skins and probably other eastern trade goods, especially the much-desired turquoise and fibrolite.

It seems likely that this group was on a routine mission to the major entrepôt of Zuni, exchanging bison skins and turquoises for the shell, macaw feathers, and Hopi-derived cotton cloth so much valued along the Rio Grande. To what extent the Spaniards' arrival influenced this trading expedition is unclear, but probably Cacique and Bigotes had heard of the

Spaniards before leaving home. After all, Coronado had been in residence at Hawikuh for a month, and news traveled fast among the Pueblos.

Coronado gave presents to the party—small tinklers, glassware, and beads, which, according to the Spaniards at any rate, the Pecos group much appreciated. He listened with great interest to accounts of the eastern regions, especially the Great Plains with their vast bison herds. Coronado quickly decided to extend his explorations on to the east. It was not that he really expected Pecos and Tiguex to be very different from Cíbola-Zuni. But the general was facing a serious problem: he was going to have to winter over in this northern, mountainous area without the supplies and especially the clothing carried by Alarçón. Already he was beginning to hear horror stories of what winter was like on the cold Zuni plateau. I strongly suspect that Coronado's Zuni hosts praised the pleasant winter climate of the Rio Grande as a way of getting rid of the invaders. The chronicler for the Coronado expedition, Pedro de Castañeda, later claimed that the Pecos trading party extended a wholehearted invitation for the invaders to come east.

This invitation raises the question of Spanish and Pueblo Indian mutual understanding. For the most part, communications seem to have been pretty good between Southwestern natives and the Spanish invaders. Contact between Pimas and Spaniards on the west coast dated from as early as 1536, and both Coronado and Alarçón had Pima interpreters. Such individuals became extremely important to Alarçón because, on the trip up the Colorado, he came across Piman-speaking settlements and could obtain information quite freely.

In addition to his Hispanicized Piman Indians, Coronado had picked up other interpreters in Sonora, probably from both the Pima and Opata areas. These men spoke Zuni and perhaps Southern Tiwa, and there were certainly Cíbolans who spoke Pima and Opata. The Spanish parties going both west to Hopi and east to the Rio Grande took along Zuni interpreters. In 1540, as in later historic times, there were many Zunis who could speak the Shoshonean Hopi language. To the east, the Zunis had long been in contact with the Keresan-speakers of Acoma. And in the fifteenth and sixteenth centuries there were also important trade contacts between Zuni and the Piro-Tompiro groups, so it is extremely likely that some of the Zuni traders could speak Piro.

There are some other interesting possibilities as to linguistic contacts. At least one Mexican Indian captive at Zuni, from the group who came with Esteban in 1539, was, according to Coronado, rapidly learning Zuni. More intriguing is that Bigotes, the Pecos chief, while being held prisoner in the Tiguex area in early 1541, is supposed to have conversed with Father Juan de Padilla, one of the priests on the expedition. The two men presumably spoke in Nahuatl, the language of the Aztecs and Tlaxcalans. Padilla had been in Mexico since the late 1520s and may actually have been attached to the Tlaxcalan mission at one time. Like the central Mexican Franciscans generally, Padilla would have been able to speak at least some Nahuatl—a language used as a kind of lingua franca at least as far north as southern Sinaloa. Pueblo Indians who were involved in trade were often acquainted with several languages, and it would not be too surprising if various of them, including Bigotes, could get along in a trade jargon based on Nahuatl. "Turk" (whom we will meet shortly), from far east of the Pueblo region, was also supposed to have spoken "a little of the Mexican tongue." And of course there was always sign language, much used especially between Pueblos and plains Indians.

Even so, it is clear from the Spanish documents that obviously incorrect information was often reported. Sometimes, as may have been the case with the Pecos Indian "invitation," Coronado's men simply heard what they wanted to hear. Nowhere was this self-deception more evident than in the Quivira story that came up as a result of the expedition's first exploration eastward.

On August 29, 1540, Coronado's young lieutenant, Hernando de Alvarado, with the priest Juan de Padilla and a party of about twenty soldiers, set out for the Rio Grande. En route, Alvarado mentioned a fork in the trail, one road going to Acoma and the other to Zia Pueblo. This split actually lay somewhere in the vicinity of El Morro, and Alvarado and Padilla took the right fork. Thus they followed a trail roughly on the line of modern New Mexico Highway 53, passing by El Morro rock and over the escarpment at the south end of the Zuni Mountains. From there they struck northward, skirting the west side of the extensive *malpais*, or lava beds, and then turned eastward again, either somewhere around modern Grants or via one of the trails through the malpais.

The left fork of the trail was the one most used by the Zunis. It cut across Agua Fria and Capulin canyons and eventually followed Zuni Canyon to the Grants area. From there it was possible to reach Zia and the other Jemez River sites and Tiguex. This trail was the more common one for Spanish parties in the later sixteenth century and was likely the one used by the main Spanish army in the fall of 1540. Why Alvarado and his party chose the right-hand route is not clear. By cutting across the malpais, they would have a slightly shorter trail to Acoma, but there is some question as to whether horses could have been taken over these volcanic badlands. Possibly, certain members of the Pecos trading party wanted to visit one or more of the

Pueblo shrines that, at least in later times, dotted the highlands east of El Morro.

Alvarado and Padilla stopped at Acoma, and the chronicler, Pedro de Castañeda, says that the party met with a great deal of hostility there. The Acoma Indians, like those at Hopi a few weeks before, drew a line on the ground, challenging the Spaniards to cross. Seemingly, after a short face-off, the Acomas backed down, and Alvarado and Padilla were given a tour of the easily defended town on its steep mesa.

The party then traveled on to the Rio Grande, reaching it probably somewhere around modern Albuquerque. Alvarado and Padilla named the river the "Nuestra Señora," noted twelve Tiguex towns, and estimated that there were eighty pueblos in the general area. The count of Tiguex towns was probably correct—at any rate, Castañeda also gives that number. But for the whole Rio Grande and Pecos drainages, including the Piros and probably the Tompiros, Castañeda gives a total of only sixty-one pueblos; fifty-seven of them are named groups.

In Castañeda's list, inserted between Tutahaco and Quirix, is the notation *por abajo del rio estauan estos pueblos* (these pueblos were downriver). Since most of the remaining pueblos on the list are *upriver*, Castañeda was probably not using this *por abajo* entry as a subheading. Instead, he seems to be referring to a specific group of unnamed pueblos. That such is the case is indicated by an entry a few lines down, where the chronicler says, "The four pueblos downriver are to the southeast where the river turns to the east." The Rio Grande does make a turn to the southeast a few miles upstream from modern-day Hatch, so perhaps Castañeda was talking about the lower end of Piro country. Why these pueblos were separated out from the eight Tutahaco (Piro) towns listed in the entry just above the *por abajo* entry is not clear. The Hatch region forty years later was well downriver from Piro country, so it may be that the four downriver pueblos were Manso rather than Piro.

Alvarado and his party were well received. People from the various towns flocked to see them and to offer them food, blankets, and skins. It was a more or less standard Pueblo greeting for visitors, especially the sharing of food. Alvarado was supposed to reciprocate, and he did give the Tiguex "some small articles, whereupon they went away," satisfied or not. Hammond and Rey believed that at some point in his explorations Alvarado reached the northernmost Rio Grande settlement, the pueblo of Taos. It is generally assumed that he went up the Rio Grande, but judging from his itinerary, which included a trip to the edge of the High Plains, I have an idea that the Taos trip (if made at all) may have been up the Mora River valley

Plate 14. Ruins of the pueblo of Pecos, 1994. Photograph by the author.

and across Holman Pass. There is very little evidence for either route, however, and the description of the town is extremely vague.

Alvarado and Padilla, with their little company, were escorted by Cacique and Bigotes to Pecos, the pueblo called by the Spaniards Cicúye or Cicúique. This strongly defended town, situated just west and south of the Pecos River, maintained its autonomy throughout the early Spanish period. It sits on a low *mesilla,* or sandstone hill, about thirteen hundred feet long and four hundred feet across; the pueblo itself occupies a portion of the northern, wider section of the mesilla. The whole area was surrounded by a low wall, three to four feet high. The purpose of this wall is not clear: it may have been mainly symbolic, for it was certainly too low to be successfully defended. The massive main section of the pueblo was constructed for defense. Rebuilt in the fifteenth century, apparently as part of a unified plan, the town formed a quadrangle of coursed sandstone four stories high, with the outside walls sheer and unbroken and with large interior courtyards.

At the time of Coronado, Pecos housed around two thousand people and could, according to Castañeda, muster five hundred warriors. Pecos in the sixteenth century was probably the most important Pueblo trading center to the plains. Not only did Pecos parties go out to trade, but Plains groups such

Plate 15. Humpbacked stone figurine about eight
inches high, from Pecos Pueblo, perhaps sixteenth
century. The figure may be a representation of
Kokopelli, a flute-playing deity who carries a trader's
pack on his back. Photograph by Wyatt Davis,
courtesy Museum of New Mexico, neg. no. 43924.

as the Querechos and Teyas also came to Pecos to trade, sometimes camping
for extended sojourns outside the walls.

At Pecos, Alvarado and Padilla came across two men whom the Spaniards referred to as "slaves." These men had been captured in a battle in which the Pecos people had taken part. One of them, whom the Spaniards called Ysopete or Sopete, was from Quivira, a Wichita group of Caddoan speakers who lived in central Kansas. The other man, a major actor in the events of the next few months, the Europeans nicknamed "Turk" because of his fancied resemblance to a native of Turkey. He was from Harahey, an area east of Quivira whose people also spoke a Caddoan language. They were, most likely, proto-Pawnee. The Spaniards wanted to see the great bison herds, so Turk and Ysopete joined Alvarado's party as guides for an expedition onto the plains. This arrangement seems to have been made with the agreement of the Pecos leaders.

Turk is a most interesting person. He was skilled with languages and, like Bigotes, had been a trader. He told the Spaniards (probably through a series of interpreters) of great lands off to the east where an enormous river ran and where people used great canoes with twenty oarsmen on a side, as well as sails. Nobles traveled in those boats under canopies. There was much gold—in fact, so much that common table service was of gold and silver.

These descriptions might at first glance seem to come straight out of a European fairy tale. But in all probability Turk was describing the Mississippi River and the rich Mississippian-culture chiefdoms that formed an important part of the southeastern United States. Only the stories of gold and silver were false. The Spaniards had made it abundantly clear that they were looking for these precious metals, and the quick-witted Turk decided to take advantage of their obsession. For example, he also claimed to have owned some gold bracelets that the Pecos people had taken from him. Because he told this story while the party was exploring somewhere in the Canadian River drainage, it may be that he was simply trying to tempt Alvarado to push on north and east, giving Turk a protected trip homeward.

If this was Turk's plan, it backfired. Excited about the possibility of gold at Quivira and Harahey, Alvarado's first wish was to tell the glad tidings to Coronado and recommend an eastward exploration in force. Back at Pecos, however, the leaders of that pueblo flatly denied knowing anything about gold bracelets. After a confused series of events in which Turk escaped and was recaptured, Alvarado literally kidnapped Bigotes and Cacique and marched with them, as well as Turk and Ysopete, back to Tiguex.

Coronado, meanwhile, was waiting for Tristán de Arellano and the main army, which was slowly working its way northward. Coronado had already received an account of the Rio Grande from Alvarado and Padilla and was eager to see this new country. On the return of Cárdenas from his hapless attempt to find the lower Colorado, sometime around mid-November, 1540, Coronado sent the campmaster on to Tiguex to prepare winter quarters. Arellano arrived in Cíbola probably a few days after Cárdenas left for the Rio Grande, and Coronado ordered this commander to rest his trail-weary men and animals for twenty days, then to follow the now well-known trail eastward from Zuni to Tiguex.

Coronado himself took some thirty men to explore the Rio Grande south of Tiguex. He used an alternate trail from Zuni to the Piro-Tompiro region and was guided by Zuni Indians, eager to cooperate in order to rid themselves of the Spaniards. This trail branched off the main road between Acoma and Cíbola, probably somewhere in the vicinity of· El Morro, and cut through the eastern edge of the San Agustin Plains, more or less following the line of modern U.S. Highway 60. Coronado reached the Rio Grande in the northernmost part of the Tutahaco (Piro) region, around present-day Socorro. Sending a young subordinate officer, Francisco de Ovando, with a few men south to the edge of Piro country, Coronado turned northward to rendezvous with Cárdenas and Alvarado at Tiguex.

Campmaster Cárdenas, upon arriving at Tiguex, had evicted the natives from one of the Tiguex towns and begun to prepare it for the arrival of the massive main army. This pueblo, called by the Spaniards Coofor, from the Tiwa word *ghufoor*, "parched corn town," seems most likely to be the site called Santiago Pueblo or Bandelier's Puaray (LA 326), which sits on the west bank of the Rio Grande across from the southern end of modern-day Bernalillo (map 14). The Spaniards later claimed that the Tiguex had volunteered their town—something very unlikely, especially on the verge of winter. So hostilities were the order of the day even before Coronado arrived.

One task that Coronado had given Cárdenas was to augment the food supplies and especially to find clothing for the Spanish army. He set about this in a businesslike way, combing the Tiguex area for cotton cloth and dressed hides. His efforts met with considerable resistance, especially when Spaniards began to meet their quotas by literally taking cloaks off the backs of the Indians. The situation was exacerbated when a soldier named Juan de Villegas raped a woman at the pueblo of Arenal. This town is still not identified with complete certainty, but it is probably site LA 717, not too far from present-day Sandia Pueblo on the east side of the Rio Grande a few miles south of Bernalillo. Later in the century, Arenal was known by the Spaniards as Puaray or Puala.

By the time Coronado arrived, the situation had disintegrated. Alvarado's

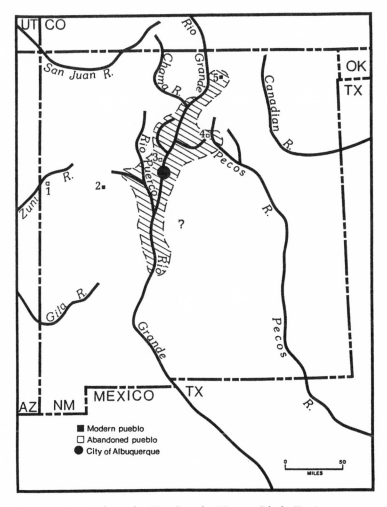

Map 14. Spaniards to the Rio Grande. Key: 1, Cíbola-Zuni; 2, Acoma; 3, Coofor; 4, Cicúye-Pecos; 5, Taos.

high-handed action in abducting Cacique and Bigotes left the pueblo of Pecos fuming. And Spanish rapacity and brutality had left Tiguex ready to burst into flames. War was at hand.

CHAPTER TWELVE

The Tiguex War

The war at Tiguex must be considered in light of general Spanish attitudes—as of 1540—toward New World native peoples. As might be expected, Spaniards of the early colonial period were, even by their own standards, something of a mixed bag. It was not a particularly moral period in European history—certainly not as modern people judge morality. The earliest Spanish invaders of the New World, beginning with Columbus and the conquest of Hispaniola, left a grim record—on Hispaniola, a trail of torture, rape, and murder. Once Spanish forces had seized practical control of the island, the native Taino groups were ruthlessly oppressed, drafted for grueling labor in the gold mines and plantations. The large native populations simply melted away and were quickly replaced by Indians from other areas, especially the Cariban-speaking populations of the Lesser Antilles, and increasingly by African natives, plucked from their homes and carried as slaves across the Atlantic.

In Europe, meanwhile, debate raged as to whether Indians were full-fledged human beings. The question was more biological (or perhaps genealogical) than it was ecclesiastical, the problem being whether Native Americans were actually children of Adam and Eve. The question had immediate practical importance, for early Spaniards had treated the Indians as creatures without souls, to be exploited like domestic animals.

The issue was quickly settled in favor of the humanness of the American Indian. Queen Isabella of Castile had no doubts on the score: she pressed for humane treatment and missionization of the native peoples. After her death in 1504, her husband and co-ruler, Ferdinand of Aragon, continued to insist on greater attention to native rights. Ferdinand, however, was also eager that the new territorial possessions pay for themselves, so in practice the ruthless exploitation of the dwindling Taino population continued with little change.

In 1510, the first Dominican friars arrived in Hispaniola and soon became a strong voice for reform. The colonists managed to blunt this reform effort, and for a few years the status quo was more or less maintained. But times were slowly changing. By the 1520s there developed two major trends in church-state policy as it affected Native Americans. One trend involved the Order of Friars Minor, or Franciscans, who came to Mexico shortly after Cortés's conquest and quickly developed a powerful millenarian movement. The early Franciscans, especially in Mexico, viewed the New World as the last great reservoir of peoples who had never heard the truths of Christianity. Once these pagans were contacted—and, to the extent possible, Christianized—the way would be clear for the Second Coming of Christ. Other missionary organizations do not seem to have made this idea central to their activities, but for the Franciscans it was a powerful and driving force.

The second trend that began to gain strength about the same time was the preparation of laws to protect the Indians against Spaniards' rapacity. Principally involved in this movement were the Dominicans, although individual Franciscan friars also fought for the same cause. The most effective crusader was Bartolomé de Las Casas, a mine owner in Hispaniola. Of a religious turn of mind, he was ordained in 1512 and served as chaplain during the Spanish invasion of Cuba, becoming an *encomendero* (a person who held rights to Indian labor). Las Casas, however, became increasingly horrified by the things he saw on the islands. In 1515 he decided to return to Spain and fight for Indian rights. He joined the Dominican order in 1523 and began to devote a lifetime to the struggle for Native American causes. Las Casas caught the attention of King Carlos I, a monarch who had been influenced by the humanist movement of the early sixteenth century. Their meeting of minds led in 1542 to the progressive "New Laws," the first of a series of legislative attempts aimed at protecting Indians from colonial misrule.

In Mexico, the Franciscan bishop, Juan de Zumárraga, was favorably disposed toward Indian rights, and the first viceroy, Antonio de Mendoza, felt the same way. These early administrators, along with the king, may actually have dreamed of eventually putting Christianized Native Americans, loyal to the Spanish Crown, in positions of power in the New World. This remained only a dream, but it did produce an atmosphere in which the rights of Indians were taken seriously.

Thus, Viceroy Mendoza had given Coronado strict orders on the treatment of Indians. They were not, for example, to serve as burden bearers, or *támenes,* something that caused a great deal of grumbling among the Spanish soldiers, who, in many cases, had to carry their own equipment. Coronado seems to have made a halfhearted attempt to carry out Mendoza's orders. During the trials that followed his return to Mexico, he denied having committed any atrocities. When asked about the activities of his various commanders, Coronado generally insisted that he saw, heard, or was told nothing amiss. His memory conveniently failed even in situations of the greatest gravity and drama—such as events at the Tiguex pueblo of Arenal, to which we shall turn shortly.

Regardless of Coronado's complicity or lack of it, his followers certainly committed a number of atrocities. Probably the most brutal of Coronado's officers were the campmaster, López de Cárdenas, and captains Pedro Tovar and Hernando Alvarado. The priest, Juan de Padilla, who gave religious sanction to maltreatment of the native Southwesterners, can also be faulted. Of these, only Cárdenas was eventually punished, though Padilla's death at the hands of Quivirans might be considered a sort of divine retribution.

The actions for which Cárdenas was to be brought to trial developed quickly out of the anger of the Tiguex people and the determined, often frantic, attempts of the Spaniards to obtain clothing and foodstuffs for the winter of 1540–41. About the time Coronado arrived in Tiguex, the people of Arenal stole a number of Spanish horses, took them to the interior courtyard of the pueblo, and shot them with arrows. Cárdenas led a party to round up the remaining loose horses, finding about twenty-five dead in the fields on the east side of the Rio Grande. The wrought-up Arenal Indians discharged arrows at the Cárdenas party. Cárdenas claimed in his trial hearings several years later that he attempted to make peace, assuring the Indians that the Spaniards "did not care at all that they had killed the horses since they had many." He asked the Arenal people to be friends and promised that they would come to no harm.

Cárdenas was under some difficulty in this particular encounter because there were no interpreters and all information had to be imparted by sign language. The Indians refused the overtures, perhaps not understanding or trusting them, and Cárdenas returned to Coofor, the town he had commandeered as Spanish headquarters, to make his report to Coronado. If Cárdenas's later testimony is to be believed, Coronado ordered him to attempt peace a second time. Again Cárdenas was rebuffed.

The Spaniards then attacked Arenal, using both Spanish soldiers and Mexican Indian allies. A number of the allies were killed and thirteen or fourteen Spaniards wounded. After a considerable amount of fighting, the attackers managed to establish footholds in the outer terraces of the town. Fighting broke off at nightfall, but the following morning the Spaniards and their Mexican allies fired the pueblo.

According to Cárdenas, Coronado had ordered the pueblo to be attacked with "blood and fire" if the Tiguex refused to submit, so he gave the command to destroy the pueblo. There was a confused scene in which various of the Indians tried to surrender under the sign of the cross. Cárdenas, presumably following Coronado's orders to allow no quarter, ordered the prisoners burned at the stake. A melee followed in which some natives of Arenal actually died at the stake, while others attempted to break out of confinement and were lanced by Spanish soldiers. It is not clear how many people were slaughtered at Arenal, but the best estimates are 130 or more.

One of the events that helped trigger Indian resentment and eventually the battle of Arenal was the treatment of the Pecos and Caddoan captives by Alvarado and Pedro de Tovar, the man who had been in charge of the first Spanish expedition to Hopi. Bigotes and Cacique, especially, were closely questioned about the gold bracelet supposedly stolen from Turk. In the process of this interrogation, Bigotes was set on by Tovar's dogs and severely bitten on an arm and both legs. At the battle of Arenal, the two Pecos captives were taken to the battle scene by order of Coronado so that they could bear witness to the invincibility of Spanish arms. Tiguex and Pecos alike were outraged by the treatment of the prisoners, and, especially after the brutal events at Arenal, a total confrontation was inevitable.

Arenal had fallen sometime around the end of the year 1540. About a week later, Cárdenas was sent with a contingent of some forty horsemen plus a number of foot soldiers to make sure of the submission of the Tiguex people. He found the various towns along the east side of the river deserted. Cárdenas burned one of the pueblos, where he discovered the carcasses of horses. The Indians, meanwhile, had fled to the mountains, probably the Sandias, which lie just to the east of Tiguex. In spite of the bitter cold of the winter of 1540, the Tiguex people remained in their mountain fastnesses; indeed, the province was not fully reoccupied until Coronado left the Southwest.

One of the war leaders who in the late fall of 1540 had resisted Cárdenas's attempt to collect blankets and food was a man whose native name was given as Xauian (probably pronounced sha-WEE-an) and whom the Spaniards called Juan Alemán (John the German) because he resembled a colonist of that name living in New Spain. By the time of the writer Father Tello in the mid-seventeenth century, the name had been transmuted to Juan Lomán, and this spelling was used by another writer, Mota Padilla, a century later.

Juan Alemán seems not only to have spearheaded resistance to the Spanish takeover, but he also had the war command of a large Tiguex town the Spaniards called Moho or Mohi. This is a somewhat mysterious pueblo. According to the rather vague Spanish accounts, Moho was located west of the Rio Grande some eight to twelve miles north of Coofor. This distance would place the town near or perhaps a little north of the Jemez River, assuming that Moho was on the Rio Grande. It is clear enough from the accounts that the pueblo was near *some* river, but whether the Rio Grande or the Jemez is unknown. To date, no site that fills this geographical description has been identified.

It is possible, of course, that Santiago Pueblo (LA 326), with its nearby encampment of Coronado's native Mexican allies, which I have taken to be Coofor, was actually Moho. A large temporary camp (designated LA 54147) was discovered in the late 1980s in the mesa country about a quarter-mile west of Santiago Pueblo. Evidence from the excavation strongly suggests that this camp was occupied by Mexican Indians. The excavators proposed that LA 54147 might represent a spillover from Coronado's main camp at Coofor (Santiago Pueblo), the pueblo itself having been used primarily by Spanish soldiers.

If, however, Santiago Pueblo was actually Moho instead of Coofor, this encampment presumably would represent the siege-camp that blocked the pueblo on its landward side. If Santiago was Moho, it could be that Coofor was what is today called the Mann-Zuris site, or Piedras Marcadas Pueblo (LA 290). This huge Tiguex pueblo (about 330,000 square feet) is situated on a low benchland on the west bank of the Rio Grande in present-day northwest greater Albuquerque, some twelve miles south of Santiago. It has never been excavated, but surface artifacts tell of an occupation from the thirteenth to the late sixteenth century. The site was probably deserted before—or at the latest, shortly after—1600, before permanent Spanish occupation really took hold in New Mexico. The only Spanish pottery that has been found is four sherds from an olive jar. These sherds are too fragmentary to be classified as to time period, but in the context of the site they are presumably sixteenth century in date.

One problem with identifying Santiago with Moho is that the site was almost completely excavated in 1934–35 and none of the siege features described for Moho were found. Nor does the area around Santiago Pueblo have the natural defenses described for Moho. At least until we have more evidence on the layout of Tiguex towns, my tentative equation of Santiago with Coofor seems most satisfactory. I would suggest that sites north of the

Jemez River on the west side of the Rio Grande be reexamined with Moho in mind. That region certainly has the proper topography, with its high, steep mesas rising precipitously from the river's floodplain.

To add to the confusion, there was, according to the chronicler Castañeda, another, smaller pueblo a mile or so beyond Moho, and this pueblo also resisted the Spaniards. By the time hostilities broke out at Moho and its smaller neighbor, the rest of the Tiguex pueblos had been looted and largely destroyed by Spaniards and Mexican allies looking for wood to burn.

Wherever located, Moho was strongly defended. It sat on an elevation, and the riverside had steep banks. The Moho people had reinforced the pueblo wall on the accessible landward side with some sort of log palisade. They began hostilities by attacking Cárdenas who, unarmed, was meeting with them under a truce. The attempt to kill or capture Cárdenas failed, but some Spaniards were wounded. Cárdenas went on to the unnamed second pueblo, where he found the defiant Indians gathered within their town. Backtracking to Moho, Cárdenas was immediately involved in hostilities. He feigned a retreat to draw the Indians out and managed to kill a number of them before the rest escaped back into their stronghold. Cárdenas then returned to Coofor to report to his chief.

Coronado decided to strike Moho in force. Bringing with him scaling ladders, he surrounded the pueblo and launched an attack. The Spaniards were caught in a fierce enfilading fire from the town walls. They attempted to break through the pueblo wall but found it too strong. Then the Spaniards attempted to climb to the top of the first terrace but were met with a hail of stones and arrows, some of the arrow points, according to the Spaniards, poisoned by snake venom. Castañeda reports that about a hundred soldiers were wounded, a number that probably included Mexican allies as well as Spaniards. Five or six Spaniards were killed outright. The most important Spanish death, from a military point of view, was that of young Francisco de Ovando, who had returned from his exploration of the Piro country just in time to enter this engagement and be killed in it.

The Spaniards' first strategy was to launch a series of attacks on the pueblo. They built homemade battering rams but these failed to breach the reinforced walls. For some reason the Spaniards did not try to burn the town, the tactic that was so successful at Arenal. Chances are that the masonry outer walls at Moho simply would not catch fire. In any case, the Spaniards were short of wood, as can be seen from their stripping of wood from the various deserted Tiguex towns. Because of the Pueblos' heavy use of wood for heating, cooking, and pottery making, any region in which Indians had lived for any length of time was apt to be deficient in wood. Coronado's underclad army of thirteen hundred or more men needed all the fuel they could find simply to stay warm during this brutal winter. Whether the Spaniards used their cannons, small brass pieces carried on mule back, is unknown. The eighteenth-century writer Mota Padilla reported that the Spaniards made some wooden tubes (*cañones*) bound with cords, like rockets (*a modo de cohetes*), which, however, failed. It is not clear just what Mota Padilla meant by this statement—perhaps that the Spaniards were attempting to make rocket launchers.

Coronado then settled down to a siege that dragged on for several weeks. The Spaniards controlled the spring from which the Indians got their water, and soldiers cut off access to the river below the town. Fortunately for Juan Alemán and his defenders, snow fell heavily and provided enough water for the town to continue fighting. The siege dragged on from mid-January till the end of March. The second, smaller, unnamed pueblo a mile or so beyond Moho was also put under siege by captains Diego de Guevara and Juan de Zaldívar, but at some point the defenders fled to the countryside and the pueblo, like the rest of the Tiguex towns, was burned and sacked. Around one hundred women and children were captured.

As March wore on, the winter snows lessened and lack of water made the situation of the besieged Moho natives more and more desperate. Sometime in mid-March, there was a temporary truce and a parley, with the defenders of Moho agreeing to surrender about a hundred women and children. It is not clear whether these were refugees from other pueblos or part of the citizenry of Moho itself.

During the siege, the people of Moho decided to dig a deep well. Unfortunately, the shaft caved in before water was reached, killing thirty of the excavators, according to Castañeda. This may have been the last straw. At any rate, fifteen days after the transfer of noncombatants, the Moho warriors decided to abandon the pueblo. They set out during the first quarter of the night, in a compact body with the women in the center. The Spaniards had forty horsemen on guard under the command of Rodrigo Maldonado, and there was a sharp battle in which the Spaniards lost one or perhaps two men and several of the defenders of Moho were killed. The rest escaped across the river, which was in flood and extremely cold, and a number of people died from wounds and exposure. The Spaniards took a considerable number of captives, mainly women and children but also some of the wounded warriors.

This action, however, did not immediately end the battle for Moho. A few inhabitants still held out in one of the roomblocks and managed to defend this part of the pueblo for a few more days before being overcome. It had been a costly war for both sides. The Spaniards lost at least six and perhaps eight or more Spanish soldiers, and many other Spaniards were wounded. The Mexican allies also suffered, though we have no details about their casualties. The Tiguex lost several hundred people, mainly fighting men, and a large number of women and children were enslaved.

While directing the mopping-up operations at Moho, Coronado learned that Tiguex Indians from other villages were trying to reoccupy their towns. He sent Maldonado with a body of soldiers to destroy these new defenses. Maldonado seems to have carried out his orders with excessive enthusiasm, wrecking any pueblos that had escaped or partially escaped earlier Spanish destruction.

While the battle for Moho was going on, Spanish parties continued to comb the area around Tiguex for food and clothing. Cárdenas himself led a party to the large pueblo of Zia in the Jemez valley, demanding cotton clothing and skins. The Zia Indians, with the example of Tiguex before their eyes, not only gave up such cotton wares as they had but also, a little later, sent a Zia delegation with turkeys and other foods to the Spanish occupying force at Moho. According to Spanish accounts, the Zias also offered to join the occupying forces. Whatever the truth of that, Coronado seems to have trusted the Zia Indians more than those of other pueblos, for he later left several disabled cannons at that town. Spanish parties visited the Quirix villages, that is, the Rio Grande Keresan towns, and collected supplies from those pueblos.

As the siege ground on, Coronado made a quick trip to Pecos, returning the old man the Spaniards referred to as Cacique. The general was received without overt hostility, and he promised the Pecos people to return Bigotes to them in the spring if they would help with the siege of Moho. The Pecos people were not enthusiastic, claiming that they were too busy with planting. (More likely, they were preparing the fields, because March is too early for planting at Pecos.) Coronado, making the best of a bad situation, conceded the point and left the return of Bigotes for later negotiations.

The trip to golden Quivira was already in the planning stages and Coronado needed Pecos's help—or at least its neutrality. Turk, still a captive at Coofor, had continued to describe Quivira in glowing terms. The great king there, a man named Tatarrax, would welcome the Spaniards with open arms.

It is fairly clear that during these months of captivity, Turk and the Pecos leaders gradually worked out what I shall call the *Pecos plot*. They envisioned leading the Spaniards east and losing them in the vast distances of the Great Plains. This new and daring strategy was likely planned in secret by Bigotes and Turk, for Ysopete, Turk's Wichita fellow slave, does not seem to have been fully aware of it. Ysopete's lack of cooperation was later to be a fatal flaw in the plan.

After the Pecos trip, Coronado returned to Moho and completion of the siege. He then moved his forces back to Coofor sometime in early April 1541. It seems likely that most or all of the Spanish soldiers were accommodated within the walls of Coofor itself, with the Mexican Indian contingent camped nearby. Coronado was now making detailed plans for the move out onto the plains.

At just about this time, he received news of Melchior Díaz's death on the return trip from the Colorado River. The soldiers bringing this news also told of increasing trouble that the commander at San Gerónimo de los Corazones in the Sonora valley was having with the natives of that region. This threat to his retreat route to Mexico was very disturbing to Coronado. He directed Pedro de Tovar to take a small group of men to reorganize the Corazones garrison and bring back part of it to join the main army. He also sent dispatches for Viceroy Mendoza. Coronado at this point probably had no suspicion that western Mexico was filled with unrest and that the savage Mixtón war was about to break out far to the south in his own province of Nueva Galicia.

In councils with his leading captains, Coronado had been advised to send a probing party to Quivira. The general, however, was determined to take the entire expeditionary force with him onto the plains. Tiguex was shattered, and the Spaniards did not expect any trouble from that quarter in the near future. Coronado believed he had mended fences with Pecos, and at any rate, the army would pay a final visit to that powerful pueblo. If Quivira was, indeed, the great kingdom he had been led to believe, Coronado felt that he needed all the firepower he could muster. So when he finally left Coofor in late April 1541, it was with the entire army and its baggage, extra horses, and herds of sheep. The Spaniards were moving in full force.

CHAPTER THIRTEEN

Turk and the Pecos Plot

 On April 23, 1541, Coronado began his move to the Great Plains and the hope of gold in Quivira (map 15; and see map 13). His massive army numbered fifteen hundred or more Spaniards and Mexican Indians. There was also an indeterminate number of slaves from the conquered Tiguex towns. These slaves are not mentioned in the accounts, except for one Caddoan woman who had been a slave in Tiguex and was either purchased by the Spaniards or taken during the capture of Moho or Arenal. The Tiguex captives must have been taken along, for no Spanish force was left behind to guard them. Some, of course, may have escaped or died in captivity, but we do know that a number were still in Spanish hands as late as the spring of 1542. Adding in the Tiguex, the total human count on this trip could have been as high as seventeen or even eighteen hundred. With the army were the remaining stock animals, primarily horses, mules, and sheep.

Everything was carried on human backs or on pack animals. One of the archival documents from the Coronado period mentions *carros de artillería*, a phrase that could refer to wheeled carriages for cannons—the wheels used to maneuver the cannon on the battlefield. With this possible exception, it seems certain that the Coronado expedition had no wheeled vehicles. Ox-drawn or horse-drawn carts and wagons came into vogue in central Mexico in the 1540s but would not be seen in the far north for some decades.

The expedition crossed the Rio Grande and followed the river northward, perhaps as far as Galisteo Wash north of modern Bernalillo. It then turned east toward the Tano towns. The Spaniards were already acquainted with this area. During the previous winter they had collected pottery from the Galisteo pueblos and very likely food and clothing as well. The Galisteo area may have been in

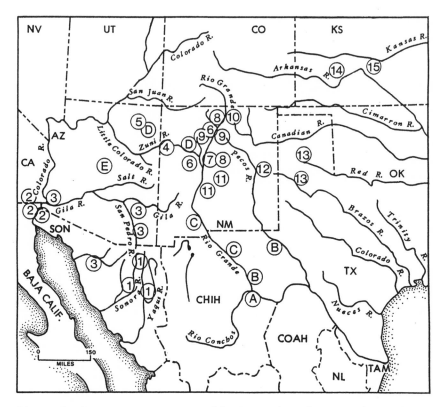

Map 15. Southwestern groups contacted by Spaniards in the sixteenth century. Key to groups identified by the Coronado expedition, 1539–42: 1, Sonoran statelets; 2, Yuman speakers; 3, upper Pima; 4, Zuni; 5, Hopi; 6, Keresan speakers; 7, southern Tiwa; 8, Tewa-Tano; 9, Towa; 10, northern Tiwa; 11, Piro-Tompiro; 12, Querecho (Apache); 13, Teya (Jumano); 14, Quivira (Wichita); 15, Harahey (Pawnee). Key to additional groups identified by the Chamuscado and Espejo expeditions, 1581–83: A, Patarabueye; B, Southern Jumano (Teya); C, Suma-Manso; D, western Querecho (Navajo or proto-Navajo); E, mountain people (Yavapai?).

some disarray, for it was in the process of recovering from an attack by nomadic Indians. This attack came sometime around 1525 and probably accounts for the desertion of Pueblo Blanco, Pueblo Colorado, and Pueblo Shé. Castañeda noted only two occupied pueblos, one that he called Ximena (probably San Lázaro) and a second, unnamed town that probably was Galisteo Pueblo. A third, presumably occupied village, San Cristóbal, was not mentioned in the narrative but was included in the overall list of pueblos.

The attack on the Galisteo pueblos around 1525 had come from the plains as hostile groups likely moved up the Cañon Blanco from the Pecos River. According to Castañeda, the attackers were Teyas, and the same group struck at Pecos but failed to breach the powerfully defended pueblo. I tentatively identify the Teyas with an archaeologically known group called the *Garza complex*, whose sites are scattered along streams at the base of the Texas Panhandle, mostly in the very upper drainage of the Brazos River. The Garza people were bison hunters who also seem to have had a certain amount of agriculture. They carried on a vigorous trade, especially with the Galisteo towns and Tunque Pueblo but also with Pecos, obtaining glazed wares, obsidian, turquoise, and Gulf of California olive shells.

The Garza people imported culinary pottery from the eastern Pueblos but, along with other archaeologically known plains groups, they also made their own cooking wares, which collectively are called Tierra Blanca Plain. These pots were pretty clearly copied from Pueblo prototypes but used local clay and temper sources. The pots tended to be somewhat smaller, with thinner walls, and were sometimes fitted with loop handles, perhaps for strapping them to backpacks or dog travois. All in all, it looks as if Garza and other southern plains protohistoric peoples known from archaeological finds were trading for Pueblo maize and beans and at the same time borrowing the ceramic technology to allow them to cook these foods most efficiently. Besides cultivated crops, pottery was probably used to boil wild seeds such as amaranth, goosefoot, and sunflower. Pots may also have been used in extracting bone grease.

Olive shell that originated in the Gulf of Mexico also shows up in Garza sites. In all probability, the Garza complex–Teyas traded mainly bison products to the Pueblos. What caused the Teyas to attack their old Galisteo trading partners is not clear. Probably the Querechos, infiltrating deeper into the Pueblo zone of influence in the later part of the fifteenth century, changed the dynamics of the western plains, straining relationships between the Pueblos and the Teyas and creating animosities where none had existed before. Or it may have been that Castañeda had his groups mixed up and it was actually Querechos who had attacked the Galisteo pueblos and Pecos.

To complicate the issue, there is this statement from the Alvarado and Padilla advance party while in the Tiguex region: "There are in this province, seven other pueblos, uninhabited and in ruins, belonging to the Indians who daub their eyes, and about whom the guides told your Lordship. They say that they border on the cattle, and that they have maize and straw houses." There is at least a possibility that this statement refers to the ruined Galisteo pueblos described by Castañeda. If so, then Alvarado must mean that the Indians with straw houses were the *attackers*. Their description does not fit the Querechos. The Teyas grew maize, but straw houses and painting of the eyes sounds more like one of the Caddoan groups. In that case not only Teyas but certain of the Caddoans, perhaps Indians of the Edwards complex, may have been involved.

Coronado is generally thought to have turned northeast from the Galisteo towns, bringing his cumbersome army into Lamy and Apache canyons and then over Glorieta Pass to Pecos-Cicuyé. An alternate route of about the same distance (sixty miles) would have the Spaniards ascending to Glorieta Mesa just east of the Galisteo basin and following the relatively flat, high country to the north and east, coming off the mesa to enter the Pecos valley near the modern town of Rowe. The journey to Pecos took four days, although that may have been the arrival time of the vanguard; the long lines of soldiers, servants, slaves, pack animals, and livestock perhaps came during the following days.

Coronado had problems on several fronts. He was concerned about Corazones and eager to hear Pedro de Tovar's report—so eager, in fact, that he had instructed this captain to rejoin the main party immediately. The general had arranged with Tovar for letters to be left under crosses at various points on the trail so that Tovar could track the expedition onto the plains. While at Pecos, Coronado released Bigotes in a calculated but futile bid for Pecos friendship. The Pecos plot, worked out between Turk and Bigotes, was already in place. Turk was to lead the group southeast into the vastnesses of the Llano Estacado. There, the Harahey native was to slip away, perhaps joining one of the Teya bands roaming the plains, and leave the Spaniards to wander aimlessly until their expedition broke up altogether. Since Coronado had carried a sea compass along on the expedition, the Spaniards would probably have been able to retrace their steps, guides or not, but Turk had no way of knowing this.

After a four-day stay among the sullen and reserved Pecos people, Coronado turned to his major task of finding Quivira and all its treasure. The great expedition moved south from Pecos, reaching one of the natural ramps that breach the north wall of Glorieta Mesa. The one just beyond modern Rowe was widely employed during the historic period as a means of easy access to the flat mesa country, and its use certainly goes back into pre-His-

Plate 16. Natural ramp onto Rowe Mesa a few miles south of Pecos Pueblo. A modern road follows the line of the historic and prehistoric trail onto the mesa top. Photograph by the author.

panic times. The Pecos Indians were well acquainted with this particular trail, for it was actually visible from Pecos Pueblo. The trail led on down the gentle southward slope of the mesa to the large Cañon Blanco, for centuries a major east-west route between the Pecos and Rio Grande valleys. In Coronado's time there seems to have been no sedentary settlement in Blanco Canyon, but the area had a sizable population up to the late thirteenth century.

From Pecos, according to Castañeda, the expedition marched for four days to the Cicúye River. This was the Pecos, probably just below where the tributary Gallinas River joins the main stream, a distance of some sixty or sixty-five miles from the pueblo of Pecos. There the Spaniards stopped and built a bridge over the swollen river. It is not entirely clear just what kind of bridge they assembled, but it was likely the floating or pontoon variety. Juan de Jaramillo, another of Coronado's soldiers who left an account of the expedition, recalls the march as taking three days, and it may be again that a fast-riding vanguard reached the spot before the main body of the expedition.

After four days the work was complete, and, in the words of Castañeda, "the entire army and livestock crossed over the bridge." Another eight days

Plate 17. Dog travois. These devices, first described by the Coronado party, were used by plains Indians until the later part of the nineteenth century. Photograph courtesy Southern Illinois University Learning Resources Service.

of travel and Coronado's people sighted their first bison. Two days later they reached an encampment of Querecho Indians, and a second Querecho group was contacted two days after the first. Several members of the expedition gave short descriptions of these Indians. According to Coronado's later letter to the king of Spain, the Querechos ate the raw meat and drank the blood of bison. They dressed in bison skins and made well-constructed, tipilike tents from sewn skins and poles.

Both Coronado and Castañeda took special note of the Querechos' use of dogs with poles strapped to their sides. The loose ends of the poles dragged the ground behind the dogs and were fitted with platforms on which tents and other belongings were placed. The dogs then became beasts of burden, dragging their loads from camp to camp. These are the first accounts of the dog travois. By the early eighteenth century, Spanish horses had spread out onto the plains and the travois was adapted to the horse, a much more efficient animal for this purpose, although the dog travois continued to be used into the nineteenth century.

Continuing onward, guided by Turk, Coronado now ascended Mescalero

Ridge and reached the Llano Estacado ("staked" or palisaded plains). This extremely flat segment of the High Plains covers about thirty thousand square miles of eastern New Mexico and northwestern Texas. Because of its low rainfall, the porosity of its surface soil, and its low gradient, the Llano Estacado undergoes a minimum of erosion. Its endless stretches of flat surface are pitted with shallow depressions, some a few feet wide, some a half mile or more, and these collect water during the seasonal rains. In this flat terrain there is very little perspective, and things often seem much nearer (or farther away) than they really are. In Coronado's time the Llano Estacado was home to many thousands of bison who took advantage of the rich growth of grass and of the ephemeral ponds and lakes.

Here the Spaniards quickly became lost. Coronado had entered the Llano Estacado somewhere south of modern Tucumcari. Turk seems to have been trying to lead the group off to the southeast, though all the information the Spaniards had collected about Quivira suggested that this mysterious place was to the northeast. At this point Ysopete entered the scene. Apparently he had never been a real partner in the Pecos plot. Turk and Bigotes may have had good reason to mistrust him, but leaving Ysopete out of the plot was to have grave consequences. The young Quiviran now decided to use the situation to his personal advantage, which in Ysopete's case was to get safely home to Quivira. Increasingly, and ever louder, he protested that the Spaniards were being led astray.

Coronado continued to trust Turk, but he was becoming seriously concerned. The water in the shallow pools was generally polluted, having been turned into buffalo wallows. Although there was meat to eat—an undreamed-of amount, not only bison but also deer, antelope, and rabbit—the Spaniards were beginning to suffer from lack of grain or other non-meat foods. The Querechos solved the metabolic and dietary problems caused by such a heavy meat diet by eating the vegetation-filled, semidigested stomach contents of bison. This dish, however, did not appeal to Spanish palates.

While the expedition wandered, parties of mounted Spaniards, scouting ahead of the main force, came across other nomadic Indians, enemies of the Querechos, but a people whose life-style and material culture were very similar. This second ethnic group on the Llano Estacado the Spaniards called Teya. Eventually, probably with Teya guidance, the Spaniards discovered a deep canyon, which the historian Herbert E. Bolton believes was Tule (locally pronounced "Tool") Canyon, where heads one of the streams that eventually runs into the Red River.

The Spaniards suffered through one of the violent hailstorms common to this area, then moved north to a place they called the "deep barranca," where they could expect better forage and a more dependable water supply. Bolton identified this barranca with Palo Duro Canyon, today a Texas state park. To someone coming over the flat and featureless Llano Estacado and suddenly arriving at the edge of this vast chasm, it is a breathtaking sight. It must surely have impressed the Spaniards. Still, Coronado's marching time on the stretches of the Llano Estacado suggests that he had penetrated farther south and east when he came into the canyon country. Along the entire eastern face of the Llano Estacado one finds what are called the "caprock canyons." Any number of them, including Palo Duro, Tule, Quitaque, Blanco, or Yellow House, could have been Coronado's "deep barranca."

The whole area was Teya country, with Indian camps spread over the barranca region. The Teyas had trade contacts with Quivira and considerable knowledge of the Quivira region. Information received from the Teyas while the Spaniards were still in the first barranca—along with increasingly strident statements from Ysopete that the army had been going the wrong way—led the general to shift his plan. Instead of leading the whole unwieldy army to Quivira, Coronado decided to push on with a small mounted party of about thirty men. The main army and the livestock would turn back to Tiguex. The deep barranca, which the expedition reached on May 29 or 30, 1541, was now to be used for a final staging area for the march to Quivira.

At this point let us pause to examine who exactly were the Querechos and Teyas (map 16). The Querechos were never lost sight of, next appearing in the records of Spanish exploring parties of the early 1580s. They clearly were Apachean speakers and represent one or more of the historic Apache groups. It is generally assumed that the Querechos on the plains can be identified with eastern Apache peoples, perhaps specifically the Lipan Apaches. Querechos farther west, in northern New Mexico and northern Arizona, come into history with the expeditions of the 1580s and are pretty clearly western Apaches and/or ancestors of the Navajos. The balance of the current evidence seems to me to point to a movement of the Querechos onto the western plains beginning around A.D. 1300, with the newcomers still spreading south and east during the Coronado period. As I discussed in chapter 7, experts are still undecided as to when the Querechos invaded northern New Mexico west of the Rio Grande.

If the Querechos were Apachean newcomers, what then of the Teyas, so important to this stage of Coronado's Quivira expedition? For many years people followed the ideas of the linguist John P. Harrington, who believed that the Teyas were Lipan Apaches. Harrington based his theory on one slim

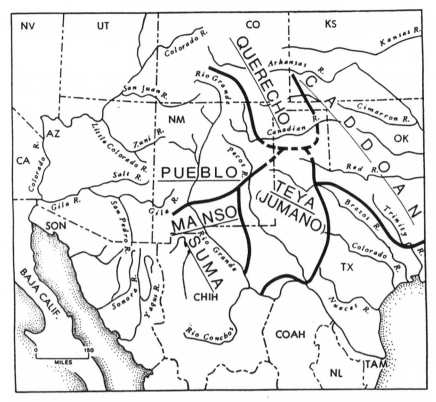

Map 16. People of the Southwest and High Plains, 1540.

bit of information—that the Jemez Pueblo people used the term *Teya* to refer
to plains Apaches. On the other hand, Teyas were clearly enemies to the
Querecho-Apaches, and Apache bands tended not to fight each other. Cultural similarities between the Querechos and Teyas have been used to argue
their linguistic kinship. But these resemblances were rather general, representing more an adaptation to plains nomadism and bison hunting than anything else. In any case, the Spaniards considered the Querechos and Teyas to
be quite separate peoples, which suggests a linguistic difference between the
two. It has also been suggested that the Teyas were a Caddoan-speaking
group. Certainly the Teyas were middlemen to the largely Caddoan-speaking
peoples of the upper Arkansas drainage and to the Caddoans of east Texas,
but this can hardly be taken to prove linguistic affinity.

What I believe to be the correct solution has been offered by the linguist
Nancy P. Hickerson. According to Hickerson, the Indians called Teya by the

Spaniards were identical with people referred to from the early 1580s on as *Jumano* (pronounced hoo-MAH-noh, the Spanish *j* being a strongly aspirated sound). A number of people, including myself, had long assumed that the Jumanos were early Apachean speakers. But Hickerson makes a strong case that these Indians may actually have spoken either Piro-Tompiro or a language or dialect closely related to Tompiro. She believes that the Suma and Manso Indians, who lived along the Rio Grande south of the Piro pueblos, were also part of this linguistic group. It seems clear enough the Jumanos had some special relationship with the Tompiros, as witness the "Pueblo of the Humanas" (today rather confusingly called "Gran Quivira") of the early Spanish accounts.

In Hickerson's scenario, the Teya-Jumanos represent a fairly old occupation in the plains, with contacts to the Pueblos going back two or three centuries before Coronado. This scenario fits reasonably well with the archaeological evidence discussed earlier, in which the Teyas were equated with the protohistoric Garza people of the Lubbock area and the southern Texas Panhandle. Apropos of that, the term *Ximena,* given by Castañeda for one of the Galisteo towns, is suggestive. Assuming, as I have done, that the Teya Indians were involved in important trade relationships with the Galisteo pueblos, the name Ximena may be parallel with "Pueblo of the Humanas"—both of them referring to towns that had important trade ties with the Teya-Jumanos. I would stress, however, that more work needs to be done on the relationships between the protohistoric archaeological cultures of the region and the early historic nomadic groups.

The Jumanos are interesting people whose descriptions, so far as they go, certainly do sound like Teyas. Cabeza de Vaca and his three companions described a nomadic, bison-hunting group that may well have been Jumanos while at or near La Junta de los Rios, the area where the Rio Grande and the Conchos River come together. The Jumanos were first identified by name by members of the Espejo party, forty-seven years after Cabeza de Vaca, in the same La Junta area. These Indians were seasonal bison hunters who returned in winter to the warmer terrain around La Junta and along the Rio Grande to the east. They were enemies of the Apaches, and also avid traders, bringing Pueblo goods to the Indians of the Conchos valley and trading bison products and other goods to Pueblo land. This distribution of Jumano Indians along the Pecos River only forty years after Coronado also strongly suggests that Jumanos and Teyas were the same people.

Marching back to Tiguex from the "deep barranca" in 1541, Coronado's party intercepted the Pecos River at a point downstream from modern Fort

Sumner. According to Castañeda, the Teya Indian guides reported that the Pecos River joined the Rio Grande "more than twenty days' travel from [the Fort Sumner area] and that it flows to the east again." The Teyas' information about the topography of the Rio Grande and Pecos valleys was strikingly correct, suggesting that they knew the entire Pecos River valley. Four decades later, Espejo, returning from the Rio Grande area to Chihuahua via the Pecos River, was guided by Jumanos. Seven years after Espejo, Castaño de Sosa, coming into the Southwest from northeast Mexico via the Pecos, also obtained information on the Jumanos. It is clear from the Espejo and Castaño accounts that the Jumanos occupied the Pecos throughout its middle and lower drainages, just as the Teyas must have done a generation or two before.

One other bit of evidence concerns Cabeza de Vaca himself. Both Castañeda and Jaramillo reported that in the barranca area they had reports of Vaca and his companions. Castañeda's account implies that the Vaca party had actually visited the barranca country, but Jaramillo makes clear that the meeting between the Teya Indians and Cabeza de Vaca took place off to the south, "closer to New Spain." If the Teyas were Jumanos, as seems likely, Jaramillo must have been referring to the La Junta de los Rios area.

Coronado, by now mistrustful of Turk and listening more and more to Ysopete, made final plans for his trip north. Cárdenas, who had broken his arm on the march to the deep barranca and was incapacitated, returned to Coofor with the main army under the command of Tristán de Arellano, reaching the unhappy Tiguex country in mid-July. On its trip back west, the main army passed a number of salt lakes, eventually reaching the Pecos River "over a more direct route," in the words of Castañeda. On this trip the Spaniards found a mass of bison bones extending for perhaps two hundred yards in a mound ten to twelve feet high on the south shore of a salt lake. Just such a collection of bones has been found on the south side of Silver Lake, about forty-five miles northwest of Lubbock, Texas. Today, Silver Lake is not salty but is certainly brackish when low. The lake is on the Yellow House drainage, and a plausible route for Coronado's army from the deep barranca to the Pecos would perhaps be up the Yellow House drainage, eventually reaching the Pecos some miles south of modern Fort Sumner.

One curious incident that took place while Coronado's main army was on its way back to the Pecos sheds some light on the far-flung contacts of the Pueblo world with regions to the east. The young Caddoan slave woman I mentioned earlier had been obtained by a Spaniard named Juan de Zaldívar. Dismayed by the army's planned return to Tiguex, she determined to escape. The young woman probably realized that from the broken country east of the caprock canyons she could easily make her way into the upper drainage of the Red River valley. She escaped and fled eastward, following a much-traveled trade route to Caddo country. Castañeda, writing years later, said that the unfortunate girl traveled some nine days and then ran headlong into a party from the de Soto expedition. There are some chronological problems with this account since de Soto was still near the Mississippi at the time the Coronado party was on the Llano Estacado. A year later, however, Luís de Moscoso was on the Trinity River in eastern Texas, where he found evidence of trade going to the Southwest. Moscoso or his men may well have contacted this woman.

During the course of the summer, Arellano attempted to collect provisions for the coming cold season. He sent one of his commanders, Velasco de Barrionuevo, north into the Jemez country and then to the Tewa towns around the mouth of the Chama River. It seems likely that Barrionuevo followed the Jemez River north, then worked his way eastward, perhaps around the south side of Valle Grande and down the escarpment of the Jemez Mountains. The Tewas of Yuque-Yunque abandoned "two very beautiful pueblos" (probably the Tewa pueblos Yungue and Okeh near the mouth of the Chama River) and retreated to fortified sites in the high country. Barrionuevo's men looted the deserted pueblos, finding, among other things, "abundant provisions, and beautiful glazed pottery of many decorations and shapes." There were also "many ollas filled with a select shiny metal [presumably lead] with which the Indians glazed their pottery"—an interesting ethnographic comment on glaze manufacturing here on the northern edge of glaze-ware distribution. Barrionuevo then moved on to Taos, which the Spaniards called Braba or Valladolid. He does not seem to have gone by way of the other northern Tiwa town, Picurís. Indeed, Picurís may have completely avoided Spanish contact during the Coronado period.

Another of Arellano's lieutenants, perhaps a man named Mondragón, made an expedition to the Piro country with uncertain results. By this time Arellano was becoming concerned about the continuing absence of Coronado. Finally, in late summer, he took forty men on a trip to Pecos, fearful that Coronado might have been ambushed on his way back from the plains. This relief party was attacked by Pecos Indians, who were driven off with considerable losses. The Pecos fighters retired to their pueblo and the battle went on for four days. The Spaniards may possibly have used their primitive cannons in this battle; at least, Castañeda remarked that a "a few shots fired into the town killed some of [the Pecos] people." Of course, he may have been referring to arquebuses, with which the expedition was well equipped, or, for that matter, even to crossbows, which the Spaniards had in some numbers.

Meanwhile, Coronado and his cavalry unit, now holding Turk prisoner, had reached Quivira. It seems likely that their line of march carried them northeast-ward from the caprock canyon country across the Texas Panhandle into extreme western Oklahoma. The Teya guides were following a major trail that ran from the Teya Indian settlements of the Garza complex. In western Oklahoma the Coronado party likely passed through the territory of Native Americans of the early *Wheeler phase* (also referred to as the *Edwards complex*). These people, like the Garza groups, combined bison hunting with agriculture, and some archae-ologists believe they were culturally and economically related to the Garza people. They also had extensive trade with both the Pueblos and the Quivirans. Their language is unknown, but it could have been Teya (that is, Tompiro or Tompiro-related) or, more probably, Caddoan.

In the Great Bend of the Arkansas, Coronado met up with Quivirans and Haraheys—Wichita and Pawnee Indians who lived, as they did two centuries later, by mixed bison hunting and agriculture. There were fair-sized popula-tions, but no gold. Coronado, in a later letter to the king, described Quivira as a land in which the people lived in houses of skins and reeds, without cotton or blankets, using hides for clothing. The inhabitants ate raw meat, as did the Querechos and Teyas. There were hostilities among the various tribes, but "they were all people of the same type." The province itself Coro-nado praised as well watered with plums, nuts, "fine sweet grapes," and mul-berries. The soil would be excellently suited for growing all the products of Spain. The only metal he found was a piece of copper that belonged to one of the Indian chiefs.

The anonymous "Relación del Suceso" from the Coronado accounts mentions that the Quivirans had maize, beans, and squash. According to this source, the copper that Coronado found was supposed to be more plentiful in Harahey. Juan de Jaramillo, who was with the Quivira party, added a number of details in his own account of the trip. Quivira consisted of six or seven towns. As Coronado had said, the land was rich, with excellent "Castil-ian plums." The area was relatively flat, with fine rivers and good soil that should be very productive. Evidence of bison was everywhere. The Quiviran house was described as round and made of straw, with the straw hanging to the ground. So far as it goes, this is a perfectly good description of a Wichita grass lodge.

The Spaniards went beyond the friendly Quiviran settlements, where they met a Harahey war party of about two hundred men. Turk attempted to get word to this military party to attack and destroy the Spaniards but failed because Coronado's party, in the words of Jaramillo, "found it out and took precautions." Turk was now clearly a liability, and the Spaniards, once again denied gold, were in a savage mood. So they garroted Turk, who seems to have been defiant to the end. Understanding that his death was imminent, he taunted the Spaniards with details of the Pecos plot. Turk and the Indians of Pecos had planned for him to lead the Coronado party astray on the Great Plains, weakening them so that even if they returned, the Pecos warriors could easily destroy them.

Hearing this news about possible trouble in the Pueblo world and realizing their exposed position, the Spaniards decided to turn back without reaching Harahey. Returning to the more friendly confines of Quivira, Coronado obtained shucked ears of corn along with dried shelled corn for the return trip. In good Spanish fashion, he had a wooden cross erected, with chiseled letters cut near the base of the upright post, telling that he had reached this place.

Leaving Ysopete with his fellow Quivirans, Coronado took guides from among them and made a quick trip back to Pueblo land, cutting southwestward through what are now the Oklahoma and Texas panhandles. He reached the outward line of march of the army somewhere around modern Tucumcari, then backtracked to the Pecos valley, joining Arellano, who was holding Glorieta Pass. The expeditionary force arrived back in Tiguex sometime around the middle of October 1541.

At this remove of four and a half centuries it is difficult to evaluate Turk. One of the great strengths of Turk's story about riches in the lands to the east was that they were *true*. This ring of truth was probably a factor in Coronado's stubborn belief in his guide. Turk was describing the advanced Mississippian culture of the eastern United States, a culture of which, as a trader, he might logically be expected to know. The large populations organized into chiefdoms and the relatively advanced technology—if not the gold—were actually there. It was simply that they did not exist in the upper Arkansas valley.

According to the Spaniards, Turk, while held captive at Tiguex, practiced black magic. His captors spied on his actions in the Tiguex prison and reported that he studied the surface of an olla of water and magically saw events he otherwise could not know. For example, Turk told the Spaniards guarding him that several of their countrymen had been killed in the fighting around Moho. Admittedly, this account is vague and secondhand, but it does suggest that Turk had shamanistic training.

The little we know about Turk and his behavior is consistent with the culture of the later Pawnee Indians. Even the term Harahey, or Orahey, used for the group to which Turk belonged, was probably an old Caddoan name for the Pawnee tribe. George E. Hyde has suggested that the Haraheys were ancestral to the Skidi Pawnees. The descriptions of Turk allow us to see in vague outline an obviously brave and resourceful man, proud, somewhat arrogant, and totally committed to carrying out the complex plan to destroy the Spaniards. He was an important person, a trader certainly and likely either a shaman or a man with strong spirit powers. Redefined in our own modern terms, Turk seems an authentic American patriot and hero with a vision that transcended narrow tribal boundaries to incorporate the greater good for his own culture world. Few of the Spaniards could claim such breadth of outlook and greatness of spirit.

CHAPTER FOURTEEN

Coronado's Failure

Arriving back at Tiguex, Coronado reported a carefully edited version of the Quivira expedition to King Carlos. He described Quivira but said little about his plans for returning there. Yet Quivira was very much on his mind. Coronado was convinced that mountains of precious metal lay just beyond the horizon, if not in Quivira then in Harahey, and if not in Harahey, then *más allá*.

Meanwhile, another winter was approaching and the provisions collected earlier by Arellano needed to be augmented. According to Castañeda, Coronado made a conciliatory visit to Pecos Pueblo on his way back from the plains, leaving the pueblo calm and peaceful. It is unlikely that the Pecos Indians were actually mollified, but some sort of truce does seem to have been worked out since the Spaniards were willing for the Franciscan friar Luís de Ubeda to remain at Pecos the following spring. Whatever the case with Pecos, the scattered Tiguex could not be lured back to their ruined towns. They preferred to remain in the cold, harsh, but relatively safe mountains, or perhaps, in individual cases, with friends or kinfolk from Tewa, Piro, or Quirix villages.

While the army was settling in, the Spaniards got mixed news from the south. Pedro de Tovar, whom Coronado had sent to check out the situation at San Gerónimo de los Corazones in the Sonora valley, returned to Tiguex. He had found Corazones in a state of uproar because of the cruel behavior of Alcaráz, the commander there. Shortly after Tovar arrived he directed Alcaráz to attack one of the rebellious towns in a place the Spaniards had named, rather uncharitably, Valle de los Vellacos (from *bellacos,* rogues or ungovernable people). It may have been one of the mountain strongholds of the statelet of Señora, in which area the second Corazones was placed. Alcaráz botched the attack and lost seventeen soldiers, mostly to poisoned arrows. The success of this mode of Indian fighting is attested by the morbid fear of such poison Spaniards expressed as late as the 1560s. The poison came from the sap of a shrublike tree, a member of the family Euphorbiaceae, and it created deep abscesses where the arrow punctured the skin. There are large numbers of euphorbs in the general area, but the specific plant is unknown today. Certainly it was one with a particularly toxic and dangerous sap.

Tovar decided to move San Gerónimo a second time and relocated it farther north at a place the Spaniards called Suya, probably somewhere north of present-day Arizpe, in or near the statelet of Guaraspi. He had already collected dispatches that had reached San Gerónimo from Nueva Galicia, and he now divided the San Gerónimo garrison in half, taking the most trustworthy men and returning to the Rio Grande area. He reached Tiguex in the late fall to report the uncertain situation in the area of the Sonoran statelets.

Among the letters from Mexico was news for Cárdenas that his older brother had died and a large inheritance awaited him in Spain. One of the letters received by Coronado was an official dispatch from the viceroy that must have contained news of the Mixtón War. After several years of unrest and increasingly violent resistance on the part of Indians of west Mexico, a furious conflict had broken out in April 1541. This threat to the province of Nueva Galicia, of which Coronado was the absentee governor, must have been one reason why Coronado gave up the expedition and retreated to Mexico in the spring of 1542. In fact, by the time Coronado received his dispatches, the war was winding down, the last major Mixtón stronghold near Guadalajara having surrendered in December 1541. But Coronado had no way of knowing this.

Nor did the Spaniards quite realize what an explosive situation remained in Sonora. It was not long before Alcaráz found himself in an impossible dilemma. This greedy and stupid man quickly fell out with part of his remaining contingent of soldiers. One group returned to Culiacán, leaving Alcaráz very shorthanded. Alcaráz, in spite of his dangerously weak military position, continued to insist on heavy tribute, and this quickly led to a revolt. According to a story told twenty years later by Baltasar de Obregón, who talked to Spanish survivors, Alcaráz kept a regular harem of native women. When the revolt came, Alcaráz was sleeping between two women who, under the pretense of helping him into battle dress, killed him by thrusting arrows through the seams of his cotton armor. Several of the remaining Spanish soldiers were also killed and the rest fled back to Culiacán.

Meanwhile, López de Cárdenas, with his broken arm, was released by

Coronado so that he could go immediately back to Spain to take up his inheritance. Arriving in the upper San Pedro drainage—present-day southeast Arizona—he heard that San Gerónimo had been sacked and the Spaniards scattered. Cárdenas, prudently, returned to Coronado's camp on the Rio Grande with this unpleasant news.

One other Spanish party, twenty-three soldiers under Juan Gallego, came through the statelet area in the early part of 1542. Gallego had been with Coronado in Cíbola but had returned south with Díaz and Marcos de Niza, going on to Mexico City on a supply mission. Delayed by the Mixtón war, he was finally escorting the supply train northward. Taking an advance guard of commandos—seven or eight cavalrymen—Gallego fought his way up the Sonora River, murdering and burning as he went. Historians have usually considered this a kind of military marvel, but in all probability the native warriors had pulled back into their mountain fortresses. The people Gallego killed with such impunity were noncombatants: women, children, and old people who remained in the towns. Likely, such defenseless people were considered "off limits" in the warlike but chivalrous culture of the statelets. The Spaniards played by another, more sinister, set of rules. In any case, by the time Gallego met Coronado in the San Pedro valley, the Spaniards were already in retreat from the new lands.

Scholars have often assumed that a major target of Gallego's attack was the statelet of Corazones. But Gallego was hardly likely to have attacked Corazones, a polity that seems to have been friendly to the Spaniards from Cabeza de Vaca's day. Castañeda's statement that Gallego savaged the *town* of Corazones surely refers to the area around San Gerónimo de los Corazones, either the one in the Señora valley or its successor at Guaraspi. As we shall see, the Corazones people, like those of Batuco, remained either friendly or neutral in their dealings with Coronado.

The Spaniards made many misjudgments during this first exploration of the Southwest, but none quite so drastic as their misreading of the situation in the Sonoran statelets. Parenthetically, I would caution the nonspecialist reader, when perusing the discussion below, that my reconstruction of the cultures of northeastern Sonora is not accepted by all archaeologists and ethnohistorians who have worked in that area. Some scholars believe that the Sonoran area did not have as complex a culture as I describe. For more on this, see the sources for this chapter.

I coined the term "statelet" a number of years ago in order to avoid semantically laden terms like "chiefdom," since we have no real information about the sociopolitical and economic organization of protohistoric northeast Sonora. What we *do* know is that these small polities were heavily engaged in trade and were extremely warlike. They were organized for the latter purpose into two major confederacies—one, primarily or entirely Opata speaking, dominated by Señora in the Sonora valley, and the other, by Piman-speaking Oera in the Nuri Chico drainage. The statelet of Batuco, located in the mid-Moctezuma valley, likely was a frontier state, shifting its alliance from one confederacy to the other but basically hostile to both. Corazones, which I consider to have been a Piman-speaking statelet in an area where most of the other groups spoke Opata, was also in a frontier situation, situated for trade with the Seri Indians of the coast (see map 12). It was too near powerful Señora to be completely unaffected by the northern confederacy but may have maintained some independence from it.

The statelet peoples had first met Spaniards when Cabeza de Vaca and his three companions entered their territory early in 1536. These four refugees were met with courtesy, given gifts, and helped along their way. Possibly they were considered to be traders fallen on hard times. The kind treatment of Cabeza de Vaca seems to indicate that such parties, great and small, had reasonably free access to statelet territory, something to be expected in these trading centers. Coronado in 1540 had maintained good relations with these northern Sonoran Indians and established some special tie with Batuco in the Moctezuma valley.

However, Coronado *had* ordered the building of San Gerónimo, which was staffed by Arellano's main army, following behind Coronado's vanguard. The actual seizure of statelet territory by the Spaniards must have come as a surprise and a shock, especially to the people of Señora, who bore the burden of the occupation. Revolt was certainly in the cards, but it may be that the leaders of these tiny states were playing a waiting game, expecting the Spaniards to move on shortly.

Now Alcaráz's brutality was too outrageous to bear, and a war flared up, very likely involving the whole northern confederacy. The Oera group held aloof, not being directly threatened, and Batuco welcomed any weakening of the Señora confederation. In other words, Batuco decided to back the new Spanish force against a current enemy. This deadly and destructive game had already been played two decades before by the Tlaxcalans when they chose the Spaniards over the Aztecs. The situation of the statelet people vis-à-vis the Spaniards was still more or less the same in 1564 when Ibarra invaded northern Sonora. He was welcomed at Oera and seems to have had no problems with Batuco (though he tended to avoid the latter statelet since it was involved in a war with Oera). At Señora, however, Ibarra was met with savage hostility.

But that lay in the future. By the end of 1541, things were going very wrong for the Coronado party. Officially, Coronado still planned to return to Quivira in the spring of 1542. Whether he had any great support for this within the army as a whole is problematic. Certainly the Spaniards had suffered hardships since arriving in the Southwest, and precious metals seemed as far away as ever.

Then came one of those deciding events in which a private action seems to wield a disproportionate effect on historical process. On December 27, 1541, the general, riding as he often did for recreation, was racing with Rodrigo Maldonado, one of his officers. Coronado had been issued a new saddle girth from the Spanish commissary, which had become rotten in storage. The girth broke and Coronado fell under the hooves of Maldonado's fast-moving horse. Struck on the head, he was unconscious for some time. From descriptions, especially in the Castañeda account, it is clear Coronado suffered a severe concussion. For a time he lay near death, and a number of weeks passed before he was able to reassume leadership.

The general had shaken off the most immediate effects of his head wound when López de Cárdenas returned with the grim news about the collapsing situation in Sonora. This caused Coronado a relapse, and when he finally recovered enough to retake command of the army, he was brooding, vastly homesick, and somewhat mystical. For the balance of the expedition, and perhaps for the rest of his life, Coronado was a changed man—morose where he had been cheerful, indecisive and vacillating where he had been firm. His vagueness in later trial hearings, and especially his inability to remember events of the Tiguex War, possibly could have been more than the "convenient failure of memory" I suggested in chapter 12. Perhaps his head injury actually left Coronado with a muddled recollection of past events.

Castañeda tells a curious story that Coronado is supposed to have related to his soldiers at this time: "[Coronado] remembered that at Salamanca a mathematical friend of his had told him that he would find himself in strange lands, that he would become mighty and powerful, and that he was to suffer a fall from which he would be unable to recover. This thought of death made him desire to go back to die near his wife and children."

But even if Coronado's injury precipitated the retreat from the Southwest, there were other important reasons for the Spaniards to return to New Spain. The loss of San Gerónimo had cut their lifeline to the south. Supplies were short, especially basic food and clothing. The Pueblo area had been thoroughly looted, and it may have seemed unlikely to Coronado that he could sustain himself for another year in Pueblo land. Even if Quivira and Harahey proved to have riches in metals, removal to those regions would place the Spanish army several hundreds of miles farther from their base of supplies and leave them increasingly vulnerable to attack. Another factor that loomed larger with every passing day was the spiraling cost of the expedition. Already Coronado and his wife were facing financial hardship, nor would the viceroy, who had personally invested in the Cíbola venture, welcome throwing good money after bad. And last, Coronado was still not sure of the outcome of the Mixtón War.

According to Castañeda, a petition orchestrated by Coronado but circulated by various of his captains asked that the Spaniards return to New Spain. The petition was then presented to the general, who "agreed," under pressure as it were. There was a reaction to this decision, and a counterpetition was circulated. It seems that about sixty members of the expedition wanted to stay in the Southwest, presumably in the Rio Grande area. Their request was refused, and the Spanish party began preparations to leave for New Spain.

In spite of Coronado's determination to take his party home, there were defections. Father Juan de Padilla, who seems to have felt certain that somewhere beyond Quivira were the mystical Seven Cities of Antillia with their transplanted Portuguese population, chose to return to the plains. He took with him two young Tarascan Indians who were *donados,* that is, they had been "donated" to the missionaries as tiny children to the service of the church. Also making the journey to Quivira was a mounted Portuguese soldier named Andrés do Campo, whom Juan de Padilla had persuaded to go, probably to serve as a translator for the hypothetical Portuguese of Antillia. Coronado apparently had no control over his Franciscans, but the layman, do Campo, did have to get special permission from the general.

Along with Padilla and do Campo went a half dozen Quivirans, the same Indians who had guided Coronado back from Quivira in the fall of 1541. According to three of the Coronado accounts—those of Castañeda, Jaramillo, and the anonymous Relación del Suceso—there was a black man who also went with Padilla. Jaramillo called this man "a free negro interpreter, who went as a tertiary and became a Franciscan friar." The man might well have been a member of the layman's third, or tertiary, order of the Franciscans (probably many of the party, perhaps including Coronado himself, belonged to it), but he could not have been made a friar. Blacks, like Indians, were barred from full membership in the Franciscan order during this period. Both Jaramillo and Castañeda mention a "mestizo" (that is, a person of mixed Indian and European ancestry) who was with the Padilla party. The historian López de Gómara, writing a few years later, said that some dozen Tarascan Indians were also in the party.

The party took some of the sheep and mules, and one horse for do Campo. Gómara adds that Spanish chickens were also taken along to Quivira, the only indication we have that the Coronado expedition brought chickens with them. However, Castañeda did remark that Castilian chickens were noted by the Spanish party at Suya, somewhere in the northern part of the Sonoran River drainage. Chickens do not seem to have reached the upper Southwest from northern Sonora, nor did the chickens (if indeed there were any) brought by Coronado survive in the area; at least, none of the Spanish expeditions of the later part of the sixteenth century mention them.

While Padilla was planning his expedition, another friar, Luís de Ubeda (sometimes called Escalona in the Coronado narratives), decided to stay and missionize Pecos. According to Jaramillo, a black slave boy named Cristóbal, two other blacks, and several Mesoamerican Indians remained with Ubeda. One of the black men had a wife and children, the implication being that they were on the expedition and stayed behind in the Southwest, although this is not entirely clear.

We do not know what Coronado thought about these lunatic ideas of Father Padilla and Friar Ubeda, but, as I mentioned, the missionaries were not under his direct control. He made the best of a bad situation, sending a mounted group of twenty soldiers to escort Padilla and Ubeda and their followers as far as Pecos. A short time later, when the main army was preparing to leave Tiguex, a small party brought some additional sheep to Ubeda. This group met the friar on the road to Galisteo, where he intended to preach. Castañeda reported that Ubeda told the Spanish party that "the old men were deserting him and he believed that they would end by killing him."

Coronado, in the early spring of 1542, turned back to Mexico. According to Castañeda, he ordered that all the slaves captured during the Tiguex wars be released. I doubt that there was much altruism involved in this decision. Coronado must have realized that unless put in chains or otherwise closely guarded, his prisoners would slip away as the army retreated. The expedition was a grand failure, and Viceroy Mendoza was not going to be happy with him in any case. The Crown was bound to investigate the events that led to the battles at Tiguex. To return without precious metals but with a gang of slaves obtained through a questionable military operation might be tempting fate.

Even so, at least one Southwestern native did make her way to Mexico. One of the soldiers, Juan de Troyano, had married a native woman, probably a Pueblo from the Rio Grande area. According to Troyano, in a 1568 letter, this native Southwesterner was the only woman who came back to central Mexico with Coronado. Sixty-six years after the Coronado expedition, Juan de Oñate brought from Mexico a woman from the Galisteo pueblo of San Cristóbal. Called doña Inés by the Spaniards, she was supposed to have been carried off by the Castaño party in 1591. However, there is reason to think that this woman had lived for many years in Mexico, and she may possibly have been Troyano's wife. We will return to the curious story of doña Inés in chapter 17.

The trip from Tiguex to Cíbola-Zuni was hard. The expedition's horses began to sicken, and by the time the army reached Cíbola, some thirty of them were dead. All the way south to Culiacán horses perished. It is not clear whether bad diet, some poison plant, or even deliberate poisoning killed them. One educated guess might be that the horses were eating the spring shoots of datura (*Datura meteloides*). Local Indians used this widespread Southwestern variety of jimsonweed both medicinally and ritually as a hallucinogen—but without careful preparation, it can be extremely poisonous.

The army reached Cíbola-Zuni and halted there to regroup for the long, dreary march home. For two or three days after the army turned south across the *despoblado* and back toward Mexico, the people of Cíbola followed, picking up discarded pieces of baggage and, according to Castañeda, coaxing the Mexican allies to stay behind. It is not entirely clear why the people of Cíbola would want to do this except possibly as a last attempt to divide and weaken the Spanish army. More likely, some of the Mexican Indians decided on their own not to return with Coronado to their homeland. Castañeda commented on the defections: "As a result there must be fine interpreters there at present."

Toiling its way across the empty country of the San Francisco River, Coronado's army reached the upper Gila drainage and eventually the ruined town of Chichilticalli. Then his men turned south and west, toward the San Pedro River. On the second day out from Chichilticalli, Coronado met Juan Gallego and his supply train—no doubt a welcome surprise. Gallego, however, who had heard that Coronado was in distant Quivira and expected to catch up with him there, was not pleased to find the explorer returning empty-handed. His little band had been battered in almost daily confrontations with the Sonoran Indians but so far had remained buoyed by the dream of Quiviran gold at the end of the trail.

Again, the question of a settlement, perhaps in the Gila or the San Pedro valley, was discussed. There was a suggestion that the army make a colony somewhere in the region, with a special party to go on south and inform the viceroy. In settling the Gila valley or that of the San Pedro, the Spaniards would have nearby populations of Piman-speaking peoples to exploit. Even so, the region probably could not support a conquest army, especially with no sign of precious metals. The Spaniards, lacking agricultural tools, were not equipped to begin a secular settlement. In any case, a settlement would involve families, and we know of only three wives of Spanish soldiers— although one was the redoubtable Francisca de Hozes, who, with her husband, Alonso Sánchez, was among the group who had petitioned to stay at Tiguex. Francisca and her husband had brought a child north with them, and one and possibly two others had been born on the road. Of course, there were other ways to start families. At Culiacán the settlers had taken Indian wives and concubines, and they might have done the same in southern Arizona.

But the army was sick of the Southwest, and the dispirited Coronado agreed with them. There would be no settlement and everyone would return to Mexico. The southward march through Sonora represented a slight detour from the route north to Cíbola. Coronado, probably on Gallego's advice, decided not to fight his way through hostile Guaraspi and Señora and took a somewhat longer route, marching south and east from the upper San Pedro into the Nacozari area and then on to the Moctezuma River and Batuco. There he encountered people whom Castañeda called "friendly Indians from the valley of Corazones." These Corazones natives probably actually traversed the southern part of Señora territory, reaching Batuco by a trail that left the Sonora River and crossed the Sierra de Bacachi at Mazocahui near the north end of the Ures Gorge. One wonders what the Señorans felt about a Corazones embassy crossing their territory to meet and confer with the enemy. This ancient road, however, was one of the trade routes linking the Sonora and upper Yaqui drainages. In areas where people live and die by trade, such routes tend to be open to all, and passage of small or nonthreatening parties is not contested.

After being entertained by the Batuco people and meeting with those of Corazones, the Spaniards followed the difficult trail along the Moctezuma and Yaqui rivers, downstream toward the coast. They ran short of supplies again in northern Sinaloa and had to raid surrounding areas. The road-weary army reached Culiacán around the middle of June 1542. Spain's first attempt to dominate the Southwest had ended, and ended in failure.

CHAPTER FIFTEEN

A Short Freedom

The Pueblo Indians were safe once more. They had seen the last of Coronado and his marauding army and no doubt breathed a collective sigh of relief. The Spaniards had left them considerable equipment, some of it useful, the rest a matter of curiosity only. Some items were likely picked up and taken to the various pueblos as keepsakes or souvenirs. Indeed, when some Spaniards returned in the 1580s they remarked on finding a trunk and a book (title not specified) at Zuni, and there must have been a great many more things—bits and pieces of metal, worn-out parts of saddles and other leather goods, and perhaps cooking pots. There is no evidence that the Pueblos added significantly to their material culture inventory as a result of such leavings, even though a number of Mexican Indians, both from the Valley of Mexico and environs and from the Tarascan region, stayed behind, and these people were well acquainted with Spanish manufactures.

It is perhaps not surprising that iron-working techniques failed to catch on, even though a considerable amount of meteoritic iron is scattered in fragments throughout New Mexico, and hematite and other iron ores are widespread. The Coronado group probably included one or more blacksmiths, although none is actually mentioned in accounts of the expedition. But at that time, any blacksmiths would have been Spaniards, and most likely the technical skills needed for iron casting—not to mention the equipment—were lacking among Mexican Indians who stayed in the Southwest.

More puzzling is the lack of Spanish influence on various ceramic wares of the Pueblo Indians. The Spaniards in all probability brought large numbers of a pervasive ceramic vessel known as an "olive jar" (often called *botijuela* in the Spanish records), a globular, narrow-necked, lugged amphora used

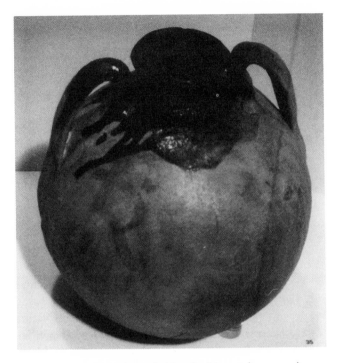

Plate 18. Reconstruction of old-style (sixteenth century) olive jar. Photograph courtesy Richard and Shirley Cushing Flint.

mainly for storing and carrying liquids. A sherd from what seems to be an early form of this jar has been found near the mouth of Santa Fe Canyon. The sherd, found in conjunction with a Pecos Glaze Polychrome vessel with a Glaze E rim, could actually date from Coronado's time—or at least from the sixteenth century. As I mentioned in chapter 12, four sherds from a wheel-made olive jar, terracotta with an exterior cream slip and an interior brown glaze, were found at the Mann-Zuris site (LA 290) in the Albuquerque area. These also seem likely to be sixteenth century in date. There is no indication that Native Americans copied these olive jars either during or after Coronado's visit.

Coronado and his senior captains probably carried at least a small amount of the popular majolica pottery, since we know that they carried glassware. Majolica, or maiolica, developed in Moorish Spain and was a painted ceramic ware glazed with lead admixed with tin oxide. It appears in New World Spanish sites from the late fifteenth to the nineteenth century. The

CHEVRON

NUEVA CÁDIZ PLAIN

Figure 11. Sixteenth-century European trade beads.

name majolica was given to the pottery by Italians who received it from western Spain via the island of Majorca and who erroneously considered it to have been made there. This ceramic style was very popular in western Europe; Italian faience pottery and Dutch and English delftwares were essentially copies of majolica. In Coronado's day, not only was majolica imported to New Spain, but native workshops were also springing up in the area of Mexico City. No majolica has ever been found, however, that dates from the Coronado expedition, and, as is the case with the olive jars, no tradition of copying majolica seems to have developed among the sixteenth-century Pueblos.

The Spaniards were known to have brought with them a number of trade items, including beads, various "glasswares," and bronze or brass bells or tinklers. One would not expect the Pueblo Indians to have been able to duplicate these, but the originals should appear archaeologically. Unfortunately, only a few examples of beads that probably date from the mid-sixteenth century have been found. In excavations at Hawikuh, several graves yielded glass beads. Two of these represented a sixteenth-century type called the "star" chevron that was made by banding patterns of various colors—green, white, blue, and red (fig. 11). On the other side of the Pueblo world, archaeologists discovered a short, square-sided blue glass bead of a type known as Nueva Cádiz. This bead was a surface find at the Goodwin-Baker site (of the Edwards complex) in western Oklahoma. Nueva Cádiz beads mostly went out of fashion around 1560, though the shorter variety may have been used sporadically until around 1600. In the 1880s a geologist named J. A. Udden discovered two beads and a fragment of chain mail in McPherson County, Kansas, northeast of the great bend of the Arkansas River in what may have been Harahey country. He thought that these could have been from the Coronado expedition. Sadly, these specimens have been lost.

It is likely that the Coronado expedition brought both the Nueva Cádiz and star chevron beads. The Nueva Cádiz bead found in Oklahoma, however, need not have been dropped or traded by Coronado's men on their way to Quivira. It could instead have been obtained at Pecos, Tiguex, or the Galisteo towns and traded perhaps to Querecho or Teya Indians, subsequently reaching western Oklahoma. Future excavation with better temporal controls in early historic sites, both in the Pueblo area and on the western plains, may give more information on this matter.

Coronado's departure left behind not only Mexican Indians but certain Spaniards. The mad little Padilla expedition seems to have left for Quivira about the same time Coronado headed back to Mexico. Because three members of the expedition eventually returned to Mexico, there was some later news of its fate, although the accounts are somewhat garbled. The black and mestizo members were not heard of again. Father Padilla himself was killed in Quivira or possibly at Harahey, according to the chronicler Gómara, who had the story indirectly from Andrés do Campo. Castañeda also says that Father Padilla died in Quivira, and Jaramillo, probably getting his information from the Tarascan *donados*, added that the Quiviran guides themselves killed him for the livestock and baggage. The Franciscan Father Pedro Oroz, writing in 1587, simply says that he was killed by warlike Indians.

In any case, the dozen Tarascan Indians and do Campo, with the party's one horse, fled southward. Virtually nothing is known of their trip, but do Campo was captured somewhere on the plains and held for several months. Eventually he escaped and in 1543 finally reached Pánuco on the east coast of Mexico.

The two donados, Lucas and Sebastián, retreated back toward the Southwest, eventually reaching the Mexican west coast. Whether they revisited the Pecos, Tiguex, or Cíbolan regions is unknown. Since a number of Tarascan Indians stayed behind when Coronado left, it might have been logical for the donados to get fresh supplies on their way south. Unfortunately, we know virtually nothing of their trips except that they survived and took up their missionary duties in west Mexico. Sebastián died shortly after the return, but Lucas continued the work of conversion for many years. Because of racism among the Franciscans of that period, he never became more than a catechist and was essentially a servant. Because of his great piety and success in missionizing, there was an attempt late in his life to make him a friar, but this was rejected by the order because "it might open the door to other Indians."

Nothing more was ever heard of Luís de Ubeda, who, in Spanish eyes at any rate, was a saintly man who, unlike Padilla, had not promoted the Spanish carnage at Arenal and Moho. Ubeda's fate can only be guessed at. I think it very likely that he was killed as soon as the Spaniards were safely out of sight. Pecos had suffered at the hands of the Spaniards and the Pecos people were understandably bitter. The brutality of Coronado and Cárdenas would not have been quickly forgotten. It may well be that Luís de Ubeda was in the process of permanently moving to the Galisteo towns when last seen by the Spaniards. These towns had suffered less at Coronado's hands, although demands were made on them for provisions. If the Tano Pueblos of Galisteo actually granted Ubeda asylum, however, they would have come under serious pressure from their Tiguex neighbors, who had no reason to love any Spaniard.

I suspect that both Ubeda and his flock of sheep (the latter consigned to the cookpots) were dead long before Coronado reached Mexico City. This would not necessarily be true of Cristóbal or the other black people and certainly not of the Indians from central and west Mexico who also stayed at Pecos. They would likely have been considered as much victims of the Spaniards as the Pecos people themselves. In fact, one of the Mexican Indians was still alive in 1583 when Espejo visited Pecos. Chances are that blacks and Mexican Indians gradually merged into the Pecos population. Perhaps some of their descendants can still be found today at Jemez, where the remnants of the Pecos tribe migrated during the early nineteenth century.

We really do not know just how many central Mexican natives remained behind. The Spanish expeditions of the early 1580s mention only five—four of them by name. At Cíbola-Zuni were Andrés and Gaspar, brothers from the city of Mexico, Martín from Tonalá, and Antón from the Guadalajara region. Sixteen years later, Oñate remarked that he had interviewed Gaspar's two sons. The one Mexican native mentioned for Pecos is unnamed in the chronicles. Against this low head count we have the statements of Castañeda that quite a number of Mexican Indians stayed behind, especially at Zuni.

All in all, it seems likely that we are talking about a significant number of

Indians from Mesoamerica who remained in the Southwest. Considering that there were some thirteen hundred Mexican Indians in the party, several dozen or as many as a hundred or even two hundred defectors would not be a surprising number. Few of them would have had any reason to welcome the Spaniards back, particularly those who remained at hostile Tiguex and Pecos. The four named individuals from Zuni who greeted the later Spanish expeditions probably represented the exception rather than the rule.

The big question is the extent to which these native Mexicans influenced the culture of the Pueblo Indians in the Rio Grande and elsewhere. Certain things they did *not* do. Other than crosses in the Zuni area, reported by Espejo in 1583, there is absolutely no evidence that any of the uses of Christianity ever developed among the Pueblos as a result of their absorbing the expatriate Mexicans. The crosses, if they actually were Christian in origin, were perhaps being used for magical purposes. In 1540 it seems likely that conversion of many central Mexican Indians still ran only skin deep. And those who chose not to return to a Mexico dominated by Spaniards were probably not the firmest of Christian converts.

Nor did the newcomers introduce anything in the way of exotic animals to the Pueblos. We know that Luís de Ubeda had a flock of sheep with him, and sheep herding was making great headway in Mexico by 1540. Surely some of the Mexican Indians who remained in the Southwest were familiar with the techniques of herding and raising sheep. But there is simply no evidence that sheep survived; they most likely disappeared into the stomachs of the Pecos or Tanos people. And in spite of Gómara's statement about European chickens, there is no indication that such fowls were maintained by the Pueblos after Coronado left the region.

In terms of plants, chili (*Capsicum annuum*), which was extremely popular in central Mexico, would be a likely domesticate to have reached the Southwest with Coronado. However, it does not seem to have been introduced until Espejo's day (1582–83) at the very earliest. A wild form of chili, *chiltepín,* was probably already in use, and the domesticated varieties did not really catch on until the seventeenth century.

Of European cultigens, only melons perhaps reached the upper Southwest before the time of Oñate, whose colonizing group arrived in the Rio Grande in 1598. In 1564, Obregón, in Sonora, heard of European melons "from seeds that were left when Alcaráz was killed" and of "frijol de Castilla." The latter may or may not have been chickpeas. That melons, at any rate, should have spread rapidly is no surprise, for they were easy to adapt to the native agricultural system and their high sugar content made them very desirable. If the settlers at San Gerónimo de los Corazones had melon seeds, then in all probability Coronado carried some into the Zuni and Rio Grande areas. As early as the beginning of March 1599, Juan de Oñate writes of watermelons—at a time before his colonists could possibly have harvested their own melons. Two years later, in the Valverde inquest on Oñate's colonists, there is the clear statement that "maize, beans, fine [cantaloupe?] melons, and watermelons" were found among the Rio Grande Pueblos. The implication is very strong that they were considered "native" as of Oñate's time.

Another type of plant is also a candidate for entry into the Southwest in this period. Peyote (*Lophophora williamsii*), a small cactus that contains several psychoactive alkaloids, including mescaline, has a long history in west and central Mexico. It is mentioned by Sahagún for Aztec times and remains important among the Huichol Indians of western Mexico, where it is central to the religious system. There is some evidence that peyote was used at Casas Grandes, at least by the fourteenth or fifteenth century. The Suma Indians in the old Casas Grandes area had the drug at least by the eighteenth century. It appears in the Rio Grande valley in very early Spanish records (1631–32), at which time Mexican Indians, mestizos, and Pueblo Indians were all involved in its use.

It is possible that peyote was actually pre-Columbian in the Southwest, coming over the trade routes, but no direct evidence of it has been found in a prehistoric context. If peyote was introduced, either aboriginally or in the sixteenth century, its use never became firmly implanted in Pueblo ceremonial structures. The modern Native American Church with its peyote rituals represented an introduction or reintroduction of the plant during the nineteenth century, and the Pueblos have been generally resistant to the Native American Church movement. I think it most likely that peyote was introduced from Mexico in post-Spanish days. It may have arrived as early as Coronado's time, but on balance, my vote is for an introduction by Spanish or Mexican Indian settlers who came with Oñate. Whatever the time of arrival, the Pueblos seem to have taken up peyote only peripherally and atypically.

One might also expect that a considerable number of Mexican Indians living permanently in the Southwest would produce certain identifiably Mexican artifacts. It might be too much to expect to find Mexican pottery, since pottery making in the Aztec and Tarascan areas was generally specialist work or, in some localities, a woman's occupation. It seems rather unlikely (though certainly not impossible) that professional potters were among the Indian warrior contingent. And we simply have no idea whether there were women among the Mexican allies. Aztec armies, at any rate, tended to travel without camp followers, although women might be brought on a military expedition as part of the commissary unit. In any case, there is virtually no evidence of sixteenth-century Mexican pottery in our area. One undated sherd of "probably central Mexican" pottery was found in A. V. Kidder's excavations at Pecos, but its provenance is unclear.

A few curiosities appear. At Pecos were found a series of human, animal, and bird effigies—tiny, crudely made clay objects—that stratigraphically date to the sixteenth century. They seem out of place in protohistoric Pecos, and Kidder suggests that they may have been introduced, or at least their manufacture influenced, by Mexican Indians with the Coronado expedition. They do not, however, look particularly Mesoamerican.

One site where Mexican Indian materials have been found is LA 54147, near Santiago Pueblo, probably the town called Coofor by Coronado and occupied by the Spaniards from late 1540 until the late winter or early spring of 1542. At Santiago Pueblo itself a considerable number of metal artifacts have been found, and some of them—for example, crossbow boltheads—are of sixteenth-century provenance. LA 54147 appears to be the campsite of some or all of Coronado's Mesoamerican Indian allies. Spanish artifacts were also found at this campsite: nails, a clothes hook, a jack plate from a coat of armor, and several small, miscellaneous pieces, all of iron. Large amounts of ceramic wares, mostly Glaze E pottery from up and down the Rio Grande valley, were found at LA 54147, but no ceramics of either European or Mesoamerican manufacture.

Certain artifacts of stone, however, did suggest the presence of Mexican Indians. These included a number of *comales,* implements that are widespread in Mesoamerica. The ones found at LA 54147 are flat sandstone slabs that show obvious use signs and were probably employed in cooking tortillas. These comales, according to the excavators, "appear to differ from the griddles or piki stones found in contemporaneous Rio Grande sites." Whoever procured them went to a certain amount of trouble, for they likely came from the Placitas area on the flanks of the Sandia Mountains to the east, or perhaps from near San Ysidro in the Jemez River region to the west. There was also a blade segment of green volcanic glass that most probably came from the Cerro de las Navajas near Mexico City. A projectile point at LA 54147 has been tentatively identified as a Texcoco point, found in the valley of Mexico during this time period.

A large portion of LA 54147 is still unexcavated, and doubtless more Spanish and Mexican Indian artifacts remain to be found. I should stress, however, that these particular artifacts, although pretty clearly related to Coronado's Mexican allies, are also dated specifically to the Coronado period, 1540–42, and almost certainly were brought from Mexico by members of the native forces or, in the case of the comales, made from local materials but as copies of Mesoamerican prototypes. They throw no light on the activities of Indians from Mesoamerica after the Spanish expedition left the Southwest.

One Mesoamerican trait found among modern Pueblos that may well date from a sixteenth-century introduction by central Mexican Indians is the game of *patolli*. This game has a long history in Mexico. It was popular among the Aztecs, from which the name patolli comes, but the game was also found from Yucatán to Jalisco in Mexico and by Aztec times had been played in Mesoamerica for at least a thousand years. The game is somewhat like pachisi, a board game that probably originated in south Asia but has spread all around the world. It has even been suggested that patolli originated from pachisi, but the balance of evidence seems to show that patolli was independently invented in the New World. In the Southwest the game is played with three split willow dice. According to the throw of the dice, players move markers around a circle of stones. Among the Pueblos, patolli has religious significance and is usually played in the kivas.

Because it is widespread and ancient in Mesoamerica, it may well be that the game spread from Mexico to the Pueblo area in prehistoric times. But the Pueblo game is quite similar to the Aztec one in its rules of play, and, more strikingly, the name *patol* that the Pueblos use was almost certainly derived from the Nahuatl or Aztec word *patolli*. Of course, patolli might have been introduced into the Southwest at some later historic time, perhaps by the Tlaxcalan Indians who settled in the Santa Fe area in the seventeenth century. However, the game has spread to the Apaches and Navajos, surely through Pueblo trade or other contacts. It appears also among the Pimas and Papagos, perhaps also from an original Pueblo source. This secondary distribution suggests a considerable time depth in the Southwest—at the least a sixteenth- rather than a seventeenth- or eighteenth-century introduction. Very likely the native troops with Coronado played the game to while away the long hours of inaction in camp. Its spread to the Pueblos would not be surprising given the number of Mexican natives who remained in the Southwest in 1542. The adaptation of patolli to religious uses might be expected, considering the pervasive religious nature of Pueblo society and that among the Aztecs, too, patolli had religious connotations.

It is in the field of ceremonialism that we might expect some Mexican influence during the forty-year interregnum between Coronado and the Spanish expeditions of the 1580s. As the kachina cult attests, the Pueblo Indians were eclectic and receptive to new ceremonies that could be easily assimilated to Pueblo religion. The ethnologists and ethnohistorians of the late nineteenth century—Cushing, Bandelier, and others—were interested in the possibilities of this contact. However, throughout much of the twentieth century, Southwestern archaeologists and historians were so influenced by models of autonomous growth of native institutions that they tended to discount diffusion into the area, whether prehistoric or protohistoric.

One exception was the ethnologist Elsie Clews Parsons, who probably had a better grasp of the totality of Pueblo social, ceremonial, and religious life than any other scholar, living or dead. Parsons, in a 1933 article, speculated on contacts between Mesoamerica and the Pueblo world. She believed that a fair part of Pueblo ceremonialism came from Mexico, particularly the kachina complex. In the early 1930s there had not yet been any archaeological demonstration that the kachina complex was prehistoric, so Parsons thought more in terms of post-Columbian introduction of ceremonialism than would be the case today. This is indicated in the title of her paper: "Some Aztec and Pueblo Parallels." With sixty years' hindsight we know that Pueblo contacts with Mesoamerica were mainly with west Mexico and that direct Aztec influence came only after the Spaniards had largely destroyed the bases of Aztec culture. And indeed, Parsons recognized that some of the similarities she saw between the Pueblo world and Mexico were from the west rather than from central Mexico.

In her paper Parsons lists a whole series of religious similarities between Mesoamerica and the Pueblos, especially the western Pueblos, Zuni and Hopi. I have discussed some of these in chapters 7 and 8, using present-day archaeological knowledge to suggest at least broad time periods and general points of origin for Pueblo ceremonialism. Although Parsons saw many likenesses, she was a little puzzled that she could find no point-by-point similarities between specific Pueblo and Mesoamerican ceremonies. Today, realizing that ceremonies such as the kachina cult came mainly from the archaeologically less-well-known west of Mexico, we would not be surprised at this lack of specificity.

There was, however, one ceremony among the modern western Pueblos (though not the Rio Grande groups) for which Parsons could find strong parallels. This was the Zuni Shalako ceremony, which Parsons compares in detail with Aztec ceremonies of the twelfth month of the Aztec calendar, Teotleco or Teutleco. I might say at the very outset that the two ceremonies do not match up calendrically. Shalako is celebrated in early December, about two weeks before the winter solstice, whereas Teotleco falls in September. Still, the resemblances are striking. According to Parsons:

A SHORT FREEDOM

The exception [to the rather scattered parallels between Pueblo and Mexican ceremonialism] is the Koko awia or Shalako of Zuñi and the ceremony of the Aztec twelfth month, Teotleco. Here are so many points of resemblance in the ceremonial complex that some equation has to be made. In both Zuñi and Nahuatl the name of the ceremony refers to the arrival of the gods who are "said to have gone to other parts." The first god to arrive in both ceremonies is a "bachelor" or virgin god. . . . The older gods arrive the following day. . . . The Aztec made a mound of corn[meal] which was watched overnight by the head priest to see when the gods made a footprint on it in token of arrival. The Zuñi make two mounds of sand covered with meal which is also watched for omens, and possibly, for the coming of the gods because a "road" of meal leads to the mounds. Should a Shalako impersonator fall in the running ritual he would be exorcised (or punished as Sahagún would say). Running ritual and a taboo against stumbling or falling are Aztec traits. In the Aztec ceremony there is a midnight drinking party, which was not uncommon in other ceremonials. In the Zuñi ceremony there is also a midnight feast, which is uncommon, in fact unique, in Zuñi ceremonialism, and, curiously enough, before prohibition enforcement there was much drinking this night, nonritualistic drinking, but drinking which would not be tolerated at other ceremonies. The Aztecs made a fire around which danced "certain young men disguised as monsters." When Shulawitsi comes in in the Zuñi ceremony he kindles several large bonfires at which their dance is performed by the Sayatasha group. Their horned masks might be described as monsters. . . . One of the Aztec gods was the fire god; the Zuñi virgin god is the so-called little fire god.

Parsons listed a series of other traits that were Aztec, though not necessarily from the Teotleco itself:

> There are still other Aztec traits that we may note in Shalako. The impersonators of the gods serve for a year, and some of them are referred to during their services by their god's name. For example, the impersonator of Sayatasha will be called Sayatasha in the familiar daily speech of the townspeople. When the Shalako masks leave town it is said that they are struck at and thrown down, which is suggestive of the killing of the god. This ritual no white has ever been allowed to see. The Shalako are or were thought of as warriors (in Aztec terms prisoners of war) for in their belts they carry war clubs. The attachment of feathers to the blanket costume of the Shalako, a very elaborate arrangement on First Mesa [Hopi], suggests an Aztec technique. Finally we note that one of the Shalako day counts is by ten, an Aztec and *not* a Pueblo count.

This great, enigmatic Shalako ceremony seems to have originated among the Zunis and spread to the Hopis. It is generally assumed by modern anthropologists that the Rio Grande Pueblos became acquainted with Shalako only after the migrations westward of Tiguex and Tano Indians after the Pueblo Revolt of 1680. But this is a somewhat gratuitous assumption since we definitely lack details on seventeenth-century Rio Grande Pueblo masked dances. It may well be that Shalako was introduced to the Rio Grande region from Zuni after 1542 and then was successfully suppressed in the seventeenth century. Spanish control of the eastern Pueblos was too firm to allow a ceremony as spectacular as the Shalako to survive.

If Mexican Indians from the Coronado party actually did introduce Shalako, the Hopis could have received it before the Spaniards overran the Southwest in the two or three decades following 1598. Alternatively, it may have reached the Hopis after the Pueblo Revolt, at which time the Hopis shook themselves free of Spanish domination and the Zunis became very loosely attached to the Spanish imperium.

The Shalako ceremony is the final event in the yearly kachina cycle and represents the coming of the gods to Zuni. Shalako is of great importance at Zuni for it is the hinge of the ceremonial year and comes at the "turning of the sun," the winter solstice. Because it is a western Pueblo, not a Rio Grande Pueblo, ceremony—at least in modern times—I will not discuss Shalako in more detail; there are ample descriptions in the literature.

Even though Shalako, as a ceremonial complex, may have been introduced in the sixteenth century, elements of it are certainly earlier. Zuni rock art shows various aspects of Shalako dancers, and although some of these are clearly post-Spanish, others date from the earlier part of the protohistoric period. Shalako figures also appear in the rock art of the Galisteo basin. Hopi Shalako figures have been found on pots, one of which—a Jeddito Black-on-yellow bowl—dates to perhaps A.D. 1375. If Shalako was actually introduced in the mid-sixteenth century as a new ceremonial complex, it was surely reinterpreted in light of the earlier kachina cult. Although Zuni Shalako figures, unlike the Hopi ones, are not technically kachinas, the Shalako cult certainly belongs to the conceptual world of the kachina. Some of the Shalako icons, gods, and costumes were most likely borrowed from earlier kachina ceremonies.

It is perhaps unfortunate that excavation of some of the most spectacular Pueblo sites, large towns that extended into the historic period, took place when the techniques of archaeology were still relatively primitive. It would be extremely valuable if future archaeological work in the Rio Grande valley, especially work on the Tiguex towns, could be directed specifically toward this interregnum period (1542–81). From what we do know, both from archaeology and from the later Spanish accounts, the Tiguex sifted back to their burned-out towns and began the task of reconstruction. Most or all of the towns seem to have been reoccupied; at any rate, the pueblo count for Tiguex in the 1580s was higher than it was in Coronado's day.

The Keresan-speaking Quirix pueblos were somewhat less involved in the Spanish occupation than their Tiguex neighbors, although certain Quirix pueblos, especially Zia, had been the focus of considerable food and cloth collecting on the part of the Spaniards. The Jemez River Towas, the Tewas, and the northern Tiwas had relatively less contact, and their towns were essentially intact when Coronado left the Southwest. The Tewas continued to experiment with their pottery designs, and the beautiful Sankawi Black-on-cream pottery, ancestor to the Tewa sculptured wares of the seventeenth century, was introduced about 1550.

Another event that probably can be dated to the period between 1540 and 1580 is the movement of certain of the Querecho bands into the northern Rio Grande westward as far as Hopi country. In 1629 they were identified by the Franciscan friar Estévan de Perea simply as "Apache," but there is a good chance that some of them were ancestral Navajos. The Coronado expedition did not report Querechos west of the Pecos River and the Rio Grande. Only the indirect evidence of the name Tusayán, Coronado's word for the Hopi country, suggests Athabascan connections at that early time. Tusayán sounds like a Navajo word (see chapter 8), although not too much reliance should be placed on one isolated place name.

In 1583, however, the Espejo party had considerable contact with Querechos both around Hopi and near Acoma. From the descriptions of the chronicler Luxán, it would seem that Querecho bands had been living in the area for at least a generation or two. They were interacting with the Pueblos in what seemed to be fairly well-worn patterns of behavior. The first Spaniards to explore the middle and upper Rio Chama valley were colonists who came with Oñate beginning in 1598. Shortly after that time, there were groups, recognizably Navajo, living in the Chama valley.

This situation has been discussed in earlier chapters; to summarize, let me say that there are two conflicting hypotheses. The first holds that after 1540 there was a westward drift of Querechos—ancestral Navajos and western Apaches, living in extreme northeast New Mexico and adjacent states. Nomadic settlements in the San Juan area that predate Coronado (if they indeed

Plate 19. Tyuonyi Pueblo, Frijoles Canyon, inhabited in Coronado's time. Photograph by Jesse L. Nusbaum, about 1910, courtesy Museum of New Mexico, neg. no. 28693.

exist) may be protohistoric Ute. A second explanation is that Querechos settled the San Juan basin in pre-Hispanic times and, after 1540, drifted into Black Mesa, the Mt. Taylor region, and perhaps the Chama valley.

Whether reacting to a new threat from Querechos or to some other demographic factor, the Pueblos do seem to have undergone some consolidation around the Rio Grande valley during this period. In the Frijoles area (modern Bandelier National Monument), the large town of Tyuonyi along Frijoles Creek was deserted around 1550, as was nearby Tsankawi in Sandia Canyon. There does not seem to be much evidence that European diseases brought by the Coronado expedition had any significant effect on the Pueblo populations, something rather startling in view of the large number of people involved in this expedition. Malaria, introduced from Africa with the early slave trade, was beginning to sweep across the New World, but the high-altitude Southwest probably did not provide a good environment for the vectors of this dread disease.

The Coronado expedition was probably free of certain of the so-called child-hood diseases. Indeed, these diseases may not even have reached the New World during the sixteenth century because the viruses that cause chicken pox, mumps, and rubella could not have maintained themselves during what amounted to an involuntary quarantine of human shipboard populations during the long sea voyages. The same would be true of influenza.

Common measles also belongs to this group; however, there is a reference to *sarampión,* a term that normally meant measles, by the Franciscan Moto-linía during the central Mexican epidemic of 1531. What may have been the same disease swept up the west coast of Mexico in the early 1530s, reaching to central Sinaloa. In addition, the word *sarampión* is used in an entry of the Códice Aubin (Anales Coloniales de Tlatelolco) for the year 1563. European adults normally were immune to measles, but it is possible that by 1531 a ship traveling to the New World had carried enough children to keep a measles infection alive and bring it to the indigenes. Of course, the disease may have been misidentified. Scarlet fever (caused by the bacterium *Streptococcus pyogenes*) has been suggested as the possible infectious agent, at least for the 1531 epidemic. In any case, one exception among the childhood ailments, the bacterial infection pertussis or whooping cough, with its longer period of communicability, could likely have survived the Atlantic voyages.

Smallpox, because the dried virus can be transmitted on clothing, is easier to spread and definitely did reach central Mexico around 1520. There is no indication, however, that Coronado's army carried either smallpox or whooping cough. So far as the present evidence goes, the first secure documentation of smallpox in Pueblo country comes in the eighteenth century, though in all probability the disease made a considerable impact on the seventeenth-century Southwest. Syphilis and/or its more benign cousin, yaws, could well have been carried north by the soldiers and would surely have spread to some degree among the Pueblos, although we have no evidence for it in the mid-sixteenth century. A little later on in the century, plague, caused by the bacillus *Pasteurella pestis* and transmitted from rodents through fleas to human beings, was recorded for both Mesoamerica and South America. Today, plague is endemic in the Southwest, but there is no reason to believe that it was introduced as early as Coronado's time.

The vector of typhus is the louse *Pediculus humanus,* which carries the microorganism *Rickettsia prowazekii.* The louse is found in both the Old World and the New, but the Rickettsia organism was presumably Old World in distribution. Typhus (called *tabardillo*) was well known in Spain and probably was introduced into Mexico in the sixteenth century, perhaps as early as the Cortés invasion. It is possible that Coronado's forces brought typhus to the Southwest, but there is no evidence that such was the case.

Generally speaking, the Pueblo population decline during the middle decades of the sixteenth century, though considerable, was gradual and may have been caused as much by social disruption, especially in the Tiguex area, as by actual diseases. Population had stabilized again by 1590 or 1600 and then steadily sagged during the seventeenth century. If the Coronado-period Rio Grande had fifty thousand Pueblo Indians, only four-fifths of that number were there to greet Oñate in 1598. Yet the Pueblo area seems to have avoided the catastrophic population collapse that marked the spread of Euro-African disease in the Serrana area of Sonora.

CHAPTER SIXTEEN

Return of
the Spaniards

 When Castañeda came to write his account of the Coronado expedition sometime in the early 1560s, the Spaniards were already thinking of a shorter path to Quivira "by way of the land of the Guachichules," a tribe living in the basin country of north-central Mexico. But Castañeda, a resident of Culiacán in the far northwest of New Spain, did not understand that the Southwest could be more easily reached through the interior of Mexico. In his book, which was dedicated to an unnamed individual—probably Francisco Ibarra, the first governor of the newly founded province of Nueva Vizcaya—Castañeda assured the reader that the west coast route was the only way to get to Tiguex.

Ibarra himself seems to have agreed. In exploring the northern frontiers of his new province, he made a frightening trip across the Sierra Madre Occidental to central Sinaloa and marched northward to explore the Sonoran statelets. With him went members of the Culiacán community, including Castañeda, who died during the expedition. Ibarra, astoundingly, recrossed the sierra somewhere along the boundary between modern Sonora and Chihuahua, eventually reaching and describing the great ruin of Casas Grandes. Ibarra did not seem to realize that from Casas Grandes he could reach his new province of Nueva Vizcaya by marching south along the eastern flanks of the Sierra Madre. In any case, he had left soldiers behind in northern Sinaloa, and so he crossed the mountains a third time, struggling through the wild country of the Aros and upper Yaqui drainages. His aim was to cut back to the coast far enough south to avoid the dreaded statelet of Señora, where he had already fought a major battle. Following the Yaqui River to the coast, Ibarra turned south and eventually reached Culiacán.

By Ibarra's time the Spaniards were well on their way to overrunning the northern interior of Mexico. The machine that drove this rapid northward advance was silver. Rich veins of this precious metal were discovered in Zacatecas in 1546. There was an immediate rush to the new mines, and settlement spread to the lush grasslands of the Guadiana valley in present-day southern Durango, where cattle ranches quickly sprang up to supply the mines. In 1562, Francisco Ibarra was appointed governor of the new state of Nueva Vizcaya, which incorporated these pioneer lands north and west of Zacatecas. The following year he established his temporary capital and head-quarters at San Juan del Rio, north of the present-day city of Durango. From there he launched his arduous expedition to the west coast.

Silver-hungry Spanish miners now moved to the north of Durango and then into present-day southern Chihuahua. Ibarra himself seems to have dis-covered the mines at Indé in northern Durango and may have been the first Spanish captain to reach the Conchos River in its upper course. The Indé mining area was settled in 1567 by a lieutenant of Ibarra's named Rodrigo del Río. Santa Bárbara in southern Chihuahua, with its extensive mines, was colonized by the same man later that year. Santa Bárbara initially had some thirty Spanish families surrounded by natives of the Concho tribe. Sometime after 1579, the population of Santa Bárbara was augmented by large numbers of Tlaxcalan Indians. The town was said to have seven thousand inhabitants by the year 1600. Franciscan missionaries were not far behind. Around 1570 a convent was established at San Bartolomé (modern Allende) some twenty-five miles east of Santa Bárbara.

It was from the Santa Bárbara region that the expeditions of the 1580s were launched. Shortly after settling this portion of the Conchos drainage, the Spaniards, hungry for slaves to work the mines, began raiding the regions roundabout for victims. The raids quickly made the Europeans realize that the Conchos drained into another river coming from the north and west. It soon became clear that this river was Coronado's Nuestra Señora—in other words, the Rio Grande. It is likely that one or another Spanish raiding party, having second- or thirdhand knowledge of the Coronado expedition, made probes in the direction of the Southwest. There is at least a possibility that the Spaniards, sometime in the 1570s, had reached the edge of Piro country.

The viceroy and the church quickly became concerned about events on the wild northern frontier of New Spain. Indeed, the Crown and the Coun-cil of the Indies in Spain had for decades been distressed over the brutal Spanish treatment of the native population. The "New Laws" of 1542, partly a reaction to the crimes of Nuño de Guzmán, had attempted to control, soften, and regulate Spanish treatment of native populations. In 1573 a second series of laws was aimed at providing peaceful penetration into unconquered areas with a large amount of mission control. Under these new regulations there was to be a different attitude toward exploration and settlement of new lands. The word *conquista* was forbidden to be used, and discoveries were to be undertaken "with peace and mercy." Leaders of such expeditions were to be peace-loving men who would not allow harm to come to the Indians. It was forbidden to make war on the Indians, to take them from their homes, or to side militarily with one tribe against another. Priests and other missionaries were to be favored on such expeditions and given every facility for conversion. No exploration by either missionaries or laymen would be allowed without specific license from the Crown. It was a noble, if somewhat paternalistic, code, but a difficult one to enforce.

There was still a great deal of talk about the Coronado expedition, and stories of the wealth of Quivira continued to reverberate in New Spain. The possibility that the Southwest might have rich mines decidedly interested both government officials and private entrepreneurs. The Franciscans still had no information on Luís de Ubeda with his flock of sheep at Pecos. And now there seemed to be a simpler route to the Southwest, following the Conchos to its juncture with the Rio Grande and the latter river up to the land of the Pueblos.

Such an expedition got under way in early June of 1581, leaving Santa Bárbara with nine Spanish soldiers, three Franciscan friars, nineteen Indian servants—two of them women—six hundred head of stock (cattle, sheep, goats, and pigs), and ninety horses. The little expedition was led by Captain Francisco Sánchez Chamuscado and Friar Agustín Rodríguez of the San Bartolomé mission. Although Chamuscado was the overall leader, he probably had been nominated by Rodríguez. In keeping with the new legalities, the expedition was officially authorized and had as major goals the conversion of the Indians and the exploration of the country for possible mineral wealth.

The Spaniards traveled the Conchos River to its mouth, where they contacted towns of settled agricultural people whom they called Patarabueyes and nomadic, bison-hunting Indians who, from the 1580s on, would be called Jumanos. I suggested in chapter 13 that these Jumanos were the Teyas of the Coronado period—the term *Teya* disappearing from the Spanish lexicon of native names at just this time. Chamuscado and his men began to pick up information at La Junta de los Ríos (where the Conchos and Rio Grande meet) about people living in large houses entered with ladders, who had much agriculture and who wove cotton and kept turkeys. Chamuscado's chronicler, the soldier Hernán Gallegos, saw someone with a copper bell, and the informants were wearing red and white coral and turquoise. One Indian had an iron bar about two feet long which he claimed came from the people of the large houses.

Chamuscado and his men at La Junta were on one of the trade routes connecting La Junta with the Southwest. The main route reaching La Junta very likely ran from Pecos and the Tompiro pueblos down the Pecos River and was operated by the Jumanos in their seasonal shifts from the bison area to wintering grounds at La Junta. There was a secondary trail, however, that followed the Rio Grande and cut across Suma country. The Spaniards, perhaps under Indian advice, took this trail and saw other evidence of trade as they went upriver (map 17). At one Suma village, for example, they found headdresses of macaw feathers.

If it had arrived from the Southwest, the iron bar must have been a discard from Coronado's army somewhere in Pueblo country, unless, of course, Gallegos misunderstood his informant and it had actually been carried by some Indian or Spaniard down the Conchos from Santa Bárbara. The latter is a distinct possibility because, as of Chamuscado's time, there had already developed much traffic between Chihuahua and La Junta. Some of this traffic involved Patarabueye Indians captured near La Junta and enslaved in the Santa Bárbara mines. Indeed, the very name "Patarabueye" seems to be a derogatory Spanish slang term—"ox foot," or some such meaning. The Jumanos wintered at La Junta and had a friendly relationship with the town-dwelling Patarabueyes that dated back at least to Cabeza de Vaca's time and probably for many decades before that. What the Patarabueyes spoke is still unclear, though it seems extremely likely to have been a Uto-Aztecan tongue. Their language probably was very similar to that of the upriver Suma and Manso. It has also been suggested that Patarabueye speech was related, perhaps at the dialect level, to the language of the Jumanos. Even if the languages were not mutually intelligible, the two groups must have had considerable bilingualism after so many years of intimate contact.

In the La Junta area, Fray Agustín Rodríguez persuaded a Patarabueye Indian whom the Spaniards called Juan Cantor, who could speak Nahuatl, to join the party. Chamuscado and his tiny band followed the Rio Grande upstream. They traversed both Suma and Manso territory, and in late August 1581 reached the Piro region. There they found deserted villages, the Indians having fled. At first glance this seems a rather strange reaction to such a small group, and it deepens my suspicion that Spanish slavers, sometime between about 1570 and 1581, had raided this southernmost Piro area.

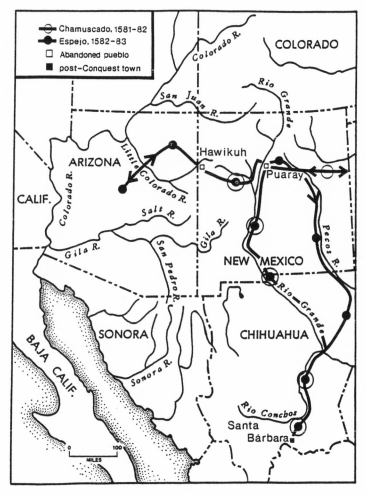

Map 17. Spanish exploration in the Southwest, 1581–1583.

The first Piro town was encountered just south of modern Milligan's Gulch, a large, east-draining arroyo that joins the Rio Grande south of historic San Marcial. Naming this first town San Felipe, Chamuscado and his party took formal possession of the entire region under the name San Felipe del Nuevo México, a name perhaps intended to honor the Spanish king, Philip (Felipe) II, as well as the saint. This title had a very brief vogue, and its shortened form, Nuevo México, quickly became the norm.

As Chamuscado and his men continued on upriver, they went by a number of large towns. Somewhere around modern Socorro they found a series of pueblos, one of which was in the process of construction. This "Pueblo Nuevo" probably was on the northern fringe of Piro country. In his account, dating to about 1630, the Franciscan *custos,* or head of the local order, Alonso de Benavides, stated that there was a gap of about eighteen miles between the northernmost Piro town and the southernmost Tiguex town. The idea of a spatial gap was reinforced in modern times by the archaeologist H. P. Mera, who failed to find protohistoric period sites in the region south of modern Isleta Pueblo. However, recent work by archeologists Curtis F. Schaafsma, Michael P. Marshall, and Henry Walt makes it clear that there were, in fact, several large pueblos in the area. So Gallegos's account, describing Indian towns in a continuous distribution from San Marcial to the Albuquerque and Bernalillo area, seems to indicate that in 1581 the Piro and Tiguex provinces more or less adjoined each other. The Tiguex region began somewhere around where the west-draining Abó Arroyo joins the Rio Grande. The line of modern U.S. Highway 60 can be taken as a general border marker.

The southernmost Tiguex town cannot be identified with any great certainty from the Gallegos lists. The northernmost of the Piro towns, later called Sevilleta, may have been a pueblo named Mexicalcingo by Gallegos. If so, the beginning of Tiguex country would be at nearby Tomatlán on the eastern bank of the Rio Grande. Or perhaps Tomatlán was Sevilleta and the first Tiguex town was Taxumulco, across the river on the west side.

Unfortunately, the Gallegos names generally do not relate to either the native languages or the geography of the Rio Grande basin. For the most part they were never used again and so are difficult to correlate with later names and places. One of the few Gallegos town names to survive was Puaray, or Puarai, which, as I pointed out some years ago, was very likely the Arenal of Coronado's period. The Espejo expedition members in the following year, 1582, called this place Puala or Puara.

Even in Benavides's time there were "fifteen or sixteen pueblos," and in 1581 there may have been as many as twenty Tiguex towns strung along the Rio Grande. Some of the pueblos were fairly small. Just how small is not entirely clear because both Gallegos and members of the Espejo party a year later described them in terms of "houses." What fourteen or fifteen two-story houses actually meant in the way of rooms or families occupying them is uncertain, but probably we are talking of structures with a hundred or more separate rooms. It suggests that Tiguex, since the desolation of Coronado's time, had been rebuilt with a larger number of pueblos but that the pueblos themselves were generally smaller than the earlier towns.

The itinerary of the Chamuscado expedition is somewhat confused because of the lack of firm dates in the Gallegos account. On the other hand, the chronicler does give a considerable amount of cultural and physical information about the natives, though usually we have no idea which group he is talking about. For example, Gallegos remarks that the Pueblos were "handsome and fair-skinned" and that some of the women "have light hair, which is surprising." If Gallegos was at Tiguex when he made these observations, it might suggest genetic mixture from Coronado's men, since large numbers of Tiguex women were enslaved after the Arenal and Moho battles.

Although lack of dates makes it unclear just where Chamuscado's Spaniards were at any given time, they did explore the Tiguex area and reached as far north as the Keresan towns, including a visit to Zia on the Jemez River. They seem to have touched on the Towa towns of the Jemez River and definitely went on to Acoma and Zuni, both identified by name. At Zuni they heard about (but did not visit) Hopi. They also reached the Galisteo towns and somewhere in the area stopped by a large settlement they called Nueva Tlaxcala. Most scholars have identified Nueva Tlaxcala with Pecos.

On September 10, 1881, one of the three friars, Juan de Santa María, decided to return to Mexico. His reasons are unknown, but possibly some personality conflict caused him to give up the expedition. Chamuscado was unhappy to see the missionary go. Reading between the lines of the various accounts, it seems that the expedition was under some threat, and loss of even one member was worrisome—not to mention the danger to Friar Juan himself, traveling alone through hostile country. Juan de Santa María, however, was adamant.

The lone missionary left the Spanish party somewhere on the edge of Tiguex country, most likely at the pueblo of Tunque, which lies at the north end of the Sandia Mountains between Tiguex and the Galisteo basin. The linguistic affiliation of Tunque may have been Tiwa or Keresan, or perhaps its people spoke both tongues. Tunque was probably not part of the Tiguex hegemony, but it had close ties with Tiguex.

According to the Gallegos account, the Chamuscado party left for a trip to the plains immediately after Friar Juan's departure. Chamuscado requested guides from one of the Tano towns in the Galisteo basin, but the Indians refused. The Tanos did give directions, and the Spaniards struck out alone. It is impossible to be sure of their route, but it seems likely that they

Plate 20. Reconstructed kiva entrance at Pecos Pueblo. Photograph courtesy Museum of New Mexico, neg. no. 41072.

swung south of Glorieta Mesa, getting into the upper reaches of Blanco Canyon. This took them through wooded country and eventually to the Pecos River. The party then pushed on to the east and ran across an encampment of nomadic Indians. Because the Spaniards were forced to use sign language, I believe that these nomads were Querechos rather than Teya-Jumanos. From the vague accounts it seems that the Spaniards penetrated as far as the Canadian River, traveling without guides. Eventually they found a bison herd and slaughtered some forty animals for food. On October 19, after about a month of exploration, the party turned back, finally reaching the Galisteo basin sometime in late October 1581.

Bad news awaited the Spaniards on their return to the Rio Grande valley:

Fray Juan de Santa María had been killed after two or three days' travel to the south. In spite of this clear indication of Indian feeling, the remaining two missionaries decided to stay in the Southwest. They kept with them three Concho Indian servants, Francisco, Gerónimo, and Andrés, and a mestizo man named Juan Bautista. That the servants stayed on under duress or without enthusiasm is suggested by the statement of Hernando Barrado, a member of the expedition, that some "native boys" also in the party "remained of their own free will." It is unclear what tribe these boys came from.

The decision of friars Agustín Rodríguez and Francisco López to remain left Chamuscado in something of a quandary. He fully realized the danger to the friars and feared that officials in Mexico City would blame him personally for their foolish decision. To tempt fate even further, the two Franciscans chose to stay at Puaray, the old town of Arenal, Coronado's burning of which had launched the Tiguex war. Elsewhere I have suggested that the Franciscans deliberately picked the town that represented the epitome of Spanish repression and cruelty; "if Puaray could be missionized, surely any Rio Grande pueblo would receive missionaries. It was a noble idea and one that took courage on the parts of friars Rodríguez and López. It also makes understandable the frenetic attempts of the pragmatic Chamuscado to persuade the friars to return to Mexico."

The best that Chamuscado could do was to draw up an affidavit protesting the decisions of Rodríguez and his companion to remain in New Mexico. This was dated February 13, 1582, although, according to the Gallegos account, the little expedition departed Puaray on January 31. Possibly they dawdled at some nearby town for a few days to give the friars a chance to change their minds.

The expedition, sans missionaries, marched downriver, stopping to explore some mines, perhaps in the Magdalena Mountains near modern Socorro. Chamuscado seems to have been ill, as were several of the other soldiers. The group followed the Rio Grande southeast to the Conchos, Chamuscado becoming weaker and weaker. He was exhausted from the march, and following the maniacal medical practice of the day, he was bled, the soldiers using a horseshoe nail "as soldiers do in time of need" in lieu of a proper lancet. This treatment, coming on top of a grueling journey, finished off Chamuscado. He died and was buried along the Conchos several days' journey north of Santa Bárbara. At least Chamuscado was saved having to explain to the viceroy's officials why he had allowed the Franciscans to remain unprotected in New Mexico.

The next expedition for New Mexico, launched in 1582, had rather mixed motives. Its leader, Antonio de Espejo, a relative newcomer to New Spain, had arrived in 1571 and settled in the Querétaro area. He soon became involved in a murder trial, being accused of complicity in the killing of an Indian *vaquero,* or cowboy. He was fined for his part in the murder but escaped payment by fleeing to the wild northern frontier of Santa Bárbara. Espejo was in residence when the bedraggled Chamuscado party made its way back to the settlement.

Fears for the safety of the two friars left at Puaray made another expedition desirable from the viewpoint of the Spanish authorities, and this fitted nicely into Espejo's plans to search for new mines. While he was making these plans the Indian servant, Francisco, who had remained with the friars at Puaray turned up in Santa Bárbara. According to Francisco, Friar Francisco López had been murdered in the vicinity of Puaray. Francisco, who had witnessed López's burial, rushed to inform Friar Agustín and then, with the other servants, fled the region, apparently just in time. As they hurried away they heard a terrible commotion in Puaray, making them sure that Friar Agustín and the faithful "native boys" had also been killed.

Espejo managed to get his expedition together and left the area on November 10, 1582, with a small force of fourteen men, a number of servants, and 115 horses and mules. Astonishingly, one of the soldiers, Miguel Sánchez Valenciano, brought his wife and three sons, the two younger children only three and a half years and twenty months old. This expedition included just one Franciscan, Fray Bernardino Beltrán. There were perhaps forty to fifty people in all, counting the children. One very useful member of the party was a Patarabueye Indian boy named Pedro, about thirteen years old. Pedro had been captured on a slaving raid as a child and had grown up in the household of Diego Pérez de Luxán, a member of the party and its main chronicler. Young Pedro was a relative of Juan Cantor, who had guided Chamuscado the previous year.

Like the Chamuscado group, Espejo and his party followed the Conchos downriver to its junction with the Rio Grande. The Patarabueye Indians at La Junta were hostile, but Pedro diplomatically managed to smooth things over. Their expedition was given new urgency when, calling on Juan Cantor, they heard a rumor that the friars in Tiguex country were not really dead. According to Cantor, the Concho Indians who had brought the news south had simply deserted the Franciscans and were lying to cover up this fact.

The Espejo party followed the Rio Grande to the Piro towns. Continuing north, the group reached the edge of Tiguex country on February 8, 1583. Luxán called this province "Puala," and the town of Puaray he also referred

to as Puala. There the Spaniards learned the truth: friars Rodríguez and López had indeed been killed at Puaray. At the edge of Tiguex, Espejo settled
the party in a camp along the Rio Grande while he, with Luxán and one
other companion, made a trip to the Tompiro villages, following the line of
modern U.S. Highway 60 eastward through Abó Pass. The little party reported eleven pueblos in this Tompiro and eastern Tiwa region. They also
discovered that natives of the area had killed Friar Juan de Santa María, the
first of Chamuscado's friars to die. Espejo then rejoined his main party on
the Rio Grande and continued north. Among the Tompiros and especially
among the Tiguex the Spaniards were met with great suspicion. Reaching the
town of Puala, they found it deserted. The party continued on upriver to the
somewhat more friendly Keresan villages.

The identification of specific pueblos is a little clearer in the Luxán accounts than are those given in the Chamuscado expedition reports. Puaray
(Puala or Puara) can be recognized, and of course Acoma, which was named
by both expeditions. For the Tiguex, Luxán also identified a pueblo called
Guagua that is probably the modern Kuaua at Coronado State Monument.
None of his other Tiguex towns, however, can be equated with Coronado-
period sites, with those listed by the Chamuscado party, or with later, historic
pueblos. The reader has more luck as Luxán moves north to the Quirix region. His Sieharan is the Zia or Sia of Coronado's and later historic time.
Catiete seems to be San Felipe, whose Keresan name is Katishtya. Gigue can
be identified with Santo Domingo, Tipolti with Santa Ana, and Cochita
with the historic and modern pueblo of Cochiti.

Espejo's main objective was to find rich mines, so his party continued on
to Zuni and then Hopi. There the expedition divided and a party of five, led
by Espejo, traveled on to central Arizona, eventually reaching the Jerome area
in the Verde valley. Returning via Hopi to Zuni, they were reunited with the
other members of the party who had backtracked there. The reunion was
short-lived, for several of the party were determined to return immediately to
Chihuahua. Among those leaving were Friar Bernardino and Miguel Sánchez
Valenciano, with his wife (now pregnant again) and children. These defections left only nine members of the expedition, plus servants.

When the small group reached Acoma in early June of 1583, three of the
servants, two of them husband and wife, deserted. The husband was murdered shortly afterward by Acomas, and the second man fled back to Zuni.
The wife, a Concho Indian woman, was rescued by the Spanish party.

The Acomas were now up in arms, and a band of nearby Querechos also
threatened hostilities. It was with these Querechos that the truncated Espejo

party had an adventure that sheds considerable light on the movement of nomadic people in the sixteenth century. I discussed the sixteenth-century Apachean situation west of the Rio Grande in earlier chapters. Here, let me simply say that by the early 1580s, Apachean-speaking Querechos had reached the Hopi area. A case can be made that these Apachean Indians were ancestral Navajos who initiated the long-standing "trade and raid" relationship between Hopis and Navajos. Querechos were also operating in the region around Acoma and seem to have had friendly relations with that pueblo. Espejo gave a thumbnail description of these migratory Indians in the Acoma area: "The mountain dwellers, who are called Querechos, came down to serve the people in the towns, mingling and trading with them, bringing them salt, game (such as deer, rabbits, and hares), dressed chamois skins, and other goods in exchange for cotton blankets and various articles accepted in payment."

While at Hopi, Espejo and his men had been given some female Querecho captives whom they brought back with them into the Rio Grande drainage. One of these captives fled to the nearby Querecho group. The Espejo party attacked the Querecho *ranchería,* probably located at modern Acomita west of present-day Laguna Pueblo, and captured a local Querecho woman. After several days of skirmishes, the Indians approached Espejo with an offer to trade the escapee for the local woman in Spanish hands. The trade turned out to be a ruse, for the escapee had already been sent back to her home band near Hopi. A relative acted the part of the escaped captive, putting on her "feather crest" to fool the Spaniards. Espejo's interpreter to the Querechos, also a woman captive of the Spanish, was involved in the plot to separate the small Spanish party and thus allow the Querechos to take back their own woman and kill as many of the Europeans as possible. Luxán seized the disguised woman, but in the melee, which the interpreter joined, was forced to let her go. The Spaniards seem to have maintained possession of the local Querecho girl and the interpreter.

This dramatic and somewhat confused episode presaged the future when Spaniards would barter for Apache and other nomadic captives as part of a flourishing slave trade. In 1583, however, only a decade after the new regulations to protect Indians had been put in place, such slaving may not have been altogether pleasing to the Spanish authorities. This would explain the fact that Espejo, in his formal report to the viceroy, ignored the entire incident.

Espejo also diplomatically failed to report another dramatic happening of this same period. Continuing on from Acoma, the Spaniards returned to Tiguex. They reached the Puaray area on June 20, and after camping for a day attacked that pueblo on June 22. The Tiguex had fled to the mountains and all that remained in Puaray were some thirty people, most likely old men and women. The pueblo was set on fire and the Indians in residence were rounded up and put in a kiva, then taken out two by two and shot or garroted. Following this slaughter the Spaniards marched north into Keresan country. According to Luxán, the people in the Keresan towns were very much afraid and brought offerings of "many turkeys." From one unspecified town, the Tiguex were summoned to a peace treaty. Understandably, they refused to come out of the mountains.

Disappointed by his failure to find any significant amounts of silver ore, Espejo determined to leave New Mexico. He seems to have heard of other mines near a town called Santa Catalina, fifteen or twenty miles away. It seems very likely that Santa Catalina was Tunque Pueblo and that the mines were in the Cerrillos area. How the Spaniards arrived at the name Santa Catalina is unknown. Luxán claims that this was the same town as that named by the Chamuscado party two years before. Chamuscado's Santa Catalina, however, was one of the southernmost Tiguex pueblos and must have been a separate place.

From Santa Catalina (Tunque), Espejo and his men moved to the nearby Tano pueblos, but finding them hostile went on to Pecos, arriving on the third of July. The Pecos people were equally hostile but, reacting to threats, gave a certain amount of food to the Spaniards. Two days later, after kidnapping two Pecos Indians to serve as guides, Espejo set off down the Pecos River. Unlike Coronado and his shortcut across Rowe Mesa, the party seems to have skirted the northern flanks of that mesa, going through the juniper and piñon region north of the high mesa and south of the Pecos. They reached the Pecos River somewhere in the vicinity of the later San Miguel del Vado and followed it south. In the region around modern Villanueva the small party may have climbed onto Rowe Mesa and crossed the relatively flat country to Blanco Canyon. At any rate, Luxán said that the party went "five leagues through the forest, by a good trail, stopping by a stream of water which we called Arroyo de los Alamillos." The Cañón Blanco is not a perennial stream today, though it does contain water after upstream rains. In the sixteenth century, before sheep herding and other ranching and agricultural activities lowered the water table, it may have run all or most of the year.

The trip south from Pecos makes it obvious that Espejo had received information at La Junta about the general topography. It is also clear that the lad Pedro, Luxán's servant, had considerable geographical knowledge.

Plate 21. The Pecos River about three miles northwest of San Miguel del Vado. Photograph by the author.

Moving quickly southward, following the Pecos River, Espejo and his men came across a band of Jumano Indians, probably in the region around the modern city of Pecos, Texas. Using Pedro as interpreter, Espejo persuaded the Jumanos to guide the Spaniards to La Junta. From there they journeyed via the Conchos to Santa Bárbara.

One thing is clear about the general knowledge of the upper Southwest as of 1580. The Spaniards at Santa Bárbara had ample contact down the Conchos, raiding and enslaving the Patarabueyes and other groups. From the actions of the Piro Indians when Chamuscado approached, scattered slave raids may have occurred as far north and west as the Rio Grande above El Paso. Knowledge of the Southwest was rapidly being fleshed out, and Pueblo country was no longer terra incognita. Espejo, especially, seems to have been an able leader with a keen feeling for the lay of the land. His return to Chihuahua by way of the Pecos River was a bold pioneering effort.

Generally, there seems to have been rather free intercourse between Pueblo country and the La Junta area during this period. The willingness of Juan Cantor to go with the Chamuscado group must have been based to some degree on self-interest—probably commercial. The Jumanos at this time were the major middlemen between the Pueblos and the plains groups and Indian tribes farther south. Cantor's home was up the Rio Grande from the main La Junta groups, and it may well be that he wanted to exploit this secondary trail to the Pueblos. Clearly, the Jumanos utilized and probably dominated the Pecos River line for their moves north and south. Their main contacts among the Pueblos were at Pecos, the Galisteo towns, and especially the Tompiro villages. The route up the Rio Grande bypassed these places but led directly to Piro country and beyond that to Tiguex, with its wealth of turquoise and much-desired cotton cloth.

CHAPTER SEVENTEEN

Occupation

The Chamuscado and Espejo expeditions left the Pueblo area shaken and apprehensive. Once again, as after the Coronado expedition, the luckless Tiguex towns tried to pull themselves together. Fire-blackened Puaray was again rebuilt, the dead were mourned, and the Tiguex groups tentatively began to reconstruct their lives. But a cloud of dread must have descended onto the Pueblo world. Not only was there the gloomy expectation of an eventual Spanish return, but also the weather gods seemed to be out of sorts. A period of substandard rainfall beginning about 1560 lasted through the 1580s. A number of winters during these last decades of the sixteenth century were severe. Rivers froze and snow fell heavily in the higher elevations.

Contacts with the rapidly expanding new power to the south were now becoming commonplace. Information from the Conchos River people reached the Pueblos with every trading season, and the Pueblos learned that Indian groups were being pressured all along the new Spanish border. Slaving raids continued along the frontier in spite of the new laws, and the victims, derisively called *piezas* (a slang term for animals being hunted), were scattered throughout the mines and ranches of the frontier provinces. The government in New Spain made repeated attempts to protect native peoples against the rapacity of the mine operators and ranchers, but such attempts were all too often ineffective on this wild frontier.

The church, with its own agenda for conquest, did not always shield its potential devotees from attacks by bands of settlers and from governmental authorities. Some churchmen may even have argued that slavery in the mines could be justified in that it contributed to saving souls. In fairness to the

Spaniards, however, this cynical religious defense of colonialism was much more widespread among English and—in later years—American missionaries.

The next Spanish expedition to the Southwest of which we have any knowledge was not long in coming. It was launched from the new Spanish province of Nuevo León, founded and headed by Luís de Carbajal. This province, situated in what are now the states of Nuevo León and Coahuila in northeast Mexico, suffered a blow in 1589 when Carbajal was arrested and charged with apostasy. The Carbajal family were *conversos,* members of a segment of the Jewish population of Spain that had been forcibly converted to Christianity in the fifteenth and sixteenth centuries. Eventually, several people from this large and influential family were executed for returning to the Jewish faith. Carbajal himself died in prison in Mexico City.

The province had been a disappointment to both Carbajal and the Nuevo León settlers. It had not produced any great wealth in silver, so the colonists turned to slave raiding to augment their income. At the time of Carbajal's arrest, the person next in line of command in Nuevo León was the lieutenant governor, Gaspar Castaño de Sosa. Castaño, perhaps also from a converso family, was an energetic and aggressive man who had come to Nuevo León around 1582 or 1583, serving as *alcalde mayor* of the settlement of San Luís (present-day Monterrey) before being appointed lieutenant governor. With the arrest of Carbajal, Castaño became head of the province. For some time garbled rumors had been creeping in about wealth off to the northwest in the newly named New Mexico. Castaño seems also to have heard a version of the old Quivira story. At any rate, he made the fateful decision in the summer of 1590 to move the entire Nueva León colony westward.

Castaño tried to get permission from the viceroy to settle New Mexico. But Carbajal's arrest on suspicion of heresy did not dispose the Mexico City authorities to quickly grant any request from Nuevo León. In fairness to the viceregal authorities, the religious situation was probably not the main reason for their reservations about the Nuevo León colony. Castaño was strongly implicated in slaving activities—much more so than Governor Carbajal himself. Castaño sent a deputation to Mexico City in May 1590 asking for a license to remove the colony from Almadén (present-day Montclova), his new headquarters, and to take the colonists to New Mexico. The head of this deputation, a trusted aide named Francisco Salgado, was perhaps was not the best person to represent the colony, for he had notorious slave-raiding proclivities.

In any case, Castaño was served notice in June 1590 by one of the viceroy's commanders, Captain Juan Morlete, to stop slave raiding and to remain in Nuevo León. Invited to return with Morlete to Mexico City to further plead the case for a New Mexico colony, Castaño decided to send a petition instead. It is fairly clear that Castaño was determined to found his new colony, come what might. Before any answer to his petition could possibly be received, the lieutenant governor left Almadén with the men, women, and children of the settlement, 160 to 170 people in all, along with livestock and supplies carried in a wagon train. It was a daring and risky journey into the unknown.

Castaño and his settlers struck out north and east across the stretch of Coahuila desert that lies between Almadén and the Rio Grande. Reaching the river somewhere downstream from modern Del Rio, the party worked its way up the north side of the Rio Grande, eventually cutting across country in a northeasterly direction and reaching the Pecos probably not too far from the modern Interstate Highway 10 bridge. Somewhere in the lower Pecos region the party met Jumano Indians and were in contact with them sporadically. It is likely that these Indians gave advice about the best route to Pueblo country, although Castaño's relations with the Jumanos were not very friendly.

On December 26, after a long journey, Castaño and his settlers arrived in the vicinity of the juncture of the Gallinas and Pecos rivers. A small probing party had just been roughed up at Pecos Pueblo and had lost a considerable amount of equipment. Castaño left his settlers behind and, with an advance guard of some forty men, reached the town of Pecos on December 30. He attacked the pueblo the following day, after trying to give presents and make peace—or so, at least, he claimed. Whatever his intentions might have been, it is clear that the inhabitants of Pecos were determined to defend their pueblo, for after considerable fighting Castaño and his men succeeded in occupying only one of the roomblocks. On the night of January 1, however, the Pecos Indians decided to make a tactical withdrawal from their town. The lieutenant governor and his men looted a considerable store of foodstuffs on January 2 and stayed in the vicinity for several more days, but the Pecos people refused to return.

On January 6 the advance party left the pueblo to search for mines, taking along two captured Pecos Indians to act as guides. In the following months Castaño explored the Galisteo, Tewa, and Keresan country, though generally keeping clear of the Tiguex who, in any case, fled once more to the mountains. Everywhere he was met with mistrust and hostility—information that seeps through the otherwise upbeat and propagandistic pages of Castaño's *Memorial.* In late January 1591, Castaño returned for the colonists in their Pecos River encampment, probably going down the Cañón Blanco. Retracing his steps the same way, with the remaining party and livestock, Castaño reached the Galisteo towns around the middle of February. Eventually the colonists settled down near a Keresan town to which Castaño gave its modern Hispanic name, Santo Domingo. Hardships and the harsh winter with its heavy snows were beginning to tell on settler morale, and in early March Castaño had to quell a revolt by dissatisfied soldiers.

What his eventual plans might have been is very hard to tell. Unable to find mines, Castaño may have planned to settle down and divide the pueblos into *encomiendas* for more efficient exploitation of the Indians. Encomiendas were grants of Indian labor to the government or to individuals. They had been part of Spanish-Indian relations in central Mexico since Cortés's time and had spread all over Spanish America. Eventually the Crown outlawed the holding of encomiendas by individuals, but the practice was to be followed in New Mexico throughout the seventeenth century.

Of more immediate significance, Castaño took possession of the various pueblos in the name of the Crown and appointed native governors, *alcaldes* (council members), and *alguaciles* (constables with police functions). What the Indians thought of this change in their social and political structure is unknown. Nor do we have any real idea how the new officers were chosen or with what reception they met. Generally speaking, there seems to have been little enthusiasm on the part of the various pueblos for any of Castaño's actions.

In any event, Castaño's colonization of the Rio Grande came to a sudden end. Hearing news of the desertion of Nuevo León by Castaño and the settlers, the viceroy sent Juan de Morlete to bring the errant group back to Mexico and free any slaves they might have taken. Morlete arrived at Santo Domingo on March 29. The colony immediately surrendered and an unspecified number of Indian captives were released. Castaño, who was away on an inspection tour, was arrested on his return and taken back to Mexico City in chains. He was later exiled for six years in the Philippines, where he was to continue service to the Crown under orders of the governor of that new Spanish province. Castaño died in the Philippines. It would seem that many of the settlers who followed him to New Mexico trickled back to Nuevo León.

The Pueblo Indians must have realized by now that the Spaniards were not going to go away. Castaño's appointment of officers in the various pueblos sent a clear message that the newcomers considered the Rio Grande area their own domain. Still, there is no evidence that the Pueblos made any concerted effort to unite and block the next Spanish move northward. No mechanism for this kind of interpueblo cooperation existed in Coronado's day, and it was still lacking half a century later in the wake of Castaño's attempted settlement. The Keresan Pueblos on the Rio Grande and lower

Plate 22. San Ildefonso Pueblo from the air. Photograph by Tyler Dingee, courtesy Museum of New Mexico, neg. no. 74174.

Jemez River, and to some degree the Tewas, had cooperated with the Spaniards, beginning with Coronado. On the other hand, Tiguex, Acoma, Pecos, and the Galisteo towns had been generally hostile. In the seventeenth century, under Spanish rule, the river Keresans and the Tewas paid the price for their cooperation. At the center of the Franciscan bureaucratic system, they were constantly pressured to give up paganism and Pueblo ways. Their unwillingness to do so would eventually culminate in their taking the forefront in the Pueblo Revolt of 1680.

About three years after Castaño de Sosa's attempted settlement of New Mexico there followed a small, unauthorized expedition under Antonio Gutiérrez de Humaña and Francisco Leyva de Bonilla. Setting out from Santa Bárbara, Humaña, Leyva, and their little band utilized the old path taken by Chamuscado and Espejo down the Conchos and up the Rio Grande. They settled at the Tewa Pueblo of San Ildefonso south of the modern town of Española and remained for about a year, exploring the Pueblo area and presumably looking for mines.

Finally the group decided to go in search of Quivira and reached as far as central Kansas, where Humaña killed Leyva in a quarrel. The small group was then wiped out by plains Indians, except for a servant of Humaña's named Jusepe, a native of Culhuacán north of Mexico City. Jusepe escaped but was taken prisoner by Apaches, who held him captive for a year before he again fled. He reached safety at Pecos and was living there when Juan de Oñate arrived in 1598. Little is known about the sojourn of the Humaña party among the Rio Grande Pueblos. Like Castaño's settlers, this group seems to have avoided Tiguex. It is unlikely that the Humaña and Leyva *entrada* had much direct effect even on the Tewas.

Meanwhile, the fate of the Rio Grande Pueblos was being decided by the Spanish Crown and the Council of the Indies, the governing body for the Spanish New World. A number of people were eager to conquer and settle the region. In spite of previous expeditions' failure to find rich mineral deposits, hope of another silver strike seems to have hung on. Aside from the possibility of mining, three rather different agendas occupied the minds of would-be colonizers. Various border-country entrepreneurs recognized that although there might not be immediate profits from mining, the large, sedentary, agricultural populations in the Rio Grande and Pecos drainages offered their own kind of wealth. This was the assignment of Indian productive labor to the provincial officials or to well-connected settlers in the form of encomiendas. Failing encomiendas, the settlers might expect grants of land, especially for herding purposes, with the native population as a rich potential labor supply. A third agenda would have Spaniards take over the lucrative trade, especially trade to the plains Indians.

And of course there was a fourth agenda, that of the Franciscans. The order wanted to establish a series of missions in New Mexico. One goal was to make the missions self-supporting with Indian labor and European-introduced animals, especially sheep. Expansionism was part of this plan. The Franciscan order desired to build a rich and influential missionary province, perhaps under the control of a Franciscan bishop. Competition and sometimes open warfare between power brokers in church and state led to double exploitation of native New Mexicans and laid the foundations for the explosive revolt of 1680.

But all this was yet to come. By 1595 the Crown and Council of the Indies had tentatively decided on a leader for the New Mexico colonists, a man named Juan de Oñate from a rich Basque mining family, who was appointed governor and captain general of the expedition. His father, Cristóbal de Oñate, had served as lieutenant governor of Nueva Galicia under Coronado and was in charge of that new province during Coronado's expedition to the Southwest. Oñate, therefore, had an interest in the Rio Grande and probably some knowledge of the region gained through his family connections. Parenthetically, Oñate's wife was the granddaughter of Hernán Cortés and great-granddaughter of the Aztec emperor, Moteuczoma II.

Oñate's appointment did not go smoothly at first. Rivals continued to press their claims, and it was not until January 21, 1598, that the expedition completed its final inspection. There were 129 soldiers and an unrecorded number of women, children, servants, and slaves. The governor provided more than 3,000 sheep and goats, precursors of the great herds that would be built up over the next eighty years. He also brought some 200 horses, mares, and colts. There were about 800 head of cattle plus 500 calves, in addition to pigs, mules, and donkeys. The many carts were pulled primarily by oxen. Supplies were plentiful: iron tools, equipment for horses, armor, cooking ware, sewing paraphernalia, foodstuffs including wine, oil, and sugar, writing paper, medicines, blacksmithing tools, horseshoes and nails, weapons, gunpowder and lead, quicksilver (for mining purposes), and more. The governor also took a great variety of trade items, including perhaps 80,000 glass beads of various kinds, rosaries, sacred images of tin, amulets and medals, clay whistles, knives, mirrors, needles, thread, thimbles, rings, glass earrings, and hawks' bells, among other things. Clearly, Oñate expected great profit from trade.

In addition to what Governor Oñate contributed, the individual colonists had their own mounts and equipment, household goods, carts and wagons, weapons, cattle, mules and donkeys, and large numbers of extra horses. It was a well-equipped expedition and obviously one that came intending to stay.

The Franciscan contingent of ten, led by the *comisario*, Fray Alonso Martínez, caught up with the expedition on March 3. Oñate decided to try a bold new route. Instead of creeping down the Conchos and up the Rio Grande he would strike out northward across Chihuahua and intercept the Rio Grande at its great bend in the modern El Paso area. Thus Oñate pioneered the southern end of the *camino real* that would be used by supply trains, traders, missionaries, and government officials for the next two and a half centuries. Indeed, this route is still used today, for it is basically the line of Mexican Federal Highway 45.

The party reached the Rio Grande on April 20, 1598, and marched upriver toward the El Paso area. On April 30 the party took possession, in the name of King Philip II, of "all the kingdoms and provinces of New Mexico" and paused for celebrations. El Paso, with its ford, was reached on May 4, and the expedition continued on upriver. There is reason to believe that previous

Plate 23. The barren Jornada del Muerto. Photograph courtesy Archives of the Laboratory of Anthropology/MIAC, Santa Fe, N.M., no. 70.11338.

expeditions had clung to the main river valley insofar as possible. Oñate, however, with his cumbersome carts, realized the need for a detour in the region from about modern Hatch to historic San Marcial. In this area the Rio Grande describes a large curve. Flanking it to the east are mountains, and to the west the terrain is cut by a number of deep arroyos. It is possible that Oñate had received information about this shortcut—the *jornada del muerto,* or "dead man's passage"—from Juan de Morlete, who had brought the Castaño party back from the Southwest eight years previously. Because Castaño's settlers had carts, Morlete may also have been forced to use this new route.

Leaving the carts and wagons to travel at their own speed, Oñate, with an advance force, pushed on across the Jornada del Muerto, a ninety-mile stretch of flat, almost waterless desert, coming out at the south end of Piro country on May 28. There, the inhabitants fled their town as they had when Chamuscado approached seventeen years before. The Spaniards then moved upriver and camped for a number of days to replenish their supply of maize and wait out the illness of the Franciscan commissary, Fray Martínez. Finally, in mid-June, the advance party moved forward again. The group received more maize at a pueblo named Teypana, which the Spaniards rechristened

Socorro (help or succor) because the people supplied them with food. For the most part, however, Oñate found the Piro pueblos deserted.

On June 15 the Spaniards reached a small pueblo which they named Nueva Sevilla. This town, under its later name, Sevilleta, saw major growth in the seventeenth century, for it became an important mission station during that period. As we saw in the previous chapter, Sevilleta has tentatively been identified with either Mexicalcingo or Tomatlán on Gallegos's list of Rio Grande pueblos. While Oñate's advance party waited in this area for more maize to be collected, a small exploring group followed the well-worn trail up the Abó Arroyo to the Tompiro country, essentially retracing the footsteps of Espejo in this regard.

On June 21 the party marched into hostile Tiguex country. Making some ten miles that day, the Spaniards reached the pueblo that Oñate had called San Juan Bautista. Finding it deserted but with a large supply of corn, the group settled down for several days, receiving visitors and envoys. They then continued north to Puaray and on to the Keresan town of Santo Domingo, which had been chosen by the Franciscans as their order's future headquarters.

On July 4, Oñate sent his nephew and maestro de campo, Juan de Zaldívar, south to help escort the lagging cart train. On the seventh he held a meeting with "seven Indian chieftains" from the various provinces, who may have been war or bow chiefs. At any rate—according to Oñate—they pledged obedience to the Spaniards in the name of their various groups. What they actually thought they were promising is unclear.

The governor then established his headquarters at the Tewa pueblo of Okeh, the future San Juan Pueblo, in the lower Chama valley. Following this act, the governor apparently visited Santa Clara Pueblo in the Tewa group and pushed northward to the northern Tiwa towns of Picurís and Taos. The Spanish party also visited the Galisteo region. It was during this visit that doña Inés, whom we met in chapter 14, was reintroduced to her Tano people: "She is an Indian woman we brought from Mexico like a second Malinche, but she does not know that language nor any other spoken in New Mexico, nor is she learning them. Her parents and almost all of her relatives were already dead, and there is hardly anyone who remembered how Castaño had taken her away."

Of course, it could hardly have been Castaño who took the woman from her home, since he returned to New Mexico under arrest. In any case, doña Inés surely would not have forgotten her language completely in seven years, nor would one expect her parents and "almost all" her relatives to have died and herself to be virtually forgotten in the pueblo. I am reasonably sure that Inés was taken south by the Coronado expedition. How she was dragooned into being "another Malinche" and coming on this expedition is unknown. Whatever the reason, it must have seemed an alien land to Inés after a fifty-six-year absence.

On July 25 Oñate went to Pecos. A Pecos native kidnapped by Espejo had been sent in the mid-1580s to the Franciscan convent at Tlanepantla, where he took the name Pedro Oroz—the original Oroz being the Franciscan commissary general for New Spain, who perhaps stood as his baptismal sponsor. With an eye to eventually missionizing the Southwest, the Franciscans had Oroz teach the Towa language to several Indian donados. Oroz died before the Oñate expedition, but one of the donados, Juan de Dios, who had learned Towa, came along with Oñate.

The main party, with the carts and wagons, reached Okeh on August 18. A church, San Juan Bautista, was quickly begun and was consecrated on September 8. The Oñate party seemed to have remained at Okeh for about a year. By March 22, 1601, they had taken over the nearby pueblo of Yungue and were rebuilding it to suit Spanish specifications. This town, San Gabriel del Yungue, remained the capital of the province of New Mexico until 1610.

During his first few months in New Mexico, Oñate assigned pueblos to the various Franciscan missionaries and took declarations of obedience and vassalage in a number of towns. He sent one of his captains, Marcos Farfán de los Godos, to explore the mines that Espejo had discovered in the Verde valley. *Sargento mayor* (major) Vicente de Zaldívar was sent with some sixty soldiers to explore the plains. They saw a great many buffalo and ran into encampments of Querechos, who now were called *Vaqueros*. These Indians asked Zaldívar for aid against their enemies, the Jumanos. It would seem that the enmity between the Querechos and Teyas of Coronado's time still lived among their descendants. It is not clear how far Zaldívar penetrated into the plains, but he probably reached as far east as the Canadian River valley in what is now the western Texas Panhandle.

The Indian population of the Rio Grande and Pecos valleys in 1598 has been a matter of some disagreement. I suggest that in Oñate's day there may have been some forty thousand Native Americans in this area, perhaps a 20 percent decrease from the Coronado period. The population would decline steadily during the seventeenth century. At the time of the Pueblo Revolt in 1680 there may have been fifteen thousand Indians in the upper Rio Grande and upper Pecos drainages.

For the most part the Pueblos capitulated to Oñate and his army with scarcely a whimper. Even Pecos, which received its missionaries on July 25, accepted the new rule. One notable exception was Acoma. This proud and confident pueblo had been read the Act of Obedience and Homage in late October. It may have taken a little while for the implications of this act to sink in. At any rate, when the campmaster, Juan de Zaldívar, arrived with a party of thirty men on December 4, he was allowed onto the fortresslike Acoma mesa and then suddenly attacked. Thirteen Spaniards were killed, including Zaldívar and two of his officers.

A retaliatory party of some seventy men was quickly organized under the sargento mayor, Vicente de Zaldívar, reaching Acoma on January 21, 1599. In a battle that lasted at least into a second day and perhaps into a third, the Spaniards managed to overrun the village. About five hundred Acoma Indians were captured, with Indian casualties estimated at from six hundred to eight hundred. In 1601, Luís Gasco de Velasco, treasurer of the expedition, accused Zaldívar of murdering many Acomas after they had surrendered by throwing them off the cliffs. Then Zaldívar ordered the pueblo to be set ablaze, and a number of Indians, especially women and children, lost their lives in the fire. It is not clear how many Spanish soldiers died in the attack.

In a so-called trial held at Santo Domingo in February 1599, all male Acomas over the age of twenty-five were sentenced to have one foot cut off and to endure twenty years of servitude; males between the ages of twelve and twenty-five and all women over twelve were sentenced to servitude without mutilation. According to later testimony, twenty-four Acoma natives had their feet severed. The captives were distributed among the officers and soldiers of the expedition. Boys and girls under twelve years seem to have been apportioned out to various monasteries in New Spain to be taught Christianity. Men and women too old to be effective servants were subsequently freed and "entrusted to the Indians of the province of the Querechos that they may support them and may not allow them to leave their pueblos." Two bystanders from the Hopi area who happened to be at Acoma had their right hands cut off and were sent home as a warning.

It would seem that some of the children were actually sent to Mexico. At least, Gaspar de Villagrá, one of the captains and the poet of the expedition, claimed that he personally took sixty or more young girls to Mexico City to be distributed among various convents. The older Indians who were handed over to local Querechos probably quickly made their way back to Acoma. As early as Espejo's time (and probably for a decade or more before that) these Querechos, perhaps ancestral Navajos, had been living in the vicinity of Acoma and had friendly relations with the Acoma Indians.

It is also likely that at least some of the enslaved people soon escaped and went back to the Acoma mesa, which may have lain unoccupied for only a few months. There seems to have been no contact between Acomas and Spaniards for a number of years, and Acoma was not included in the encomiendas, the granting of which began with Oñate's successor, Governor Pedro de Peralta, founder of the city of Santa Fe. Indeed, Acoma seems to have been something of a refuge area for Indians escaping the exactions of church and state. It was not until the 1620s, perhaps as late as 1629, that a mission was firmly established at Acoma. By that time the mesa had been largely resettled.

Unimpressed by the Spaniards' ferocious treatment of the Acoma Indians, the Tompiro pueblos now rose in rebellion. Trouble began in 1599 when attempts by Oñate's soldiers to obtain blankets and other provisions from the Tompiros led to the Spaniards' killing a number of natives of the area. A major explosion, probably in the winter of 1601, was set off by the murder of two renegade Spaniards at Abó. A retaliatory attack by Oñate left a number of Tompiro Indians dead and many more captured, although these escaped fairly quickly. This may have been the attack described by the treasurer of the expedition, Luís Gasco de Velasco. According to Velasco, more than nine hundred Indians were killed, three of their pueblos were burned, and two hundred prisoners were taken. Since Velasco writes of a pueblo "belonging to the Jumanos," one of the towns was presumably Humanas, now called Gran Quivira. Although Velasco does not identify it by name, another victimized town was Abó.

New colonists for the New Mexico province arrived at the end of 1600. Oñate explored widely, reaching as far northeast as central Kansas and as far southwest as the lower Colorado River. His governance of the province, however, came under increasing attack both from within the colony—by friars and colonists—and from officials in Mexico City and Spain. On August 24, 1607, Oñate submitted his resignation and warned the viceroy that his settlers were planning to leave New Mexico the following year unless relief came in the form of reinforcements and supplies. For several months in 1607 and 1608 the fate of the Spanish province of New Mexico hung in the balance. Then, in December 1608, the announcement of returning Fray Lázaro Ximénez that seven thousand Indians had been baptized and many thousands more were ready for baptism tipped the scales. In January 1609 the viceregal authorities decided to continue the province, if on a reduced scale, with an end to expansion beyond the Pueblo area.

In 1609 Pedro de Peralta was appointed governor with orders to reorganize the colony. As part of that reorganization, Peralta moved his capital from San Gabriel de Yungue in the Tewa area to a more central and defensible area on the Santa Fe River. The villa of Santa Fe dates from the spring of 1610 though it may have been built on a slightly earlier settlement made in 1607 or 1608 by one of Oñate's officers, Juan Martínez de Montoya. Peralta's villa contained not only official buildings but also houses and gardens for Spanish residents and a barrio or district called Analco on the south side of the Santa Fe River for Mexican (probably mainly Tlaxcalan) Indians who had accompanied the colonizing expedition. Peralta and the Spaniards faced a large, restless Pueblo population, uncooperative and unhappy but for the moment passive and afraid. The missionaries moved rapidly to consolidate their hold on the Pueblos, and civilian settlements and ranches were established up and down the Rio Grande. The next seventy years would make an indelible mark on the human world of the Rio Grande.

CHAPTER EIGHTEEN

A Century of Change

 Spanish domination of the upper Rio Grande during the seventeenth century was harsh and generally uncompromising. The most powerful force operating directly on the Indians was that of the missionaries. Franciscan control of the pueblos commenced the same year as Oñate's invasion, various pueblos having been assigned to specific missionaries. But progress was slow in the first decade of the new century. The New Mexico undertaking flagged, and the original ten missionaries shrank to two or three. Missionizing during the later part of the Oñate period seems to have come pretty much to a standstill, in spite of the claim by Fray Ximénez in 1608 that there had been seven thousand converts.

In 1610, nine missionaries arrived with Governor Peralta. Two years later an additional eight missionaries reached the new mission province, and another seven in 1616 or early 1617. With their arrival, the missionizing effort developed rapidly. By 1616, missionaries resided at several of the Keresan and Tewa towns and at two in Tiguex. In addition, there were a number of *visitas,* smaller mission churches where services were performed on a visiting basis by friars from the nearest permanent mission.

That same year the New Mexico missions, centered at Santo Domingo Pueblo, were given the administrative status of *custodia,* a ranking one step below that of full ecclesiastical province. As it turned out, the New Mexico Franciscan custodia was never made a province but remained always under the control of the Province of the Holy Gospel in Spain. In the early days, however, the desire to be something greater ran strong. Alonso de Benavides, the brilliant and ambitious *custos,* or head of the custodia, was appointed in October 1623 (though he did not arrive in New Mexico until January 1626).

Plate 24. Spaniards among the Jemez. Early seventeenth-century ruins of the Franciscan mission at Guisewa, a few miles from modern Jemez Pueblo. Photograph courtesy Museum of New Mexico, neg. no. 6400.

Benavides served until the fall of 1629, and then, returning to Spain, he advertised New Mexico in a way that might make a modern public-relations person jealous. Benavides dreamed of establishing a mission see in New Mexico with himself as the first bishop. This grandiose plan never came to fruition.

Although he is undoubtedly the best known religious figure in New Mexico at the beginning of the mission period, Benavides was actually less important to the overall mission effort than was Estevan de Perea, who had first come to New Mexico in 1610. Except for a few years in central Mexico in the 1620s, Perea spent his entire time in the new custodia, finally dying there in 1638. Perea brought an additional thirty friars when he arrived from his Mexico sojourn to replace Benavides as custos in 1629. By the early 1630s, the missions had expanded to forty-six friars in thirty-five missions and their attached visitas, and all corners of the Pueblo world had been filled in. The non-native population of New Mexico in 1630 has been estimated at about 750, and it included Spaniards, Mexican Indians, blacks, and various mixtures of the three. This population would grow very slowly, reaching a num-

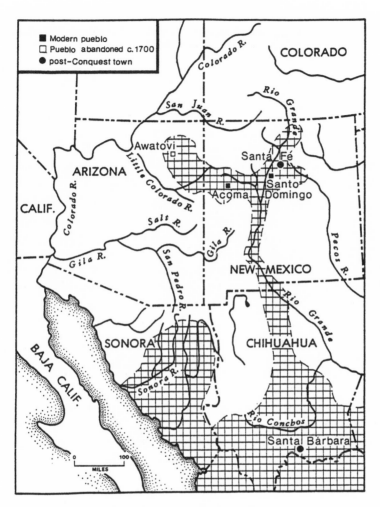

Map 18. Spanish control of the Southwest, 1680.

ber between two and three thousand (estimates range from 2,500 to 2,900) in
the fatal year 1680 (map 18).

Perea was a man of vigorous, even violent, opinions, and he made himself
a power in New Mexico. In 1611 or 1612 a rift developed between the Franciscans and Governor Peralta, the beginning of a church-state power struggle
that would dominate New Mexico politics for the next seventy years. Perea
was involved in this struggle, for he served as Peralta's jailer after the governor was arrested by Fray Ysidro Ordóñez, the mission head. Ordóñez

claimed, falsely it would seem, that he was acting under a warrant from the Spanish Inquisition. This attempt simply foreshadowed the use of actual inquisitorial powers that were given to Perea in 1630—powers that would be used by the missionaries as a powerful weapon of last resort in their struggle with the civil authorities.

The reason for this struggle was primarily economic, although personalities, personal ambitions, and various other side issues often exacerbated the conflict. Because New Mexico was a mission province, the church considered the function of the state to be primarily that of protecting and forwarding the missions' work. The governors and their entourages, however, had rather different plans for the province. There was money to be made in New Mexico, partly from trade but also, importantly, from the exploitation of Pueblo Indians held in encomienda. As the century wore on, *estancias,* or ranches, were developed for cattle raising and sheep herding. Sheep expanded with explosive rapidity. The sheep were *churros,* a Spanish breed somewhat deficient in wool but well adapted to the semidesert conditions of the Southwest. The missions pioneered the raising of sheep, as is indicated by a document of the Santa Fe cabildo in 1639 which states that "each friar possesses one or two thousand sheep, whereas there are few citizens who have as many as five hundred." A later, partial count of herds at certain of the missions makes it clear that by the late 1660s there were vast numbers of sheep, certainly many tens of thousands. Probably the majority of these animals were owned by the various missions, but there also were large flocks on the estancias of Spanish settlers.

By assigning encomiendas, Spanish governmental officials helped pay for military operations. *Encomenderos,* the owners of encomiendas, were obligated to provide military service to the Crown and formed the officer corps for the local militia and the work forces of Pueblo Indians. Occasionally the militia would be called on for guard service in outlying pueblos. For their duties the encomenderos were given a specific amount of tribute from the pueblos they held. They were forbidden to live in these pueblos or to draft Indians for personal services—but both of these prohibitions were apparently widely ignored in New Mexico.

Trade was another vital necessity to the governor and his party. A great deal of this trade was directed to the Great Plains. Important incoming trade items were antelope, deer, and bison skins and enslaved nomadic Indians. Many of the latter were sold in Chihuahua for work in the mines and ranches, and slaves were occasionally sent as gifts to Mexico City by the governor and the wealthier New Mexico settlers. Large numbers of slaves, however, also remained in New Mexico. In the eighteenth century they became the basis of the *genízaro* group. Genízaros (the word is derived from Turkish *yenicheri,* compare English *janizary*) were the descendants of these nomadic captives who were eventually absorbed into the New Mexican population and were settled in border communities on the Chama, the Pecos, and at various points along the Rio Grande.

Throughout the seventeenth century the civil government drafted Pueblo Indians to assist in these slaving raids onto the plains. The practice certainly elevated the office of war leader and, by giving the Pueblos some training in European tactics and logistics, probably was a factor in their success when they finally rose in rebellion. It also had the advantage for Pueblo soldiers that they, too, could take slaves, who were then often traded to Spanish settlers for horses or cattle.

Other goods going south—some to Chihuahua, some to central Mexico—included salt, piñon nuts, coarse cotton and wool cloth (much of it woven by Pueblo Indians), and livestock, primarily horses, cattle, and sheep. Most of the goods seem to have gone with the great mission supply-wagon trains that traversed the long road from Mexico to Santa Fe with a round trip every three years. These same trains brought both necessities and luxury goods to the missions and the settlers.

In an attempt to regulate Pueblo life and protect the new subjects of the Crown from abuse, the authorities in New Spain instituted a certain amount of self-rule for the native towns. A series of regulations promulgated in 1620 set pueblo elections for local officials annually on January 1, with the stipulation that neither the civil authorities nor the Franciscans should interfere or even be present. The economic use of Pueblo people by encomenderos and missionaries—especially the use of women as servants in Spanish houses—was strictly regulated. Making the Indians támenes or burden bearers was absolutely forbidden. Cutting the hair of Indians for minor offenses was also forbidden. Long hair in certain situations had and has ceremonial meaning for Pueblo men, and it seems that the missionaries were using every excuse to clip the heads of their new parishioners. One result in the early years of such hair cutting and other abuses was that recalcitrant Indians fled to the freedom of Acoma.

There is no question but that governmental authorities in Spain and Mexico City were making a serious attempt to protect the native New Mexicans. Their first objective, however, was to Christianize the Pueblos and, to whatever extent possible, the surrounding Apaches and other nomads. So the missionaries had to be given considerable latitude. In addition, the

seventeenth-century government of New Spain was chronically short of
money. There was hope that both the Franciscan custodia and the civil province of New Mexico would eventually pay for themselves, and this, too,
blunted reform measures aimed at protecting the Pueblo population.

The feud between the missions and the secular government raged on
throughout much of the seventeenth century. Several governors were
hounded by missionaries and by factions within the Spanish secular population. One governor was murdered, others were tried by the Holy Office of
the Inquisition. The Pueblo Indians were caught between the contending
parties. Each side, missionary and governor, accused the other of exploiting
and brutalizing the Indians.

Again the quarrel was a matter of different approaches. Whereas the civil
authorities dealt with the Pueblos mainly in economic terms, the Franciscans
were primarily interested in remaking Pueblo culture to fit into the mission
pattern. Certain new European materials and ideas were eagerly accepted by
the Indians: iron tools such as axes and hoes, and new building techniques
such as Spanish-introduced fireplaces and adobe ovens. More advanced
methods for making adobe bricks appeared, although there seems to have
been little modification in house types generally.

Spanish animals were also quickly accepted, especially sheep, the raising of
which was a mission specialty. Cattle were somewhat less popular, but the
horse, a prestige animal, gradually filtered both to the Pueblos and the nomadic Apaches and Navajos. Spanish chickens also seem to have been a seventeenth-century introduction, though of course they competed with the native domesticate, the turkey.

Sheep were important for their meat but especially for their wool. The
Rio Grande Pueblos had grown cotton since prehistoric times, but the plant
is somewhat marginal in the upper Rio Grande and probably was not grown
much beyond Cochiti, the northernmost Keresan pueblo. The churro breed
of sheep yields wool that is coarse but easy to work by hand, producing a
rough-textured but serviceable cloth. The spread of sheep during the seventeenth century, however, did lead to a considerable amount of overgrazing
with contingent arroyo cutting. Another animal that made a significant impact on Pueblo life was the burro or donkey. This beast of burden allowed
much more efficient utilization of wood for building and for cooking and
heating, especially now that metal axes were available for tree cutting. This
practice eventually altered the ancient balance between humans and forest.

There were new food crops: wheat, cabbages, lettuce, chilis, onions, rad-
ishes, cucumbers, peas, chickpeas, and exotic varieties of maize. Peach, plum,

apricot, and cherry trees had an early seventeenth-century introduction and became extremely popular with the Pueblo Indians. As we have already seen, melons, important and widespread plants among the Pueblos, may have arrived with Coronado. Wheat was a very early domesticate. The first planting at Yungue in 1599 was of seven *fanegas* (about 62 acres) of spring wheat. Two years later, in 1601, the settlers at Yungue planted about 450 acres of irrigated land and produced between 3,500 and 4,000 bushels of wheat. This grain quickly became important, especially in the Tewa region. Wheat eventually found its way into the ceremonial life of the Rio Grande Pueblos, and today the grain plays a role in planting ceremonials. Whether wheat achieved this ceremonial status as early as the seventeenth century is not certain, for it was at this precise time that a major and sustained attack was made on the entire religious and ceremonial complex of the Pueblos.

The destruction of Pueblo religion took the highest priority among seventeenth-century New Mexico missionaries. There was no question in the minds of the Franciscans that in order to make good Christians out of the Pueblo people, they first had to wipe out pagan ways. Because Pueblo social and political systems were thoroughly interwoven with religion, all these things had to be done away with. The missionaries directed their attacks toward the great ceremonials with special vigor. To the Franciscans, the masked kachina dances were satanic celebrations that must be ruthlessly suppressed.

Pueblo languages, though not actually forbidden, tended to be discouraged. In other parts of the New World—for example, in central Mexico— the first missionaries had learned the native languages and used them extensively in teaching Christian doctrine. This was especially true of the Franciscans, who also made attempts to isolate the Indians from Spanish settlers. Although their philosophical background was different, the Jesuits continued to use this approach until their expulsion from the New World in the mid-eighteenth century.

There was nothing to prevent this happening in New Mexico, and certainly some of the friars in the Rio Grande area did learn Tanoan or Keresan. By the seventeenth century, however, the Franciscan order had largely accepted the idea of acculturating Indian populations to Spanish language and culture. In addition, the Pueblo area had several distinct languages, and missionaries were moved around a great deal. So in New Mexico the missionaries largely gave instruction in Spanish. It was the most practical way of handling the language situation and it certainly speeded up Hispanicization.

The Franciscans in central Mexico in the first decades after Cortés's conquest had especially targeted the children of the Aztecs and Tlaxcalans for intense and continuous training. This strategy was employed along the Rio Grande as well, with considerable success. For a Pueblo Indian born after about 1630—in some cases after 1610—the mission effect was pervasive. The child attended church services, learned the rites and rituals of Christianity, was taught Spanish, and had constantly drummed into his or her head that the Pueblo fertility and weather-control ceremonies were wicked and depraved. These same ceremonies, when held at all, usually had to be conducted in secrecy. After two generations under this kind of attack, it is amazing that so much native religion survived in 1680.

The Pueblos, of course, fought back, and religious officers at the various towns were at the forefront of the struggle. From time to time they found a curious ally in the person of the governor. The governors, generally, had a stake in exploiting the Indians but an even larger stake in limiting the power of the clergy in New Mexico. All in all, they were not a particularly pious lot. One early governor, Juan de Eulate, refused to use civil authority to suppress ceremonial dances and what the friars called "idol worship." Governor López de Mendizábal a few years later actually encouraged Indian dances.

The missionaries had considerable latitude for disciplinary actions against Pueblo members. Whipping, usually carried out by a *fiscal* (a low-ranking native officer) on the orders of the missionary, was a common method of punishment, and there is considerable evidence that some Franciscans overstepped their bounds. A particularly savage case was reported at Hopi, where Father Salvador de Guerra flogged a man to death and regularly whipped boys and girls, often for trivial offenses, and followed the beatings with an application of hot turpentine. Guerra was also charged with forcing Indians to weave cotton and woolen cloth, whipping them if quotas were not met. Guerra was admonished and sent back to Mexico, but he returned a short time later and within a few years was appointed an officer in the New Mexico branch of the Inquisition. The practice of beating certainly did not diminish. Indians were flogged for missing mass, for infidelity, for casual sexual encounters, and for a variety of other minor offenses. Whipping was sometimes combined with hair cutting in spite of prohibitions against such practices.

Another kind of abuse was that of friars' sexual misconduct with their Pueblo parishioners. At least, a continuing series of accusations was made by both Pueblo Indians and certain of the civil authorities about sexual irregularities. If the accusers are to be believed, such abuse was endemic in some mission stations. We should be cautious, however, about accepting these accusations at face value. The horror with which the Franciscans held sexual irregularities and the rigor with which Native Americans were punished for sexual infractions made it very tempting to bring this particular kind of charge against the missionaries themselves. A fair judgment might be that with so much smoke there was probably some fire, but not a raging conflagration. In all probability, the irregularities occurred mainly in isolated stations like Taos and the Tompiro towns and involved only a small fraction of the friars.

Some governors attempted to alleviate the severity of high-handed punishments dealt out by the clergy, as well as extortions by the settlers. Governor Bernardo López de Mendizábal, who took office in 1659, seems often to have taken the side of the Pueblo Indians. One of his first actions upon taking office was to increase the rate of pay for Indian labor from one-half real per day to one real, plus rations. López later stated that he had heard stories even before coming to New Mexico of the shamefully meager compensation given Pueblo Indians. His action, however, was unpopular with many of the encomenderos and estancia owners.

Parenthetically, a real was worth about one-eighth of a peso, the peso having a book value of roughly one ounce of silver. Probably in New Mexico, where coins were scarce, much payment was made in produce or handled in some sort of bookkeeping operation with no money actually changing hands. Establishing the peso in terms of modern buying power is very difficult, but in the early eighteenth century one ewe sheep was considered to be worth two pesos, and a ram, four pesos. Prices in Mendizábal's time were probably comparable.

Our information on seventeenth-century Native American wages is not very good, but records for the seventeenth century elsewhere in the New World suggest that the New Mexico wage of one-half real was abnormally low. In any case, pay of a half-real per day did not go very far. Most Pueblo workers in pre-López times would probably never make more than ten to fifteen pesos per year, and since work tended to be seasonal, normally a great deal less. Out of their wages, people would have had to supply their own food and contribute to the support of their families. This latter obligation varied a great deal, for it depended on the interlocking kin system of the Pueblos and the extent to which any given person functioned in the Pueblo economic structure. The sweatshop level of pay did make warfare on the eastern frontier attractive to Pueblo men, for an enslaved Apache girl or boy could bring as much as forty pesos—several years' wages.

During López's term of office a Pueblo man named Esteban Clemente, who had some form of leadership over the eastern Tiwa and the Tompiro pueblos, became a very successful trader to the Apaches in the western plains and a power broker among the Tompiros. López worked closely with this Pueblo leader, lending him goods for the Apache trade, probably on some sort of profit-sharing basis. Clemente is an interesting character who lived at Abó and who was described as "native Indian governor" over the Salinas pueblos. One document indicates that he was governor of Pecos as well, and another calls him "governor of the pueblos of Las Salinas and Tanos." Clemente, who spoke several Indian languages and could write as well as speak Spanish, was favorably quoted by both sides in the church-state controversy. For example, he served as interpreter for Nicolás Aguilar, López's alcalde mayor for the Salinas region, in a case where one Indian woman accused Fray Diego de Parraga, priest at Tajique, of rape and a second woman charged Parraga with fathering her child. On the other hand, in a letter of November 30, 1660, Clemente gave a deposition in which he characterized the kachina dances in pejorative terms and accused Aguilar of having "commanded" the Indians to dance the kachinas. No accusations were made against López de Mendizábal.

It is dangerous to put too much reliance on Clemente's deposition for it is not clear to what extent the statement was dictated or suggested by the Franciscans. Clemente seems to have been trying to walk a tightrope in a period when any successful Pueblo leader had to dissemble and try to balance conflicting factions—the missionaries, Pueblo conservatives, Indians favorable to the new teachings, the governor's party, and the settlers.

In any case, the Tompiro pueblos were in particular turmoil around 1660, and accusations of malfeasance on the part of both mission fathers and secular officials were especially rife. Alcalde mayor Aguilar was constantly involved in trying to stop cases of Indian mistreatment by missionaries. At least, this was Aguilar's position. The friars counterclaimed that Aguilar abused Indians who were performing religious duties, something the alcalde mayor vigorously denied.

López's public highlighting of cases of immorality among the missionaries created strong antagonisms, partly because of the nature of the offenses but also because in the eyes of the Franciscans it threatened clerical control over their own personnel. Still, it was perhaps López's policy of allowing Pueblo Indians to publicly perform their ritual dances that caused the most hostile reaction from the Franciscans. This policy undercut the vital missionary project of destroying native religion lock, stock, and barrel.

A new governor, Diego de Peñalosa, took office in 1661 and arrested López. A *residencia* (a hearing on the activities of López while governor) was begun, and in 1662 the *audiencia*—the judicial and legislative body sitting in Mexico City—handed down its verdict. Though upholding the ecclesiastical privileges of the Franciscans, it did refuse to censure López for his attempts to allow Pueblo ceremonial dances. The Franciscans now played their Inquisition card, and López de Mendizábal's trial was shifted to a higher and darker court. On April 10, 1663, he was thrown in prison by the Holy Office of the Inquisition. His trial was still dragging on when López died on September 16, 1664.

It is difficult to evaluate the short rule of López de Mendizábal in terms of what it meant to the native population of the Rio Grande. He has gotten a bad press from latter-day scholars, who as a group have generally accepted the Franciscan version of events. In the missionary view, López was a heartless exploiter of the Pueblos and a diabolical enemy of the church. Documents analyzed by the historian France V. Scholes, however, tell a somewhat more complex story. Some of López's activities could certainly be faulted. Like all the seventeenth-century governors, he was interested in making a profit out of his office. He was very much an entrepreneur, shipping sugar, chocolate, and European manufactured goods to be resold in New Mexico. He also seems to have sometimes been remiss in paying for contract work, whether performed by Pueblo Indians or Spaniards. And he was often less than tactful, thus creating enemies in the close-knit New Mexico colony.

Still, the governor was generally sympathetic to the Pueblo cause, attempting to control and lessen the harsh treatment dealt out by the missionaries, especially their excessive use of corporal punishment. He also resisted the friars' habit of drafting Indian labor for personal service and for mission-organized processing of cloth. Something that outraged the missionaries was that López often remitted the brutal punishments the Franciscans dealt out for Indian couples living in adultery. López argued before the Inquisitors that such persons were often willing to marry and that was a better solution than whipping. His unilateral doubling of Indian wages can best be explained as genuine altruism because López, as a major labor contractor, stood to lose by such a decision.

He also gave the Indians some protection in practicing their religious rituals. It may be that the governor realized the dangers of the repressive mission policy, though probably he did not foresee a major revolt. However, he honestly seems to have looked on the kachina dances as harmless, eye-pleasing folk ceremonials. A case can be made that López de Mendizábal and his wife (an educated Italian woman who brought Ariosto's *Orlando Furioso* to New Mexico for reading pleasure) were more sophisticated and urbane than were the New Mexico settlers and clergy. Obviously, the governor operated to some degree from motives of self-interest, but his liking for and interest in protecting the Pueblo population seem to have been genuine.

At any rate, tension between the Indians and the missionaries and settlers was growing year by year. Sometime around 1640 the Indians of Taos killed their resident priest. A rebellion at Jemez in 1649, in conjunction with Apachean speakers, involved the murder of a Spaniard. The revolt was put down and twenty-nine Indians were hanged, others flogged, and still others imprisoned. The following year various Tewa towns were involved with Apaches in a plot to kill the local friars and resident soldiers. Around 1653 there was a general rebellion by two of the Tiguex towns, some Keresan towns, and the Jemez, in conjunction with Apache groups. This revolt was defeated and nine participants hanged.

Tensions were made all the worse by the fact that since Oñate's time, Pueblo population had been declining. As stated in chapter 17, the forty thousand eastern Pueblos that I estimate for Oñate's time had, by the last decades of the seventeenth century, dropped to perhaps fifteen thousand. Diseases, largely introduced by the Spaniards by way of the Camino Real, helped fuel this decline. These diseases are not as well documented as are the great Southwestern epidemics of the eighteenth century, but it seems likely that smallpox, probably certain of the "childhood diseases," and typhus were involved. Unfortunately, the newcomers could provide little or no remedy; the primitive European medical system proved hopelessly inadequate to the task.

The situation was exacerbated by a drought that lasted from 1667 to 1672. The missionaries attempted to alleviate famine conditions by freely giving out livestock and supplies from the mission stations, but they could not prevent tremendous suffering. Apache raids also began to pick up in intensity. At some point in the 1670s the Salinas region was largely deserted, and some of the outlying Zuni towns may have been abandoned too. The official Spanish governmental view, gained from reports by the governors and missionaries in New Mexico, was that Apache raids were to blame for these desertions. Raids may well have have been a factor, and drought certainly was. However, there is some reason to believe that by the 1660s and 1670s, scattered Pueblo revolts, especially in the outlying areas, were becoming endemic and the Pueblo population was simply moving away.

The precise events that led to the great Pueblo Revolt of 1680 began in 1675, when forty-seven religious leaders of the northern Rio Grande pueblos were arrested and charged with plotting to overthrow the government. Of these, three were executed and the rest brutally punished. Among the latter was a ceremonial leader from the Tewa pueblo of San Juan, a man named Popé. Determined on revenge, Popé eventually withdrew from San Juan to Taos, a pueblo that had been smoldering for decades. By the spring of 1680, if not before, Popé was constructing an alliance made up of the northern Tiwa, Tewa, Keresan, Tano, and Jemez pueblos along with Pecos, Zuni, and Hopi. Only the old Tiguex area and the Piro towns failed to join wholeheartedly in the rebellion. Popé's revolt had strong millenarian overtones, springing not only from the burden of Spanish rule but surely also from the losing struggle with disease and the attendant population decline. One promise given by the supernatural figures who "underwrote" the rebellion was that abundant health would return once the Spaniards were driven away.

Various Apaches and Navajos joined in the revolt. They were motivated by the chance to share in the vast Spanish herds, especially horses, that were beginning to change the culture of both the Southwest and the western Great Plains. Moreover, both Apaches and Navajos, with eighty years of organized slave raiding to remember, had their own reasons to hate the Spaniards. Even some people who were part of the Spanish cultural tradition may have aided in the Pueblo Revolt. The Franciscan historian Fray Angelico Chavez suggested a number of years ago that members of the mixed black and Mexican-Indian Naranjo family, whose founder had come as a freed slave to New Mexico in 1600, were importantly involved in planning the revolt. After all, slaves and servants, both black and Indian, had no great stake in the future of a Spanish New Mexico, and a number of them may have drifted to the Pueblo side.

But basically the Pueblo Revolt was a native uprising, led by Pueblo religious leaders and war captains and directed most violently against the Franciscan missionaries. It certainly had wide support among the Pueblo population. Extraordinary factors in the revolt were its careful planning, extreme secrecy, and the acceptance by other Pueblos of the leadership of Popé and his lieutenants.

The revolt was planned for August 11, 1680. On August 9, however, two messengers from the Tewa town of Tesuque, near Santa Fe, who were carrying detailed plans of the uprising were arrested by Spanish authorities. From Tesuque, word went out that hostilities must start immediately, so August 10 saw a unified revolt beginning at dawn. By August 15 an Indian army had set siege to Santa Fe, and the governor of New Mexico, Antonio de Otermín, was trapped in the capital city. Handicapped by a thousand or so refugee

Spaniards and weakened by the continuing attacks of the united northern Pueblos, Otermín a few days later fought his way out of Santa Fe and moved south as rapidly as possible.

As I mentioned in chapter 17, there was also a considerable population of central Mexican Indians, possibly several hundred, living in the barrio of Analco in the southern part of Santa Fe. There is no evidence that this group favored the revolt. Presumably the Analco contingent retreated south with Otermín and were reckoned with the Europeans in the head count of escapees.

The Tiguex town of Isleta was in the hands of Otermín's lieutenant governor, Alonso García of the Rio Abajo district. Once the escaping settlers moved south of Isleta, attacks by the rebellious northern Pueblos slackened, allowing the majority of the colonists to escape to the mission area of El Paso. The southernmost Tiwas and the Piros for the most part fled with the Spaniards, fearing retaliation for their lack of support for the Pueblo cause. Twenty-one of the thirty-three missionaries in New Mexico in 1680 were killed, along with about 380 colonists.

The unity of the diverse pueblos in 1680 was remarkable, but it was not to last. The centrifugal tendencies that had kept the pueblos from uniting to face Coronado were still operating in 1680. Mechanisms of government that could function over time, space, and diversity were simply not in place. The Pueblo Indians might have succeeded had they copied the Spanish governmental structure, appointing or electing a pan-Pueblo governor, regional alcalde mayores, and other intertribal officers and investing these people with real power. But the Spanish offices introduced in the early seventeenth century were utilized only at the village level, and interpueblo cohesion maintained itself, when at all, only along certain linguistic lines. Crosscutting organizations such as the kachina cult, the war societies, and the curing and clown societies, which had functioned so well in uniting the large Pueblo IV towns, simply were not an adequate framework for Pueblo-wide organizations. In addition, the Navajo and Apache allies maintained their own, different vision of the future and had no interest in bolstering a strong Pueblo nation.

After twelve years, the Spaniards came back. Partly their return was a matter of geopolitics, for the Spanish Crown harbored exaggerated fears of the French, who were beginning a push into the lower Mississippi River valley. Convinced that the French incursion might threaten Spain in the world political arena, the Crown decided it had to reassert itself in the Southwest. The reconquest, which began in 1692 under an able Spanish commander named Diego de Vargas, was not easy. There was savage fighting, especially in 1696, but by the first years of the eighteenth century the eastern Pueblos were once again under Spanish rule. Only distant Hopi managed to escape the Spanish net. All the Rio Grande pueblos were reoccupied and remained under foreign control—first that of Spain, then Mexico, and finally the United States.

In candidly discussing the shortcomings of Spanish rule, especially missionary rule, I emphatically do *not* wish to perpetuate the "Black Legend" that the Spaniards were monsters in their treatment of native peoples. Compared to the colonial activities of the English, Dutch, and French, Spain's record in the New World is a good one. The Spanish Crown from the time of Isabella made serious and sustained efforts to protect native populations and guarantee their welfare. Many Spanish laws were models of humane legislation for their time. If one compares the Spanish attitude toward native peoples in seventeenth-century New Mexico with attitudes of the Puritan settlers of New England during the same period, the Spaniards look very good indeed. New Mexico saw none of the English mixture of hypocritical piety and ruthless underlying policy that had as its final aim the destruction or removal of all native groups. The reconquest led by Vargas was far from being a reenactment of New England's King Philip's War (1675–76) and its aftermath, the devastation of regional Indian populations. Spain's relatively benign attitude toward native peoples owed a great deal to the pressures of churchmen and missionary groups.

However, I equally wish to avoid the habit of certain modern-day apologists who, when they criticize the Spaniards in New Mexico, make an absolute distinction between the good missionary and the bad governor. Missionaries are cast not only as self-sacrificing teachers of Native Americans but also as their staunch and fearless defenders against rapacious settlers and secular officials.

The missionaries, specifically the Franciscans in New Mexico, numbered many courageous and dedicated men, committed to the welfare of their charges. Still, as we have seen, the record of both lay and missionary groups in New Mexico was spotty. Individual governors and encomenderos *and* individual missionaries all too often were capable of cruelty and greed.

We especially need to understand and explain the fact that it was against the *missionaries,* not the settlers or the governors, that the Pueblo Indians directed their special fury. I think the reason can be found in one activity that was absolutely central and crucial to the missionary program, especially in seventeenth-century New Mexico. Whether their individual feelings and actions toward Pueblo Indians were kind or cruel, all the missionaries were united in what amounted to cultural genocide. For the Indians' own welfare, to save their very souls, the Franciscans set out to destroy all vestiges of native

Plate 25. Corn dance at Santo Domingo Pueblo, about 1890. Photograph courtesy Museum of New Mexico, neg. no. 109020.

religion. The friars saw only too clearly that in order to eliminate Pueblo religion it would be necessary to cut away the innermost fabric of Pueblo life. It was in an attempt to prevent loss of identity at the most basic level—a veritable struggle against cultural death—that the Pueblos directed their violent reactions toward missionary teaching and missionary control.

This frantic resistance to the destruction of their lifeways served the Pueblos well in the long run. Returning Spaniards lost their taste for some of the extreme behavior of the seventeenth century. Eighteenth-century mission policy was much more tolerant of native "superstitions," as the ceremonials increasingly were called. As the non-Pueblo population grew and the hold of the missions weakened, Pueblo Indians in their daily lives were increasingly left alone. The modern religious synthesis among Rio Grande Pueblos is a complex of traits, some age-old and some from prehistoric Mexico, the whole interlaced with Spanish folk Catholicism. Curiously, the kachina cult for which the Rio Grande Pueblos fought so valiantly in 1680 has lost some of its content along the Rio Grande and is found in its greatest ceremonial glory only among the western Pueblos of Zuni and Hopi. It is not clear why this should be. Possibly, competing colorful and emotion-laden ceremonies drawn from Catholicism have proved to be acceptable substitutes for the fully functioning kachina cult among the Rio Grande Pueblos.

The heartland of the Rio Grande Pueblos includes descendants of the old provinces of Tiguex, Quirix, and the Tewa, Towa, and northern Tiwa towns—regions where Pueblo religion is still vital. The sociopolitical systems of the Native Americans in this heartland are still recognizably Puebloan but have been much modified by centuries of European contact. The heartland languages endure, both Keresan and the Tanoan tongues. Technology derived from Spaniards, Mexicans, and Anglo-Americans was from early times gracefully accepted, and it has been used to better deal with economic and social problems that lie deep in Pueblo history.

For the most part, the outliers of the Rio Grande Pueblo world are gone. The Tompiro pueblos crumbled even before the Pueblo Revolt, and their fellow Piro towns are also deserted. No one has spoken Piro for many years, and too little of the language's vocabulary and grammar remains for proper study by linguists. Pecos was deserted by the late 1830s, its people being absorbed by linguistic kinfolk at Jemez. The Tano peoples are scattered, some to Hopi and others to Tewa kin on the Rio Grande. Even in the heartland, the southern Tiwa—the historic Tiguex—are very acculturated, although the Tiwa language is still spoken. The northern Tiwa Indians at Taos and Picurís have also undergone considerable acculturation.

Still, the Rio Grande Pueblos maintain some inner strength, some notion of being, that holds together the deep heart of their culture. The fertility and rain ceremonies go on, season after season. It is true that they are now interspersed with Christian elements, but the older gods and ceremonies are basic. The central core of Pueblo ceremonialism is very much alive—indeed, during the last thirty or forty years it has undergone something of a renaissance. The Pueblos may never again dominate the world of the Rio Grande; a second Pueblo Revolt is no longer feasible. But the spirit of the Pueblo world is still strong in northern New Mexico and that spirit will enrich the lives of all New Mexicans for many years to come.

Sources and
Commentary

Introduction

A recent work by R. A. Gutiérrez, *When Jesus Came, the Corn Mothers Went Away: Marriage, Sexuality, and Power in New Mexico, 1500–1846* (Stanford University Press, 1991) takes a very different orientation from mine. Gutiérrez describes an aboriginal Pueblo people for whom religion involved a dynamic tension between the sexes. According to Gutiérrez, women's role in the pueblos had its supernatural reflection in the Corn Mothers, female deities who were arbiters of sexual and social behavior. Into this setting came the Spaniards, with their arrogant, male-oriented society and religion, and the power struggle that followed involved sexual as well as socioeconomic politics. In Gutiérrez's view, the Pueblo Indians saw the Spaniards as a species of kachina or divine being, and so Pueblo women offered the newcomers intimate favors, "cooling" and transforming them by the power of their sexuality.

Gutiérrez offers a number of provocative ideas. Unfortunately, his use of source materials often leaves something to be desired. For a detailed analysis of Gutiérrez's work by Native American scholars, see "Commentaries on *When Jesus Came . . .*" compiled by the Native American Studies Center, University of New Mexico (*American Indian Culture and Research Journal*, vol. 17, no. 3, 1993, pp. 141–77).

Chapter 1

On Pueblo Indian names for the Rio Grande and Rio Chama, see J. P. Harrington, *Ethnogeography of the Tewa Indians* (Annual Report of the Bureau of American Ethnography, Washington, D.C., no. 29, 1907–1908, pp. 79, 95, 100). Navajo names for the Rio Grande are courtesy of Pearl Sunrise,

Museum of New Mexico. Sixteenth- and seventeenth-century Spanish names for the Rio Grande are given in G. P. Hammond and A. Rey, *Narratives of the Coronado Expedition, 1540–42* (University of New Mexico Press, 1940, pp. 183, 292); *The Rediscovery of New Mexico* (University of New Mexico Press, 1966, pp. 74, 76, 77, 160, 162–65, 211, 250, 306, passim); and *Don Juan de Oñate, Colonizer of New Mexico* (University of New Mexico Press, 1953, vol. I: pp. 311, 314, 330, 425, 480; vol. II: 624, 638, 812, 819, 1012, passim).

Sixteenth-century maps appear in A. E. Nordenskiöld, *Facsimile-Atlas to the Early History of Cartography* (Dover Publications, 1973). For eighteenth- and nineteenth-century Spanish-Mexican and American names for the river, see E. Adams and A. Chavez, *The Missions of New Mexico, 1776* (University of New Mexico Press, 1956, pp. 64, 84, 92, 111, 130, 144, 150, 160, 202, passim); R. H. Dillon, *Meriwether Lewis* (Coward McCann, New York, 1965, p. 50); M. Salinas, *Indians of the Rio Grande Delta* (University of Texas Press, 1990, pp. 181, 183, 185); and F. A. Wislizenus, *A Tour to Northern Mexico, 1846–47* (Rio Grande Press, Glorieta, N.M., 1969, pp. 26–27, endmap).

Chapter 2

For early observations on the Rio Grande and its tributaries, see R. Folansbee and H. J. Dean, *Water Resources of the Rio Grande Basin, 1888–1913* (United States Geological Survey, Water Supply Paper 358, 1915, pp. 98–141, 166–69, 414–15, 435, 440–43, 676); and W. E. Hale, L. J. Reiland, and J. P. Beverage, *Characteristics of the Water Supply in New Mexico* (New Mexico State Engineer, Technical Report 31, 1965, pp. 20, 44–45, 72). Information on general landforms, geology, climate, and topography is contained in J. L. Williams, ed., *New Mexico in Maps* (second edition, University of New Mexico Press, 1986); and P. W. Christiansen and F. E. Kottlowski, *Mosaic of New Mexico's Scenery, Rocks, and History* (State Bureau of Mines and Mineral Resources, Scenic Trips to the Geologic Past, no. 8, 1967).

For information on natural features, especially on flora and fauna, consult C. L. Riley, *The Frontier People* (University of New Mexico Press, 1987, pp. 218–21, 253–56). Additional information on plant life can be found in E. L. Little, *Southwestern Trees* (USDA Agricultural Handbook no. 9, 1968); R. C. Stebbins and H. D. Harrington, *Edible Native Plants of the Rocky Mountains* (University of New Mexico Press, 1967, pp. 53–103, passim); F. H. Elmore, *Shrubs and Trees of the Southwest Uplands* (Southwest Parks and Monuments Association, Popular Series no. 19, 1976); N. N. Dodge, *Flowers of the Southwest Deserts* (seventh edition, SPMA, Popular Series no. 4, 1969, pp. 9–108);

and P. M. Patrow, *Flowers of the Southwest Mesas* (fourth edition, SPMA, Popular Series no. 5, 1964, pp. 8–105).

For additional information on Southwestern fauna, see R. C. Stebbins, *Field Guide to Western Reptiles and Amphibians* (Houghton Mifflin, 1966); and G. Olin, *Mammals of the Southwestern Desert* (fourth edition, SPMA, Popular Series no. 8, 1970, pp. 11–107). For minerals, see S. A. Northrop, *Minerals of New Mexico* (revised edition, University of New Mexico Press, 1955, pp. 130–31, 200, 248–55, 314–15, 340–42, 380–85, 420–23, 464–65).

Chapter 3

An excellent overview of early New World cultures is given in J. D. Jennings, "Origins" (in *Ancient Native Americans*, J. D. Jennings, ed., W. H. Freeman Co., San Francisco, 1978, pp. 1–41). For early languages, see J. H. Greenberg, *Language in the Americas* (Stanford University Press, 1987, pp. 123, 144, 378–87); J. H. Greenberg, "The American Indian Language Controversy" (*Review of Archaeology*, vol. 11, no. 2, 1990, pp. 5–14); and J. H. Greenberg and M. Ruhlen, "Linguistic Origins of Native Americans" (*Scientific American*, vol. 267, no. 5, November 1992, pp. 94–99).

The mtDNA evidence for early Americans and its relationship to the Greenberg linguistic hypothesis is discussed in T. G. Schurr et al., "Amerindian Mitochondrial DNAs Have Rare Asian Mutations . . ." (*American Journal of Human Genetics*, vol. 46, 1990, pp. 613–23). The mtDNA comparison of Pima, Maya, and Ticuna Indians, as well as various Na-Dene peoples, is given by D. C. Wallace and A. Torroni, "American Indian Prehistory as Written in the Mitochondrial DNA: A Review" (*Human Biology*, vol. 64, no. 3, 1992, pp. 403–16). See also A. Torroni et al., "Native American Mitochondrial DNA Analysis Indicates that the Amerind and Nadene Populations Were Founded by Two Independent Migrations" (*Genetics*, vol. 130, 1992, pp. 153–62). For the size of the ancestral Amerind group, refer to Thomas H. Maugh, Los Angeles *Times*, July 28, 1990. I will say here that I consider the "four females" idea rather improbable, but the point is that very small populations were surely involved. See also comments by Harold C. Fleming, "mtDna and the Americas" (*Mother Tongue*, issue 13, April 1991, pp. 1–6).

For a consideration of pre-Clovis sites, see J. L. Hofman, "Prehistoric Culture History—Hunters and Gatherers in the Southern Great Plains" (in *From Clovis to Comanchero: Archeological Overview of the Southern Great Plains*, J. L. Hofman et al., eds., Arkansas Archeological Survey Research Series no. 35, 1989, pp. 25–60); and S. J. Fiedel, *Prehistory of the Americas*

SOURCES AND COMMENTARY

(Cambridge University Press, 1987, pp. 39–56). The Pendejo Cave site is reported by R. S. MacNeish, *The Fort Bliss Archaeology Project: Excavation of Pintada and Pendejo Caves near Orogrande, New Mexico: 1991 Annual Report* (Andover Foundation for Archaeological Research, Andover, Mass., 1991, pp. 6–27). For a popular account of the excavations at Pendejo Cave, see R. Nelson, "Discovering Orogrande Man" (*New Mexico Magazine*, vol. 70, no. 2, February 1992, pp. 58–63).

A balanced discussion of early humans in the Americas is given by D. J. Meltzer, "Why Don't We Know When the First People Came to North America?" (*American Antiquity*, vol. 53, no. 3, 1989, pp. 471–90); see also R. L. Humphrey and D. Stanford, eds., *Pre-Llano Cultures of the Americas: Paradoxes and Possibilities* (Anthropological Society of Washington, D.C., 1979). A defense of the pre-Clovis hypothesis can be found in D. S. Whitley and R. I. Dorn, "New Perspectives on the Clovis vs. Pre-Clovis Controversy" (*American Antiquity*, vol. 58, no. 4, 1993, pp. 626–47).

A statement on the relationship of Nenana to Clovis is given in J. F. Hoffecker, W. R. Powers, and T. Goebel, "The Colonization of Beringia and the Peopling of the New World" (*Science*, vol. 259, January, 1993, pp. 46–53). C. V. Haynes, Jr., in "Clovis Origin Update (*The Kiva*, vol. 52, no. 2, 1987, pp. 83–93), suggests that the Clovis ancestral group may have left Beringia sometime between 13,000 and 12,000 years ago and adapted to mammoth hunting south of the ice fields.

For recent redating of the Clovis complex, see Hoffecker, Powers, and Goebel, "The Colonization of Beringia," p. 51; also Whitley and Dorn, "New Perspectives," p. 632. These draw from C. V. Haynes, Jr., "Geoarchaeological and Paleohydrological Evidence for a Clovis-Age Drought in North America and Its Bearing on Extinction" (*Quaternary Research*, vol. 35, 1991, pp. 438–50). The possibility of boat transport in Paleoindian times is discussed by G. Wisner, "Mollusks, Not Mammoths: The Case for a Pacific Rim Migration" (*Mammoth Trumpet*, vol. 8, no. 4, September 1993, pp. 4–5).

Old World archaeologists occasionally rush in where some Americanists fear to tread. For example, C. Renfrew, in "World Linguistic Diversity" (*Scientific American*, vol. 270, no. 1, 1994, pp. 116–23), states categorically (p. 118) that "by perhaps as early as 37,000 years ago—and no later than 16,000 years ago—Asian pioneers had crossed the Bering Strait, beginning the settlement of the New World."

A discussion of Sandia Cave is given by M. J. Berman, *Cultural Resources Overview of Socorro, New Mexico* (USDA Forest Service, Albuquerque, N.M., and Bureau of Land Management, Santa Fe, N.M., 1979, pp. 10–11);

see also J. C. Winter, *The Excavation of Sevilleta Shelter* (Office of Contract Archaeology, University of New Mexico, 1980, p. 23). Arguments for a pre-Clovis age for Sandia are given by F. C. Hibben, "Specimens from Sandia Cave and Their Possible Significance" (*Science*, vol. 122, no. 3872, 1955, pp. 688–89); and H. M. Wormington, *Ancient Man in North America* (Denver Museum of Natural History, Popular Series no. 4, 1957, p. 89).

For the Clovis hunters, consult W. J. Judge, *Paleoindian Occupation of the Central Rio Grande Valley in New Mexico* (University of New Mexico Press, 1973, pp. 73, 86, 94, 247–57); T. R. Lyons, "A Study of the Paleo-Indian and Desert Culture Complexes of the Estancia Valley Area, New Mexico" (Ph.D. dissertation, Department of Anthropology, University of New Mexico, 1970, pp. 132–40, 145–55); G. C. Frison and L. C. Todd, *The Colby Mammoth Site* (University of New Mexico Press, 1986, pp. 27–32, 91–114, 120–34, 191–205, passim); Hofman, "Prehistoric Culture History," pp. 29–34; and Fiedel, *Prehistory of the Americas,* pp. 56–73, 80.

The Midland skeletal finds are discussed in F. Wendorf, A. D. Krieger, C. C. Albritton, and T. D. Stewart, *The Midland Discovery* (University of Texas Press, 1955, pp. 90, 97–100). For carbon 14 redating of the Midland skeleton, see C. R. McKinney, "Antiquity of Oldest American Confirmed" (*Science News,* vol. 142, no. 20, November 1992, p. 334). For a cautionary note, however, see V. T. Holliday and D. J. Meltzer, "Geoarchaeology of the Midland (Paleoindian) Site and Age of the Midland Skull" (*Current Research in the Pleistocene,* vol. 10, Center for the Study of the First Americans, Oregon State University, 1993, pp. 41–43). Holliday and Meltzer "find no compelling evidence that the human remains from the Midland site are older than Folsom age" (pp. 42–43).

Analysis of the spear-thrower is found in R. Hassig, *Aztec Warfare* (University of Oklahoma Press, 1988, pp. 75–79). Whereas Southwestern Clovis hunters seem to have considered the Pleistocene elephants primary hunting targets, Clovis peoples in other parts of North America may have concentrated on other game. For example, at the Udora site in Ontario, peoples of the Clovislike Gainey complex (dating to perhaps 11,000–10,500 B.P.) possibly utilized the caribou. See P. L. Storck and A. E. Spiess, "The Significance of New Faunal Identifications Attributed to an Early Paleoindian (Gainey Complex) Occupation . . ." (*American Antiquity,* vol. 59, no. 1, 1994, pp. 121–42).

For a discussion of shamanism, see P. Farb, *Man's Rise to Civilization* (revised second edition, E. P. Dutton, 1978, pp. 50–54, 135). Women's roles in ancient societies and feminist approaches in archaeology are discussed in M. W.

Conkey and J. D. Spector, "Archaeology and the Study of Gender" (in *Advances in Archaeological Method and Theory*, vol. 7, M. B. Schiffer, ed., Academic Press, 1984, pp. 1–38); M. W. Conkey and J. M. Gero, "Tensions, Pluralities, and Engendering Archaeology: An Introduction to Women and Prehistory" (in *Engendering Archaeology: Women and Prehistory*, J. M. Gero and M. W. Conkey, eds., Basil Blackwell, Ltd., Oxford, 1991, pp. 3–30); and J. M. Gero, "Genderlithics: Women's Roles in Stone Tool Production" (in *Engendering Archaeology*, pp. 163–93).

The Goshen complex is outlined by Hofman, "Prehistoric Culture History," p. 34. Hofman draws on an unpublished paper by G. C. Frison, "The Goshen Paleoindian Cultural Complex: A Possible Clovis Variant and Technological Predecessor of Folsom" (Paper presented at the 44th Annual Plains Conference, Denver, 1986). For the Folsom culture, consult G. C. Frison and D. J. Stanford, *The Agate Basin Site* (Academic Press, 1982, pp. 37–71, passim); Judge, *Paleoindian Occupation*, pp. 66–69, 163–210, passim; Hofman, "Prehistoric Culture History," pp. 30, 34–37; and Lyons, "A Study," pp. 80–85, 114, 157–59, passim.

Paleoindian technology is discussed by G. C. Frison, *Prehistoric Hunters of the High Plains* (Academic Press, 1978). Discussion and advantages of foreshafts on spears or darts is given on p. 333. Discoveries at the Theo Lake site are described in B. R. Harrington and K. L. Killen, *Lake Theo: A Stratified Early Man Bison Butchering and Camp Site, Briscoe County, Texas* (Panhandle-Plains Historical Museum, Special Archeological Report 1, 1978, pp. 20–21, 89).

For post-Folsom periods, see Judge, *Paleoindian Occupation*, pp. 71–74, 210–47, passim; Lyons, "A Study," pp. 72–80, 144–75; C. Irwin-Williams, *Archaic Culture History in the Southwestern United States* (Eastern New Mexico University Contributions in Anthropology, vol. 1, no. 4, 1968); and C. Irwin-Williams, *The Oshara Tradition: Origins of Anasazi Culture* (Eastern New Mexico University Contributions in Anthropology, vol. 5, no. 1, 1973).

Chapter 4

To get an overview on the Archaic in the Southwest, consult A. H. Simmons et al., *Human Adaptations and Cultural Change in the Greater Southwest* (Arkansas Archeological Survey Research Series no. 32, 1989, pp. 39–74). For climatic conditions, see E. Antevs, "Geologic-Climatic Dating in the West" (*American Antiquity*, vol. 20, no. 4, 1955, pp. 317–35); and W. J. Judge, "The Paleo-Indian and Basketmaker Periods: An Overview and Some Research

Problems" (in *The San Juan Tomorrow*, F. Plog and W. Wait, eds., National Park Service, Southwest Region, 1982, pp. 46–48). Another viewpoint on post-Pleistocene climates can be found in T. R. Van Devender and W. G. Spaulding, "Development of Vegetation and Climate in the Southwestern United States" (*Science*, vol. 204, 1979, pp. 701–10).

For the Oshara tradition, see especially Irwin-Williams, *The Oshara Tradition;* C. Irwin-Williams and C. V. Haynes, "Climatic Change and Early Population Dynamics in the Southwestern United States" (*Quaternary Research*, vol. 1, 1970, pp. 57–71); C. Irwin-Williams, "The Seasonal Strategy" (paper presented at a School of American Research Advanced Seminar on "Seasonal Economic Patterns," Santa Fe, December 1971); Simmons et al., "The Archaic" (in Simmons et al., *Human Adaptations*, pp. 39–74, esp. pp. 43–47); and J. A. Tainter and F. Levine, *Cultural Resources Overview: Central New Mexico* (Bureau of Land Management, Santa Fe, 1987, pp. 26–31).

For earlier work on Osharalike materials, see K. Bryan and J. H. Toulouse, Jr., "The San José Non-ceramic Culture and Its Relation to a Puebloan Culture in New Mexico" (*American Antiquity*, vol. 8, no. 3, 1943, pp. 269–80). I have examined lithic material from both the Gallinas and Tecolote valleys now in collections of New Mexico Highlands University and have gone over site reports from the Rio Grande and the Pecos and Canadian river drainages at the Laboratory of Anthropology, Museum of New Mexico, Santa Fe. In the Gallinas-Tecolote area, an Oshara presence seems to have begun at least by the San José phase and probably by the Bajada phase.

Discussion of the Cochise-Oshara boundary is found in P. H. Beckett, "Cochise Culture Sites in South Central and North Central New Mexico" (M.A. thesis, Eastern New Mexico State University, 1973); and Winter, *Excavation of Sevilleta Shelter*, p. 24. An excellent overview of the Archaic in the middle Rio Grande valley is found in Berman, *Cultural Resources Overview*, pp. 17–27. For southern manifestations of the Oshara tradition, consult P. H. Beckett, "The Archaic Prehistory of the Tularosa Basin: 5500 B.C.–A.D. 400" (in *The Prehistory of Rhodes Canyon*, P. L. Eidenbach, ed., Human Systems Research, Inc., Tularosa, N.M., 1983, pp. 105–110). For the Chihuahua tradition, see R. S. MacNeish and P. H. Beckett, *The Archaic Chihuahua Tradition of South-Central New Mexico and Chihuahua, Mexico* (COAS, Monograph no. 7, 1987).

The origin of agriculture in the Southwest is still controversial and has been treated by a number of authors, including P. E. Minnis, "Domesticating Plants and People in the Greater Southwest" (in *Prehistoric Food Production in North America*, R. I. Ford, ed., Anthropological Papers of the Museum of Anthropology, University of Michigan, no. 75, 1985, pp. 309–40); P. E. Minnis, "Earliest Plant Cultivation in the Desert Border-lands of North America" (in *The Origins of Agriculture,* C. W. Cowan and P. J. Watson, eds., Smithsonian Institution Press, 1993, pp. 121–41); W. H. Wills, *Early Prehistoric Agriculture in the American Southwest* (School of American Research Press, Santa Fe, 1988, pp. 10–11, 33–41); W. H. Wills, "Patterns of Prehistoric Food Production in West-Central New Mexico" (*Journal of Anthropological Research,* vol. 45, no. 1, 1989, pp. 129–57); S. Upham et al., "Evidence Concerning the Origin of Maiz de Ocho" (*American Anthropologist,* vol. 89, no. 2, 1987, pp. 410–19); and R. G. Matson, *The Origins of Southwestern Agriculture* (University of Arizona Press, 1991, esp. pp. 267–77).

Women's role in agriculture in the Archaic of the eastern United States is discussed in P. J. Watson and M. C. Kennedy, "The Development of Hor-ticulture in the Eastern Woodlands of North America: Women's Role" (in Gero and Conkey, eds., *Engendering Archaeology,* pp. 255–75). For other as-pects of maize agriculture, see P. E. Minnis, *Social Adaptation to Food Stress* (University of Chicago Press, 1985, pp. 108–13, 119–32); and R. I. Ford, "Gar-dening and Farming before A.D. 1000" (*Journal of Ethnobiology,* vol. 1, no. 1, 1981, pp. 6–27). A commentary on the importance of maize in Basketmaker and Pueblo times is made in P. E. Minnis, "Prehistoric Diet in the Northern Southwest: Macroplant Remains from Four Corners Feces" (*American An-tiquity,* vol. 54, no. 3, 1989, pp. 543–63).

Chapter 5

For discussions of Basketmaker culture, see L. S. Cordell, *Prehistory of the Southwest* (Academic Press, 1984, pp. 213–30); P. S. Martin, G. I. Quimby, and D. Collier, *Indians before Columbus* (University of Chicago Press, 1947, pp. 111–20); Simmons et al., *Human Adaptations;* F. H. H. Roberts, Jr., *Shabik'eshchee Village* (Bureau of American Ethnology Bulletin 92, 1929, esp. pl. 1). A good general discussion of dendrochronology, or tree-ring dating, is given in J. C. McGregor, *Southwestern Archaeology* (second edition, Univer-sity of Illinois Press, 1965, pp. 75–90). For Hohokam and Mogollon, see Cordell, *Prehistory of the Southwest,* pp. 107–18.

For Basketmaker and Pueblo periods generally, see L. S. Cordell, "North-ern and Central Rio Grande" (in *Dynamics of Southwestern Prehistory,* L. S. Cordell and G. J. Gumerman, eds., Smithsonian Institution Press, 1989, pp. 293–314, 390–97); F. Plog, "Prehistory: Western Anasazi" (in *Handbook of North American Indians,* vol. 9, A. Ortiz, ed., Smithsonian Institution Press, 1979, pp. 108–31); L. S. Cordell, "Prehistory: Eastern Anasazi" (in *Handbook,* vol. 9, 1979, pp. 131–51). A useful survey of research developments in northern Mogollon and Anasazi archaeology between 1988 and 1993 is contained in T. A. Kohler, "News from the Northern American Southwest: Prehistory on the Edge of Chaos" (*Journal of Archaeological Research,* vol. 1, no. 4, 1993, pp. 267–321).

A discussion of climatic conditions is found in W. J. Judge, "The Paleo-Indian and Basketmaker Periods" (in *San Juan Tomorrow,* pp. 486–48, 455–56). For overviews, consult S. Peckham, "The Anasazi Culture of the Northern Rio Grande Rift" (*New Mexico Geological Society Guidebook,* 35th Field Conference, 1984, pp. 275–81); and Simmons et al., *Human Adaptation,* pp. 75–118). Information on agriculture is given in Minnis, "Prehistoric Diet," pp. 549–51.

For ceramic studies, see E. Blinman, "Anasazi Pottery" (*Expedition,* vol. 35, no. 1, 1993, pp. 14–22); and D. A. Breternitz, *An Appraisal of Tree-Ring Dated Pottery in the Southwest* (Anthropological Papers of the University of Arizona, no. 10, 1966). Blinman (p. 15) dates the beginning of Anasazi pottery at A.D. 200. Also consult the following chapters in A. H. Schroeder, ed., *Southwest Ceramics: A Comparative Review* (Arizona Archaeological Society, no. 15, 1982): A. H. Schroeder, "Historical Overview of Southwestern Ceramics," pp. 1–26; S. A. LeBlanc, "The Advent of Pottery in the Southwest," pp. 27–52; D. A. Breternitz, "The Four Corners Anasazi Ceramic Tradition," pp. 129–48; and R. W. Lang, "Transformation in White Ware Pottery of the Northern Rio Grande," pp. 129–48.

Evidence for the Southwestern origin of turkeys can be found in E. Breitburg, "Prehistoric New World Turkey Domestication, Origins, Developments, and Consequences" (Ph.D. dissertation, Department of Anthropology, Southern Illinois University, 1988, pp. 96–99, 102–9). For dogs, see N. J. Akins, "Prehistoric Faunal Utilization in Chaco Canyon, Basketmaker III through Pueblo III" (in *Environment and Subsistence of Chaco Canyon, New Mexico,* F. J. Mathien, ed., Publications in Archaeology 18E, National Park Service, Albuquerque, 1985, pp. 305–445, esp. pp. 314, 319).

The function of pithouses is discussed by R. Y. Farwell, "Pit Houses: Prehistoric Energy Conservation?" (*El Palacio,* vol. 87, no. 3, 1981, pp. 43–47). Late pithouses in the upper Rio Grande basin are discussed by J. W. Allen and C. H. McNutt, "A Pit House Site near Santa Ana Pueblo, New Mexico" (*American Antiquity,* vol. 20, no. 3, 1955, pp. 241–62); R. G. Vivian and N. W. Clendenen, "The Denison Site: Four Pit Houses near Isleta, New

Mexico" (*El Palacio,* vol. 73, no. 2, 1965, pp. 5–26); H. W. Dick, C. F. Schaaf-
sma, D. Wolfman, and M. Wolfman, *Picuris Pueblo Excavations* (National
Park Service, Southwest Region, Santa Fe, N.M., 1965); T. R. Frisbie, "The
Excavation and Interpretation of the Artificial Leg Basketmaker III–Pueblo I
Sites near Corrales, New Mexico" (M.A. thesis, Department of Anthropol-
ogy, University of New Mexico, 1967); N. S. Hammack, A. Ferg, and B. Brad-
ley, *Excavations at Three Developmental Period Sites near Zia and Santa Ana
Pueblos, New Mexico* (CASA Papers, no. 2, Cortez, Colo., 1983); and A. E.
Ward, "Two Dead Juniper Village" (*CAS Newsletter,* winter and spring, 1993,
pp. 1–6).

Information on the Anasazi pithouse dwellers in the Gallinas-Tecolote region comes from my colleague Robert Mishler of New Mexico Highlands
University (personal communication). Mishler has done extensive archaeological fieldwork on various prehistoric cultures of the upper Tecolote and
Gallinas valleys. His data are as yet largely unpublished.

Chapter 6

For the Chaco and Mesa Verde areas generally, see Martin, Quimby, and
Collier, *Indians before Columbus,* pp. 129–49; Cordell, *Prehistory of the Southwest,* pp. 246–48, 253–61, 266–74, 304–25; and the following chapters in P. L.
Crown and W. J. Judge, eds., *Chaco and Hohokam* (School of American Research Press, Santa Fe, 1991): W. J. Judge, "Chaco: Current Views of Prehistory and the Regional System," pp. 11–30; S. H. Lekson, "Settlement Pattern
and the Chaco Region," pp. 31–55; and R. G. Vivian, "Chacoan Subsistence," pp. 57–76. Also see R. Flint and S. C. Flint, *A Pocket Guide to Chaco
Canyon Architecture* (Central Graphics Printing, 1987); *Chacoesque* (Century
Graphics, Albuquerque, 1989); *Mesa Verde Architecture* (Century Graphics,
1991); A. H. Rohn, "Northern San Juan Prehistory" (in Cordell and Gumerman, eds., *Dynamics of Southwest Prehistory,* pp. 149–77); W. J. Judge,
"Chaco Canyon–San Juan Basin" (in *Dynamics,* pp. 209–61); and
A. C. Hayes, D. M. Brugge, and W. J. Judge, *Archeological Surveys of Chaco
Canyon, New Mexico* (University of New Mexico Press, 1981). A survey of
various explanations for the Chaco phenomenon can be found in L. Sebastian, *The Chaco Anasazi* (Cambridge University Press, 1992, pp. 82–97).

Plant utilization is discussed in Minnis, "Prehistoric Diet," pp. 547–51,
559–60; M. A. Stiger, "Mesa Verde Subsistence Patterns from Basketmaker to
Pueblo III" (*The Kiva,* vol. 44, no. 2–3, 1979, pp. 133–44); and L. J. Scott,
"Dietary Inferences from Hoy House Coprolites" (*The Kiva,* vol. 44, no.

2–3, 1979, pp. 237–81, esp. pp. 266–67). Turkeys are discussed in Akins, "Prehistoric Faunal Utilization," pp. 323, 326.

Size and other differentiations between Chaco and Mesa Verde kivas are discussed in Martin, Quimby, and Collier, *Indians before Columbus*, pp. 132–36. Population in Chaco Canyon is considered by L. M. Pierson, "The Prehistoric Population of Chaco Canyon, New Mexico" (M.A. thesis, Department of Anthropology, University of New Mexico, 1949); see also Hayes, Brugge, and Judge, *Archeological Surveys of Chaco Canyon*, pp. 49–51.

Roads in the Chaco area are summarized by J. R. Roney, "Prehistoric Roads and Regional Integration in the Chacoan System" (in *Anasazi Regional Organization and the Chaco System*, D. E. Doyel, ed., Maxwell Museum of Anthropology, Anthropological Papers no. 5, 1992, pp. 123–31). Discussion of the northern outlier of Chaco at Aztec, especially information on the great kiva there, can be found in R. H. Lister and F. C. Lister, *Aztec Ruins on the Animas* (University of New Mexico Press, 1987). For consideration of possible moiety structures in the Chaco area, see R. G. Vivian, "An Inquiry into Prehistoric Social Organization in Chaco Canyon, New Mexico" (in *Reconstructing Prehistoric Pueblo Societies*, W. A. Longacre, ed., University of New Mexico Press, 1970, pp. 59–83).

For Mesoamerican and other trade contacts in the Pueblo period, see J. C. Kelley and E. A. Kelley, "An Alternative Hypothesis for the Explanation of Anasazi Culture History" (in *Collected Papers in Honor of Florence Hawley Ellis*, T. R. Frisbie, ed., Papers of the Archeological Society of New Mexico, no. 2, 1975, pp. 178–223, esp. pp. 201–9); T. Holien, "Pseudo-cloisonné in the Southwest and Mesoamerica" (in Frisbie, ed., *Collected Papers*, pp. 157–77, esp. pp. 159, 162–64); and J. E. Reyman, "A Reevaluation of Bi-wall and Tri-wall Structures in the Anasazi Area" (in *Contributions to the Archaeology and Ethnohistory of Greater Mesoamerica: Essays in Honor of Carroll L. Riley*, W. J. Folan, ed., Southern Illinois University Press, 1985, pp. 293–334).

On trade in minerals, see F. J. Mathien, "Ornaments and Minerals from Pueblo Alto" (in *Investigations at the Pueblo Alto Complex, Chaco Canyon, New Mexico*, T. C. Windes, ed., National Park Service, Santa Fe, 1987, pp. 381–428); J. E. Pogue, *The Turquoise* (Rio Grande Press, Glorieta, N.M., 1975 [originally published in 1915], pp. 100–101); R. N. Wiseman and J. A. Darling, "The Bronze Trail Site Group: More Evidence for a Cerrillos-Chaco Turquoise Connection" (in *By Hands Unknown: Papers on Rock Art and Archaeology, in Honor of James G. Bain*, A. Poore, ed., Archaeological Society of New Mexico, no. 12, pp. 115–43); G. Harbottle and P. C. Weigand,

"Turquoise in Pre-Columbian America" (*Scientific American*, vol. 26, no. 2, February 1992, pp. 78–85); P. C. Weigand, "The Macroeconomic Role of Turquoise within the Chaco Canyon System" (in Doyel, ed., *Anasazi Regional Organization*, pp. 169–73); and G. M. Bockley-Fisher, "Raw Materials and Lithic Distributions" (in *Economy and Polity in Late Rio Grande Prehistory*, S. Upham and B. D. Staley, eds., New Mexico State University Occasional Papers no. 16, 1990, pp. 277–306, esp. pp. 279–81).

For more information on trade and interregional relations, see the following chapters in J. E. Smith, ed., *Proceedings of the Anasazi Symposium, 1981* (Mesa Verde Museum Association, 1983): S. H. Lekson, "Chacoan Architecture in Continental Context," pp. 183–94; F. J. Mathien, "The Mobile Trader and the Chacoan Anasazi," pp. 197–205; and T. R. Frisbie, "Anasazi-Mesoamerican Relationships . . ." pp. 215–26. Also see L. L. Hargrave, *Mexican Macaws* (Anthropological Papers of the University of Arizona, no. 10, 1970, pp. 28–33, 53); and J. E. Reyman, "Pochteca Burials in Anasazi Sites?" (in *Across the Chichimec Sea: Papers in Honor of J. Charles Kelley*, C. L. Riley and B. C. Hedrick, eds., Southern Illinois University Press, 1978, pp. 242–59).

On the distribution of Chaco turquoise, consult F. J. Mathien, "Economic Exchange Systems in the San Juan Basin" (Ph.D. dissertation, Department of Anthropology, University of New Mexico, 1981, pp. 192–217). For the viewpoint that Chaco trade did not represent massive or even significant Mesoamerican intrusion, see T. C. Windes, ed., *Investigations at the Pueblo Alto Complex, Chaco Canyon, New Mexico* (National Park Service, Santa Fe, vol. 1, 1987, pp. 407–9); also R. G. Vivian, *The Chacoan Prehistory of the San Juan Basin* (Academic Press, 1990, pp. 416–19); and F. J. Mathien, "External Contact and the Chaco Anasazi" (in *Ripples in the Chichimec Sea*, F. J. Mathien and R. H. McGuire, eds., Southern Illinois University Press, 1986, pp. 224–32).

I must say that I am somewhat on middle ground in my belief in the importance of Mesoamerican influence on the Chaco region and the later prehistoric Southwest. My reconstruction of pre-Hispanic trade, Chacoan as well as in later periods, has certainly been criticized as overemphasizing the importance of Mesoamerica. See, for example, F. J. Mathien, "The Mobile Trader," pp. 200, 204–5. On the other hand, an enthusiastic Mesoamericanist, J. Charles Kelley, considers that "Riley only pays lip service to the concept of Greater Mesoamerica" (p. 229 in J. C. Kelley, "Zenith Passage: The View from Chalchihuites," in *Culture and Contact: Charles C. Di Peso's*

SOURCES AND COMMENTARY

Gran Chichimeca, A. I. Woosley and J. C. Ravesloot, eds., University of New Mexico Press, 1993, pp. 227–50).

Astronomical observations in the Chaco region are discussed by M. Zeilik in "Archaeoastronomy at Chaco Canyon" (in *New Light on Chaco Canyon,* D. G. Noble, ed., Exploration, Annual Bulletin of the School of American Research, 1984, pp. 63–72); also J. E. Reyman, "Astronomy, Architecture and Adaptation at Pueblo Bonito" (*Science,* vol. 193, 1976, pp. 957–62). Arguments for the calendrical importance of Fajada Butte can be found in A. Sofaer and R. M. Sinclair, "Astronomical Marking at Three Sites on Fajada Butte (paper in the library of the Laboratory of Anthropology, Museum of New Mexico, Santa Fe, 1984); for lunar positions, see esp. pp. 11–13. M. Zeilik (in Noble, ed., *New Light,* p. 72) believes that the supposed calendrical site on Fajada Butte was a sun shrine visited by the Sun Priest for prayer and ceremonial offerings.

Ideas about abandonment of the Chaco and San Juan areas are found in Cordell, *Prehistory of the Southwest,* pp. 303–25; see also Rohn, "Northern San Juan," p. 16, and S. A. LeBlanc, "Cibola: Shifting Cultural Boundaries," pp. 337–69, esp. pp. 359–62, both in Cordell and Gumerman, eds., *Dynamics.* A discussion of the relationship between climate and the power structure in Chaco is found in Sebastian, *The Chaco Anasazi,* esp. pp. 147–52.

For a discussion of the Rio Grande area in early Pueblo III times, see Peckham, "Anasazi Culture," pp. 275–79; D. E. Stuart, *The Magic of Bandelier* (Ancient City Press, Santa Fe, 1989, pp. 55–56, 60–62, 66–74, passim); D. E. Stuart and R. P. Gauthier, *Prehistoric New Mexico* (University of New Mexico Press, 1988, pp. 51–52, 93–94); C. L. Riley, "San Juan Anasazi and the Galisteo Basin" (*El Palacio,* vol. 59, no. 3, 1952, pp. 77–82); F. Wendorf, "A Reconstruction of Northern Rio Grande Prehistory" (*American Anthropologist,* vol. 56, no. 2, 1954, pp. 200–227, esp. pp. 208–12); Tainter and Levine, *Cultural Resources Overview,* pp. 35–41; and M. P. Marshall and H. J. Walt, eds., *Rio Abajo: Prehistory and History of a Rio Grande Province* (New Mexico Historic Preservation Program, Santa Fe, 1984). Specifically for the northern Tiwa region, consult A. I. Woosley, "Puebloan Prehistory of the Northern Rio Grande: Settlement, Population, Subsistence" (*The Kiva,* vol. 51, no. 3, 1986, pp. 143–64, esp. pp. 147–49, 160–62).

The history of Chupadero pottery is discussed in R. N. Wiseman, *An Initial Study of the Origins of Chupadero Black-on-white* (Albuquerque Archaeological Society, Technical Note no. 2, 1986, pp. 1–6). Wiseman (p. 4) suggests that the beginning date for Chupadero may be A.D. 1100 or possibly even

A.D. 1050. A caution that not all Rio Grande culture came from the San Juan Basin is found in C. F. Schaafsma, "Linked to a Larger World" (review of *Anasazi Ruins of the Southwest,* by W. M. Ferguson and A. H. Rohn, in *Colorado Heritage,* issue 2, 1988, pp. 45–47). For the development of northern Rio Grande kivas from the local pithouse tradition, see Dick et al., *Picuris Pueblo Excavations,* esp. pp. 121–22. For comments on population decline, consult LeBlanc, "Cibola," pp. 359–62.

The spread of Mesa Verde–type peoples to Chacra Mesa is discussed by L. Jacobson and J. Roney, "Reconnaissance of the Chaco Mesa for the Bureau of Land Management" (Nominations to the National Register of Historic Places, unpublished site forms in files of the Laboratory of Anthropology, Museum of New Mexico, Santa Fe, 1984); see also Vivian, *Chacoan Prehistory,* pp. 387–89.

One possible exception to the desertion of the Pecos–Tecolote–Gallinas region by around A.D. 1300 may be the site of Tecolote on the south side of the Tecolote River about a mile southeast of the present Interstate 25 bridge. There, chemists Joseph A. Schufle and Phillip Baca did a study of ion exchange in the sodium and potassium components of the Tecolote sediments. They suggested a site occupation from about A.D. 1300 to 1350.

I must say, however, that I question the validity of these dates. Pottery on the site (studied by Robert Mishler and Mary Tinsley) better fits an occupation before 1300. The ion exchange method of dating sediments has been tested in various regions of the arid Southwest. There are several variables (annual rainfall, average soil percolation, moisture lost to runoff or evaporation) that are not well controlled, so the method seems most useful in producing "ball park" dates. For dating on the Tecolote site, see J. A. Schufle, P. Baca, R. Mishler, and M. Tinsley, "Ion Exchange Dating and Cultural Remains Associated with a Rio Tecolote Sediment in Northern New Mexico" (*Texas Journal of Science,* vol. 27, no. 3, 1976, pp. 377–81). For a discussion of the ion exchange method, see J. A. Schufle, F. E. Kottlowski, and B. C. Beckhart, "Dating of Recent Arid Zone Sediments" (*Texas Journal of Science,* vol. 18, no. 3, 1966, pp. 317–23); and J. A. Schufle and G. Brassell, "Dating of Conchos River Sediments, New Mexico" (*Nature,* vol. 223, no. 5213, 1969, p. 1356).

For early Apacheans, especially the Navajos, consult C. L. Riley, "A Survey of Navajo Archaeology," (University of Colorado Studies, Series in Anthropology no. 4, 1954, pp. 45–60); and D. M. Brugge, "Navajo Prehistory and History to 1850" (in *Handbook of North American Indians,* vol. 10, A. Ortiz, ed., Smithsonian Institution Press, 1983, pp. 489–501, esp. pp. 489–91). On

Apachean movements into the San Juan and Chama basins, see C. F. Schaaf-sma, "Early Apacheans in the Southwest: A Review" (in *The Protohistoric in the North American Southwest:* A.D. 1450–1700, D. R. Wilcox and W. B. Masse, eds., Arizona State University, Anthropological Research Papers no. 24, 1981, pp. 291–320); and D. R. Wilcox, "The Entry of Athapaskans into the American Southwest: The Problem Today" (in Wilcox and Masse, eds., *The Protohistoric,* pp. 213–56). For early Ute occupation of the San Juan basin, see A. H. Schroeder, "A Brief History of the Southern Utes" (*Southwestern Lore,* vol. 30, no. 4, March 1965, pp. 53–78).

Chapter 7

For terminology, see F. H. H. Roberts, Jr., "A Survey of Southwestern Archaeology" (*American Anthropologist,* vol. 37, no. 1, 1935, pp. 1–35); J. O. Brew, "On the Pueblo IV and on the Katchina-Tlaloc Relations" (in *El norte del México y el sur de los Estados Unidos,* A. Caso et al., Tercero reunión de la mesa redonda de la Sociedad Mexicana de Antropología, 1943, pp. 241–45); and F. H. H. Roberts, Jr, "Archaeology in the Southwest" (*American Antiquity,* vol. 3, no. 1, 1937, pp. 3–33).

The question of crosscutting, integrative mechanisms in the post-1300 Southwest is treated by W. A. Longacre, "Archaeology as Anthropology: A Case Study" (*Science,* no. 144, 1964, pp. 1454–55); see also P. Schaafsma, "Kachinas in Rock Art" (*Journal of New World Archaeology,* vol. 4, no. 2, 1981, pp. 24–32); and P. Schaafsma, *Indian Rock Art of the Southwest* (University of New Mexico Press, 1980, pp. 244–45).

Language origins and distribution are vexed questions. For various viewpoints, see I. Davis, "The Kiowa-Tanoan, Keresan, and Zuni Languages" (in *The Languages of Native America,* L. Campbell and M. Muthun, eds., University of Texas Press, 1979, pp. 390–443, esp. 398–410, 413–21); R. I. Ford, A. H. Schroeder, and S. L. Peckham, "Three Perspectives on Puebloan Prehistory" (in *New Perspectives on the Pueblos,* A. Ortiz, ed., University of New Mexico Press, 1972, pp. 19–39); Riley, *Frontier People,* pp. 256–59; A. J. Jelinek, *A Prehistoric Sequence in the Middle Pecos Valley, New Mexico* (University of Michigan Museum of Anthropology, Anthropology Papers no. 31, 1967). Interesting speculation on language distribution during the Archaic is given in C. Irwin-Williams, "Prehistoric Cultural and Linguistic Patterns in the Southwest since 5000 B.C." (paper read at the annual meeting of the Society for American Archaeology, Portales, N.M., 1967).

The idea that the Kiowas may be descendants of the Jumanos is contained in N. P. Hickerson, "Ethnogenesis in the South Plains: Jumano to Kiowa?" (manuscript in the author's possession, 1994). For thoughts on an ancient connection of ancestral Apacheans with Sino-Tibetans, see J. W. Palmer, "Migrations of the Apachean Dineh" (*North American Archaeologist,* vol. 13, no. 2, 1992, p. 196). On a possible Dene-Caucasian superfamily, see M. Ruhlen, "An Overview of Genetic Classification" (in *Evolution of Human Language,* J. A. Hawkins and M. Gell-Mann, eds., Santa Fe Institute, Studies in the Sciences of Complexity, Proceedings, vol. 11, 1992, pp. 159–85, esp. p. 179).

A model in which the Tanoans came into the Rio Grande valley from the east around the beginning of the Rio Grande Classic period has been tentatively advanced by D. H. Snow, "Prologue to Rio Grande Prehistory" (in *Collected Papers in Honor of Harry L. Hadlock,* N. L. Fox, ed., Papers of the Archaeological Society of New Mexico, no. 9, 1984, pp. 125–32). Suggestion of early Apachean settlement of the San Juan basin has been made by Brugge, "Navajo Prehistory," p. 490; see also Palmer, "Migrations of the Apachean Dineh," pp. 203–4; and D. M. Brugge, "Thoughts on the Significance of Navajo Traditions in View of the Newly Discovered Early Athabaskan Archaeology North of the San Juan River" (in *Why Museums Collect: Papers in Honor of Joe Ben Wheat,* M. S. Duran and D. T. Kirkpatrick, eds., Papers of the Archaeological Society of New Mexico, no. 19, 1993, pp. 31–38).

Information on the eastward movement of Shoshoni speakers into western Colorado can be found in J. D. Jennings, *Prehistory of Utah and the Eastern Great Basin* (University of Utah, Anthropological Papers no. 98, 1973, pp. 235–37); also A. R. Reed and S. A. McDonald, *Archaeological Investigations at Three Lithic Scatters . . . Montezuma and Dolores Counties, Colorado* (National Park Service, Interagency Archeological Service, Denver, April 1988, pp. ii, 36–37, 52). Curtis Schaafsma (personal communication) has given me his own ideas about Utes and later Apacheans on the San Juan River; also see C. F. Schaafsma, "The Piedra Lumbre Phase and the Origins of the Navajos" (paper presented at the 58th annual meeting of the Society for American Archaeology, St. Louis, May, 1993, copy in files of the Laboratory of Anthropology, Museum of New Mexico, Santa Fe); Schaafsma, "Early Apacheans," pp. 291–94; and Wilcox, "Entry of Athapaskans," pp. 229–36. A statement generally opposed to the Schaafsma-Wilcox position is made by David M. Brugge, "Comments on Athabaskans and Sumas" (in Wilcox and Masse, eds., *Protohistoric in the North American Southwest,* pp. 282–90, esp. pp. 286–89). Arguments for a very late arrival of the Apacheans into the southern plains can be found in J. H. Gunnerson and D. A. Gunnerson,

SOURCES AND COMMENTARY

Ethnohistory of the High Plains (Colorado State Office, Bureau of Land Management, Denver, 1988, pp. 1–2).

For the development of Classic or Pueblo IV sites along the Rio Grande, see P. F. Reed, "A Spatial Analysis of the Northern Rio Grande Region . . ." (in *Economy and Polity in Late Rio Grande Prehistory,* S. Upham and B. D. Staley, eds., New Mexico State University Museum, Occasional Papers no. 16, 1990, pp. 1–89, esp. pp. 20, 75–76); W. Creamer and J. Haas, "Warfare, Disease, and Colonial Contact in the Pueblos of Northern New Mexico" (ms. P-1727, library of the Laboratory of Anthropology, Museum of New Mexico, Santa Fe, 1988); Tainter and Levine, *Cultural Resources Overview,* pp. 42–55; and F. Wendorf and E. K. Reed, "An Alternative Reconstruction of Northern Rio Grande Prehistory" (*El Palacio,* vol. 62, nos. 5–6, 1955, pp. 131–73). A warning about the dangers of estimating population from room counts is found in W. Creamer, "The Transition to History in the Rio Grande: Recent Work at Pueblo Blanco, New Mexico" (paper presented at 65th Pecos Conference, Pecos, N.M., August 14–15, 1992).

Discussions of pottery distribution can be found in Cordell, *Prehistory of the Southwest,* pp. 337–41; R. L. Carlson, "The Polychrome Complexes" (in Schroeder, ed., *Southwestern Ceramics,* pp. 201–34); D. H. Snow, "The Rio Grande Glaze, Matte-Paint, and Plainware Tradition" (in Schroeder, ed., *Southwestern Ceramics,* pp. 235–78, esp. pp. 245–47, 250–54, 260–65); and H. P. Mera, *Style Trends of Pueblo Pottery* (Laboratory of Anthropology Memoirs, no. 3, Santa Fe, 1939).

The dating for coursed adobe is given by Dick et al., *Picuris Pueblo Excavations,* pp. 82, 85. For various types of kivas in the Pueblo III and IV Rio Grande, see Wendorf and Reed, "An Alternative Reconstruction," pp. 144–47, 151–52, 157; Martin, Quimby, and Collier, *Indians before Columbus,* p. 150; S. A. Stubbs, "Summary Report on an Early Pueblo Site in the Tesuque Valley, New Mexico" (*El Palacio,* vol. 61, no. 2, 1954, pp. 43–45); and S. A. Stubbs and W. S. Stallings, Jr., *The Excavation of Pindi Pueblo* (Monographs of the School of American Research and Laboratory of Anthropology, Santa Fe, no. 18, 1953, pp. 39–47).

For a discussion of the kachina cult, see P. Schaafsma and C. F. Schaafsma, "Evidence for the Origins of the Kachina Cult" (*American Antiquity,* vol. 39, no. 4, 1974, pp. 535–45). For an opposing view of kachina origins, consult E. C. Adams, *The Origin and Development of the Pueblo Katsina Cult* (University of Arizona Press, 1991, pp. 185–91); also H. K. Crotty, "Masks Portrayed in Pueblo IV Kiva Murals: New Evidence for the Origins of Pueblo Ceremonialism" (ms. in files of the Laboratory of Anthropology, Museum of

New Mexico, Santa Fe., n.d.); and F. G. Anderson, "The Pueblo Kachina Cult: A Historical Reconstruction" (*Southwestern Journal of Anthropology*, vol. 11, no. 4, 1955, pp. 404–19).

The name kachina or katsina is something of a mystery. The term is Hopi but seems to be a word borrowed into the Hopi language, probably from outside the Pueblo area (see Adams, *Pueblo Katsina Cult*, p. 4). The relationship of the kachina cult and the war, hunt, and medicine sodalities is discussed by P. Schaafsma, "Imagery and Magic: Petroglyphs at Comanche Gap, Galisteo Basin, New Mexico" (*Archaeology, Art, and Anthropology: Papers in Honor of J. J. Brody*, M. S. Duran and D. T. Kirkpatrick, eds., Archaeological Society of New Mexico, no. 18, 1992, pp. 157–74); and P. Schaafsma, *Rock Art in New Mexico* (Museum of New Mexico Press, 1992, pp. 130–31).

For kiva murals and their implications for Mesoamerican contacts, see Cordell, *Prehistory of the Southwest*, pp. 343–46; Kelley and Kelley, "An Alternative Hypothesis," pp. 203, 210–13; F. C. Hibben, "A Possible Pyramidal Structure and Other Mexican Influences at Pottery Mound, New Mexico" (*American Antiquity*, vol. 31, no. 4, 1966, pp. 522–29); J. J. Brody, "Pueblo Fine Arts" (in *Handbook of North American Indians*, vol. 9, 1979, pp. 603–8; B. P. Dutton, *Sun Father's Way* (University of New Mexico Press, 1963); and J. J. Brody, "The Kiva Murals of Pottery Mound" (*Verhandlungen des XXXVIII. Internationalen Amerikanistenkongresses*, Stuttgart-München, 1968, Band II, 1970, pp. 101–10). On the kachina cult among the Tiwas, see Schaafsma and Schaafsma, "Evidence," pp. 540–41; Dutton, *Sun Father's Way*, pp. 200–204, passim; Brody, "Kiva Murals," pp. 103–4; and J. J. Brody, *Anasazi and Pueblo Painting* (University of New Mexico Press, 1991, pp. 98–113, esp. p. 112).

Quetzalcoatl and Tlaloc influences in northern Mexico and the Southwest are discussed in J. C. Kelley, "Archaeology of Zacatecas and Durango" (in *Archaeology of Northern Mesoamerica*, G. F. Ekholm and I. Bernal, eds., *Handbook of Middle American Indians*, vol. 11, 1971, pp. 768–801, esp. pp. 794–95); C. C. Di Peso, "Casas Grandes and the Gran Chichimeca" (*El Palacio*, vol. 75, no. 4, 1968, pp. 47–61); R. L. Beals, "Northern Mexico and the Southwest" (in *El norte del México*, Tercero mesa redonda, 1943, pp. 191–99); Brew, "On the Pueblo IV," p. 244; Riley, *Frontier People*, pp. 204, 207, 210–11; and E. C. Parsons, "Some Aztec and Pueblo Parallels" (in *The Mesoamerican Southwest*, B. C. Hedrick, J. C. Kelley, and C. L. Riley, eds., Southern Illinois University Press, 1974, pp. 131–46, 165–72). Trade into and across the Southwest is discussed in great detail in Riley, *Frontier People,* pp. 236–40, 267–81, 319–21.

Chapter 8

Information on the Dulmo voyage was derived from S. M. Wilson, "Columbus's Competition" (*Natural History,* January 1992, pp. 27–29). Columbus's first voyage is discussed in C. O. Sauer, *The Early Spanish Main* (University of California Press, 1966, pp. 12–23). Parenthetically, Sauer (p. 16) suggests that the Spanish sovereigns may have expected Columbus to discover only empty islands or areas not settled by civilized people.

For climatic and dendroclimatological data, see M. R. Rose, J. S. Dean, and W. J. Robinson, *The Past Climate of Arroyo Hondo, New Mexico* (School of American Research Press, Santa Fe, 1981, pp. 91–106). On archaeoastronomy, see J. E. Reyman, "The Nature and Nurture of Archaeoastronomical Studies" (in *Archaeoastronomy in Pre-Columbian America,* A. F. Aveni, ed., University of Texas Press, 1975, pp. 206–15, esp. pp. 206–8). For full moon positions over time, consult H. H. Goldstine, *New and Full Moons 1001 B.C. to A.D. 1651* (American Philosophical Society, Philadelphia, 1973). In 1492 the full moon fell on December 4 of the Julian calendar. Adjusted for Gregorian dating this would be mid-December, with the new moon falling on December 27 or 28. The solstice and moon watchers would actually have had better luck at the end of 1491, when the full moon fell on December 16 of the Julian calendar—about December 25 by Gregorian reckoning, and thus pretty close to the solstice.

I must admit to a certain amount of creative speculation in my discussion of the attempts by Pueblo priests in 1492 to match the full moon with the winter solstice. Such attempts have been documented for the historic Zunis, but so far as I know, not for the eastern Pueblos. I suspect that the simpler astronomical system found today among the eastern Pueblos is the result of long and intimate European occupation and influence. In pre-Spanish times I would expect to find a somewhat more elaborate system of measurements of sun and moon positions. For a consideration of solstice–full-moon matching at Zuni, see J. E. Reyman, "The Predictive Dimension of Priestly Power" (in *New Frontiers in the Archaeology and Ethnohistory of the Greater Southwest,* C. L. Riley and B. C. Hedrick, eds., Transactions of the Illinois State Academy of Science, vol. 72, no. 4, 1980, pp. 40–59, esp. pp. 44–47, 55—a note by physicist Harold J. Born).

SOURCES AND COMMENTARY

A discussion of Pueblo names can be found in Riley, *Frontier People,* pp. 182–83, 252–53; F. Eggan, "Pueblos: Introduction" (in *Handbook of North American Indians,* vol. 9, pp. 224–35, esp. pp. 234–35); and A. H. Schroeder, "Pecos Pueblo" (in *Handbook,* vol. 9, pp. 430–37, esp. pp. 436–37). Edmund J. Ladd, of the Museum of New Mexico, believes that the *si:wolo* explanation for the name Cíbola may be correct. The particular form of the word *Pecos* used by the Spaniards may have come from the Keresan form of the name. See E. L. Hewett, *Ancient Communities in the American Desert* (translated by M. T. Rodack from the 1908 French version, A. H. Schroeder, ed., Archaeological Society of New Mexico, Monograph Series, no. 1, 1993, p. 36).

Thoughtful commentary on complexity among the protohistoric western Pueblos is found in K. W. Kintigh, "Protohistoric Transitions in the Western Pueblo Area" (in *Perspectives on Southwestern Prehistory,* P. E. Minnis and C. L. Redman, eds., Westview Press, Boulder, Colo., 1990, pp. 258–75. "Banking" is discussed by Riley, *Frontier People,* p. 326. For a discussion of Juan Alemán, see Hammond and Rey, *Narratives of the Coronado Expedition,* pp. 224–26. The situation with Francisco de Espeleta is discussed by C. L. Riley, "The Hopi" (ms. in files of the library of the Laboratory of Anthropology, Museum of New Mexico, Santa Fe).

On subsistence, see Riley, *Frontier People,* pp. 232–35, 260–64; E. Garber, "Analysis of Plant Remains" (in *Tijeras Canyon: Analyses of the Past,* L. S. Cordell, ed., University of New Mexico Press, 1980, pp. 71–87); G. Young, "Analysis of Faunal Remains" (in Cordell, ed., *Tijeras Canyon,* pp. 88–120, esp. pp. 98–104); and C. R. McKusick, "The Faunal Remains of Las Humanas" (in *Contributions to Gran Quivira Archeology,* A. C. Hayes, ed., National Park Service Publications in Archeology, no. 17, 1981, pp. 39–65). At Pecos, bison were probably eaten from earliest times. According to the excavator, A. V. Kidder (*The Artifacts of Pecos,* Yale University Press, 1932, p. 196), bison bones "occurred at all levels but were most numerous in the upper deposits." However, a study of isotope ratios from human skeletal material at Pecos suggests that there was no significant increase in the amount of bison consumed (relative to other foodstuffs) during the later periods when Pecos was an important gateway for plains trade. See K. A. Spielmann, M. J. Schoeninger, and K. Moore, "Plains-Pueblo Interdependence and Human Diet at Pecos Pueblo, New Mexico" (*American Antiquity,* vol. 55, no. 4, 1990, pp. 745–65, esp. p. 760).

Protein values for various foods can be found in B. K. Watt and A. L. Merrill, preparers, *Handbook of the Nutritional Contents of Foods* (USDA Handbook no. 8, Washington, D. C., 1963). On *Ephedra* (Mormon tea), consult M. Moore, *Medicinal Plants of the Mountain West* (Museum of New Mexico Press, Santa Fe, 1979, pp. 109–10); and L. S. M. Curtin, *Healing Herbs of the Upper Rio Grande* (Laboratory of Anthropology, Museum of New Mexico, Santa Fe, 1947, pp. 49–51). Datura is discussed by W. J. Litzinger, "Ceramic Evidence for the Prehistoric Use of *Datura* in Mexico and the Southwestern United States" (*The Kiva*, vol. 44, no. 2–3, 1979, pp. 145–58). For the medical used of dogbane, see Moore, *Medicinal Plants*, pp. 70–72.

Costume is considered in Riley, *Frontier People*, pp. 208–10, 283–84. Modern social and ceremonial structures of the Rio Grande Pueblos are discussed in B. P. Dutton, *American Indians of the Southwest* (University of New Mexico Press, 1983, pp. 18–31); E. P. Dozier, *The Pueblo Indians of North America* (Holt, Rinehart and Winston, 1970, pp. 142–76, esp. pp. 165–66); F. Hawley (Ellis), "Big Kivas, Little Kivas, and Moiety Houses in Historical Reconstruction" (*Southwestern Journal of Anthropology*, vol. 6, no. 3, 1950, pp. 286–302); and P. Schaafsma, "Imagery and Magic," pp. 167–71. For the twin god complex, consult M. Thompson, "Codes from the Underworld: Mimbres Iconography Revealed" (paper presented at the sixth Biannual Mogollon Conference, October 1990).

For a discussion of pottery in the Rio Grande valley, see Snow, "Rio Grande Glaze" (in Schroeder, ed., *Southwestern Ceramics*, pp. 250, 254–56, 261); and F. M. Hawley, *Field Manual of Southwestern Pottery Types* (University of New Mexico Bulletin, Anthropological Series, vol. 1, no. 4, 1936, pp. 85, 89). Keresan "ownership" of certain of the Cerrillos mines is suggested by A. F. Bandelier; see C. H. Lange and C. L. Riley, *The Southwestern Journals of Adolph F. Bandelier, 1880–82* (University of New Mexico Press, 1966, p. 109). A cautionary note on the firmness of ceramic dates is given by D. H. Snow, "Por alli no hay losa, ni se hace: Gilded Men and Glazed Pottery on the Southern Plains, Some Observations" (paper read at the symposium "Where Did the Encuentro Happen in the Southwest?," Las Vegas, N.M., August 1992). Trade in the Rio Grande area is extensively discussed in Riley, *Frontier People*, pp. 236–40, 267–77, 302–4, 319–27, passim.

Chapter 9

For the settlement of the West Indies beginning with Columbus's first voyage in 1492, see I. Rouse, *The Tainos* (Yale University Press, 1992, pp. 6–7, 150–61); Sauer, *Spanish Main*, pp. 29–34, 71–103; and J. B. Brebner, *The Explorers of North America* (Doubleday Anchor Books, 1955). Information

SOURCES AND COMMENTARY

on earlier prehistoric periods in central Mexico is given in T. P. Culbert, "Mesoamerica" (in Jennings, ed., *Ancient Native Americans,* pp. 403–53, esp. pp. 424–31, 441–44, 448–50). For information on the Córdova and Grijalva expeditions, see Sauer, *Spanish Main,* pp. 214–17; and R. C. Padden, *The Hummingbird and the Hawk* (Harper and Row, 1967, pp. 116–20, 138–42).

On the Aztecs and Spanish conquest of central and west Mexico, see B. C. Brundage, *A Rain of Darts* (University of Texas Press, 1972); Padden, *Hummingbird and Hawk;* and C. O. Sauer, *The Road to Cíbola* (*Ibero-Americana,* no. 3, 1932, esp. pp. 1–8). For Aztec life and culture, see A. Chavero, ed. and annot., *Obras históricas de don Fernando de Alva Ixtlilxochitl* (Editora Nacional, México, D.F., 1952); M. D. Coe, *Mexico* (Thames and Hudson, London, 1962, pp. 152–75); H. Cortés, *Letters* (F. A. MacNutt, ed. and trans., Rio Grande Press, Glorieta, N.M., 1977 [reprint of the A. H. Clark Co. edition, 1908]); and A. R. Reyes, *Perfil histórico del Tlacaelel* (Edamex, México, 1986).

On the importance of human sacrifice and its impact on the Aztecs, see S. F. Cook, "Human Sacrifice and Warfare as Factors in the Demography of Pre-Colonial Mexico" (*Human Biology,* vol. 18, 1946, pp. 81–102). A discussion of exaggeration in the Aztec human sacrificial "body count" can be found in A. M. Reed, *El remoto pasado de Mexico* (M. L. Perea, trans., Editorial Diana, México, 1972, pp. 103–5). For the idea that human sacrifice alleviated population pressure, see E. R. Wolf, *Sons of the Shaking Earth* (University of Chicago Press, 1959, p. 145). In fairness, Wolf does not consider this a sufficient explanation. A different perspective on human sacrifice is given by M. Harner, "The Ecological Basis for Aztec Sacrifice" (*American Ethnologist,* vol. 4, pp. 117–35). Harner believes that cannibalism (as an adjunct of sacrifice) among the Aztecs was an important source of protein. For a discussion of the many problems of interpreting Aztec sacrifice, see N. Davies, *The Aztec Empire* (University of Oklahoma Press, 1987, pp. 217–42).

A character sketch of Moteuczoma is given in Padden, *Hummingbird and Hawk,* esp. pp. 81–82, 85–89, 92–93. A more favorable assessment of the emperor is contained in C. A. Burland, *Montezuma: Lord of the Aztecs* (G. P. Putnam's Sons, 1973). Information on Marina is given in Cortés, *Letters,* vol. 1, pp. 328–29. The luxury of Moteuczoma's everyday life is described in Cortes's second letter (*Letters,* vol. 1, pp. 266–68); and Bernal Dias del Castillo, *Verdadera historia de los sucesos de la conquista de la Nueva España* (Madrid, Imprenta de Don Benito Cano, 4 vols., 1796, vol. 2, pp. 91–99).

A superior short summary of Cortés's war with the Aztecs can be found in F. Horcasitas, *The Aztecs Then and Now* (Editorial Minutiae Mexicana,

México, D.F., 1979, pp. 74–82). Another good, if rather impressionistic, summary is C. Fuentes, *The Buried Mirror* (Houghton Mifflin, 1992, pp. 110–17). Spanish introduction of smallpox is discussed in Padden, *Hummingbird and Hawk*, pp. 206, 210; and Brundage, *Rain of Darts*, pp. 278–79, 330. For the final days of the war consult Brundage, *Rain of Darts*, pp. 289, 332 n. 19.

Chapter 10

A discussion of the history of the *requerimiento* can be found in A. R. Pagden, trans. and ed., *Hernán Cortés: Letters from Mexico* (Grossman Publishers, New York, 1971, 453–55). For an account of the Tarascans, see E. R. Craine and R. C. Reindorp, trans. and eds., *The Chronicles of Michoacán* (University of Oklahoma Press, 1970, esp. pp. xi–xvi, 70–100). For events on the west coast, consult Sauer, *Road to Cíbola*, pp. 1–8; C. O. Sauer and D. Brand, *Aztatlán* (*Ibero-Americana*, no. 1, 1932, pp. 41–51); H. H. Bancroft, *History of the North Mexican States and Texas, vol. 1, 1531–1800* (A. L. Bancroft and Co., San Francisco, 1884, pp. 12–23, 32–44); and B. C. Hedrick and C. L. Riley, *Documents Ancillary to the Vaca Journey* (University Museum, Southern Illinois University, Carbondale, University Museum Studies no. 5, 1976, pp. 16–32, 34–35, 39 -54, 56–57).

Along with most researchers in this area, I have identified the village called Yaquimi by Guzmán, and its river, as the lower Yaqui region. One exception to this consensus, however, was C. C. Di Peso, who believed that Guzmán's Yaquimi was actually on the lower Mayo River. Consult C. D. Di Peso, J. B. Rinaldo, and G. J. Fenner, *Casas Grandes: A Fallen Trade Center of the Gran Chichimeca*, vol. 4 (Northland Press, Flagstaff, 1974, pp. 46–47). For a discussion of the journey of Cabeza de Vaca, see A. N. Cabeza de Vaca, *Naufragios* (Editorial Layac, México, D.F., 1944, esp. pp. 61–64); and B. C. Hedrick and C. L. Riley, *The Journey of the Vaca Party* (University Museum, Southern Illinois University, University Museum Studies no. 2, 1974, esp. pp. 59–67). The de Soto expedition is succinctly but authoritatively treated in J. R. Swanton, *Indians of the Southeastern United States* (Bureau of American Ethnology Bulletin 137, Washington, D.C., 1946, pp. 39–59). The Seven Cities of Antillia are discussed in Fray A. Chavez, *Coronado's Friars* (Academy of American Franciscan History, Washington, D.C., 1968, pp. 14–16).

For the Marcos journey and the trip northward by Coronado, consult Hammond and Rey, *Narratives of the Coronado Expedition*, esp. pp. 44–49 (Coronado's letter to the king, July 15, 1539), pp. 63–82 (Marcos's report), pp.

162–70 (Coronado to Mendoza, August 3, 1540), and pp. 202–13 (Castañeda). Also see M. T. Rodack, "Cíbola Revisited" (in *Southwestern Culture History, Collected Papers in Honor of Albert H. Schroeder,* C. H. Lange, ed., Papers of the Archaeological Society of New Mexico, no. 10, pp. 163–82). Edmund Ladd, curator of ethnology at the Laboratory of Anthropology, Museum of New Mexico, and a Zuni tribal member, believes that the Cíbolans considered Esteban a spy for Spanish slave-raiders (personal communication; also see Ladd's comments in the 1992 PBS television documentary *Surviving Columbus*).

From my reading of the Spanish documents I have no doubt that Esteban was black in the sense the word is used in the modern world. See C. L. Riley, "Blacks in the Early Southwest" (*Ethnohistory*, vol. 19, no. 3, 1972, pp. 247–60). At one time, however, this was a hotly argued question, perhaps because of reluctance to give a black man credit for pioneering the trail to Arizona and New Mexico. As recently as 1949, Cleve Hallenbeck, in an edition of Fray Marcos's account, insisted that Esteban was a "Moor." David J. Weber has surveyed the evidence on Esteban's racial status in his introduction to the re-publication of the Marcos journey. See D. J. Weber, "Introduction" (in *The Journey of Fray Marcos de Niza,* C. Hallenbeck, ed., Southern Methodist University Press, 1987, pp. vii–l). Hallenbeck's own comment on the matter comes on p. 98.

For Marata, Totonteac, and Acus, consult C. L. Riley, "The Sonoran Statelets Revisited" (in *Clues to the Past, Papers in Honor of William M. Sundt,* M. S. Duran and D. T. Kirkpatrick, eds., Archaeological Society of New Mexico, no. 16, 1990, pp. 229–35). Information on the makeup of the Coronado expedition is contained in Hammond and Rey, *Narratives of the Coronado Expedition,* pp. 87–108 (muster roll). For the nationalities involved, see H. E. Bolton, *Coronado: Knight of Pueblos and Plains* (University of New Mexico Press, 1964 [first published in 1949], p. 71). The name Yancuictlalpan for the Southwest is given in J. E. L. Monjarás-Ruiz and M. de la Cruz Pailles eds., *Tlatelolco: Fuentes e historia* (vol. 2 of *Obras de Robert H. Barlow,* Instituto Nacional de Antropología e Historia, Mexico, D.F., 1989, p. 232). I have rounded off the numbers of Europeans in the expedition to 350. G. D. Inglis, in "The Men of Cíbola: New Investigations on the Francisco Vázquez de Coronado Expedition" (*Panhandle-Plains Historical Review,* vol. 55, 1982, pp. 1–24, esp. p. 4), was able to identify 338 individuals, but this was probably not the full roster.

Coronado's route to Cíbola is reexamined in C. L. Riley, "Coronado in the Southwest" (*Archaeology, Art, and Anthropology: Collected Papers in Honor of J. J. Brody,* M. S. Duran and D. T. Kirkpatrick, eds., Papers of the Archaeological Society of New Mexico, no. 18, 1992, pp. 147–56). My belief that the northeast Sonoran area contained statelets has certainly been disputed (see sources for chapter 14), as has my routing of Coronado's journey. Indeed, there are almost as many proposed routes for Coronado as there are experts on Coronado matters. A summary of some of these routes has been published by the National Park Service in J. E. Ivey, D. L. Rhodes, and J. P. Sanchez, eds., *The Coronado Expedition of 1540–42: A Special History Report Prepared for the Coronado Trail Study* (U. S. Department of the Interior, National Park Service, 1991). Parenthetically, the alternate routes I proposed in Ivey et al. are ones I have now discarded. For an identification of Ko:thlu-wala:wa, see E. J. Ladd, "Zuni on the Day the Men in Metal Arrived" (paper given at the conference "Where Did the Encuentro Happen in the South-west?," Las Vegas, N.M., August 1992).

Chapter 11

For the capture of Hawikuh, see Hammond and Rey, *Narratives of the Coronado Expedition,* pp. 168–69 (Coronado's letter to Viceroy Mendoza), pp. 208–9 (Castañeda's history), and pp. 323, 345 (subsequent testimony of Coronado and López de Cárdenas). Much of the information on the Coronado expedition can be found in Hammond and Rey's easily available *Narratives,* which includes dependable translations of most of the major extant documents of the expedition.

There is also considerable information, especially on Spanish activities in the Rio Grande, in the mid-seventeenth-century writings of A. Tello, O.F.M., *Libro segundo de la crónica miscelanea* (Imprenta de "La Republica Literaria," Guadalajara, 1891, esp. pp. 414–24). In the mid-eighteenth century, Matías de Mota Padilla also gave an account of the Coronado period. Like Tello, he utilized documents now lost—for example, the papers of Pedro de Tovar. See M. de la Mota Padilla, *Historia de la conquista de la provincia de la Nueva-Galicia* (Publicado de la Sociedad Mexicana de Geografía y Estadística, Imprinta del Gobierno en Palacio, México, 1870, pp. 158–70). To the best of my knowledge, neither Tello's nor Mota Padilla's work has been published in English translation in its entirety. However, a translation of Mota Padilla's account of the Coronado expedition appears in A. G. Day, "Mota Padilla on the Coronado Expedition" (*Hispanic American Historical Review,* vol. 20, no. 1, 1940, pp. 88–110).

For an extended discussion of sixteenth- and seventeenth-century sources for the greater Southwest, see Riley, *Frontier People,* pp. 329–45. A good secondary account, not only of Coronado's and later Southwestern expeditions but also of those of the eastern United States during the same period, is one by D. J. Weber, *The Spanish Frontier in North America* (Yale University Press, 1992, esp. pp. 30–146).

Spanish activities at Hopi are discussed in Hammond and Rey, *Narratives,* pp. 213–15 (Castañeda). Information that Tovar actually destroyed a Hopi town is given in Luxán's account in Hammond and Rey, *Rediscovery of New Mexico,* pp. 188–89; and in M. Cuevas, ed., *Historia de los descubrimientos antiguos y modernos de la Nueva España, escrita por el conquistador Baltasar de Obregón, año de 1584* (Departamento Editorial de la Sría. de Educación Pública, México, 1924, p. 294). A discussion of communication problems in the Coronado period can be found in C. L. Riley, "Early Spanish Indian Communication in the Greater Southwest" (*New Mexico Historical Review ,* vol. 46, no. 4, 1971, pp. 285–314). For the possibility that some Nahuatl was spoken in the sixteenth-century Southwest, see the testimony of Gaspar de Saldaña (AGI [General Archives of the Indies, Seville, Spain] Justicia, legajo 1021, pieza 3); also Riley, "Communication," pp. 304, 313; and Sauer and Brand, *Aztatlán,* pp. 56–58. Information on Father Padilla is contained in Chavez, *Coronado's Friars,* pp. 14–27.

For the trip eastward by Padilla and Alvarado, consult C. L. Riley and J. L. Manson, "The Cibola-Tiguex Route (*New Mexico Historical Review,* vol. 58, no. 4, 1983, pp. 347–67, esp. pp. 353–56); and Hammond and Rey, *Narratives of the Coronado Expedition,* pp. 182–84, 217–220. A recent investigator of Coronado's route, Douglas Preston (*Cities of Gold,* Simon & Schuster, 1992, pp. 384–89), crossed the *malpais* west of Acoma on horseback. The prepared trail he used is old, but I doubt that it dates to Coronado's time. Hammond and Rey, in *Narratives,* p. 183, n. 9, identify Alvarado's town "located among some banks" as Taos. Castañeda's list of pueblos is in Hammond and Rey, *Narratives,* pp. 258–59. For the historic distribution of Manso Indians (possibly Castañeda's four downriver pueblos), see P. H. Beckett and T. L. Corbett, *The Manso Indians* (COAS Publishing and Research, Las Cruces, N.M., 1992, esp. p. 40). Beckett and Corbett (p. 48) believe the Manso to be direct descendants of the El Paso phase of the Jornada Mogollon.

The best account of Spanish military activities in the Rio Grande valley in 1540–41 is found in Castañeda's account in Hammond and Rey, *Narratives,* pp. 223–33; see also Tello, *Libro segundo,* pp. 418–27. For Mota Padilla's account, see *Historia de la conquista,* pp. 160–62. Turk's account of the wonders of Quivira can be found in Hammond and Rey, *Narratives,* p. 221 (Castañeda); see also Riley, "Communication," pp. 304–305.

For locations of various of the Tiguex pueblos, see G. Vivian, "A Re-study of the Province of Tiguex" (Master's thesis, Department of Anthropology, University of New Mexico, 1932); C. L. Riley, "Puaray and Coronado's Tiguex" (in *Papers in Honor of Erik K. Reed,* A. H. Schroeder, ed., Archaeological Society of New Mexico, no. 6, pp. 197–213); and B. J. Vierra, *A Sixteenth Century Spanish Campsite in the Tiguex Province* (Museum of New Mexico Research Section, LA Notes 475, 1989, esp. pp. 223–27). Also see S. M. Hordes, "Historical Context of LA 54147" (in Vierra, *Sixteenth Century Campsite,* pp. 207–18); and D. H. Snow, "The Identification of Puaray Pueblo" (in Frisbie, ed., *Collected Papers in Honor of Florence Hawley Ellis,* pp. 463–80). For an opposing view of the location of Arenal, see A. H. Schroeder and D. Matson, *A Colony on the Move: Gaspar Castaño de Sosa's Journal, 1590–1591* (School of American Research, Santa Fe, 1965, p. 171).

Chapter 12

For the attitudes of Isabella and Ferdinand toward the Indians, see C. H. Haring, *The Spanish Empire in America* (Oxford University Press, 1947, pp. 42–48). Though less concerned than Isabella about the welfare of Indians, Ferdinand did sponsor the 1512 Laws of Burgos, which gave Native Americans their first comprehensive protection within the Spanish system (Haring, p. 48). For a consideration of the Franciscan "millenarian" attitude, consult J. Lafaye, *Quetzalcóatl and Guadalupe* (University of Chicago Press, 1976, pp. 30–37). A discussion of Las Casas's contributions can be found in Sauer, *Spanish Main,* pp. 38–39, 197. Biographical information on Las Casas is given in G. Sanderlin, trans. and ed., *Bartolomé de Las Casas: A Selection of His Writings* (Alfred A. Knopf, 1971, pp. 3–24).

Two modern writers who have given detailed, dramatic, and well-written accounts of the "Tiguex war" are Bolton, *Coronado,* pp. 201–37, and A. G. Day, *Coronado's Quest* (University of California Press, 1940, pp. 196–210). Bolton is especially valuable because of extensive archival research on the Coronado period and "on the ground" tracing of Coronado's route. However, the reader should be cautioned that both these writers are heavily prejudiced toward the Spanish point of view.

An account of the Tiguex war, as well as Alvarado's activities in regard to the Pecos prisoners, is found in Hammond and Rey, *Narratives,* pp. 223–31

(Castañeda), pp. 325–35 (Coronado's testimony), and pp. 347–61 (Cárdenas's testimony). The supposed Indian name of Juan Alemán is given by Cárdenas (in *Narratives*, p. 359). Additional testimony about these events can be found in manuscript sources: AGI Justicia, legajo 1021, pieza 4 (Información contra . . . Coronado), and AGI Justicia, legajo 1021, pieza 3 (Relación sacada de la probanza . . . que trata con Dn. García Ramirez de Cárdenas). For a seventeenth-century account using documents now lost, see Tello, *Libro segundo*, pp. 415–24; for an eighteenth-century account, see Mota Padilla, *Historia de la conquista*, pp. 161–63.

The story of the arrow poison used at Moho is given in Tello, *Libro segundo*, p. 424. The identical number of women and children taken from the unnamed pueblo and from Moho, before the final attack on the latter pueblo, makes one wonder if Castañeda (Hammond and Rey, *Narratives*, pp. 229–31) may not be duplicating his data. The question of the location of Coofor and Moho is discussed in Vierra, *Sixteenth Century Campsite*, pp. 223–27. For the view that Moho is LA 326, see A. H. Schroeder, "Vásquez de Coronado and the Southern Tiwa Pueblos" (in Duran and Kirkpatrick, eds., *Archaeology, Art, and Anthropology*, pp. 185–91). A good description of the Mann-Zuris site (LA 290) is contained in M. P. Marshall, *An Archeological Survey of the Mann-Zuris Pueblo Complex* (Report to the New Mexico Historic Preservation Commission and Miller-Brown Land Co., Albuquerque and Santa Fe, Phase II, 1988). For Spanish contacts with the Keresan towns during the Moho siege, see Hammond and Rey, *Narratives*, p. 233, 331; and Bolton, *Coronado*, pp. 225–26.

The name Tatarrax appears in F. Lopez de Gómara, *Historia general de las indias* (Calpe, Madrid, 1922, tomo II, p. 234). Barrionuevo's trip to Taos is reported by Castañeda in Hammond and Rey, *Narratives*, pp. 244–45. Information on the status of Picurís during the Coronado expedition can be found in A. H. Schroeder, *A Brief History of Picuris Pueblo* (Adams State College, Series in Anthropology, no. 2, 1974, p. 1).

Chapter 13

The date April 23 is given in Coronado's letter to the king (Hammond and Rey, *Narratives*, p. 186). Castañeda (in *Narratives*, p. 234) gives the date May 5. However, the one extant Castañeda manuscript was copied about 1595, after the date (1582) that Pope Gregory ordered a change to the Gregorian calendar. It has been suggested that the scribe adjusted the date to fit the new calendar. If so, it was a two-day overadjustment.

SOURCES AND COMMENTARY

For information on the Tano pueblos of the Galisteo basin and on Cicúye, or Pecos, see Hammond and Rey, *Narratives,* pp. 234–35, 257–59 (Castañeda). On the possibility of wheeled vehicles, there is a curious comment by Juan de Troyano in "Información contra Coronado" (AGI Justicia, legajo 1021). According to Troyano, he had been sent from the Tiguex area to Cíbola in the winter of 1540–41 to bring back *carros de artillería* that had been left there. It is not clear what these implements were. As suggested in the text, possibly they were cradles or carriages for the small cannons which may have been equipped with wheels for better maneuverability on the battle field. Some of the cannons, perhaps all of them, were left behind at Zia when the army left for the plains.

The citation from Alvarado and Padilla about straw houses is from *Narratives,* p. 183. See also A. H. Schroeder, "Pueblos Abandoned in Historic Times" (*Handbook of North American Indians,* vol. 9, pp. 247–48); and J. L. Kessell, *Kiva, Cross, and Crown* (University of New Mexico Press, 1987, pp. 3–27). That the Spaniards collected pottery from the Galisteo pueblos seems to be indicated by Galisteo pottery at the Coronado campsite (LA 54147); see Vierra, *Sixteenth Century Campsite,* pp. 75–76. For the trip onto the plains and the return to Tiguex, consult Hammond and Rey, *Narratives,* p. 183 (Discovery of Tiguex by Alvarado and Padilla), pp. 186–90 (Coronado to King), pp. 290–94 (Relación del suceso), pp. 235–40, 256–64 (Castañeda), pp. 300–307 (Jaramillo), pp. 310–12 (Relación Postrera), p. 336 (Coronado testimony), and pp. 362–63 (Cárdenas testimony).

The first delineation of a Garza site (though not by name) seems to have come with W. C. Holden, "Blue Mountain Rock Shelter" (*Texas Archeological and Paleontological Society,* vol. 10, 1938, pp. 208–21). Since that time, a number of Garza sites have been found on the southern part of the Llano Estacado and beyond it into the Pecos drainage. A summary of the Garza complex, with a bibliography of various site reports and other publications, is contained in T. G. Baugh, "Culture History and Protohistoric Societies in the Southern Plains" (in *Current Trends in Southern Plains Archaeology,* T. G. Baugh, ed., Plains Anthropologist, Memoir 21, 1986, pp. 176–81). See also J. L. Hofman, "Protohistoric Culture History on the Southern Great Plains" (in *From Clovis to Comanchero,* J. L. Hofman et al., eds., Arkansas Archeological Survey Research Series, no. 35, 1989, pp. 91–100, esp. pp. 98–99). Hofman (p. 98) draws his definition of the Garza complex from J. T. Hughes, "Cultural Developments during the Archaic and Neoindian Stages on the Texas High Plains" (ms. in files of the Oklahoma Archeological Survey, Norman).

For Garza trade patterns and ceramic ware, consult J. A. Habicht-Mauche, "Evidence for the Manufacture of Southwestern-Style Culinary Ceramics on the Southern Plains" (in *Farmers, Hunters, and Colonists: Interaction between the Southwest and the Southern Plains,* K. A. Spielmann, ed., University of Arizona Press, 1991, pp. 51–70, esp. pp. 56–57, 60, 67). See also J. A. Habicht-Mauche, "An Analysis of Southwestern Style Utility Ware Ceramics from the Southern Plains . . ." (Ph.D. dissertation, Department of Anthropology, Harvard University, 1988). An argument that the Garza people were Apaches or possibly Caddoans is given in J. T. Hughes, "Prehistoric Cultural Developments on the Texas High Plains" (*Bulletin of the Texas Archaeological Society,* Austin, vol. 60, 1989–91, pp. 1–55, esp. pp. 34–36).

For a discussion of Coronado's route from Pecos to central Kansas, see Riley, "Coronado in the Southwest," pp. 152–55. See R. Flint and S. C. Flint, "The Location of Coronado's 1541 Bridge" (*Plains Anthropologist,* vol. 36, no. 135, 1991, pp. 171–76, esp. p. 175), for speculation as to the kind of bridge; see also R. Flint and S. C. Flint, "The Coronado Expedition: Cicuye to the Rio de Cicuye Bridge" (*New Mexico Historical Review,* vol. 67, no. 2, 1992, pp. 123–38); and R. Flint, "Who Designed Coronado's Bridge across the Pecos River?" (*The Kiva,* vol. 57, no. 4, 1992, pp. 331–42).

For a different viewpoint of this portion of Coronado's route, consult A. H. Schroeder, "A Reanalysis of the Routes of Coronado and Oñate into the Plains" (*Plains Anthropologist,* vol. 7, no. 15, pp. 2–23); also A. H. Schroeder, "The Locale of Coronado's 'Bridge' " (*New Mexico Historical Review,* vol. 67, no. 2, 1992, pp. 115–22). Schroeder believed that Coronado's bridge was across the Canadian River, near present-day Conchos Dam. There is a detailed discussion of the route in Bolton, *Coronado,* pp. 238–304, well worth reading. Identification of Coronado's route on the Llano Estacado is still very much a matter of controversy. See Bolton, *Coronado,* pp. 266–67, for arguments that the deep barranca was Palo Duro. A more recent evaluation of evidence for the Coronado route can be found in W. R. Wedel, J. T. Hughes, and W. M. Wedel, "A Survey of Western Approaches to the Llano Estacado" (ms. in author's possession, 1991), and in D. J. Blakeslee, "Which Barrancas? Narrowing the Possibilities" (paper given at the symposium, "Where Did the Encuentro Happen in the Southwest?," Las Vegas, N.M., August 1992).

For the identification of the Querechos and Teyas, see J. P. Harrington, "Southern Peripheral Athapaskan Origins, Divisions, and Migrations" (in *Essays in Historical Anthropology of North America, Published in Honor of John R. Swanton,* Smithsonian Publication 3588, Washington, D.C., 1940, pp. 503–32, esp. p. 512). See also D. A. Gunnerson, *The Jicarilla Apache* (Northern Illinois University Press, 1974, pp. 17–21). For the possible Caddoan affiliation of the Teyas, see A. H. Schroeder, "A Study of the Apache Indians, Part 1, The Apaches and Their Neighbors" (ms. in files of the Laboratory of Anthropology, Museum of New Mexico, Santa Fe, pp. 35–36); this material was later published by Garland Press, New York. See also J. A. Habicht-Mauche, "Coronado's Querechos and Teyas" (*Plains Anthropologist,* vol. 37, no. 140, 1992, pp. 247–59.) A good summary of Apachean origins and a cautionary note on classifications of both Querechos and Teyas is found in M. E. Opler, "The Apachean Culture Pattern and Its Origins" (*Handbook of North American Indians,* vol. 10, pp. 368, 381–83, 387).

An argument that the Jumanos were Uto-Aztecan speaking comes from T. H. Naylor, "Athapaskans They Weren't: The Suma Rebels Executed at Casas Grandes in 1685" (in Wilcox and Masse, eds., *Protohistoric,* pp. 275–81); see also F. V. Scholes and H. P. Mera, "Some Aspects of the Jumano Problem" (Carnegie Institution of Washington, Contributions to American Anthropology and History, vol. 6, no. 34, 1940, pp. 265–99). An argument that the Jumanos were possibly Apachean speaking is found in J. C. Kelley, *Jumano and Patarabueye: Relations at La Junta de los Rios* (Anthropological Papers, Museum of Anthropology, University of Michigan, no. 77, 1986 [reprint of 1947 dissertation], p. 143). I originally concurred in this identification (see Riley, *Frontier People,* p. 297), but have since changed my position.

For a new interpretation of the Teyas and Jumanos, see N. P. Hickerson, *The Jumano: Hunters and Traders of the South Plains* (University of Texas Press, 1994, pp. 220–30); "The Linguistic Position of Jumano" (*Journal of Anthropological Research,* vol. 44, no. 3, 1988, pp. 311–26); "Jumano: The Missing Link in South Plains History" (*Journal of the West,* vol. 29, no. 4, 1990, pp. 5–12); and "Diachronic Aspects of the 'Jumano' Problem" (paper read at the annual meeting of the American Society for Ethnohistory, November 1991). Teya Indian accounts of Cabeza de Vaca are contained in Hammond and Rey, *Narratives,* pp. 237–38 (Castañeda), and pp. 301–2 (Jaramillo). Differences between Jumanos and Teyas are indicated in "Relación del suceso" (Hammond and Rey, *Narratives,* p. 292).

Evidence for a more direct return route for the main army is contained in D. J. Blakeslee, "Coronado Route Project, Preliminary Report" (ms. in author's possession, 1991); see also Castañeda (in Hammond and Rey, *Narratives,* pp. 242–43, 279). Blakeslee has speculated on a Yellowhouse route for the return army, as has E. L. Kiser in "The Re-examination of Pedro de Castañeda's Bone Bed by Geological Investigations" (*Texas Archeological Society*

Bulletin, vol. 49, 1978, pp. 332–39). The story of the Caddoan woman is given by Castañeda (Hammond and Rey, *Narratives,* p. 243). The Spanish text of Castañeda's account (G. P. Winship, *The Coronado Expedition,* Rio Grande Press, Chicago, 1964 [reproduced from the Smithsonian Institution Annual Report of 1892–93, pub. 1896], p. 146), referred to her as "una india labrada" (a painted or tattooed Indian woman).

Barrionuevo's trip to the upper Rio Grande country is told by Castañeda in Hammond and Rey, *Narratives,* pp. 244–45. Identification of Yungue and Okeh (San Juan Pueblo) can be found in F. Hawley Ellis, "The Long Lost 'City' of San Gabriel del Yungue . . ." (in *When Cultures Met: Remembering San Gabriel del Yunge Oweenge,* papers from a conference held at San Juan Pueblo, N.M., October 1984, Sunstone Press, Santa Fe, 1987, pp. 10–44, esp. pp. 15–17). See also F. Hawley Ellis, *San Gabriel del Yungue* (Sunstone Press, 1989). Castañeda (Hammond and Rey, *Narratives,* pp. 201, 244) says that a Francisco Barrionuevo, otherwise identified as "a caballero from Granada," went on the Taos expedition. However, there were only two Barrionuevos on the primary muster roll—Velasco and his brother, Rodrigo (Hammond and Rey, *Narratives,* pp. 95, 105 n. 87). I have identified Barrionuevo as Velasco, following Bolton, *Coronado,* p. 310. Still, the muster roll is incomplete, and a Francisco Barrionuevo who led the expedition to Taos may have actually existed.

For a discussion of the Great Bend aspect and the first part of the Wheeler phase (Edwards complex), as well as the Garza complex, see Baugh, "Culture History," pp. 167–83; Hofman, "Protohistoric Culture History," pp. 94–99; and W. R. Wedel, *An Introduction to Kansas Archeology* (Bureau of American Ethnology, Bulletin 174, Washington, D.C., 1959, pp. 571–89).

The account of Coronado's dash to Quivira and the treatment of Turk is found in Hammond and Rey, *Narratives,* pp. 187–89 (Coronado to King), pp. 235–32, 241–42 (Castañeda), pp. 291–92 (Relación del suceso), and pp. 303–6 (Jaramillo). On Turk's personality, see various of the *Narratives,* but particularly pp. 234–40, 245–46 (Castañeda). Discussion of the Wichitas is contained in M. M. Wedel, "The Wichita Indians in the Arkansas River Basin" (in *Plains Indian Studies: A Collection of Essays in Honor of John C. Ewers and Waldo Wedel,* D. H. Ubelaker and H. J. Viola, eds., Smithsonian Contributions to Anthropology, Washington, D.C., 1982, pp. 118–34). For the Harahey identification as Pawnee, see G. E. Hyde, *The Pawnee Indians* (University of Oklahoma Press, 1974 [original edition 1951], p. 33); Wedel, *Introduction to Kansas Archeology,* p. 61; and Riley, *Frontier People,* p. 21. Turk's involvement in the Pecos plot is described by Castañeda in Hammond and

Rey, *Narratives,* pp. 241–42. Historians in the past have dealt harshly with Turk, ignoring his heroism and loyalty and assuming that it was somehow his *duty* to aid the Spaniards (see, for example, Bolton, *Coronado,* pp. 300–303; Day, *Coronado's Quest,* pp. 248, 254–55).

Chapter 14

For Coronado and Quivira, consult the general's letter to the king (in Hammond and Rey, *Narratives,* pp. 185–90). The plan to return to Quivira is discussed in Hammond and Rey, *Narratives,* p. 246 (Castañeda). This chronicler, who was bitter at the retreat to New Spain, also described the dissension in the Spanish camp over Coronado's plans (pp. 266–68).

For the troubles in Sonora, see Hammond and Rey, *Narratives,* pp. 264–265, 268–70 (Castañeda); and Cuevas, ed., *Historia de los descubrimientos . . . escrito por . . . Obregón,* pp. 152 -53. See also the comments of Bolton, *Coronado,* pp. 317–25; and Day, *Coronado's Quest,* pp. 286–94. Some light is shed on Alcaráz's behavior in testimony by Cristóbal de Escobar in trial hearings conducted by Lorenzo de Tejada in 1544 (AGI Justicia, legajo 1021, pieza 4). See also Castañeda's comments in Hammond and Rey, *Narratives,* pp. 268–70; also, Cuevas, *Historia,* pp. 152–53. The "poison tree" is discussed by Riley, *Frontier People,* p. 94. A brief summary of the cultural situation in northeast Sonora can be found in Riley, "View from the Protohistoric" (in P. E. Minnis and C. L. Redman, eds., *Perspectives on Southwestern Prehistory,* Westview Press, Boulder, Colo., 1990, pp. 230–34); see also C. L. Riley and J. L. Manson, "The Sonoran Connection: Road and Trail Networks in the Protohistoric Period" (in *Ancient Road Networks and Settlement Hierarchies in the New World,* C. D. Trombold, ed., Cambridge University Press, 1991, pp. 132–44).

By no means do all experts agree with me on the Sonoran situation. For criticisms, see W. H. Doelle's review of *The Frontier People* (*The Kiva,* vol. 54, no. 2, pp. 165–68); also B. L. Fontana, "Were There Indian Statelets in the Río Sonora Valley?" (*Newsletter,* Southwestern Mission Research Center, vol. 23, no. 79, June 1989, p. 8). A defense of my statelet position is given in W. E. Doolittle, "Settlements and the Development of 'Statelets' in Sonora, Mexico" (*Journal of Field Archaeology,* vol. 11, 1984, pp. 13–24).

For the attack by Gallego, see Castañeda in Hammond and Rey, *Narratives,* pp. 276–78; and Riley, *Frontier People,* pp. 90–92. The injury to Coronado and his subsequent morose behavior is described by Castañeda in Hammond and Rey, *Narratives,* pp. 266–68. The Salamanca story can be found on pp. 266–67, and the petition and counterpetition regarding permanent settlement, on pp. 267–68.

Further information on attempts by certain Spaniards to stay in the Southwest is found in testimony by Francisca de Hozes and her husband, Alonso Sánchez, in the Tejada hearings of 1544 (AGI Justicia, legajo 1021, pieza 4). For the Spaniards, blacks, and Indians who remained in the Southwest, see Hammond and Rey, *Narratives,* pp. 270–301 (Castañeda), p. 294 (Relación del suceso), and p. 306–7 (Jaramillo); Chavez, *Coronado's Friars,* pp. 41–43, 59–74; C. L. Riley, "Mesoamerican Indians in the Early Southwest" (*Ethnohistory,* vol. 21, no. 1, 1974, pp. 25–36, esp. pp. 29 -30); Riley, "Blacks in the Early Southwest," pp. 253–54; and López de Gómara, *Historia,* p. 288.

The trip of one Pueblo individual to Mexico can be documented in a letter of Juan Troyano to King Philip II, Mexico, December 20, 1568 (F. del Paso y Troncoso, *Epistolario de Nueva España 1505–1818,* Antigua Librería Robredo, 16 vols., México, 1939–42, vol. 10, pp. 262–77). The remark by Castañeda on Castilian chickens in northern Sonora is found in Hammond and Rey, *Narratives,* p. 251. Coronado's return home is chronicled by Castañeda (Hammond and Rey, *Narratives,* pp. 272–74).

Chapter 15

For metallurgy, see M. Simmons and F. Turley, *Southwestern Colonial Iron-work* (Museum of New Mexico Press, Santa Fe, 1980, p. 23). Meteoritic and other forms of iron are discussed in Northrop, *Minerals of New Mexico,* pp. 283–87, 301–12, 336–39, passim. For possible sixteenth-century Spanish olive jars, see M. P. Marshall, *El Camino Real de Tierra Adentro: An Archeological Investigation* (New Mexico Historic Preservation Division Survey, Santa Fe, 1991); and Marshall, *The Mann-Zuris Pueblo Complex;* see also J. M. Goggin, *Indian and Spanish Selected Writings* (University of Miami Press, 1964). For a study of early majolica, see F. C. Lister and R. H. Lister, *Sixteenth Century Majolica Pottery in the Valley of Mexico* (University of Arizona Press, 1982, esp. pp. vii, 13–14, 45).

Trade goods among the Spaniards are mentioned by Hammond and Rey, *Narratives.* These include goods carried by Marcos and Alarcón as well as by the Coronado party itself. For Castañeda's comments, see p. 217. More information on beads found archaeologically is given in Wedel, *Introduction to Kansas Archeology,* p. 86; B. Sudbury, "A Sixteenth Century Spanish Colonial Trade Bead from Western Oklahoma" (*Oklahoma Anthropological Society*

SOURCES AND COMMENTARY

Bulletin, vol. 33, 1984, pp. 31–36); W. C. Orchard, *Beads and Beadwork of the American Indians* (Heye Museum Contributions, vol. 13, 1929, pp. 83–84); and M. T. Smith and M. E. Good, *Early Sixteenth Century Glass Beads in the Spanish Colonial Trade* (Cottonlandia Museum Publications, Greenwood, Miss., 1982, pp. 28, 33, 42–43).

Concerning the fate of Padilla and Ubeda, the *donados,* and of the various Mexican Indians left in the Southwest, see Chavez, *Coronado's Friars,* pp. 64 –74; López de Gómara, *Historia,* p. 288; Hammond and Rey, *Narratives,* pp. 270–72 (Castañeda), p. 294 (Relación del suceso), and pp. 306–7 (Jaramillo); Riley, "Mesoamerican Indians," pp. 28–30; and Fray P. Oroz, "Relación de la descripción de la provincia del sancto Evangelio que es en las Indias occidentales, que llaman la Nueva España, 1585" (ms. in files of the Middle American Research Institute, Tulane University, pp. 132–33 [also see photographic reproduction of ms. pages in Chavez, *Coronado's Friars*]). Padilla's involvement in the massacre at Arenal is found in Hammond and Rey, *Narratives,* p. 333 (Coronado's testimony). Crosses in the Zuni area in 1583 are mentioned by Espejo in Hammond and Rey, *Rediscovery,* p. 225. Conceivably, the crosses could have been erected by Coronado's men. For Mesoamerican Indians remaining in the Southwest, consult Castañeda in Hammond and Rey, *Narratives,* p. 272.

Rapid spread of certain European plants into Sonora is mentioned in Cuevas, *Historia,* p. 149. The pre-Oñate appearance of melons is discussed in Hammond and Rey, *Don Juan de Oñate,* vol. 1, p. 484, vol. 2, pp. 626, 634, 645, 660. For indications of peyote use in Casas Grandes, see Di Peso, Rinaldo, and Fenner, *Casas Grandes,* vol. 2, p. 573. On Aztec use of peyote, consult A. J. O. Anderson and C. E. Dibble, *Florentine Codex* (School of American Research and University of Utah Press, Book 11, 1963, pp. 129, 147). Peyote among the Suma is documented by A. F. Bandelier, *Final Report on Investigations in the Southwest, Part 1* (Archaeological Institute of America, American Series, vol. 3, 1990, p. 88). For peyote among Southwestern Pueblos, see F. V. Scholes, "The First Decade of the Inquisition in New Mexico" (*New Mexico Historical Review,* vol. 10, no. 3, 1935, pp. 219–20, 232); C. L. Riley, *Sixteenth Century Trade in the Greater Southwest* (Mesoamerican Studies no. 10, Research Records of the University Museum, Southern Illinois University, 1976, p. 40); and E. C. Parsons, *Pueblo Indian Religion* (University of Chicago Press, 1940, pp. 1029–30).

For Mesoamerican traits (pottery and figurines) at Pecos, see Riley, *Frontier People,* p. 276; and A. V. Kidder, *Artifacts of Pecos* (Yale University Press, 1932, p. 133). A discussion of LA 54147 is found in Vierra, *Sixteenth Century*

SOURCES AND COMMENTARY

Campsite, pp. 75–76, 119, 121–22, 125, 223–27. For *comales* found at site LA 54147, see Vierra, p. 130. Discussions of *patolli* in Mesoamerica and the Southwest appear in J. B. Mountjoy and J. P. Smith, "An Archaeological Patolli from Tomatlán, Jalisco, Mexico" (in Folan, ed., *Contributions,* pp. 240–62); and H. F. McGee, Jr., "Playing at Knowing: Patol and Pueblo World View" (in Folan, ed., *Contributions,* pp. 263–92). On the American origin of patolli, see C. J. Erasmus, "Patolli, Pachisi, and the Limitation of Possibilities" (*Southwestern Journal of Anthropology,* vol. 6, no. 4, pp. 369–87); and R. L. Rands and C. L. Riley, "Diffusion and Discontinuous Distribution" (*American Anthropologist,* vol. 60, no, 2, 1958, pp. 274–97, esp. pp. 277, 279–82).

For the Shalako ceremony, see Parsons in Hedrick, Kelley, and Riley, eds., *Mesoamerican Southwest,* pp. 128–30, 141–42. The two long quotes are from pp. 141 and 142, respectively. Parsons's account of the Teotleco ceremony came from F. R. Bandelier, *Fray Bernardino de Sahagún, 1547–1577, A History of Ancient Mexico* (Fisk University Press, Nashville, 1932, pp. 60–61, 118 –120). For more information on Shalako, see M. J. Young, *Signs from the Ancestors: Zuni Cultural Symbolism and Perceptions of Rock Art* (University of New Mexico Press, 1988, esp. pp. 63–92); K. A. Hays, "Shalako Depictions on Prehistoric Hopi Pottery" (in Duran and Kirkpatrick, eds., *Archaeology, Art,* pp. 73–97); and P. Schaafsma, "Imagery and Magic," in that same publication, pp. 167–68. See also P. Schaafsma, *Rock Art,* p. 126. A good short description of the ceremony is found in C. Gonzales, *The Shalakos Are Coming* (Museum of New Mexico, 1972). A popular account of Shalako appears in the Zuni section of E. Wilson, *Red, Black, Blond, and Olive, Studies in Four Civilizations: Zuñi, Haiti, Soviet Russia, Israel* (Oxford University Press, 1956).

For pottery trends in the sixteenth century, see F. H. Harlow, "Traditional Pueblo Pottery, 1500–1700" (paper in files of the Laboratory of Anthropology, Museum of New Mexico, Santa Fe, 1988). The position of the Querecho Apaches in the Hopi and Acoma country in 1583 has been discussed by C. F. Schaafsma, *The Cerrito Site (AR-4): A Piedra Lumbre Phase Settlement at Abiquiu Reservoir* (School of American Research, Santa Fe, 1979, esp. p. 23). See also Gunnerson, *Jicarilla,* p. 73. Perea's identification of the nomadic people near Hopi as Apaches is found in L. B. Bloom, "Fray Estevan de Perea's Relacion" (*New Mexico Historical Review,* vol. 8, no. 3, pp. 211–35, esp. p. 231).

A discussion of New World diseases is found in A. F. Ramenofsky, *Vectors of Death: The Archaeology of European Contact* (University of New Mexico

Press, 1987, pp. 140, 151, 156–160, 170–71). The possibility that the *sarampión* of 1531 was in fact scarlet fever is suggested by H. J. Prem, "Disease Outbreaks in Central Mexico during the Sixteenth Century" (in *Secret Judgments of God*, N. D. Cook and W. G. Lovell, eds., University of Oklahoma Press, 1991, pp. 20–48, esp. pp. 28–29). See also N. D. Cook and W. G. Lovell, "Unraveling the Web of Disease" (in *Secret Judgments*, pp. 213–242, esp. pp. 220–22 [measles] and pp. 225–27 [typhus]). The ravages of European diseases in the statelet area of northern Sonora are discussed in D. T. Reff, "Contact Shock and the Protohistoric Period in the Greater Southwest" (in *Perspectives on Southwestern Prehistory*, P. E. Minnis and C. L. Redman, eds., Westview Press, Boulder, Colo., 1990, pp. 276–88, esp. pp. 279–81).

For sixteenth-century mentions of measles (or at least of sarampión), see Fray T. de Benavente (Motolinía), *Memoriales* (UNAM, Instituto de Investigaciones Históricas, México, p. 22). For the Códice Aubinsee, see Monjarás-Ruiz and de la Cruz Pailles, *Tlatelolco: Fuentes e historia*, p. 280. D. T. Reff, *Disease, Depopulation, Culture Change in Northwestern New Spain 1518–1764* (University of Utah Press, 1991, pp. 108–11), believes that a measles pandemic spread up the coast of west Mexico, reaching to the Tahue region in the early 1530s. Beginning around 1545 another epidemic, referred to by the Aztecs as "the great matlazahuatl," appeared on the west Mexican coast. Reff considers this disease likely to have been typhus. For smallpox and other diseases in seventeenth-century New Mexico, see Reff, *Disease*, pp. 121, 164 -67.

Chapter 16

For a consideration of alternate routes to the Southwest, see Hammond and Rey, *Narratives*, pp. 281–82 (Castañeda). A. G. Day, in *Coronado's Quest*, p. 383, makes a cogent case for Castañeda's having been on the Ibarra expedition. For this expedition see Cuevas, *Historia;* the initial expedition across the sierra is described on pp. 55–64, and Ibarra's adventures in northern Sonora and Chihuahua, on pp. 139–221. For the early settlements in Durango and Chihuahua, consult J. L. Mecham, *Francisco de Ibarra and Nueva Vizcaya* (Greenwood Press, New York, 1968 [first published 1927], pp. 73–186). Additional information on development of the interior frontier is found in T. H. Naylor and C. W. Polzer, S.J., *The Presidio and Militia on the Northern Frontier of New Spain, 1570–1700* (University of Arizona Press, 1986, esp. pp. 20–29). For the settlement of Santa Bárbara, see Mecham, *Francisco de Ibarra*, pp. 230–32; and Hammond and Rey, *Rediscovery*, pp. 4–5.

For the revised code of 1573 as it related to the Indians, see Hammond and

Rey, *Rediscovery*, pp. 6–7. That Jumanos and Patarabueyes may have spoken the same language is suggested by C. O. Sauer, *The Distribution of Aboriginal Tribes and Languages in Northwestern Mexico* (*Ibero-Americana*, no. 5, 1934, p. 66). In fact, Sauer considered Patarabueye to be simply a subgroup of Jumano. This is unlikely, considering their differences in economy and settlement patterns (see Riley, *Frontier People*, pp. 298–302). However, the two groups may have spoken related languages. Hickerson, *Jumano*, p. 12 n. 7, argues that "[The language of] the Jumano (together with the Suma and Manso) was the same as or closely affiliated with that of the Piro." This is the position I tentatively take in this book (see chapter 13), although I must caution that there is very little purely linguistic evidence on the matter.

Information on the makeup of the Chamuscado party is given in J. L. Mecham, "The Second Spanish Expedition to New Mexico" (*New Mexico Historical Review*, vol. 1, no. 3, 1926, pp. 265–323, esp. pp. 267–68). I have not discussed the Suma and Manso in this book for they are somewhat peripheral to upper Rio Grande peoples. A good discussion of them can be found in Beckett and Corbett, *Manso Indians*. A good thumbnail sketch of the Suma is given by R. E. Gerald, "The Suma Indians of Northern Chihuahua and Western Texas" (in *The Changing Ways of Southwestern Indians*, A. H. Schroeder, ed., Rio Grande Press, Glorieta, N. M., 1973, pp. 1–33).

For the identification of Pueblo towns, see Hammond and Rey, *Rediscovery*, pp. 102–6 (Gallegos), and pp. 115–20 (Martín de Pedrosa). For the boundaries of Tiguex and the numbers and identification of the Tiguex towns, see C. F. Schaafsma, "The Tiguex Province Revisited: The Rio Medio Survey" (in *Papers in Honor of Richard A. Bice*, Papers of the Archaeological Society of New Mexico, no. 13, 1987, pp. 6–13); C. F. Schaafsma, M. P. Marshall, and H. Walt, "Register of Historic Places Inventory—Nomination Form for Pueblos Casa Colorado and Los Trujillos" (in files of the Laboratory of Anthropology, Museum of New Mexico, n.d.); Marshall and Walt, *Rio Abajo*, esp. p. 140; H. P. Mera, *Population Changes in the Rio Grande Glaze-Paint Area* (Technical Series Bulletin, no. 9, Laboratory of Anthropology, Museum of New Mexico, Santa Fe, 1940); Vivian, "Tiguex"; P. P. Forrestal and C. J. Lynch, eds., *Benavides's Memorial of 1630* (Academy of American Franciscan History, Washington, D.C., 1954, pp. 18–20); and E. K. Reed, "The Southern Tewa Pueblos in the Historic Period" (*El Palacio*, vol. 50, no. 12, 1943, pp. 276–88). Reed considered Piedrahita to have been Pecos. Kessell (*Kiva, Cross, and Crown*, pp. 38–39) believed Pecos to have been Nueva Tlaxcala, and I think this is the best, though not completely certain, identification. A discussion of Tunque Pueblo can be found in A. H. Schroeder,

"Tunque Pueblo—Who Lived There?" (in Duran and D. T. Kirkpatrick, eds., *Clues to the Past*, pp. 259–64).

Information on the physical appearance of the Pueblos is contained in Hammond and Rey, *Rediscovery*, pp. 85–86 (Gallegos). The friar's decision to remain at Puaray is explained in Riley, "Puaray," p. 210. The return journey of Chamuscado is found in Hammond and Rey, *Rediscovery*, pp. 109–12 (Gallegos). Information on the friars' fate is reported by Hernando Barrado (Hammond and Rey, *Rediscovery*, pp. 139–40; see also Luxán's account, p. 165). For the makeup of the Espejo party see *Rediscovery*, pp. 153–55 (Luxán), and p. 214 (Espejo); also Cuevas, *Historia*, p. 284.

For the events in Tiguex, see *Rediscovery*, pp. 176–77, 203–4 (Luxán); for the splitting of the Spanish party, pp. 199, 225–26 (Espejo); concerning the events at Acoma and the fight with the Querechos, pp. 200–202 (Luxán); and for a description of the Querechos, pp. 224–25 (Espejo). Consult Cuevas, *Historia*, p. 296, for the split-up in the Spanish party; for the fight at Acoma, p. 297. For the Espejo party's return via the Tano pueblos, Pecos, and the Pecos River, see Hammond and Rey, *Rediscovery*, pp. 205–11 (Luxán), and pp. 228–29 (Espejo); also Cuevas, *Historia*, pp. 299–302. For Luxán's comments that perhaps relate to Blanco Canyon, see *Rediscovery*, p. 210.

Chapter 17

For a discussion of Gaspar Castaño de Sosa and an account of his expedition, see Hammond and Rey, *Rediscovery*, pp. 28–50, 245–320. For comments on Luís de Carbajal and on slaving activities, see J. P. Sánchez, *The Rio Abajo Frontier, 1540–1692* (Albuquerque Museum History Monograph, 1987, pp. 42–44). An excellent analysis of the expedition's route can be found in Schroeder and Matson, *Colony on the Move*. These authors provide a series of maps giving their reconstruction of Castaño's route. Castaño's dealings with Pecos can be found in Hammond and Rey, *Rediscovery*, pp. 271–80; with the Rio Grande pueblos, pp. 281–95. For the Morlete expedition, see Hammond and Rey, *Rediscovery*, pp. 39–48, 298–301 (Instructions to Morlete), pp. 301–2 (Viceroy Velasco to King), and pp. 303–5 (fragment of letter from Morlete to viceroy).

The account of the Leyva and Humaña expedition comes primarily from an Indian servant of Humaña's who was found by Oñate in the Pecos area; see Hammond and Rey, *Rediscovery*, pp. 323–26. See also the summary of that expedition on pp. 48–50.

An excellent biography of Juan de Oñate is contained in M. Simmons,

SOURCES AND COMMENTARY

The Last Conquistador: Juan de Oñate and the Settling of the Far Southwest (University of Oklahoma Press, 1991). Many of the basic documents of the Oñate period were published in Hammond and Rey, *Don Juan de Oñate;* a summary of the period is contained in vol. 1, pp. 1–38. For the makeup of the expedition, see pp. 215–301 (Inspection by Juan de Frías Salazar, January 1958). A sometimes day-to-day itinerary of the expedition was kept; see esp. pp. 318–21.

Material on the *camino real,* including the *jornada del muerto,* is contained in G. G. Palmer, ed., *El Camino Real de Tierra Adentro* (Bureau of Land Management, Santa Fe, Cultural Resources Series, no. 11, 1993). See especially M. Simmons's chapter in that volume, "Opening the Camino Real," pp. 29–34. J. F. Bannon, in *The Spanish Borderlands Frontier: 1513–1821* (Holt, Rinehart and Winston, 1970, p. 38), says that there were 83 carts and 7,000 head of livestock. For the doña Inés story see Hammond and Rey, *Oñate,* p. 321; also C. L. Riley, *Pueblo Indians in Mesoamerica: The Early Historic Period* (in Frisbie, ed., *Collected Papers in Honor of Florence Hawley Ellis,* p. 459). For don Pedro Oroz, see *Pueblo Indians,* pp. 459–60; *Oñate,* p. 32 (Hammond and Rey give the name as Orez); and Kessell, *Kiva, Cross, and Crown,* pp. 43, 45, 77–78. For the population of the Rio Grande, see Riley, *Frontier People,* pp. 230–31. Somewhat lower figures are given by J. P. Wilson, "Before the Pueblo Revolt" (in *Prehistory and History in the Southwest: Collected Papers in Honor of Alden C. Hayes,* N. Fox, ed., Archaeological Society of New Mexico, no. 11, 1985, pp. 113–20).

Details of the battle at Acoma and its aftermath are given in Simmons, *The Last Conquistador,* pp. 132–46. See also W. A. Minge, *Acoma, the Sky City* (University of New Mexico Press, 1976, pp. 10–17). Gasco de Velasco's account of the battle can be found in Hammond and Rey, *Oñate,* vol. 2, pp. 614–15. For the sentencing of the Acoma Indians, see *Oñate,* vol. 1, pp. 477–78. For the actual number of individuals suffering amputation, see Sánchez, *Rio Abajo Frontier,* p. 72. Concerning the disposition of Acoma children, see G. Espinosa, ed., *History of New Mexico by Gaspar Pérez de Villagrá* (Quivira Society, Los Angeles, 1933, p. 32). Minge, in *Acoma,* p. 150 n. 15, states that there is no evidence that Acoma was ever included in the encomienda system.

For the attacks on the Tompiro pueblos, see Hammond and Rey, *Oñate,* vol. 2, p. 615 (Gasco de Velasco), and pp. 650–51, 795–96; also see Simmons, *Last Conquistador,* pp. 150–52. See also J. D. Forbes, *Apache, Navajo, and Spaniards* (University of Oklahoma Press, 1959, pp. 93–94). Although they print the accusatory Gasco de Velasco document, Hammond and Rey play down this attack. Forbes essentially accepts Gasco's figures. The last years of Oñate's rule are competently summarized by Hammond and Rey, *Oñate,* vol. 1, pp. 31–36. For the settlement of Santa Fe, see S. M. Hordes, "The History of the Santa Fe Plaza, 1610–1720" (*Santa Fe Historic Plaza Study,* L. Tigges, ed., Santa Fe City Planning Department, 1990, pp. 3–36). The 1607 or 1608 date for the founding of Santa Fe is given in F. V. Scholes, "Juan Martínez de Montoya: Settler and Conquistador of New Mexico" (*New Mexico Historical Review,* Vol. XIX, no. 4, 1944, pp. 337–42. Papers relating to the possible Martínez Montoya settlement have recently been acquired by the Museum of New Mexico, Santa, Fe.

Chapter 18

An account of the early development of the Franciscan missions in New Mexico is given by F. V. Scholes and L. B. Bloom, "Friar Personnel and Mission Chronology, 1598–1629" (*New Mexico Historical Review,* vol. 19, no. 4, 1944, I, pp. 319–36, and vol. 20, no. 1, 1945, II, pp. 58–82). A concise summary of early mission work is found in J. M. Espinosa, *The Pueblo Indian Revolt of 1696 and the Franciscan Missions in New Mexico* (University of Oklahoma Press, 1988, pp. 9–32). For the makeup of New Mexico's population, see Espinosa, *Pueblo Indian Revolt,* pp. 11–12. For firsthand accounts by Franciscans of the first decades of Spanish rule, consult Bloom, "Perea's Relacion"; Forrestal and Lynch, eds., *Benavides' Memorial of 1630;* and F. W. Hodge, G. P. Hammond, and A. Rey, trans. and annot., *Fray Alonso de Benavides' Revised Memorial* (University of New Mexico Press, 1945).

The beginning of the quarrel between church and state is related by L. B. Bloom, "Perea's Relacion," pp. 215–18; and F. V. Scholes, "First Decade of the Inquisition." An extraordinary amount of information for seventeenth-century New Mexico, especially treatment of Indians and the wars between the clergy and the governors, can be found in F. V. Scholes, "Troublous Times in New Mexico, 1659–1670" (*New Mexico Historical Review,* vol. 12, no. 2, 1937, pp. 134–74; vol. 12, no. 4, 1937, pp. 380–452; vol. 13, no. 1, 1938, pp. 63–84; and vol. 15, no. 4, 1940, pp. 369–417). Information on *encomiendas* in New Mexico is contained in vol. 12, no. 4, pp. 388–90. Further information on seventeenth-century New Mexico is to be found in C. W. Hackett, ed., *Historical Documents Relating to New Mexico, Nueva Vizcaya, and Approaches Thereto, to 1773* (Carnegie Institute of Washington, Publication 330, vol. 3, 1937, pp. 128–279).

The 1639 Santa Fe cabildo statement on sheep is cited in Scholes, "Church and State in New Mexico" (*New Mexico Historical Review,* vol. 11, no. 4, 1936, p. 313). Flock size during the 1660s is given in "Mission Report of 1672" (Scholes Collections, archive 360, box VII-1, item 1-C, University of New Mexico Library, Albuquerque). Trade in seventeenth-century New Mexico is discussed by F. V. Scholes, "The Supply Service of the New Mexican Missions in the Seventeenth Century" (*New Mexico Historical Review,* vol. 5, no. 1, 1930, p. 115; vol. 5, no. 2, pp. 186–210); Scholes, "Troublous Times," vol. 12, no. 4, 1937, pp. 397–98; J. O. Baxter, "Livestock on the Camino Real" (in Palmer, ed., *Camino Real,* pp. 101–11, esp. pp. 105–8); and D. H. Snow, "Purchased in Chihuahua for Feasts" (in *Camino Real,* pp. 133–46).

The Genízaro situation is discussed by Fray A. Chavez, "Genízaros" (*Handbook of North American Indians,* vol. 9, pp. 198–200); and C. H. Lange, "Relations of the Southwest with the Plains and Great Basin" (*Handbook,* vol. 9, pp. 201–5). For the regulations on treatment of Pueblo Indians issued by the viceroy in 1620, consult L. B. Bloom, "A Glimpse of New Mexico in 1620" (*New Mexico Historical Review,* vol. 3, no. 4, 1928, pp. 357–80, esp. pp. 373–76). For accounts of treatment of Indians, see Scholes, "Troublous Times," vol. 12, no. 2, 1937, pp. 142, 144–48, 162–63.

An excellent discussion of the impact of Spanish animals, plants, and technology on the Rio Grande Pueblos is found in R. I. Ford, "The New Pueblo Economy" (in *When Cultures Meet,* pp. 73–91, esp. pp. 76–80, 81, 85). See p. 76 for the Spanish experiment in growing wheat in the San Gabriel region. The accusations against Father Guerra are given in Scholes, "Troublous Times," vol. 12, no. 2, 1937, pp. 145–46. For the López de Mendizábal story, see Scholes, "Troublous Times," vol. 12, no. 4, 1937, pp. 380, 396, 400–421; vol. 15, no. 4, 1940, especially Aguilar's trial, pp. 398–407. For comparison of wages among the Pueblos with wages in other parts of the Spanish New World, see R. K. Barber, "Indian Labor in the Spanish Colonies" (*New Mexico Historical Review,* vol. 7, no. 2, 1932, pp. 105–42; vol. 7, no. 3, 1932, pp. 233–72; vol. 7, no. 4, 1932, pp. 311–47, esp. pp. 336–39). Material on Esteban Clemente is found in Scholes, "Troublous Times," vol. 12, no. 4, p. 396; and Hackett, ed., *Historical Documents,* pp. 146, 156, 159, 165, 170–71, 176, 184. A balanced view of the López de Mendizábal period is presented in Sánchez, *Rio Abajo Frontier,* pp. 101–19. The economic situation in colonial times is treated in L. H. Warner, "Conveyance of Property, the Spanish and Mexican Way" (*New Mexico Historical Review,* vol. 6, no. 4, 1931, pp. 327–59).

Unrest among the Pueblos is described in D. E. Worcester, "The Beginnings of the Apache Menace of the Southwest" (*New Mexico Historical Re-*

view, vol. 16, no. 1, 1939, pp. 1–14, esp. p. 9); and Espinosa, *Pueblo Indian Revolt,* pp. 30–31. For a view that officially reported "Apache raids" may have been partly Pueblo revolts, see Wilson, "Before the Pueblo Revolt," pp. 113–14, 118.

Various population figures have been given for the Pueblos at 1680. E. H. Spicer, in *Cycles of Conquest* (University of Arizona Press, 1976, p. 162), suggests a population of 25,000 to 30,000. M. Simmons, in "History of Pueblo-Spanish Relations to 1821" (*Handbook of North American Indians,* vol. 9, p. 186), believes that the total Pueblo Indian number in 1680 was approximately 17,000. D. Reff, in *Disease,* p. 229, concurs in this figure. Some years ago, I suggested (Riley, *Frontier People,* p. 231) that the population figure for the Pueblo world in 1680 might have been around 16,500, basing my figure in part on the unpublished work of S. J. Baldwin of the University of Calgary (see especially *Frontier People,* p. 384).

The millenarian aspects of the Pueblo Revolt are discussed by D. T. Reff, "The 'Predicament of Culture' and the Spanish Missionary Accounts of the Tepehuan and Pueblo Revolts" (*Ethnohistory,* in press). The suggestion that the revolt may have been masterminded by a brilliant leader of black and Indian ancestry is given by Fray A. Chavez, "Pohé-Yemo's Representative and the Pueblo Revolt of 1680" (*New Mexico Historical Review,* vol. 42, no., 2, 1967, pp. 85–126). Accounts of the revolt can be found in C. W. Hackett and C. C. Shelby, eds. and trans., *Revolt of the Pueblo Indians of New Mexico and Otermín's Attempted Reconquest, 1680–82* (University of New Mexico Press, 1942, 2 vols.); J. S. Sando, "The Pueblo Revolt" (*Handbook,* vol. 9, pp. 194–97); Espinosa, *Pueblo Indian Revolt,* pp. 32–36; and Dozier, *Pueblo Indians,* pp. 55–60.

The retreat of the Spaniards to El Paso is discussed by R. Hendricks, "Road to Rebellion, Road to Reconquest" (in Palmer, ed., *Camino Real,* pp. 77–83 , esp. pp. 77–79). The Pueblo side of the revolt is told by F. Folsom, *Red Power on the Rio Grande* (Council for Indian Education, Billings, Mont., 1973). A good modern source for King Philip's War is R. Bourne, *The Red King's Rebellion: Racial Politics in New England, 1675–1678* (Atheneum, 1990).

Information about Vargas can be found in publications of the Vargas Project: J. L. Kessell, ed., *Remote Beyond Compare* (University of New Mexico Press, 1989), and J. L. Kessell and R. Hendricks, eds., *By Force of Arms* (University of New Mexico Press, 1992). See J. L. Kessell, "Spaniards and Pueblos: From Crusading Intolerance to Pragmatic Accommodation" (in *Columbian Consequences,* vol. 1, D. H. Thomas, ed., Smithsonian Institution Press, 1989, pp. 127–38), for insightful comments on the readjustment that both Pueblos and Spaniards made in the eighteenth century. An excellent overall discussion of relationships of Native Americans to Hispanics at various stages of European colonization is found in W. R. Swagerty, "Spanish-Indian Relations, 1513–1821" (in *Scholars and the Indian Experience,* W. R. Swagerty, ed., Indiana University Press, 1984, pp. 36–78).

The permutations of the kachina cult are discussed by R. L. Bunzel, *Zuñi Katcinas* (47th Annual Report, Bureau of American Ethnology, 1932, pp. 899–903). Bunzel makes the point that "although less exuberant," the Keresan kachina cult was similar to that of Zuni, but that the cult among the Tanoans was far weaker and in some cases nonexistent. For a brief summary discussion of the Pueblo Indians in post-Spanish centuries, see C. L. Riley, "A View from the Protohistoric" (in Minnis and Redman, eds., *Perspectives on Southwestern Prehistory,* pp. 236–37).

Index of Initial Citations

In the Sources and Commentary section of this book, only the initial citation for each author contains the full bibliographic reference. This index gives the page number of that complete citation. The index does not list entries such as archival documents and personal communications since these are adequately cited at each appearance.

INDEX OF INITIAL CITATIONS

INDEX OF INITIAL CITATIONS

INDEX OF INITIAL CITATIONS

INDEX OF INITIAL CITATIONS

INDEX OF INITIAL CITATIONS

General Index

Abalone. *See* Shell

Abo. *See* Tompiro

Acoma, early accounts of, 121; early date of, 98, 102; hostile to Spaniards, 245; hostilities at, 251; Indians flee to, 259; named by Marcos, 152; Querecho near, 221; resettlement of, 252; visited by Alvarado, 165–66; visited by Chamuscado, 231, visited by Espejo, 235–36

Acomita, battle near, 236

Adams, E. Charles, and kachina cult, 110–11

Adams, Eleanor, xiv

Adobe, in Rio Grande, 90, 107, 260

Acus, described by Marcos, 152

Africans, as slaves in Caribbean, 135; as slaves in New World, 173. *See also* Slavery

Agincourt, 148

Agriculture (Native Southwest), beans in, 57, 64, 69, 70, 74, 122, 124, 132, 185; grid gardens in SW, 91, 124; in BM-II, 60; in Chaco, 75–76; in Golden Age, 123; in Hohokam 64; in Oñate period, 215; in Oshara, 57–61; lagenaria in, 57; maize in, 57–61, 64, 74–75, 122, 124, 132, 185; origins of in Rio Grande, 52, 57, 63;

squash in, 58–59, 64, 75, 132. *See also* Cotton

Agriculture, (Spanish in SW), chickpeas and melons in Sonora, 214–15; chili introduced, 214; European crops in NM, 260–61; fruit trees and wheat in NM, 260–61

Aguilar, Jerónimo de, among Maya, 142

Aguilar, Nicolas (alcalde mayor at Tompiro), 264

Ahacus, 152

Ahuítzotl, 138

Alarçón, Hernando de, 214; and Pima interpreter, 164; Díaz sent to meet, 162; reaches Colorado R, 156

Alcaráz, Diego de, 199; at Corazones, 162; brutality of, 202; killed in Sonora, 200

Alectrion. *See* Shell

Alemán (Loman), Juan (leader of Tiguex), 122, 176–77

Alibates, trade in, 42, 117–18. *See also* Trade

Alta Vista, turquoise in, 83

Altithermal, 49, 52, 56

Alvarado, Pedro de, contacts Aztecs, 143; cruelty of, 144

GENERAL INDEX

Boat transport, in Paleoindian times, 38

Bois d'arc, traded to SW, 117, 130

Bolton, Herbert E., and Coronado Route, 189–90; view of Spaniards, 299

Bow and arrow, in Anasazi, 69–70; in Hohokam, 64; in Mogollon, 65

Bow priests, at Zuni, 127

Braba (Taos Pueblo), 194

Brazil, Portuguese awarded, 148

Brew, J.O., and Golden Age, 93

Brody, J.J., 109

Brugge, David M., 104

Burgos, Laws of, 299

C-14. See Carbon-14

Cabeza de Vaca, Alvar Nuñez de, at La Junta, 228; in Sonora, 116; on Rio Grande, 12; sees Jumano, 192–93; travels of, 150–52

Cabildo, among historic Pueblos, 125; Spanish in Vera Cruz, 143

Cacique, abducted, 169, 171; office of, 126; set free, 180; trader at Zuni, 163

Caddoan Indians, ceramic borrowing from, 132; contacts with Pueblos, 12; meet Coronado, 186

Cáhitan Indians, with Marcos, 152

Camino Real, and trade, 113; pioneered by Oñate, 247–48

Canes of Office, among historic Pueblos, 126; in prehistory, 126

Cannons, left at Zia, 180; use by Spaniards, 179; used at Pecos, 194; wheeled, 183

Cantor, Juan, as relative of Pedro, 234; as trader, 239; guides Spaniards, 228

Carbajal, Gov. Luís de, as converso, 242

Carbon-14 dating, 32, 33

Cárdenas, García López de, at Hawikuh, 162; at Tiguex, 170;

atrocities by, 175, 213; explores Grand Canyon, 163; gives news of Sonora, 203; in Tiguex war, 176, 178–79; returns from Plains, 193; trip of to Sonora, 200–201;

Carlos I (King of Spain), supports Las Casas, 174

Casa Rinconada, great kivas in, 76, 78; solstice observations at, 86

Casas Grandes, adobe construction in, 107; decay of, 94, 112; major period at, 94–95; Mogollon origins of, 65; peyote in, 215; trade in, 105, 112; visited by Ibarra, 225

Castañeda de Nájera, Pedro de, 199; and bridge, 187; and Pecos traders, 164; at Galisteo, 185–86; describes Coronado's injury, 203; escape from of Caddoan woman, 194; on Moho, 178–79; on Mexican deserters, 213; on Quivira, 212; on Sonora, 207; on Suya chickens, 205; on Vaca party, 193; Pueblo list of, 166; reports Marcos trip, 153

Castaño de Sosa, Gaspar, and Inés, 206, 249–50; guided by Jumano, 193; on expedition, 243–45; on Rio Grande, 13

Castillo Maldonado, Alonso de, with Vaca party, 150

Catiete (San Felipe), identified by Luxán, 235

Cattle, introduced into New Mexico, 260

Cazonci, Tarascan, murdered by Spaniards, 149

Ce acatl (one reed), and Quetzalcoatl's return, 142

Central Amerind, 97

Ceramics, Native, Chupadero b-w in SW, 88; decoration of, 69; diffusion of to Anasazi, 68; glaze wares, 105–7; gray coiled wares, 68–69; in

of, 50, 53–54; later development of, 64; Mexican influence in, 63

Cochiti, early Spanish accounts of, 121; history of, 98; Keres speakers in, 102

Cody Tradition, 46, 47, 50, 51

Columbus, Christopher, 119

Comales, found at site 54147, 216–17

Compass, with Coronado party, 186

Coofor, 175; and location of Moho, 177; and Mexican material found at LA 54147, 216–17; soldiers in, 181; Spanish evict Indians from, 170

Cooperton site, 35

Copper, among Aztecs, 138; among Toltecs, 136; in Chaco trade, 76, 85

Coral, at La Junta, 228; in SW trade, 115, 131

Corazones, San Gerómino de, building of, 202; founded, 162; loss of, 203; Tovar sent to, 181; troubles in, 199; 3rd settlement of, 200–201

Corazones (statelet), as friendly to Coronado, 207; Coronado in, 157, 159; melons in, 215; not attacked by Gallego, 201; Piman language in, 202; Vaca party in, 151

Corner kivas, 107

Coronado, Francisco Vázquez de, xiv, 12, 17, 23, 132, 152–209, 212, 214, 227, 230–31, 246–47; appointed governor, 152; at Coofor, 216; at Moho, 181; brought seeds to Rio Grande, 215; brought trading goods, 211; brutality of, 213; contacts Querecho, 90; departs SW, 203–5; disease introduced by, 224; expedition of invades SW, 4, 120–21; influence on SW, 216–17, 220–22; lacks info. on Mixtón war, 200; on Plains, 186–96; on trail to SW, 155–58; reaches Culiacán, 207; release of Cacique by, 180; Sonoran problems

of, 202; to Rio Grande, 170; treatment of Indians by, 174–75

Cortés, Hernán, defeats Aztecs, 145; early life of, 142; invades Colima, 149; invades Mexico, 142–45; in west Mexico, 148–49; perhaps brings typhus, 224; ties of with Oñate family, 247

Costume, in BM-II, 60; in Golden Age, 124–25; in Oshara, 54

Cotton, blankets of as currency, 138; grown in Rio Grande, 122, 260; used in trade, 116–17, 131, 163, 239, 259; weaving of, 105. See also Agriculture

Council of Indies, 246

Crab Nebula, 86

Cremations. See Disposal of Dead

Cristóbal, at Pecos, 213; with Ubeda, 205

Crossbow, at Pecos, 195; used by Spaniards, 162

Crosses, Espejo found at Zuni, 214

Cuauhtemoc, leads Aztecs, 145

Cuba, colonized by Spain, 135; Cortés and, 142–43

Cuitlahuac, becomes Aztec leader, 144; dies from smallpox, 145

Culiacán, and early settlement, 150; Coronado returns by, 207; Ibarra in, 225

Curing Societies, among Pueblos, 94, 112

Cushing, Frank H., 218

Custodia, of Franciscan New Mexico, 255

Custos, Benavides holds office, 255; replaced by Perea, 256

Datura (jimsonweed), horses die from, 206; medical uses for, 27, 123

Deep Barranca, Teya settlement in, 190, 192

GENERAL INDEX

Huitzilopochtli, 140–41
Human sacrifice, in Aztec state, 140–41; in Tlaloc and SW, 110;
Humaña, Antonio Gutiérrez de, expedition of, 245–46
Humanas, attacked by Oñate, 252; in Golden Age, 96; ties with Jumano, 192
Hunt Societies, 94, 112
Hurtado de Mendoza, Diego, shipwreck of, 150
Hyde, George E., identifies Harahey, 197

Ibarra, Francisco, in Chihuahua, 226; in Nueva Vizcaya, 225; Señora hostile to, 202
Ice Age. See Pleistocene
Inca Empire, 151
Indé, mines of, 226
Indo European, linguistic family, borrowing from, 98–99
Inés, Doña, history of, 205–6; returns to Tano, 249
Inquisition, López tried by, 265; used against governors, 258, 260
Interpreters, Cárdenas lack of at Arenal, 175; in SW, 164–65
Iron, at La Junta, 228; introduced by Spaniards, 260; techniques for lacking in SW, 202
Irrigation, at Chaco, 83; in Golden Age, 122–23; in Hohokam, 64; on Rio G., 94. See Agriculture
Irwin-Williams, Cynthia, 47, 50, 51
Isabella of Castile, and Indian "soul" controversy, 173
Isleta Pueblo, in Pueblo Revolt, 286

Jacal, in early SW, 70; in Tajo phase, 88
Jamaica, Spain colonizes, 135
Janizary. See Genízaro

Jaramillo, Juan de, 196; discusses Quivira, 205, 212; names Rio Grande, 13; on Plains, 187; reports Vaca party, 193; reports Turk's death, 195
Jeddito, at Pottery Mound, 131; ceramics at Hopi, 106; in Rio Grande, 116–17
Jefferson, Thomas, 14
Jemez Pueblo, 10, 96; relations with Navajo, 103–4; rebellion in, 266
Jesuits, techniques of conversion among, 261
Jet, as jewelry in SW, 29, 125. See also Trade
Jornada del Muerto, used by Morlete, Oñate, 248
Jornada Mogollon, 21; kachina cult in, 110; Piro spoken in, 99. See also Mogollon
Julian calendar, 291
Jumano, Chamuscado among, 227; contact of by Spaniards, 129–30; identification of, 192; in Pueblo world, 4; in 16th-cent. trade, 129, 228, 239; language of, 100–101, 129–30, 228. See also Teya
Jusepe, flees to Pecos, 246

Kachina Cult, among later Pueblos, 129, 270, 316; and art, 108–9; and kiva associations, 108, 128; defended by López, 265; in Rio Grande, 107–8; influence of, 94; meaning of, 290; origin of, 5, 107, 217; influenced by Quetzalcoatl and Tlaloc, 136; opposition of by missionaries, 261, 264
Kachinas, Spanish soldiers identified with, 273
Kawaika-a, mural paintings at, 109; reported sacked by Spaniards, 163; Tovar at, 162

Peralta, Gov. Pedro de, appointed governor, 252–53; missionaries arrive with, 255; struggle of with missionaries, 257

Perea, Fr. Estevan, brings missionaries to New Mexico, 256; given Inquisitor powers, 258; identifies Querechos, 221; struggles with Peralta, 257

Peridots, in Golden Age, 125; in SW trade, 28, 114, 116

Peyote, distribution of, 215

Philippines, Castaño exiled to, 244

Picuris Pueblo, 24, not contacted by Coronado, 194, visited by Oñate, 249

Piedrahita, identified as Pecos Pueblo, 310

Piedras Marcadas Pueblo (LA 290), 177. *See also* Mann-Zuris

Piezas. *See* Slaves

Pigments, in SW trade, 116

Pikimachay, 35

Pima Papago, collection of mtDNA from Pima, 34; developed from Hohokam, 94; interpreters in SW, 164; language in Sonora, 202; patolli introduced in, 217; shamanism in, 128

Piñon nuts, in 17th-cent. trade, 259. *See also* Trade

Pipes, in BM II, 60; in Golden Age, 123

Piro Indians, climate in area, 24; disappearance of, 271; early Spanish contact with, 226, 228–30, 234, 248-49; expedition of Coronado to, 170, 194; flight of in Pueblo Revolt, 268; language distribution of, 96, 98-100; population growth in, 95; Pueblos of, 166; Tiguex stay with, 199

Pithouse, in Hohokam, 64; in Mogollon, 64; in Rosa culture, 89; late development in Rio Grande of, 89; Tajo phase, 88

Pizarro, 151

Plague. *See* Disease

Plains Archaic, 53, 54

Plainview Tradition, 46

Plant Domestication. *See* Agriculture

Pleistocene, in North America, 31–50

Pochteca, 85; as traders, 140; in Aztec times; 139; political power of, 142, 145

Poison tree, Spanish fears of, 200

Ponce de León, Juan, 135

Popé, xiv; and Pueblo Revolt, 267

Postclassic, in Mesoamerica, 136

Potatoes, eaten in SW, 27, 123. *See also* Flora; Food production

Pottery. *See* Ceramics

Pottery Mound, desertion of, 130; mural paintings in, 108–9; trade in, 117, 130–31

Preclassic, in Mesoamerica, 136

Priesthood, among Pueblos, 122, 128

Protohistoric, definition of, 3–4, in SW, 3

Pueblos, listed, 95–96

Querecho, as enemy of Pueblos, 4; as threat to Pueblo, 132; description of, 188; identification of as Apache, 190–91; 221; met by Chamuscado, 232; met by Zaldívar, 250; on Pecos by 14th cent., 90; protects Acoma rebels, 25; reaches SW, 104; trade in, 129, 168, 185, 212

Quern, 55

Quetzalcoatl, and kachina cult, 109–10, 136; history of, 109; and divine twins, 127; in Teotihuacan, 136; Spanish as return of, 142